The MPEG Handbook

For Howard and Matthew

The MPEG Handbook

MPEG-1, MPEG-2, MPEG-4

Second edition

John Watkinson

AMSTERDAM • BOSTON • HEIDELBERG • LONDON • NEW YORK • OXFORD
PARIS • SAN DIEGO • SAN FRANCISCO • SINGAPORE • SYDNEY • TOKYO
Focal Press is an imprint of Elsevier

ELSEVIER

Focal Press

Focal Press
An imprint of Elsevier
Linacre House, Jordan Hill, Oxford OX2 8DP
30 Corporate Drive, Burlington, MA 01803

First published 2001
Second edition 2004
Reprinted 2005

British Library Cataloguing in Publication Data
A catalogue record for this book is available from the British Library

Library of Congress Cataloguing in Publication Data
A catalogue record for this book is available from the Library of Congress

ISBN 0 240 80578 X

For information on all Focal Press publications
visit our website at www.focalpress.com

Printed and bound in Great Britain

Contents

Preface

This book adds some material to the first edition which in turn completely revised the earlier book entitled *MPEG-2*. It is an interesting reflection on the rate at which this technology progresses that these frequent revisions are necessary. Perhaps after H.264 one could say that all the key work has been done and thereafter progress will be incremental. H.264, also known as AVC, is, of course, the impetus for this edition. The opportunity has also been taken to incorporate some improved explanations.

The approach of the book has not changed in the slightest. Compression is an arcane subject with its own library of specialist terminology that is generally accompanied by a substantial amount of mathematics. I have always argued that mathematics is only a form of shorthand, itself a compression technique! Mathematics describes but does not explain, whereas this book explains principles and then describes actual examples.

A chapter of fundamentals is included to make the main chapters easier to follow. Also included are some guidelines that have practically been found useful in getting the best out of compression systems. The reader who has endured this book will be in a good position to tackle the MPEG standards documents themselves, although these are not for the faint-hearted, especially the MPEG-4 and H.264 documents which are huge and impenetrable.

Acknowledgements

Information for this book has come from a number of sources to whom I am indebted. The publications of the ISO, AES and SMPTE provided essential reference material. Thanks also to the following for lengthy discussions and debates: Peter de With, Steve Lyman, Bruce Devlin, Mike Knee, Peter Kraniauskas and Tom MacMahon. The assistance of MicroSoft Corp. and Tektronix Inc. is also appreciated. Special thanks to Mikael Reichel.

1

Introduction to compression

1.1   What is MPEG?

MPEG is actually an acronym for the Moving Pictures Experts Group which was formed by the ISO (International Standards Organization) to set standards for audio and video compression and transmission.

Compression is summarized in Figure 1.1. It will be seen in (a) that the data rate is reduced at source by the *compressor*. The compressed data are then passed through a communication channel and returned to the original rate by the *expander*. The ratio between the source data rate and the channel data rate is called the *compression factor*. The term *coding gain* is also used. Sometimes a compressor and expander in series are referred to as a *compander*. The compressor may equally well be referred to as a *coder* and the expander a *decoder* in which case the tandem pair may be called a *codec*.

Where the encoder is more complex than the decoder, the system is said to be asymmetrical. Figure 1.1(b) shows that MPEG works in this way. The encoder needs to be algorithmic or adaptive whereas the decoder is 'dumb' and carries out fixed actions. This is advantageous in applications such as broadcasting where the number of expensive complex encoders is small but the number of simple inexpensive decoders is large. In point-to-point applications the advantage of asymmetrical coding is not so great.

The approach of the ISO to standardization in MPEG is novel because it is not the encoder which is standardized. Figure 1.2(a) shows that instead the way in which a decoder shall interpret the bitstream is defined. A decoder which can successfully interpret the bitstream is said to be *compliant*. Figure 1.2(b) shows that the advantage of standardizing the decoder is that over time encoding algorithms can improve yet compliant decoders will continue to function with them.

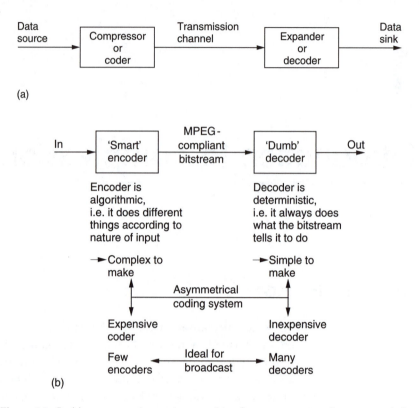

Figure 1.1 In (a) a compression system consists of compressor or coder, a transmission channel and a matching expander or decoder. The combination of coder and decoder is known as a codec. (b) MPEG is asymmetrical since the encoder is much more complex than the decoder.

It should be noted that a compliant decoder must correctly be able to interpret every allowable bitstream, whereas an encoder which produces a restricted subset of the possible codes can still be compliant.

The MPEG standards give very little information regarding the structure and operation of the encoder. Provided the bitstream is compliant, any coder construction will meet the standard, although some designs will give better picture quality than others. Encoder construction is not revealed in the bitstream and manufacturers can supply encoders using algorithms which are proprietary and their details do not need to be published. A useful result is that there can be competition between different encoder designs which means that better designs can evolve. The user will have greater choice because different levels of cost and complexity can exist in a range of coders yet a compliant decoder will operate with them all.

MPEG is, however, much more than a compression scheme as it also standardizes the protocol and syntax under which it is possible to combine or multiplex audio data with video data to produce a digital

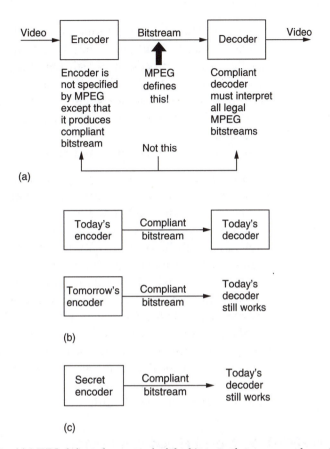

Figure 1.2 (a) MPEG defines the protocol of the bitstream between encoder and decoder. The decoder is defined by implication, the encoder is left very much to the designer. (b) This approach allows future encoders of better performance to remain compatible with existing decoders. (c) This approach also allows an encoder to produce a standard bitstream whilst its technical operation remains a commercial secret.

equivalent of a television program. Many such programs can be combined in a single multiplex and MPEG defines the way in which such multiplexes can be created and transported. The definitions include the metadata which decoders require to demultiplex correctly and which users will need to locate programs of interest.

As with all video systems there is a requirement for synchronizing or genlocking and this is particularly complex when a multiplex is assembled from many signals which are not necessarily synchronized to one another.

1.2 Why compression is necessary

Compression, bit rate reduction, data reduction and source coding are all terms which mean basically the same thing in this context. In essence the same (or nearly the same) information is carried using a smaller quantity or rate of data. It should be pointed out that in audio *compression* traditionally means a process in which the dynamic range of the sound is reduced. In the context of MPEG the same word means that the bit rate is reduced, ideally leaving the dynamics of the signal unchanged. Provided the context is clear, the two meanings can co-exist without a great deal of confusion.

There are several reasons why compression techniques are popular:

a Compression extends the playing time of a given storage device.

b Compression allows miniaturization. With fewer data to store, the same playing time is obtained with smaller hardware. This is useful in ENG (electronic news gathering) and consumer devices.

c Tolerances can be relaxed. With fewer data to record, storage density can be reduced making equipment which is more resistant to adverse environments and which requires less maintenance.

d In transmission systems, compression allows a reduction in bandwidth which will generally result in a reduction in cost. This may make possible a service which would be impracticable without it.

e If a given bandwidth is available to an uncompressed signal, compression allows faster than real-time transmission in the same bandwidth.

f If a given bandwidth is available, compression allows a better-quality signal in the same bandwidth.

1.3   MPEG-1, 2, 4 and H.264 contrasted

The first compression standard for audio and video was MPEG-1.[1,2] Although many applications have been found, MPEG-1 was basically designed to allow moving pictures and sound to be encoded into the bit rate of an audio Compact Disc. The resultant Video-CD was quite successful but has now been superseded by DVD. In order to meet the low bit requirement, MPEG-1 downsampled the images heavily as well as using picture rates of only 24–30 Hz and the resulting quality was moderate.

The subsequent MPEG-2 standard was considerably broader in scope and of wider appeal.[3] For example, MPEG-2 supports interlace and HD whereas MPEG-1 did not. MPEG-2 has become very important because it has been chosen as the compression scheme for both DVB (digital video broadcasting) and DVD (digital video disk/digital versatile disk). Developments in standardizing scaleable and multi-resolution compression which would have become MPEG-3 were ready by the time MPEG-2 was ready to be standardized and so this work was incorporated into MPEG-2, and as a result there is no MPEG-3 standard.

MPEG-4[4] uses further coding tools with additional complexity to achieve higher compression factors than MPEG-2. In addition to more efficient coding of video, MPEG-4 moves closer to computer graphics applications. In the more complex Profiles, the MPEG-4 decoder effectively becomes a rendering processor and the compressed bitstream describes three-dimensional shapes and surface texture. It is to be expected that MPEG-4 will become as important to Internet and wireless delivery as MPEG-2 has become in DVD and DVB.

The MPEG-4 standard is extremely wide ranging and it is unlikely that a single decoder will ever be made that can handle every possibility. Many of the graphics applications of MPEG-4 are outside telecommunications requirements. In 2001 the ITU (International Telecommunications Union) Video Coding Experts Group (VCEG) joined with ISO MPEG to form the Joint Video Team (JVT). The resulting standard is variously known as AVC (advanced video coding), H.264 or MPEG-4 Part 10. This standard further refines the video coding aspects of MPEG-4, which were themselves refinements of MPEG-2, to produce a coding scheme having the same applications as MPEG-2 but with higher performance.

To avoid tedium, in cases where the term MPEG is used in this book without qualification, it can be taken to mean MPEG-1, 2, 4 or H.264. Where a specific standard is being contrasted it will be made clear.

1.4 Some applications of compression

The applications of audio and video compression are limitless and the ISO has done well to provide standards which are appropriate to the wide range of possible compression products.

MPEG coding embraces video pictures from the tiny screen of a videophone to the high-definition images needed for electronic cinema. Audio coding stretches from speech-grade mono to multichannel surround sound.

Figure 1.3 shows the use of a codec with a recorder. The playing time of the medium is extended in proportion to the compression factor. In the

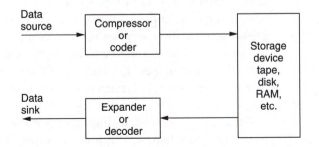

Figure 1.3 Compression can be used around a recording medium. The storage capacity may be increased or the access time reduced according to the application.

case of tapes, the access time is improved because the length of tape needed for a given recording is reduced and so it can be rewound more quickly. In the case of DVD (digital video disk aka digital versatile disk) the challenge was to store an entire movie on one 12 cm disk. The storage density available with today's optical disk technology is such that consumer recording of conventional uncompressed video would be out of the question.

In communications, the cost of data links is often roughly proportional to the data rate and so there is simple economic pressure to use a high compression factor. However, it should be borne in mind that implementing the codec also has a cost which rises with compression factor and so a degree of compromise will be inevitable.

In the case of video-on-demand, technology exists to convey full bandwidth video to the home, but to do so for a single individual at the moment would be prohibitively expensive. Without compression, HDTV (high-definition television) requires too much bandwidth. With compression, HDTV can be transmitted to the home in a similar bandwidth to an existing analog SDTV channel. Compression does not make video-on-demand or HDTV possible; it makes them economically viable.

In workstations designed for the editing of audio and/or video, the source material is stored on hard disks for rapid access. Whilst top-grade systems may function without compression, many systems use compression to offset the high cost of disk storage. In some systems a compressed version of the top-grade material may also be stored for browsing purposes.

When a workstation is used for *off-line* editing, a high compression factor can be used and artifacts will be visible in the picture. This is of no consequence as the picture is only seen by the editor who uses it to make an EDL (edit decision list) which is no more than a list of actions and the timecodes at which they occur. The original uncompressed material is then *conformed* to the EDL to obtain a high-quality edited work. When *on-line* editing is being performed, the output of the workstation is the finished product and clearly a lower compression factor will have to be used. Perhaps it is in broadcasting where the use of compression will have its greatest impact. There is only one electromagnetic spectrum and pressure from other services such as cellular telephones makes efficient use of bandwidth mandatory. Analog television broadcasting is an old technology and makes very inefficient use of bandwidth. Its replacement by a compressed digital transmission is inevitable for the practical reason that the bandwidth is needed elsewhere.

Fortunately in broadcasting there is a mass market for decoders and these can be implemented as low-cost integrated circuits. Fewer encoders are needed and so it is less important if these are expensive. Whilst the cost of digital storage goes down year on year, the cost of the electromagnetic spectrum goes up. Consequently in the future the pressure to use compression in recording will ease whereas the pressure to use it in radio communications will increase.

1.5   Lossless and perceptive coding

Although there are many different coding techniques, all of them fall into one or other of these categories. In *lossless* coding, the data from the expander are identical bit-for-bit with the original source data. The so-called 'stacker' programs which increase the apparent capacity of disk drives in personal computers use lossless codecs. Clearly with computer programs the corruption of a single bit can be catastrophic. Lossless coding is generally restricted to compression factors of around 2:1.

It is important to appreciate that a lossless coder cannot guarantee a particular compression factor and the communications link or recorder used with it must be able to function with the variable output data rate. Source data which result in poor compression factors on a given codec are described as *difficult*. It should be pointed out that the difficulty is often a function of the codec. In other words data which one codec finds difficult may not be found difficult by another. Lossless codecs can be included in bit-error-rate testing schemes. It is also possible to cascade or *concatenate* lossless codecs without any special precautions.

Higher compression factors are only possible with *lossy* coding in which data from the expander are not identical bit-for-bit with the source data and as a result comparing the input with the output is bound to reveal differences. Lossy codecs are not suitable for computer data, but are used in MPEG as they allow greater compression factors than lossless codecs. Successful lossy codecs are those in which the errors are arranged so that a human viewer or listener finds them subjectively difficult to detect. Thus lossy codecs must be based on an understanding of psycho-acoustic and psycho-visual perception and are often called *perceptive* codes.

In perceptive coding, the greater the compression factor required, the more accurately must the human senses be modelled. Perceptive coders can be forced to operate at a fixed compression factor. This is convenient for practical transmission applications where a fixed data rate is easier to handle than a variable rate. The result of a fixed compression factor is that the subjective quality can vary with the 'difficulty' of the input material. Perceptive codecs should not be concatenated indiscriminately especially if they use different algorithms. As the reconstructed signal from a perceptive codec is not bit-for-bit accurate, clearly such a codec cannot be included in any bit error rate testing system as the coding differences would be indistinguishable from real errors.

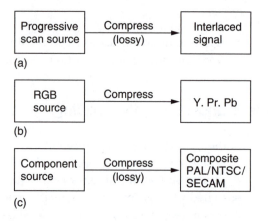

Figure 1.4 Compression is as old as television. (a) Interlace is a primitive way of halving the bandwidth. (b) Colour difference working invisibly reduces colour resolution. (c) Composite video transmits colour in the same bandwidth as monochrome.

Although the adoption of digital techniques is recent, compression itself is as old as television. Figure 1.4 shows some of the compression techniques used in traditional television systems.

Most video signals employ a non-linear relationship between brightness and the signal voltage which is known as gamma. Gamma is a perceptive coding technique which depends on the human sensitivity to video noise being a function of the brightness. The use of gamma allows the same subjective noise level with an eight-bit system as would be achieved with a fourteen-bit linear system.

One of the oldest techniques is interlace, which has been used in analog television from the very beginning as a primitive way of reducing bandwidth. As will be seen in Chapter 5, interlace is not without its problems, particularly in motion rendering. MPEG-2 supports interlace simply because legacy interlaced signals exist and there is a requirement to compress them. This should not be taken to mean that it is a good idea.

The generation of colour difference signals from *RGB* in video represents an application of perceptive coding. The human visual system (HVS) sees no change in quality although the bandwidth of the colour difference signals is reduced. This is because human perception of detail in colour changes is much less than in brightness changes. This approach is sensibly retained in MPEG.

Composite video systems such as PAL, NTSC and SECAM are all analog compression schemes which embed a subcarrier in the luminance signal so that colour pictures are available in the same bandwidth as monochrome. In comparison with a linear-light progressive scan *RGB* picture, gamma-coded interlaced composite video has a compression factor of about 10:1.

In a sense MPEG-2 can be considered to be a modern digital equivalent of analog composite video as it has most of the same attributes. For example, the eight-field sequence of the PAL subcarrier which makes editing difficult has its equivalent in the GOP (group of pictures) of MPEG.

1.6　Compression principles

In a PCM digital system the bit rate is the product of the sampling rate and the number of bits in each sample and this is generally constant. Nevertheless the *information* rate of a real signal varies.

One definition of information is that it is the unpredictable or surprising element of data. Newspapers are a good example of information because they only mention items which are surprising. Newspapers never carry items about individuals who have *not* been involved in an accident as this is the normal case. Consequently the phrase 'no news is good news' is remarkably true because if an information channel exists but nothing has been sent then it is most likely that nothing remarkable has happened.

The unpredictability of the punch line is a useful measure of how funny a joke is. Often the build-up paints a certain picture in the listener's imagination, which the punch line destroys utterly. One of the author's favourites is the one about the newly married couple who didn't know the difference between putty and petroleum jelly – their windows fell out. The difference between the information rate and the overall bit rate is known as the redundancy. Compression systems are designed to eliminate as much of that redundancy as practicable or perhaps affordable. One way in which this can be done is to exploit statistical predictability in signals. The information content or *entropy* of a sample is a function of how different it is from the predicted value. Most signals have some degree of predictability. A sine wave is highly predictable, because all cycles look the same. According to Shannon's theory, any signal which is totally predictable carries no information. In the case of the sine wave this is clear because it represents a single frequency and so has no bandwidth.

In all real signals, at least part of the signal is obvious from what has gone before or, in some cases, what may come later. A suitable decoder can predict some of the obvious part of the signal so that only the remainder has to be sent. Figure 1.5 shows a codec based on prediction. The decoder contains a predictor that attempts to anticipate the next string of data from what has gone before. If the characteristics of the decoder's predictor are known, the transmitter can omit parts of the message that the receiver has the ability to re-create. It should be clear

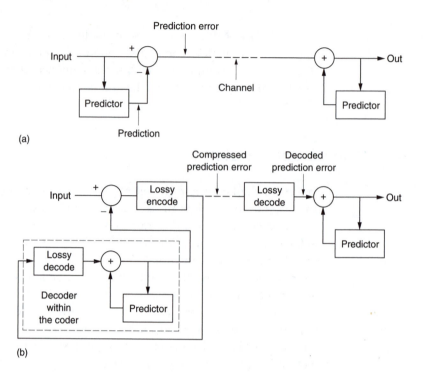

Figure 1.5 (a) A predictive codec has identical predictors in both encoder and decoder. The prediction error, or residual, is sent to the decoder which uses it perfectly to cancel the prediction error. Such a codec is lossless. (b) If the residual is subject to further lossy compression, this must take place within the encoder's prediction loop so that both predictors can track.

that all encoders using prediction must contain the same predictor as the decoder, or at least a model of it.

In Figure 1.5(a) it will be seen that the predictors in the encoder and the decoder operate with identical inputs: namely the output of the encoder. If the predictors are identical, the predictions will be identical. Thus the encoder can subtract its own prediction from the actual input to obtain a prediction error, or *residual*, in the knowledge that the decoder can add that residual thereby cancelling the prediction error.

This is a powerful technique because if all of the residual is transmitted, the codec is completely lossless. In practical codecs, lossless prediction may be combined with lossy tools. This has to be done with care. Figure 1.5(b) shows a predictive coder in which the residual is subject to further lossy coding. Note that the lossy coder is inside the encoder's prediction loop so that once more the predictors in the encoder and the decoder see the same signal. If this is not done the outputs of the two predictors will drift apart.

Clearly a signal such as noise is completely unpredictable and as a result all codecs find noise *difficult*. The most efficient way of coding noise is PCM. A codec which is designed using the statistics of real material should not be tested with random noise because it is not a representative test. Second, a codec which performs well with clean source material may perform badly with source material containing superimposed noise. Most practical compression units require some form of pre-processing before the compression stage proper and appropriate noise reduction should be incorporated into the pre-processing if noisy signals are anticipated. It will also be necessary to restrict the degree of compression applied to noisy signals.

All real signals fall part-way between the extremes of total predictability and total unpredictability or noisiness. If the bandwidth (set by the sampling rate) and the dynamic range (set by the wordlength) of the transmission system are used to delineate an area, this sets a limit on the information capacity of the system. Figure 1.6(a) shows that most real

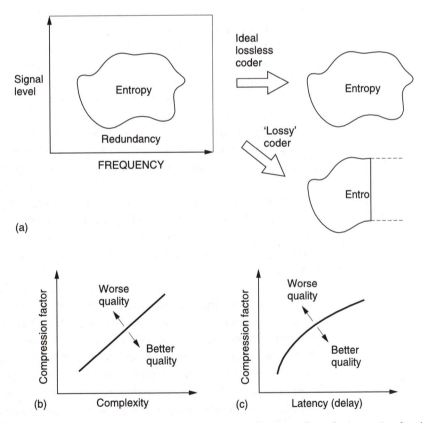

Figure 1.6 (a) A perfect coder removes only the redundancy from the input signal and results in subjectively lossless coding. If the remaining entropy is beyond the capacity of the channel some of it must be lost and the codec will then be lossy. An imperfect coder will also be lossy as it fails to keep all entropy. (b) As the compression factor rises, the complexity must also rise to maintain quality. (c) High compression factors also tend to increase latency or delay through the system.

signals only occupy part of that area. The signal may not contain all frequencies, or it may not have full dynamics at certain frequencies.

Entropy can be thought of as a measure of the actual area occupied by the signal. This is the area that *must* be transmitted if there are to be no subjective differences or *artifacts* in the received signal. The remaining area is called the *redundancy* because it adds nothing to the information conveyed. Thus an ideal coder could be imagined which miraculously sorts out the entropy from the redundancy and only sends the former. An ideal decoder would then re-create the original impression of the information quite perfectly. In this ideal case, the entropy and the residual would be the same. As the ideal is approached, the coder complexity and the latency or delay both rise. In real coders, the ideal is not reached and the residual must be larger than the entropy. Figure 1.6(b) shows how complexity increases with compression factor. The additional complexity of H.264 over MPEG-2 is obvious from this. Figure 1.6(c) shows how increasing the codec latency can improve the compression factor.

Nevertheless moderate coding gains that only remove redundancy need not cause artifacts and result in systems which are described as *subjectively lossless*. If the channel capacity is not sufficient for that, then the coder will have to discard some of the entropy and with it useful information. Larger coding gains which remove some of the entropy must result in artifacts. It will also be seen from Figure 1.6 that an imperfect coder will fail to separate the redundancy and may discard entropy instead, resulting in artifacts at a sub-optimal compression factor.

It should be clear from the above that if quality is an issue, the highest performance will be obtained using codecs in which the prediction is as powerful as possible. When this is done the residual will be smaller and so the degree of lossy coding needed to achieve a target bit rate will be reduced.

Obviously it is necessary to provide a channel that could accept whatever entropy the coder extracts in order to have transparent quality. A single variable rate transmission or recording channel is traditionally unpopular with channel providers, although newer systems such as ATM support variable rate. Digital transmitters used in DVB or ATSC have a fixed bit rate. The variable rate requirement can be overcome by combining several compressed channels into one constant rate transmission in a way which flexibly allocates data rate between the channels. Provided the material is unrelated, the probability of all channels reaching peak entropy at once is very small and so those channels which are at one instant passing easy material will make available transmission capacity for those channels which are handling difficult material. This is the principle of statistical multiplexing.

Where the same type of source material is used consistently, e.g. English text, then it is possible to perform a statistical analysis on the frequency with which particular letters are used. Variable-length coding is used in which frequently used letters are allocated short codes and letters which occur infrequently are allocated long codes. This results in a lossless code. The well-known Morse code used for telegraphy is an example of this approach. The letter e is the most frequent in English and is sent with a single dot. An infrequent letter such as z is allocated a long complex pattern. It should be clear that codes of this kind which rely on a prior knowledge of the statistics of the signal are only effective with signals actually having those statistics. If Morse code is used with another language, the transmission becomes significantly less efficient because the statistics are quite different; the letter z, for example, is quite common in Czech.

The Huffman code[5] is also one which is designed for use with a data source having known statistics. The probability of the different code values to be transmitted is studied, and the most frequent codes are arranged to be transmitted with short wordlength symbols. As the probability of a code value falls, it will be allocated longer wordlength. The Huffman code is used in conjunction with a number of compression techniques and is shown in Figure 1.7.

The input or *source* codes are assembled in order of descending probability. The two lowest probabilities are distinguished by a single

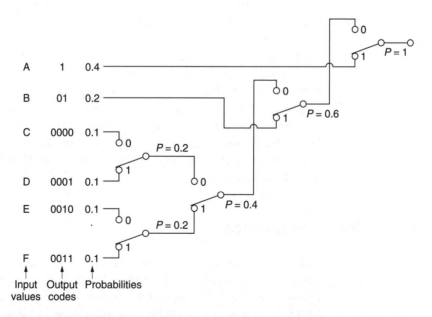

Figure 1.7 The Huffman code achieves compression by allocating short codes to frequent values. To aid deserializing the short codes are not prefixes of longer codes.

code bit and their probabilities are combined. The process of combining probabilities is continued until unity is reached and at each stage a bit is used to distinguish the path. The bit will be a zero for the most probable path and one for the least. The compressed output is obtained by reading the bits which describe which path to take going from right to left.

In the case of computer data, there is no control over the data statistics. Data to be recorded could be instructions, images, tables, text files and so on; each having their own code value distributions. In this case a coder relying on fixed source statistics will be completely inadequate. Instead a system is used which can learn the statistics as it goes along. The Lempel–Ziv–Welch (LZW) lossless codes are in this category. These codes build up a conversion table between frequent long source data strings and short transmitted data codes at both coder and decoder and initially their compression factor is below unity as the contents of the conversion tables are transmitted along with the data. However, once the tables are established, the coding gain more than compensates for the initial loss. In some applications, a continuous analysis of the frequency of code selection is made and if a data string in the table is no longer being used with sufficient frequency it can be deselected and a more common string substituted.

Lossless codes are less common for audio and video coding where perceptive codes are permissible. The perceptive codes often obtain a coding gain by shortening the wordlength of the data representing the signal waveform. This must increase the noise level and the trick is to ensure that the resultant noise is placed at frequencies where human senses are least able to perceive it. As a result although the received signal is measurably different from the source data, it can *appear* the same to the human listener or viewer at moderate compression factors. As these codes rely on the characteristics of human sight and hearing, they can only be fully tested subjectively.

The compression factor of such codes can be set at will by choosing the wordlength of the compressed data. Whilst mild compression will be undetectable, with greater compression factors, artifacts become noticeable. Figure 1.6 shows that this is inevitable from entropy considerations.

1.7   Video compression

Video signals exist in four dimensions: these are the attributes of the pixel, the horizontal and vertical spatial axes and the time axis. Compression can be applied in any or all of those four dimensions. MPEG assumes an eight-bit colour difference signal as the input, requiring rounding if the source is ten bit. The sampling rate of the

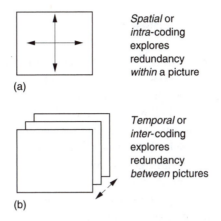

Figure 1.8 (a) Spatial or intra-coding works on individual images. (b) Temporal or inter-coding works on successive images.

colour signals is less than that of the luminance. This is done by downsampling the colour samples horizontally and generally vertically as well. Essentially an MPEG system has three parallel simultaneous channels, one for luminance and two colour difference, which after coding are multiplexed into a single bitstream.

Figure 1.8(a) shows that when individual pictures are compressed without reference to any other pictures, the time axis does not enter the process which is therefore described as *intra-coded* (intra = within) compression. The term *spatial coding* will also be found. It is an advantage of intra-coded video that there is no restriction to the editing which can be carried out on the picture sequence. As a result compressed VTRs such as Digital Betacam, DVC and D-9 use spatial coding. Cut editing may take place on the compressed data directly if necessary. As spatial coding treats each picture independently, it can employ certain techniques developed for the compression of still pictures. The ISO JPEG (Joint Photographic Experts Group) compression standards[6,7] are in this category. Where a succession of JPEG coded images are used for television, the term 'Motion JPEG' will be found.

Greater compression factors can be obtained by taking account of the redundancy from one picture to the next. This involves the time axis, as Figure 1.8(b) shows, and the process is known as *inter-coded* (inter = between) or *temporal* compression.

Temporal coding allows a higher compression factor, but has the disadvantage that an individual picture may exist only in terms of the differences from a previous picture. Clearly editing must be undertaken with caution and arbitrary cuts simply cannot be performed on the MPEG bitstream. If a previous picture is removed by an edit, the difference data will then be insufficient to re-create the current picture.

1.7.1   Intra-coded compression

Intra-coding works in three dimensions on the horizontal and vertical spatial axes and on the sample values. Analysis of typical television pictures reveals that whilst there is a high spatial frequency content due to detailed areas of the picture, there is a relatively small amount of energy at such frequencies. Often pictures contain sizeable areas in which the same or similar pixel values exist. This gives rise to low spatial frequencies. The average brightness of the picture results in a substantial zero frequency component. Simply omitting the high-frequency components is unacceptable as this causes an obvious softening of the picture.

A coding gain can be obtained by taking advantage of the fact that the amplitude of the spatial components falls with frequency. It is also possible to take advantage of the eye's reduced sensitivity to noise in high spatial frequencies. If the spatial frequency spectrum is divided into frequency bands the high-frequency bands can be described by fewer bits not only because their amplitudes are smaller but also because more noise can be tolerated. The wavelet transform (MPEG-4 only) and the discrete cosine transform used in JPEG and MPEG-1, MPEG-2 and MPEG-4 allow two-dimensional pictures to be described in the frequency domain and these are discussed in Chapter 3.

1.7.2   Inter-coded compression

Inter-coding takes further advantage of the similarities between successive pictures in real material. Instead of sending information for each picture separately, inter-coders will send the difference between the previous picture and the current picture in a form of differential coding. Figure 1.9 shows the principle. A picture store is required at the coder to allow comparison to be made between successive pictures and a similar store is required at the decoder to make the previous picture available. The difference data may be treated as a picture itself and subjected to some form of transform-based spatial compression.

The simple system of Figure 1.9(a) is of limited use as in the case of a transmission error, every subsequent picture would be affected. Channel switching in a television set would also be impossible. In practical systems a modification is required. One approach is the so-called 'leaky predictor' in which the next picture is predicted from a limited number of previous pictures rather than from an indefinite number. As a result errors cannot propagate indefinitely. The approach used in MPEG is that periodically some absolute picture data are transmitted in place of difference data.

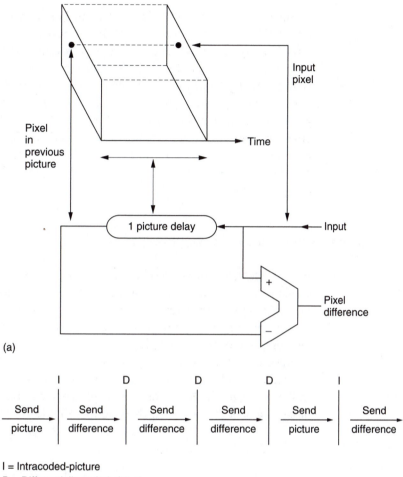

(a)

(b)

I = Intracoded-picture
D = Differentially coded picture

Figure 1.9 An inter-coded system (a) uses a delay to calculate the pixel differences between successive pictures. To prevent error propagation, intra-coded pictures (b) may be used periodically.

Figure 1.9(b) shows that absolute picture data, known as *I* or *intra pictures* are interleaved with pictures which are created using difference data, known as *P* or *predicted* pictures. The *I* pictures require a large amount of data, whereas the *P* pictures require fewer data. As a result the instantaneous data rate varies dramatically and buffering has to be used to allow a constant transmission rate. The leaky predictor needs less buffering as the compression factor does not change so much from picture to picture.

The *I* picture and all of the *P* pictures prior to the next *I* picture are called a group of pictures (GOP). For a high compression factor, a large number of *P* pictures should be present between *I* pictures, making a long GOP. However, a long GOP delays recovery from a transmission error. The compressed bitstream can only be edited at *I* pictures as shown.

In the case of moving objects, although their appearance may not change greatly from picture to picture, the data representing them on a fixed sampling grid will change and so large differences will be generated between successive pictures. It is a great advantage if the effect of motion can be removed from difference data so that they only reflect the changes in appearance of a moving object since a much greater coding gain can then be obtained. This is the objective of motion compensation.

1.7.3   Introduction to motion compensation

In real television program material objects move around before a fixed camera or the camera itself moves. Motion compensation is a process which effectively measures motion of objects from one picture to the next so that it can allow for that motion when looking for redundancy between pictures. Figure 1.10 shows that moving pictures can be expressed in a three-dimensional space which results from the screen area moving along the time axis. In the case of still objects, the only motion is along the time axis. However, when an object moves, it does so along the *optic flow axis* which is not parallel to the time axis. The optic

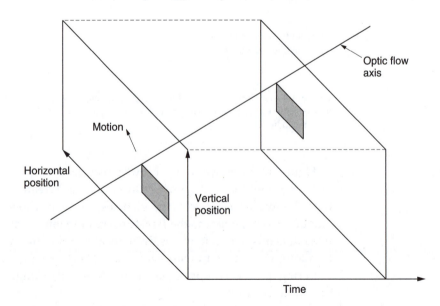

Figure 1.10 Objects travel in a three-dimensional space along the optic flow axis which is only parallel to the time axis if there is no movement.

flow axis is the locus of a point on a moving object as it takes on various screen positions.

It will be clear that the data values representing a moving object change with respect to the time axis. However, looking along the optic flow axis the appearance of an object only changes if it deforms, moves into shadow or rotates. For simple translational motions the data representing an object are highly redundant with respect to the optic flow axis. Thus if the optic flow axis can be located, coding gain can be obtained in the presence of motion.

A motion-compensated coder works as follows. A reference picture is sent, but is also locally stored so that it can be compared with another picture to find motion vectors for various areas of the picture. The reference picture is then shifted according to these vectors to cancel interpicture motion. The resultant *predicted* picture is compared with the actual picture to produce a *prediction error* also called a *residual*. The prediction error is transmitted with the motion vectors. At the receiver the reference picture is also held in a memory. It is shifted according to the transmitted motion vectors to re-create the predicted picture and then the prediction error is added to it to re-create the original.

In prior compression schemes the predicted picture followed the reference picture. In MPEG this is not the case. Information may be brought back from a later picture or forward from an earlier picture as appropriate.

1.7.4   Film-originated video compression

Film can be used as the source of video signals if a telecine machine is used. The most common frame rate for film is 24 Hz, whereas the field rates of television are 50 Hz and 60 Hz. This incompatibility is patched over in two different ways. In 50 Hz telecine, the film is simply played slightly too fast so that the frame rate becomes 25 Hz. Then each frame is converted into two television fields giving the correct 50 Hz field rate. In 60 Hz telecine, the film travels at the correct speed, but alternate frames are used to produce two fields then three fields. The technique is known as 3:2 pulldown. In this way two frames produce five fields and so the correct 60 Hz field rate results. The motion portrayal of telecine is not very good as moving objects judder, especially in 60 Hz systems. Figure 1.11 shows how the optic flow is portrayed in film-originated video.

When film-originated video is input to a compression system, the disturbed optic flow will play havoc with the motion-compensation system. In a 50 Hz system there appears to be no motion between the two fields which have originated from the same film frame, whereas between

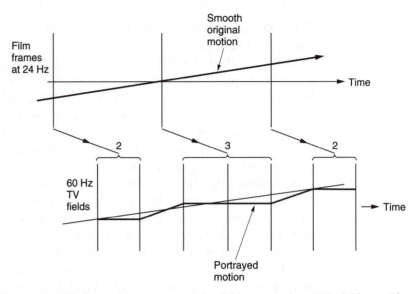

Figure 1.11 Telecine machines must use 3:2 pulldown to produce 60 Hz field rate video.

the next two fields large motions will exist. In 60 Hz systems, the motion will be zero for three fields out of five.

With such inputs, it is more efficient to adopt a different processing mode which is based upon the characteristics of the original film. Instead of attempting to manipulate fields of video, the system de-interlaces pairs of fields in order to reconstruct the original film frames. This can be done by a fairly simple motion detector. When substantial motion is measured between successive fields in the output of a telecine, this is taken to mean that the fields have come from different film frames. When negligible motion is detected between fields, this is taken to indicate that the fields have come from the same film frame.

In 50 Hz video it is quite simple to find the sequence and produce de-interlaced frames at 25 Hz. In 60 Hz 3:2 pulldown video the problem is slightly more complex because it is necessary to locate the frames in which three fields are output so that the third field can be discarded, leaving, once more, de-interlaced frames at 25 Hz. Whilst it is relatively straightforward to lock on to the 3:2 sequence with direct telecine output signals, if the telecine material has been edited on videotape the 3:2 sequence may contain discontinuities. In this case it is necessary to provide a number of field stores in the de-interlace unit so that a series of fields can be examined to locate the edits. Once telecine video has been de-interlaced back to frames, intra- and inter-coded compression can be employed using frame-based motion compensation.

MPEG transmissions include flags that tell the decoder the origin of the material. Material originating at 24 Hz but converted to interlaced video does not have the motion attributes of interlace because the lines in two fields have come from the same point on the time axis. Two fields can be combined to create a progressively scanned frame. In the case of 3:2 pulldown material, the third field need not be sent at all as the decoder can easily repeat a field from memory. As a result the same compressed film material can be output at 50 or 60 Hz as required.

Recently conventional telecine machines have been superseded by the *datacine* which scans each film frame into a pixel array which can be made directly available to the MPEG encoder without passing through an intermediate digital video standard. Datacines are used extensively for mastering DVDs from film stock.

1.8 Introduction to MPEG-1

As mentioned above, the intention of MPEG-1 is to deliver video and audio at the same bit rate as a conventional audio CD. As the bit rate was a given, this was achieved by subsampling to half the definition of conventional television. In order to have a constant input bit rate irrespective of the frame rate, 25 Hz systems have a picture size of 352×288 pixels whereas 30 Hz systems have a picture size of 352×240 pixels. This is known as *common intermediate format* (CIF). If the input is conventional interlaced video, CIF can be obtained by discarding alternate fields and downsampling the remaining active lines by a factor of two.

As interlaced systems have very poor vertical resolution, down-sampling to CIF actually does little damage to still images, although the very low picture rates damage motion portrayal.

Although MPEG-1 appeared rather rough on screen, this was due to the very low bit rate. It is more important to appreciate that MPEG-1 introduced the great majority of the coding tools which would continue to be used in MPEG-2 and MPEG-4. These included an elementary stream syntax, bidirectional motion-compensated coding, buffering and rate control. Many of the spatial coding principles of MPEG-1 were taken from JPEG. MPEG-1 also specified audio compression of up to two channels.

1.9 MPEG-2: Profiles and Levels

MPEG-2 builds upon MPEG-1 by adding interlace capability as well as a greatly expanded range of picture sizes and bit rates. The use of scaleable systems is also addressed, along with definitions of how multiple MPEG bitstreams can be multiplexed. As MPEG-2 is an extension of MPEG-1, it is easy for MPEG-2 decoders to handle MPEG-1 data. In a sense an

Profiles

Levels	Simple	Main	4:2:2	SNR	Spatial	High
High		4:2:0 1920 × 1152 90 Mb/S				4:2:0 or 4:2:2 1920 × 1152 100 Mb/S
High 1440		4:2:0 1440 × 1152 60 Mb/S			4:2:0 1440 × 1152 60 Mb/S	4:2:0 or 4:2:2 1440 × 1152 80 Mb/S
Main	4:2:0 720 × 576 15 Mb/S NO B	4:2:0 720 × 576 15 Mb/S	4:2:2 720 × 608 50 Mb/S	4:2:0 720 × 576 15 Mb/S		4:2:0 or 4:2:2 720 × 576 20 Mb/S
Low		4:2:0 352 × 288 4 Mb/S		4:2:0 352 × 288 4 Mb/S		

Figure 1.12 Profiles and Levels in MPEG-2. See text for details.

MPEG-1 bitstream is an MPEG-2 bitstream which has a restricted vocabulary and so can be readily understood by an MPEG-2 decoder.

MPEG-2 has too many applications to solve with a single standard and so it is subdivided into Profiles and Levels. Put simply a Profile describes a degree of complexity whereas a Level describes the picture size or resolution which goes with that Profile. Not all Levels are supported at all Profiles. Figure 1.12 shows the available combinations. In principle there are twenty-four of these, but not all have been defined. An MPEG-2 decoder having a given Profile and Level must also be able to decode lower Profiles and Levels.

The simple Profile does not support bidirectional coding and so only *I* and *P* pictures will be output. This reduces the coding and decoding delay and allows simpler hardware. The simple Profile has only been defined at Main Level (SP ML).

The Main Profile is designed for a large proportion of uses. The Low Level uses a low resolution input having only 352 pixels per line. The majority of broadcast applications will require the MP ML (Main Profile at Main Level) subset of MPEG which supports SDTV (standard definition television). The High-1440 Level is a high-definition scheme which doubles the definition compared to Main Level. The High Level not only doubles the resolution but maintains that resolution with 16:9 format by increasing the number of horizontal samples from 1440 to 1920.

In compression systems using spatial transforms and requantizing it is possible to produce scaleable signals. A scaleable process is one in which the input results in a main signal and a 'helper' signal. The main signal can be decoded alone to give a picture of a certain quality, but if the

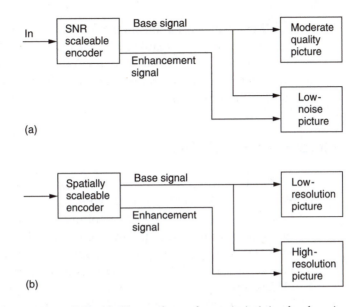

Figure 1.13 (a) An SNR scaleable encoder produces a 'noisy' signal and a noise cancelling signal. (b) A spatially scaleable encoder produces a low-resolution picture and a resolution-enhancing picture.

information from the helper signal is added some aspect of the quality can be improved.

Figure 1.13(a) shows that in a conventional MPEG coder, by heavily requantizing coefficients a picture with moderate signal-to-noise ratio results. If, however, that picture is locally decoded and subtracted pixel by pixel from the original, a 'quantizing noise' picture would result. This can be compressed and transmitted as the helper signal. A simple decoder only decodes the main 'noisy' bitstream, but a more complex decoder can decode both bitstreams and combine them to produce a low-noise picture. This is the principle of SNR scaleability.

As an alternative, Figure 1.13(b) shows that by coding only the lower spatial frequencies in an HDTV picture a base bitstream can be made which an SDTV receiver can decode. If the lower definition picture is locally decoded and subtracted from the original picture, a 'definition-enhancing' picture would result. This can be coded into a helper signal.

A suitable decoder could combine the main and helper signals to recreate the HDTV picture. This is the principle of spatial scaleability. The High Profile supports both SNR and spatial scaleability as well as allowing the option of 4:2:2 sampling (see section 2.11).

The 4:2:2 Profile has been developed for improved compatibility with existing digital television production equipment. This allows 4:2:2 working without requiring the additional complexity of using the High Profile. For example, an HP ML decoder must support SNR scaleability which is not a requirement for production.

MPEG-2 increased the number of audio channels possible to five whilst remaining compatible with MPEG-1 audio. MPEG-2 subsequently introduced a more efficient audio coding scheme known as MPEG-2 AAC (advanced audio coding) which is not backwards compatible with the earlier audio coding schemes.

1.10   Introduction to MPEG-4

MPEG-4 introduces a number of new coding tools as shown in Figure 1.14. In MPEG-1 and MPEG-2 the motion compensation is based on regular fixed-size areas of image known as *macroblocks*. Whilst this works well at the designed bit rates, there will always be some inefficiency due to real moving objects failing to align with macroblock boundaries. This will increase the residual bit rate. In MPEG-4, moving objects can be coded as arbitrary shapes. Figure 1.15 shows that a background can be coded quite independently from objects in front of it. Object motion can then be described with vectors and much-reduced residual data.

According to the Profile, objects may be two dimensional, three dimensional and opaque or translucent. The decoder must contain effectively a layering vision mixer which is capable of prioritizing image data as a function of how close it is to the viewer. The picture coding of MPEG-4 is known as texture coding and is more advanced than the MPEG-2 equivalent, using more lossless predictive coding for pixel values, coefficients and vectors.

In addition to motion compensation, MPEG-4 can describe how an object changes its perspective as it moves using a technique called mesh

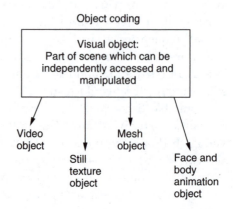

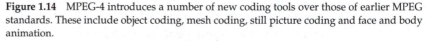

Figure 1.14   MPEG-4 introduces a number of new coding tools over those of earlier MPEG standards. These include object coding, mesh coding, still picture coding and face and body animation.

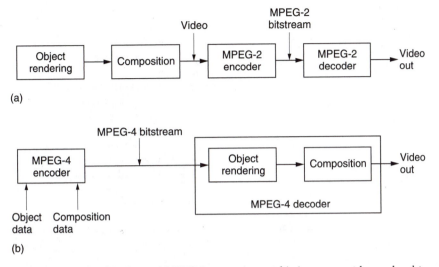

Figure 1.15   (a) In MPEG-1 and MPEG-2, computer graphic images must be rendered to video before coding. (b) In contrast, MPEG-4 may move the rendering process to the decoder, reducing the bit rate needed with the penalty of increased decoder complexity.

coding. By warping another image, the prediction of the present image is improved. MPEG-4 also introduces coding for still images using DCT or wavelets.

Although MPEG-2 supported some scaleability, MPEG-4 also takes this further. In addition to spatial and noise scaleability, MPEG-4 also allows temporal scaleability where a base level bitstream having a certain frame rate may be augmented by an additional enhancement bitstream to produce a decoder output at a higher frame rate. This is important as it allows a way forward from the marginal frame rates of today's film and television formats whilst remaining backwards compatible with traditional equipment. The comprehensive scaleability of MPEG-4 is equally important in networks where it allows the user the best picture possible for the available bit rate.

MPEG-4 also introduces standards for face and body animation. Specialized vectors allow a still picture of a face and optionally a body to be animated to allow expressions and gestures to accompany speech at very low bit rates. In some senses MPEG-4 has gone upstream of the video signal which forms the input to MPEG-1 and MPEG-2 coders to analyse ways in which the video signal was rendered. Figure 1.15(a) shows that in a system using MPEG-1 and MPEG-2, all rendering and production steps take place before the encoder. Figure 1.15(b) shows that in MPEG-4, some of these steps can take place in the decoder. The advantage is that fewer data need to be transmitted. Some of these data will be rendering instructions which can be very efficient and result in a high compression factor. As a significant part of the rendering takes place

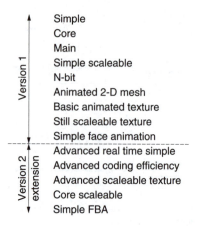

Figure 1.16 The visual object types supported by MPEG-4 in versions 1 and 2.

in the decoder, computer graphics generators can be designed directly to output an MPEG-4 bitstream. In interactive systems such as simulators and video games, inputs from the user can move objects around the screen. The disadvantage is increased decoder complexity, but as the economics of digital processing continues to advance this is hardly a serious concern.

As might be expected, the huge range of coding tools in MPEG-4 is excessive for many applications. As with MPEG-2 this has been dealt with using Profiles and Levels. Figure 1.16 shows the range of Visual Object types in version 1 of MPEG-4 and as expanded in version 2. For each visual object type the coding tools needed are shown. Figure 1.17 shows the relationship between the Visual Profiles and the Visual Object types supported by each Profile. The crossover between computer-generated and natural images is evident in the Profile structure where Profiles 1–5 cover natural images, Profiles 8 and 9 cover rendered images and Profiles 6 and 7 cover hybrid natural/rendered images. It is only possible to give an introduction here and more detail is provided in Chapter 5. MPEG-4 also extends the boundaries of audio coding. The MPEG-2 AAC technique is extended in MPEG-4 by some additional tools. New tools are added which allow operation at very low bit rates for speech applications. Also introduced is the concept of *structured audio* in which the audio waveform is synthesized at the decoder from a bitstream which is essentially a digital musical score.

1.11 Introduction to H.264 (AVC)

The wide range of applications of MPEG-4 are not needed for broadcasting purposes. However, areas of MPEG-4 such as texture

Version 1 visual profiles

Object types / Profiles	Simple	Core	Main	Simple scaleable	N-bit	Animated 2D mesh	Basic animated texture	Scaleable texture	Simple face
1. Simple	X								
2. Simple scaleable	X			X					
3. Core	X	X							
4. Main	X	X	X					X	
5. N-bit	X	X			X				
6. Hybrid	X	X				X	X	X	X
7. Basic animated texture							X	X	X
8. Scaleable texture								X	
9. Simple FA									X

Version 2 visual profiles

Object types / Profiles	Simple	Simple scaleable	Core	Core scaleable	Advanced real time simple	Advanced coding efficiency	Advanced scaleable texture	Simple FBA
V2-1. Advanced real time simple	X				X			
V2-2. Core scaleable	X	X	X	X				
V2-3. Advanced coding efficiency	X		X			X		
V2-4. Advanced core	X		X				X	
V2-5. Advanced scaleable texture							X	
V2-6. Simple FBA								X

Figure 1.17 The visual object types supported by each visual profile of MPEG-4.

coding are directly applicable to, and indeed can be interpreted as extensions of, MPEG-2. Thus a good way of appreciating H.264[8] is to consider that in developing it, every video coding tool of MPEG-4 was considered and if a refinement was possible, albeit with the penalty of increased complexity, then it would be incorporated. Thus, H.264 AVC does not do more than MPEG-2, but it does it better in that a greater coding gain is achieved for the same perceived quality. It should be noted that a significant increase in processing power is needed with AVC in comparison with MPEG-2. As before, H.264 has Profiles and Levels for the same reasons.

1.12 Audio compression

Perceptive coding in audio relies on the principle of auditory masking, which is treated in detail in section 4.1. Masking causes the ear/brain combination to be less sensitive to sound at one frequency in the presence of another at a nearby frequency. If a first tone is present in the input, then it will mask signals of lower level at nearby frequencies. The quantizing of the first tone and of further tones at those frequencies can be made coarser. Fewer bits are needed and a coding gain results. The increased quantizing error is allowable if it is masked by the presence of the first tone.

1.12.1 Sub-band coding

Sub-band coding mimics the frequency analysis mechanism of the ear and splits the audio spectrum into a large number of different bands. Signals in these bands can then be quantized independently. The quantizing error which results is confined to the frequency limits of the band and so it can be arranged to be masked by the program material. The techniques used in Layers I and II of MPEG audio are based on sub-band coding as are those used in DCC (Digital Compact Cassette).

1.12.2 Transform coding

In transform coding the time-domain audio waveform is converted into a frequency domain representation such as a Fourier, discrete cosine or wavelet transform (see Chapter 3). Transform coding takes advantage of the fact that the amplitude or envelope of an audio signal changes relatively slowly and so the coefficients of the transform can be transmitted relatively infrequently. Clearly such an approach breaks down in the presence of transients and adaptive systems are required in practice. Transients cause the coefficients to be updated frequently whereas in stationary parts of the signal such as sustained notes the update rate can be reduced. Discrete cosine transform (DCT) coding is used in Layer III of MPEG audio and in the compression system of the Sony MiniDisc.

1.12.3 Predictive coding

As seen above, in a predictive coder there are two identical predictors, one in the coder and one in the decoder. Their job is to examine a run of previous data values and to extrapolate forward to estimate or predict what the next value will be. This is subtracted from the *actual* next code value at the encoder to produce a prediction error which is transmitted. The decoder then adds the prediction error to its own prediction to obtain the output code value again.

Prediction can be used in the time domain, where sample values are predicted, or in the frequency domain where coefficient values are predicted. Time-domain predictive coders work with a short encode and decode delay and are useful in telephony where a long loop delay causes problems. Frequency prediction is used in AC-3 and MPEG AAC.

1.13 MPEG bitstreams

MPEG supports a variety of bitstream types for various purposes and these are shown in Figure 1.18. The output of a single compressor (video or audio) is known as an elementary stream. In transmission, many elementary streams will be combined to make a transport stream. Multiplexing requires blocks or packets of constant size. It is advantageous if these are short so that each elementary stream in the multiplex can receive regular data. A transport stream has a complex structure because it needs to incorporate metadata indicating which audio elementary streams and ancillary data are associated with which video elementary stream. It is possible to have a single program transport stream (SPTS) which carries only the elementary streams of one TV program.

For certain purposes, such as recording a single elementary stream, the transport stream is not appropriate. The small packets of the transport stream each require a header and this wastes storage space. In this case a program stream can be used. A program stream is a simplified

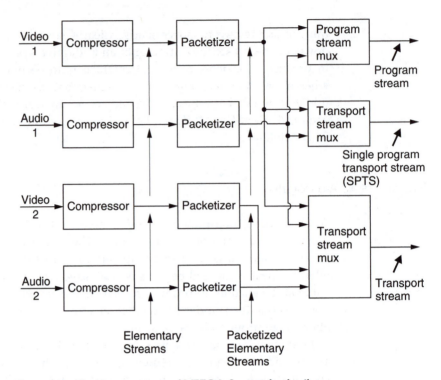

Figure 1.18 The bitstream types of MPEG-2. See text for details.

bitstream which multiplexes audio and video for a single program together, provided they have been encoded from a common locked clock. Unlike a transport stream, the blocks are larger and are not necessarily of fixed size.

1.14 Drawbacks of compression

By definition, compression removes redundancy from signals. Redundancy is, however, essential to making data resistant to errors. As a result, compressed data are more sensitive to errors than uncompressed data. Thus transmission systems using compressed data must incorporate more powerful error-correction strategies and avoid compression techniques which are notoriously sensitive. As an example, the Digital Betacam format uses relatively mild compression and yet requires 20 per cent redundancy whereas the D-5 format does not use compression and only requires 17 per cent redundancy even though it has a recording density 30 per cent higher. Techniques using tables such as the Lempel–Ziv–Welch codes are very sensitive to bit errors as an error in the transmission of a table value results in bit errors every time that table location is accessed. This is known as error propagation. Variable-length techniques such as the Huffman code are also sensitive to bit errors. As there is no fixed symbol size, the only way the decoder can parse a serial bitstream into symbols is to increase the assumed wordlength a bit at a time until a code value is recognized. The next bit must then be the first bit in the next symbol. A single bit in error could cause the length of a code to be wrongly assessed and then all subsequent codes would also be wrongly decoded until synchronization could be re-established. Later variable-length codes sacrifice some compression efficiency in order to offer better resynchronization properties.

In non-real-time systems such as computers an uncorrectable error results in reference to the back-up media. In real-time systems such as audio and video this is impossible and concealment must be used. However, concealment relies on redundancy and compression reduces the degree of redundancy. Media such as hard disks can be verified so that uncorrectable errors are virtually eliminated, but tape is prone to dropouts which will exceed the burst-correcting power of the replay system from time to time. For this reason the compression factors used on audio or video tape should be moderate.

As perceptive coders introduce noise, it will be clear that in a concatenated system the second codec could be confused by the noise due to the first. If the codecs are identical then each may well make, or better still be designed to make, the same decisions when they are in tandem. If the codecs are not identical the results could be disappointing. Signal manipulation between codecs can also result in artifacts which were previously undetectable becoming visible because the signal that was masking them is no longer present.

In general, compression should not be used for its own sake, but only where a genuine bandwidth or cost bottleneck exists. Even then the mildest compression possible should be used. Whilst high compression factors are permissible for final delivery of material to the consumer, they are not advisable prior to any post-production stages. For contribution material, lower compression factors are essential and this is sometimes referred to as *mezzanine* level compression.

One practical drawback of compression systems is that they are largely generic in structure and the same hardware can be operated at a variety of compression factors. Clearly the higher the compression factor, the cheaper the system will be to operate so there will be economic pressure to use high compression factors. Naturally the risk of artifacts is increased and so there is (or should be) counterpressure from those with engineering skills to moderate the compression. The way of the world at the time of writing is that the accountants have the upper hand. This was not a problem when there were fixed standards such as PAL and NTSC, as there was no alternative but to adhere to them. Today there is plenty of evidence that the variable compression factor control is being turned too far in the direction of economy.

It has been seen above that concatenation of compression systems should be avoided as this causes generation loss. Generation loss is worse if the codecs are different. Interlace is a legacy compression technique and if concatenated with MPEG, generation loss will be exaggerated. In theory and in practice better results are obtained in MPEG for the same bit rate if the input is progressively scanned. Consequently the use of interlace with MPEG coders cannot be recommended for new systems. Chapter 5 explores this theme in greater detail.

1.15 Compression pre-processing

Compression relies completely on identifying redundancy in the source material. Consequently anything which reduces that redundancy will have a damaging effect. Noise is particularly undesirable as it creates additional spatial frequencies in individual pictures as well as spurious differences between pictures. Where noisy source material is anticipated some form of noise reduction will be essential.

When high compression factors must be used to achieve a low bit rate, it is inevitable that the level of artifacts will rise. In order to contain the artifact level, it is necessary to restrict the source entropy prior to the coder. This may be done by spatial low-pass filtering to reduce the picture resolution, and may be combined with downsampling to reduce the number of pixels per picture. In some cases, such as teleconferencing, it will also be necessary to reduce the picture rate. At very low bit rates the use of interlace becomes acceptable as a pre-processing stage providing downsampling prior to the MPEG compression.

A compression pre-processor will combine various types of noise reduction (see Chapter 3) with spatial and temporal downsampling.

1.16 Some guidelines

Although compression techniques themselves are complex, there are some simple rules which can be used to avoid disappointment. Used wisely, MPEG compression has a number of advantages. Used in an inappropriate manner, disappointment is almost inevitable and the technology could get a bad name. The next few points are worth remembering.

- Compression technology may be exciting, but if it is not necessary it should not be used.
- If compression is to be used, the degree of compression should be as small as possible, i.e. use the highest practical bit rate.
- Cascaded compression systems cause loss of quality and the lower the bit rates, the worse this gets. Quality loss increases if any post-production steps are performed between compressions.
- Avoid using interlaced video with MPEG.
- Compression systems cause delay.
- Compression systems work best with clean source material. Noisy signals or poorly decoded composite video give poor results.
- Compressed data are generally more prone to transmission errors than non-compressed data. The choice of a compression scheme must consider the error characteristics of the channel.
- Audio codecs need to be level calibrated so that when sound pressure level-dependent decisions are made in the coder those levels actually exist at the microphone.
- Low bit rate coders should only be used for the final delivery of post-produced signals to the end-user.
- Don't believe statements comparing codec performance to 'VHS quality' or similar. Compression artifacts are quite different from the artifacts of consumer VCRs.
- Quality varies wildly with source material. Beware of 'convincing' demonstrations which may use selected material to achieve low bit rates. Use your own test material, selected for a balance of difficulty.
- Don't be browbeaten by the technology. You don't have to understand it to assess the results. Your eyes and ears are as good as anyone's so don't be afraid to criticize artifacts. In the case of video, use still frames to distinguish spatial artifacts from temporal ones.

References

1. ISO/IEC JTC1/SC29/WG11 MPEG, International standard ISO 11172, Coding of moving pictures and associated audio for digital storage media up to 1.5 Mbits/s (1992)
2. LeGall, D., MPEG: a video compression standard for multimedia applications. *Communications of the ACM*, **34**, No. 4, 46–58 (1991)
3. MPEG-2 Video Standard: ISO/IEC 13818–2: Information technology – generic coding of moving pictures and associated audio information: Video (1996) (aka ITU-T Rec. H-262 (1996))

4. MPEG-4 Standard: ISO/IEC 14496–2: Information technology – coding of audio-visual objects: Amd. 1 (2000)
5. Huffman, D.A., A method for the construction of minimum redundancy codes. *Proc. IRE*, **40**, 1098–1101 (1952)
6. ISO Joint Photographic Experts Group standard JPEG-8-R8
7. Wallace, G.K., Overview of the JPEG (ISO/CCITT) still image compression standard. ISO/JTC1/SC2/WG8 N932 (1989)
8. ITU-T H.264 Advanced video coding for generic audiovisual services (2003)

2

Fundamentals

2.1   What is an audio signal?

Actual sounds are converted to electrical signals for convenience of handling, recording and conveying from one place to another. This is the job of the microphone. There are two basic types of microphone, those which measure the variations in air pressure due to sound, and those which measure the air velocity due to sound, although there are numerous practical types which are a combination of both.

The sound pressure or velocity varies with time and so does the output voltage of the microphone, in proportion. The output voltage of the microphone is thus an analog of the sound pressure or velocity.

As sound causes no overall air movement, the average velocity of all sounds is zero, which corresponds to silence. As a result the bidirectional air movement gives rise to bipolar signals from the microphone, where silence is in the centre of the voltage range, and instantaneously negative or positive voltages are possible. Clearly the average voltage of all audio signals is also zero, and so when level is measured, it is necessary to take the modulus of the voltage, which is the job of the rectifier in the level meter. When this is done, the greater the amplitude of the audio signal, the greater the modulus becomes, and so a higher level is displayed. Whilst the nature of an audio signal is very simple, there are many applications of audio, each requiring different bandwidth and dynamic range.

2.2   What is a video signal?

The goal of television is to allow a moving picture to be seen at a remote place. The picture is a two-dimensional image, which changes as a function of time. This is a three-dimensional information source where the dimensions are distance across the screen, distance down the screen and time. Whilst telescopes convey these three dimensions directly, this cannot be done with electrical signals or radio transmissions, which are restricted to a single parameter varying with time.

The solution in film and television is to convert the three-dimensional moving image into a series of still pictures, taken at the frame rate, and then, in television only, the two-dimensional images are scanned as a series of lines[1] to produce a single voltage varying with time which can be digitized, recorded or transmitted. Europe, the Middle East and the former Soviet Union use the scanning standard of 625/50, whereas the USA and Japan use 525/59.94.

2.3   Types of video

Figure 2.1 shows some of the basic types of analog colour video. Each of these types can, of course, exist in a variety of line standards. Since practical colour cameras generally have three separate sensors, one for each primary colour, an *RGB* component system will exist at some stage in the internal workings of the camera, even if it does not emerge in that form. *RGB* consists of three parallel signals each having the same spectrum, and is used where the highest accuracy is needed, often for production of still pictures. Examples of this are paint systems and in computer aided design (CAD) displays. *RGB* is seldom used for real-time video recording.

Some compression can be obtained by using colour difference working. The human eye relies on brightness to convey detail, and much less resolution is needed in the colour information. *R*, *G* and *B* are matrixed together to form a luminance (and monochrome compatible) signal *Y* which has full bandwidth. The matrix also produces two colour difference signals, *R–Y* and *B–Y*, but these do not need the same bandwidth as *Y*, one half or one quarter will do depending on the application. Colour difference signals represent an early application of perceptive coding; a saving in bandwidth is obtained by expressing the signals according to the way the eye operates.

Analog colour difference recorders such as Betacam and M II record these signals separately. The D-1 and D-5 formats record 525/60 or 625/50 colour difference signals digitally and Digital Betacam does so using compression. In casual parlance, colour difference formats are often called component formats to distinguish them from composite formats.

For colour television broadcast in a single channel, the PAL, SECAM and NTSC systems interleave into the spectrum of a monochrome signal

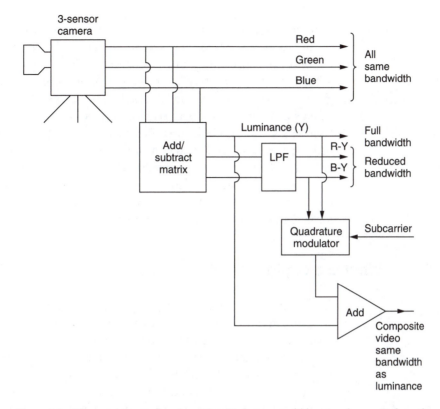

Figure 2.1 The major types of analog video. Red, green and blue signals emerge from the camera sensors, needing full bandwidth. If a luminance signal is obtained by a weighted sum of *R*, *G* and *B*, it will need full bandwidth, but the colour difference signals *R–Y* and *B–Y* need less bandwidth. Combining *R–Y* and *B–Y* into a subcarrier modulation scheme allows colour transmission in the same bandwidth as monochrome.

a subcarrier which carries two colour difference signals of restricted bandwidth. As the bandwidth required for composite video is no greater than that of luminance, it can be regarded as a form of compression performed in the analog domain. The artifacts which composite video introduces and the inflexibility in editing resulting from the need to respect colour framing serve as a warning that compression is not without its penalties. The subcarrier is intended to be invisible on the screen of a monochrome television set. A subcarrier-based colour system is generally referred to as composite video, and the modulated subcarrier is called chroma.

It is not advantageous to compress composite video using modern transform-based coders as the transform process cannot identify redundancy in a subcarrier. Composite video compression is restricted to differential coding systems. Transform-based compression must use *RGB* or colour difference signals. As *RGB* requires excessive bandwidth it makes no sense to use it with compression and so in practice only colour difference signals, which have been bandwidth reduced by perceptive coding, are used in MPEG. Where signals to be compressed originate in composite form, they must be decoded first. The decoding must be performed as accurately as possible, with particular attention being given to the quality of the Y/C separation. The chroma in composite signals is deliberately designed to invert from frame to frame in order to lessen its visibility. Unfortunately any residual chroma in luminance will be interpreted by inter-field compression systems as temporal luminance changes which need to be reproduced. This eats up data which should be used to render the picture. Residual chroma also results in high horizontal and vertical spatial frequencies in each field which appear to be wanted detail to the compressor.

2.4   What is a digital signal?

One of the vital concepts to grasp is that digital audio and video are simply alternative means of carrying the same information as their analog counterparts. An ideal digital system has the same characteristics as an ideal analog system: both of them are totally transparent and reproduce the original applied waveform without error. Needless to say, in the real world ideal conditions seldom prevail, so analog and digital equipment both fall short of the ideal. Digital equipment simply falls short of the ideal to a smaller extent than does analog and at lower cost, or, if the designer chooses, can have the same performance as analog at much lower cost. Compression is one of the techniques used to lower the cost, but it has the potential to lower the quality as well.

Any analog signal source can be characterized by a given useful bandwidth and signal-to-noise ratio. Video signals have very wide bandwidth extending over several megaHertz but require only 50 dB or so SNR whereas audio signals require only 20 kHz but need much better SNR.

Although there are a number of ways in which audio and video waveforms can be represented digitally, there is one system, known as pulse code modulation (PCM), which is in virtually universal use. Figure 2.2 shows how PCM works. Instead of being continuous, the time axis is represented in a discrete or stepwise manner. The waveform is not carried by continuous representation, but by measurement at regular intervals. This process is called sampling and the frequency with which samples are taken is called the sampling rate or sampling frequency F_s. The sampling rate is generally fixed and is not necessarily a function of any frequency in the signal, although in component video it will be line-locked for convenience. If every effort is made to rid the sampling clock of jitter, or time instability, every sample will be made at an exactly even

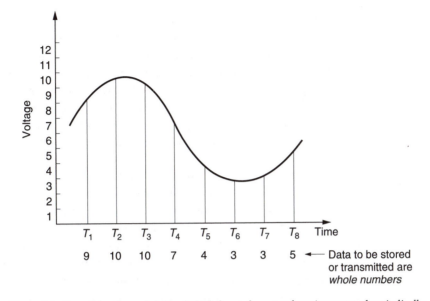

Figure 2.2 In pulse code modulation (PCM) the analog waveform is measured periodically at the sampling rate. The voltage (represented here by the height) of each sample is then described by a whole number. The whole numbers are stored or transmitted rather than the waveform itself.

time step. Clearly if there are any subsequent timebase errors, the instants at which samples arrive will be changed and the effect can be detected. If samples arrive at some destination with an irregular timebase, the effect can be eliminated by storing the samples temporarily in a memory and reading them out using a stable, locally generated clock. This process is called timebase correction which all properly engineered digital systems employ. It should be stressed that sampling is an analog process. Each sample still varies infinitely as the original waveform did.

Figure 2.2 also shows that each sample is also discrete, or represented in a stepwise manner. The length of the sample, which will be proportional to the voltage of the waveform, is represented by a whole number. This process is known as quantizing and results in an approximation, but the size of the error can be controlled until it is negligible. If, for example, we were to measure the height of humans to the nearest metre, virtually all adults would register two metres high and obvious difficulties would result. These are generally overcome by measuring height to the nearest centimetre. Clearly there is no advantage in going further and expressing our height in a whole number of millimetres or even micrometres. An appropriate resolution can be found just as readily for audio or video, and greater accuracy is not beneficial. The link between quality and sample resolution is explored later in this chapter. The advantage of using whole numbers is that they are not prone to drift. If a whole number can be carried from one place to another without numerical error, it has not changed at all. By describing waveforms numerically, the original information has been expressed in a way which is better able to resist unwanted changes.

Essentially, digital systems carry the original waveform numerically. The number of the sample is an analog of time, and the magnitude of the sample is an analog of the signal voltage. As both axes of the waveform are discrete, the waveform can be accurately restored from numbers as if it were being drawn on graph paper. If we require greater accuracy, we simply choose paper with smaller squares. Clearly more numbers are required and each one could change over a larger range.

Discrete numbers are used to represent the value of samples so that they can readily be transmitted or processed by binary logic. There are two ways in which binary signals can be used to carry sample data. When each digit of the binary number is carried on a separate wire this is called parallel transmission. The state of the wires changes at the sampling rate. This approach is used in the parallel video interfaces, as video needs a relatively short wordlength; eight or ten bits. Using multiple wires is cumbersome where a long wordlength is in use, and a single wire can be used where successive digits from each sample are sent serially. This is the definition of pulse code modulation. Clearly the clock frequency must now be higher than the sampling rate.

Digital signals of this form will be used as the input to compression systems and must also be output by the decoding stage in order that the signal can be returned to analog form. Figure 2.3 shows the stages involved. Between the coder and the decoder the signal is not PCM but will be in a format which is highly dependent on the kind of compression technique used. It will also be evident from Figure 2.3 where the signal

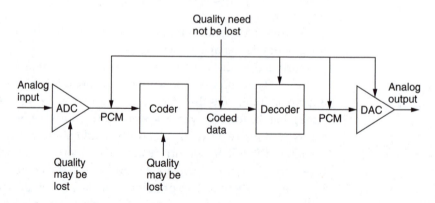

Figure 2.3 A typical digital compression system. The ADC and coder are responsible for most of the quality loss, whereas the PCM and coded data channels cause no further loss (excepting bit errors).

quality of the system can be impaired. The PCM digital interfaces between the ADC and the coder and between the decoder and the DAC cause no loss of quality. Quality is determined by the ADC and by the performance of the coder. Generally, decoders do not cause significant loss of quality; they make the best of the data from the coder. Similarly, DACs cause little quality loss above that due to the ADC. In practical systems the loss of quality is dominated by the action of the coder. In communication theory, compression is known as *source coding* in order to distinguish it from the *channel coding* necessary reliably to send data down transmission or recording channels. This book is not concerned with channel coding but details can be found elsewhere.[2]

2.5   Sampling

Sampling is a process of periodic measurement which can take place in space or time and in several dimensions at once. Figure 2.4(a) shows that in *temporal sampling* the frequency of the signal to be sampled and the sampling rate F_s are measured in Hertz (Hz), the standard unit of

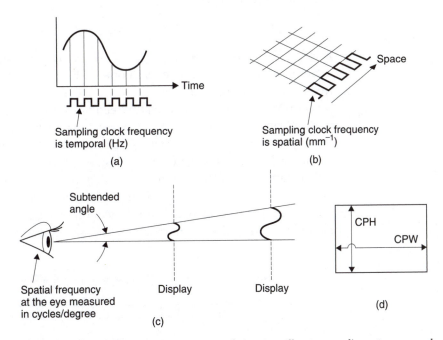

Figure 2.4   (a) Electrical waveforms are sampled temporally at a sampling rate measured in Hz. (b) Image information must be sampled spatially, but there is no single unit of spatial sampling frequency. (c) The acuity of the eye is measured as a subtended angle, and here two different displays of different resolutions give the same result at the eye because they are at a different distance. (d) Size-independent units such as cycles per picture height will also be found.

temporal frequency. In still images such as photographs there is no temporal change and Figure 2.4(b) shows that the sampling is *spatial*. The sampling rate is now a spatial frequency. The absolute unit of spatial frequency is cycles per metre, although for imaging purposes cycles-per-millimetre is more practical.

If the human viewer is considered, none of these units is useful because they don't take into account the viewing distance. The acuity of the eye is measured in cycles per degree. As Figure 2.4(c) shows, a large distant screen subtends the same angle as a small nearby screen. Figure 2.4(c) also shows that the nearby screen, possibly a computer monitor, needs to be able to display a higher spatial frequency than a distant cinema screen to give the same sharpness perceived at the eye. If the viewing distance is proportional to size, both screens could have the same number of pixels, leading to the use of a relative unit, shown in (d), which is cycles-per-picture-height (cph) in the vertical axis and cycles-per-picture-width (cpw) in the horizontal axis.

The computer screen has more cycles-per-millimetre than the cinema screen, but in this example has the same number of cycles-per-picture-height. Spatial and temporal frequencies are related by the process of scanning as given by:

Temporal frequency = spatial frequency × scanning velocity

Figure 2.5 shows that if the 1024 pixels along one line of an SVGA monitor were scanned in one tenth of a millisecond, the sampling clock frequency would be 10.24 MHz.

Sampling theory does not require regular sample spacing, but it is the most efficient arrangement. As a practical matter if regular sampling is employed, the process of timebase correction can be used to eliminate any jitter due to recording or transmission.

The sampling process originates with a pulse train which is shown in Figure 2.6(a) to be of constant amplitude and period. This pulse train can be temporal or spatial. The information to be sampled amplitude-modulates the pulse train in much the same way as the carrier is

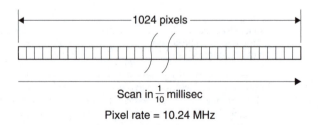

Scan in $\frac{1}{10}$ millisec

Pixel rate = 10.24 MHz

Figure 2.5 The connection between image resolution and pixel rate is the scanning speed. Scanning the above line in 1/10 ms produces a pixel rate of 10.24 MHz.

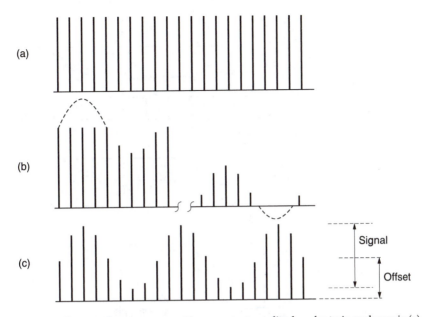

Figure 2.6 The sampling process requires a constant-amplitude pulse train as shown in (a). This is amplitude modulated by the waveform to be sampled. If the input waveform has excessive amplitude or incorrect level, the pulse train clips as shown in (b). For a bipolar waveform, the greatest signal level is possible when an offset of half the pulse amplitude is used to centre the waveform as shown in (c).

modulated in an AM radio transmitter. One must be careful to avoid over-modulating the pulse train as shown in (b) and this is achieved by suitably biasing the information waveform as at (c).

Figure 2.7 shows a constant speed rotation viewed along the axis so that the motion is circular. Imagine, however, the view from one side in the plane of the rotation. From a distance, only a vertical oscillation will be observed and if the position is plotted against time the resultant waveform will be a sine wave. The sine wave is unique because it contains only a single frequency. All other waveforms contain more than one frequency.

Imagine a second viewer who is at right angles to the first viewer. He will observe the same waveform, but at a different time. The displacement is given by multiplying the radius by the cosine of the phase angle. When plotted on the same graph, the two waveforms are *phase-shifted* with respect to one another. In this case the phase-shift is 90° and the two waveforms are said to be *in quadrature*. Incidentally the motions on each side of a steam locomotive are in quadrature so that it can always get started (the term used is quartering). Note that the phase angle of a signal is constantly changing with time whereas the phase-shift between two signals can be constant. It is important that these two are not confused.

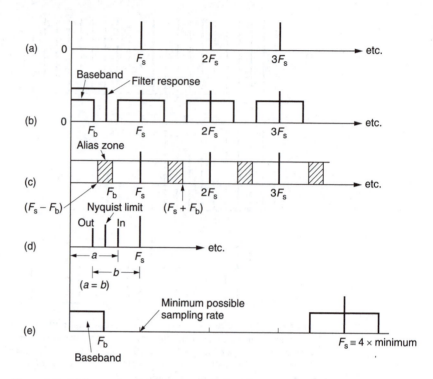

Figure 2.7 (a) Spectrum of sampling pulses. (b) Spectrum of samples. (c) Aliasing due to sideband overlap. (d) Beat-frequency production. (e) 4 × oversampling.

It was seen in Figure 2.7 that a sinusoidal function is a rotation resolved in one axis. In order to obtain a purely sinusoidal motion, the motion on the other axis must be eliminated. Conceptually this may be achieved by having a contra-rotating system in which there is one rotation at $+\omega$ and another at $-\omega$. Figure 2.8(a) shows that the sine components of these two rotations will be in the same phase and will add, whereas the cosine components will be in anti-phase and will cancel. Thus all real frequencies actually contain equal amounts of positive and negative frequencies. These cannot be distinguished unless a modulation process takes place. Figure 2.8(b) shows that when two signals of frequency $\pm\omega_1$ and $\pm\omega_2$ are multiplied together, the result is that the rotations of each must be added. The result is four frequencies, $\pm(\omega_1 + \omega_2)$ and $\pm(\omega_1 - \omega_2)$, one of which is the sum of the input frequencies and one of which is the difference between them. These are called sidebands.

Sampling is a modulation process and also produces sidebands although the carrier is now a pulse train and has an infinite series of harmonics as shown in Figure 2.9(a). The sidebands repeat above and below each harmonic of the sampling rate as shown in (b). The consequence of this is that sampling does not alter the spectrum of the

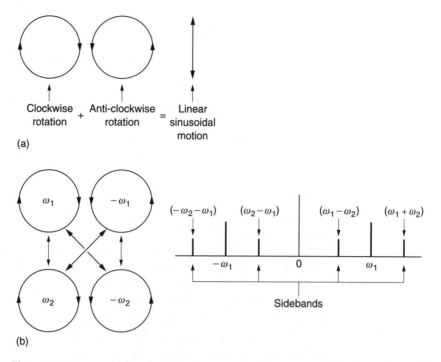

Figure 2.8 Upper and lower sidebands come about because real signals contain equal amounts of postive and negative frequencies that are revealed by modulation. See text.

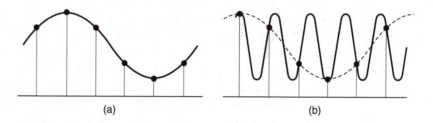

Figure 2.9 In (a) the sampling is adequate to reconstruct the original signal. In (b) the sampling rate is inadequate and reconstruction produces the wrong waveform (broken). Aliasing has taken place.

baseband signal at all. The spectrum is simply repeated. Consequently sampling need not lose any information.

The sampled signal can be returned to the continuous domain simply by passing it into a low-pass filter. This filter has a frequency response which prevents the images from passing, and only the baseband signal emerges, completely unchanged. If considered in the frequency domain, this filter can be called an anti-image filter; if considered in the time domain it can be called a reconstruction filter. It can also be considered as a spatial filter if a sampled still image is being returned to a continuous image. Such a filter will be two dimensional.

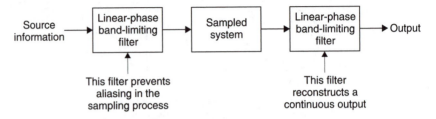

Figure 2.10 Sampling systems depend completely on the use of band-limiting filters before and after the sampling stage. Implementing these filters rigorously is non-trivial.

If an input is supplied having an excessive bandwidth for the sampling rate in use, the sidebands will overlap (Figure 2.7(c)) and the result is aliasing, where certain output frequencies are not the same as their input frequencies but instead become difference frequencies (Figure 2.7(d)). It will be seen from Figure 2.7 that aliasing does not occur when the input bandwidth is equal to or less than half the sampling rate, and this derives the most fundamental rule of sampling, which is that the sampling rate must be at least twice the input bandwidth. Nyquist[3] is generally credited with being the first to point out the need for sampling at twice the highest frequency in the signal in 1928, although the mathematical proofs were given independently by Shannon[4,5] and Kotelnikov. It subsequently transpired that Whittaker[6] beat them all to it, although his work was not widely known at the time. One half of the sampling frequency is often called the Nyquist frequency.

Whilst aliasing has been described above in the frequency domain, it can be described equally well in the time domain. In Figure 2.9(a) the sampling rate is obviously adequate to describe the waveform, but at (b) it is inadequate and aliasing has occurred. In some cases there is no control over the spectrum of input signals and in this case it becomes necessary to have a low-pass filter at the input to prevent aliasing. This anti-aliasing filter prevents frequencies of more than half the sampling rate from reaching the sampling stage.

Figure 2.10 shows that all practical sampling systems consist of a pair of filters, the anti-aliasing filter before the sampling process and the reconstruction filter after it. It should be clear that the results obtained will be strongly affected by the quality of these filters which may be spatial or temporal according to the application.

2.6   Reconstruction

Perfect reconstruction was theoretically demonstrated by Shannon as shown in Figure 2.11. The input must be band limited by an ideal linear phase low-pass filter with a rectangular frequency response and a

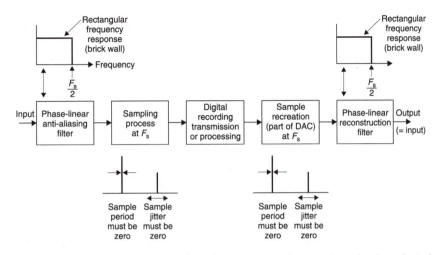

Figure 2.11 Shannon's concept of perfect reconstruction requires the hypothetical approach shown here. The anti-aliasing and reconstruction filters must have linear phase and rectangular frequency response. The sample period must be infinitely short and the sample clock must be perfectly regular. Then the output and input waveforms will be identical if the sampling frequency is twice the input bandwidth (or more).

bandwidth of one-half the sampling frequency. The samples must be taken at an instant with no averaging of the waveform. These instantaneous samples can then be passed through a second, identical filter which will perfectly reconstruct that part of the input waveform which was within the passband.

There are some practical difficulties in implementing Figure 2.11 exactly, but well-engineered systems can approach it and so it forms a useful performance target. The impulse response of a linear-phase ideal low-pass filter is a $\sin x/x$ waveform as shown in Figure 2.12(a). Such a waveform passes through zero volts periodically. If the cut-off frequency of the filter is one-half of the sampling rate, the impulse passes through zero *at the sites of all other samples*. It can be seen from Figure 2.12(b) that at the output of such a filter, the voltage at the centre of a sample is due to that sample alone, since the value of *all* other samples is zero at that instant. In other words the continuous output waveform must pass through the tops of the input samples. In between the sample instants, the output of the filter is the sum of the contributions from many impulses (theoretically an infinite number), causing the waveform to pass smoothly from sample to sample.

It is a consequence of the band-limiting of the original anti-aliasing filter that the filtered analog waveform could only take one path between the samples. As the reconstruction filter has the same frequency response, the reconstructed output waveform must be identical to the original band-limited waveform prior to sampling. A rigorous mathematical proof of reconstruction can be found in Porat[7] or Betts.[8]

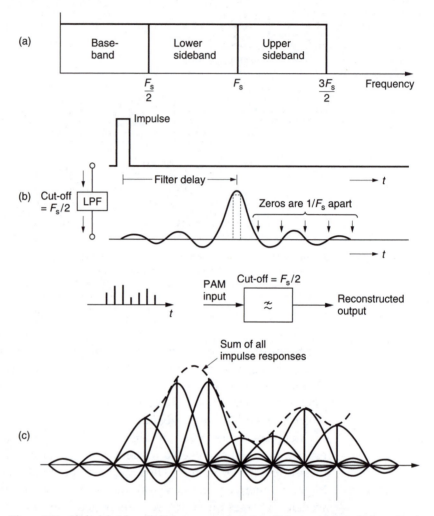

Figure 2.12 If ideal 'brick wall' filters are assumed, the efficient spectrum of (a) results. An ideal low-pass filter has an impulse response shown in (b). The impulse passes through zero at intervals equal to the sampling period. When convolved with a pulse train at the sampling rate, as shown in (c), the voltage at each sample instant is due to that sample alone as the impulses from all other samples pass through zero there.

Perfect reconstruction with a Nyquist sampling rate is a limiting condition which cannot be exceeded and can only be reached under ideal and impractical conditions. Thus in practice Nyquist rate sampling can only be approached. Zero-duration pulses are impossible and the ideal linear-phase filter with a vertical 'brick-wall' cut-off slope is impossible to implement. In the case of temporal sampling, as the slope tends to the vertical, the delay caused by the filter goes to infinity. In the case of spatial sampling, sharp-cut optical filters are impossible to build. Figure 2.13 shows that the spatial impulse response of an ideal lens is

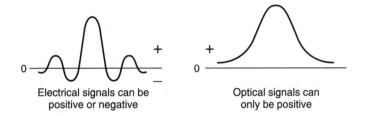

Electrical signals can be
positive or negative

Optical signals can
only be positive

Figure 2.13 In optical systems the spatial impulse response cannot have negative excursions and so ideal filters in optics are more difficult to make.

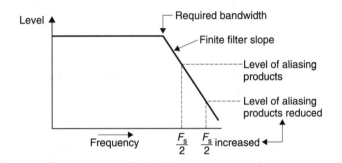

Figure 2.14 With finite slope filters, aliasing is always possible, but it can be set at an arbitrarily low level by raising the sampling rate.

a symmetrical intensity function. Note that the function is positive only as the expression for intensity contains a squaring process. The negative excursions of the $\sin x/x$ curve can be handled in an analog or digital filter by negative voltages or numbers, but in optics there is no negative light. The restriction to positive-only impulse response limits the sharpness of optical filters.

In practice real filters with finite slopes can still be used. The cut-off slope begins at the edge of the required pass band, and because the slope is not vertical, aliasing will always occur. However, it can be seen from Figure 2.14 that the sampling rate can be raised to drive aliasing products to an arbitrarily low level. The perfect reconstruction process still works, but the system is a little less efficient in information terms because the sampling rate has to be raised. There is no absolute factor by which the sampling rate must be raised. A figure of 10 per cent is typical in temporal sampling, although it depends upon the filters which are available and the level of aliasing products which is acceptable.

There is another difficulty which is that the requirement for linear phase means the impulse response of the filter must be symmetrical. In the time domain, such filters cannot be *causal* because the output has to begin before the input occurs. A filter with a finite slope has a finite window and so a linear-phase characteristic can be obtained by incorporating a delay of one-half the window period so that the filter can be causal. This concept will be expanded in Chapter 3.

2.7 Aperture effect

In practical sampling systems the sample impulse cannot be infinitely small in time or space. Figure 2.15 shows that real equipment may produce impulses whose possible shapes include rectangular and Gaussian. The result is an *aperture effect* where the frequency response of the sampling system is modified. The new response is the Fourier transform of the aperture function.

In the case where the pulses are rectangular, the proportion of the sample period occupied by the pulse is defined as the *aperture ratio* which is normally expressed as a percentage.

The case where the pulses have been extended in width to become equal to the sample period is known as a zero-order hold (ZOH) system and has a 100 per cent aperture ratio as shown in Figure 2.16(a). This produces a waveform which is more like a staircase than a pulse train.

To see how the use of ZOH compares with ideal Shannon reconstruction, it must be recalled that pulses of negligible width have a uniform spectrum and so the frequency respose of the sampler and reconstructor is flat within the pass band. In contrast, pulses of 100 per cent aperture ratio have a $\sin x/x$ spectrum which falls to a null at the sampling rate, and as a result is about 4 dB down at the Nyquist frequency as shown in Figure 2.16(b).

Figure 2.17(a) shows how ZOH is normally represented in texts with the pulses extending to the right of the sample. This representation is incorrect because it does not have linear phase as can be seen in (b). Figure 2.17(c) shows the correct representation where the pulses are extended symmetrically about the sample to achieve linear phase (d). This is conceptually easy if the pulse generator is considered to cause a half-sample-period delay relative to the original waveform. If the pulse width is stable, the reduction of high frequencies is constant and

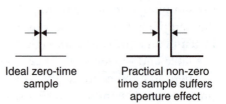

Ideal zero-time
sample

Practical non-zero
time sample suffers
aperture effect

Figure 2.15 The ideal zero duration/size sample required by Figure 2.11 is not met in practice. Typical sample impulses look like this and have a filtering action called aperture effect.

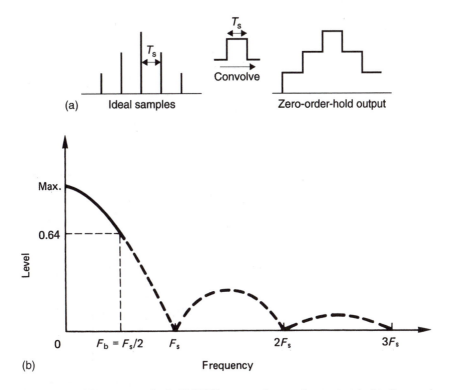

Figure 2.16 (a) In a zero-order-hold (ZOH) system, the samples are stretched to the sample period and the waveform looks like a staircase. (b) Frequency response with 100 per cent aperture nulls at multiples of sampling rate. Area of interest is up to half sampling rate.

predictable, and an appropriate filter response shown in (e) can render the overall response flat once more. Note that the equalization filter in (e) is conceptually a low-pass reconstruction filter in series with an inverse $\sin x / x$ response.

An alternative in the time domain is to use resampling which is shown in Figure 2.18. Resampling passes the zero-order hold waveform through a further synchronous sampling stage which consists of an analog switch that closes briefly in the centre of each sample period. The output of the switch will be pulses which are narrower than the original. If, for example, the aperture ratio is reduced to 50 per cent of the sample period, the first frequency response null is now at twice the sampling rate, and the loss at the edge of the pass band is reduced. As the figure shows, the frequency response becomes flatter as the aperture ratio falls. The process should not be carried too far, as with very small aperture ratios there is little energy in the pulses and noise can be a problem. A practical limit is around 12.5 per cent where the frequency response is virtually ideal.

It should be stressed that in real systems there will often be more than one aperture effect. The result is that the frequency responses of the

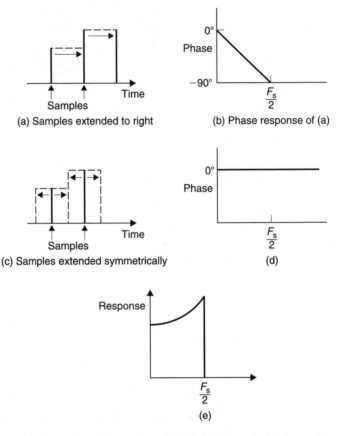

Figure 2.17 (a) Conventional description of ZOH. (b) System in (a) does not have linear phase. (c) Linear phase ZOH system in which the samples are spread symmetrically. (d) Phase response of (c). (e) Flat response can be obtained using equalizer.

various aperture effects multiply, which is the same as saying that their impulse responses convolve. Whatever fine words are used, the result is an increasing loss of high frequencies where a series of acceptable devices when cascaded produce an unacceptable result.

In many systems, for reasons of economy or ignorance, reconstruction is simply not used and the system output is an unfiltered ZOH waveform. Figure 2.19 shows some examples of this kind of thing which are associated with the 'digital look'. It is important to appreciate that in well-engineered systems containing proper filters there is no such thing as the digital look.

2.8 Choice of audio sampling rate

The Nyquist criterion is only the beginning of the process which must be followed to arrive at a suitable sampling rate. The slope of available

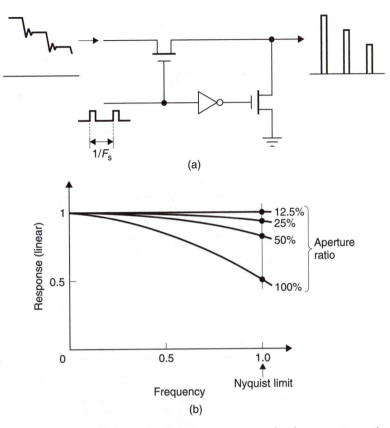

(a)

(b)

Figure 2.18 (a) Resampling circuit eliminates transients and reduces aperture ratio. (b) Response of various aperture ratios.

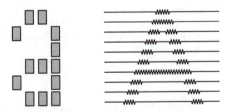

Figure 2.19 Some examples of sampled systems in which filtering is inadequate or absent.

filters will compel designers to raise the sampling rate above the theoretical Nyquist rate. For consumer products, the lower the sampling rate, the better, since the cost of the medium or channel is directly proportional to the sampling rate: thus sampling rates near to twice 20 kHz are to be expected.

Where very low bit rate compression is to be used, better results may be obtained by reducing the sampling rate so that the compression factor is not as great.

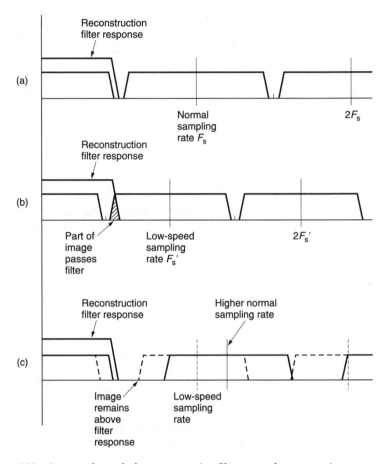

Figure 2.20 At normal speed, the reconstruction filter correctly prevents images entering the baseband, as in (a). When speed is reduced, the sampling rate falls, and a fixed filter will allow part of the lower sideband of the sampling frequency to pass. If the sampling rate of the machine is raised, but the filter characteristic remains the same, the problem can be avoided, as in (c).

For professional products, there is a need to operate at variable speed for pitch correction. When the speed of a digital recorder is reduced, the offtape sampling rate falls, and Figure 2.20 shows that with a minimal sampling rate the first image frequency can become low enough to pass the reconstruction filter. If the sampling frequency is raised without changing the response of the filters, the speed can be reduced without this problem. It follows that variable-speed recorders, generally those with stationary heads, must use a higher sampling rate.

In the early days of digital audio, video recorders were adapted to store audio samples by creating a pseudo-video waveform which could convey binary as black and white levels.[9] The sampling rate of such a system is constrained to relate simply to the field rate and field structure of the television standard used, so that an integer number of samples can be stored on each usable TV line in the field. Such a recording can be made on a monochrome recorder, and these recordings are made in two standards, 525 lines at 60 Hz and 625 lines at 50 Hz. Thus it was necessary to find a frequency which is a common multiple of the two and also suitable for use as a sampling rate.

The allowable sampling rates in a pseudo-video system can be deduced by multiplying the field rate by the number of active lines in a field (blanked lines cannot be used) and again by the number of samples in a line. By careful choice of parameters it is possible to use either 525/60 or 625/50 video with a sampling rate of 44.1 kHz.

In 60 Hz video, there are 35 blanked lines, leaving 490 lines per frame, or 245 lines per field for samples. If three samples are stored per line, the sampling rate becomes

$$60 \times 245 \times 3 = 44.1 \text{ kHz}$$

In 50 Hz video, there are 37 lines of blanking, leaving 588 active lines per frame, or 294 per field, so the same sampling rate is given by

$$50 \times 294 \times 3 = 44.1 \text{ kHz}$$

The sampling rate of 44.1 kHz came to be that of the Compact Disc. Even though CD has no video circuitry, the equipment used to make CD masters was originally video-based and determined the sampling rate.

For landlines to FM stereo broadcast transmitters having a 15 kHz audio bandwidth, the sampling rate of 32 kHz is more than adequate, and has been in use for some time in the United Kingdom and Japan. This frequency is also used in the NICAM 728 stereo TV sound system, in DVB audio and in DAB. The professional sampling rate of 48 kHz was proposed as having a simple relationship to 32 kHz, being far enough above 40 kHz for variable-speed operation, and having a simple relationship with 50 Hz frame rate video which would allow digital video recorders to store the convenient number of 960 audio samples per video field. This is the sampling rate used by all production DVTRs. The field rate offset of 59.94 Hz video does not easily relate to any of the above sampling rates, and requires special handling which is outside the scope of this book.[10]

Although in a perfect world the adoption of a single sampling rate might have had virtues, for practical and economic reasons digital audio now has essentially three rates to support: 32 kHz for broadcast, 44.1 kHz for CD, and 48 kHz for professional use.[11] In MPEG these audio sampling rates may be halved for low bit rate applications with a corresponding loss of audio bandwidth.

2.9   Video sampling structures

Component or colour difference signals are used primarily for post-production work where quality and flexibility are paramount. In colour difference working, the important requirement is for image manipulation in the digital domain. This is facilitated by a sampling rate which is a multiple of line rate because then there is a whole number of samples in a line and samples are always in the same position along the line and can form neat columns. A practical difficulty is that the line period of the 525 and 625 systems is slightly different. The problem was overcome by the use of a sampling clock which is an integer multiple of both line rates. ITU-601 (formerly CCIR-601) recommends the use of certain sampling rates which are based on integer multiples of the carefully chosen fundamental frequency of 3.375 MHz. This frequency is normalized to 1 in the document.

In order to sample 625/50 luminance signals without quality loss, the lowest multiple possible is 4 which represents a sampling rate of 13.5 MHz. This frequency line-locks to give 858 samples per line period in 525/59.94 and 864 samples per line period in 625/50.

In the component analog domain, the colour difference signals used for production purposes typically have one half the bandwidth of the luminance signal. Thus a sampling rate multiple of 2 is used and results in 6.75 MHz. This sampling rate allows respectively 429 and 432 samples per line. Component video sampled in this way has a 4:2:2 format. Whilst other combinations are possible, 4:2:2 is the format for which the majority of digital component production equipment is constructed. The D-1, D-5, D-9, SX and Digital Betacam DVTRs operate with 4:2:2 format data. Figure 2.21 shows the spatial arrangement given by 4:2:2 sampling.

Luminance samples appear at half the spacing of colour difference samples, and every other luminance sample is co-sited with a pair of colour difference samples. Co-siting is important because it allows all attributes of one picture point to be conveyed with a three-sample vector quantity. Modification of the three samples allows such techniques as colour correction to be performed. This would be difficult without co-sited information. Co-siting is achieved by clocking the three ADCs simultaneously.

For lower bandwidths, particularly in prefiltering operations prior to compression, the sampling rate of the colour difference signal can be halved. 4:1:1 delivers colour bandwidth in excess of that required by the composite formats and is used in 60 Hz DV camcorder formats.

In 4:2:2 the colour difference signals are sampled horizontally at half the luminance sampling rate, yet the vertical colour difference sampling rates are the same as for luma. Whilst this is not a problem in a

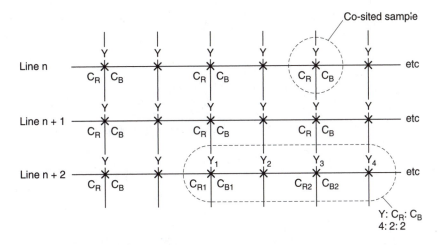

Figure 2.21 In CCIR-601 sampling mode 4:2:2, the line synchronous sampling rate of 13.5 MHz results in samples having the same position in successive lines, so that vertical columns are generated. The sampling rates of the colour difference signals C_R, C_B are one-half of that of luminance, i.e. 6.75 MHz, so that there are alternate Y only samples and co-sited samples which describe Y, C_R and C_B. In a run of four samples, there will be four Y samples, two C_R samples and two C_B samples, hence 4:2:2.

production application, this disparity of sampling rates represents a data rate overhead which is undesirable in a compression environment. In this case it is possible to halve the vertical sampling rate of the colour difference signals as well, producing a format known as 4:2:0.

This topic is the source of considerable confusion. In MPEG-1, which was designed for a low bit rate, the single ideal 4:2:0 subsampling strategy of Figure 2.22(a) was used. The colour data are vertically low-pass filtered to the same bandwidth in two dimensions and interpolated so that the remaining colour pixels are equidistant from the source pixels.

This has the effect of symmetrically disposing the colour information with respect to the luma. When MPEG-2 was developed, it was a requirement to support 4:4:4, 4:2:2 and 4:2:0 colour structures. Figure 2.22(b) shows that in MPEG-2, the colour difference samples require no horizontal interpolation in 4:4:4 or 4:2:2 and so for consistency they don't get it in 4:2:0 either. As a result there are two different 4:2:0 structures, one for MPEG-1 and one for MPEG-2 and MPEG-4. In vertical subsampling a new virtual raster has been created for the chroma samples. At the decoder a further interpolation will be required to put the decoded chroma data back onto the display raster. This causes a small generation loss which is acceptable for a single-generation codec as used in broadcasting, but not in multi-generation codecs needed for production. This problem was one of the reasons for the development of the 4:2:2 Profile of MPEG-2 which avoids the problem by retaining the colour information on every line. The term *chroma format factor* will be

```
X       X       X       X          X = Luma sample

    ( )             ( )            ( ) = Cr, Cb sample

X       X       X       X

    ( )             ( )

X       X       X       X
```

(a) MPEG-1 chroma downsampling (4:2:0)

```
X       X       X       X          X = Luma sample

( )             ( )                ( ) = Cr, Cb sample

X       X       X       X

( )             ( )

X       X       X       X
```

(b) MPEG-2 chroma downsampling (4:2:0)

Figure 2.22 (a) In MPEG-1 colour difference information is downsampled and shifted so that it is symmetrically disposed about the luminance pixels. (b) In MPEG-2 the horizontal shift was abandoned.

found in connection with colour downsampling. This is the factor by which the addition of colour difference data increases the source bit rate with respect to monochrome. For example, 4:2:0 has a factor of 1.5 whereas 4:2:2 has a factor of 2.

The sampling rates of ITU-601 are based on commonality between 525- and 625-line systems. However, the consequence is that the pixel spacing is different in the horizontal and vertical axes. This is incompatible with computer graphics in which so-called 'square' pixels are used. This means that the horizontal and vertical spacing is the same, giving the same resolution in both axes. However, high-definition TV and computer graphics formats universally use 'square' pixels. MPEG can handle various pixel aspect ratios and allows a control code to be embedded in the sequence header to help the decoder.

2.10   The phase-locked loop

All digital video systems need to be clocked at the appropriate rate in order to function properly. Whilst a clock may be obtained from a fixed frequency oscillator such as a crystal, many operations in video require *genlocking* or synchronizing the clock to an external source.

In phase-locked loops, the oscillator can run at a range of frequencies according to the voltage applied to a control terminal. This is called a voltage-controlled oscillator or VCO. Figure 2.23 shows that the VCO

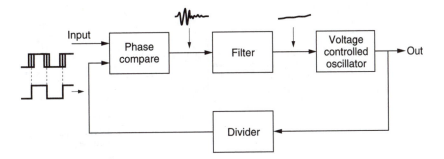

Figure 2.23 A phase-locked loop requires these components as a minimum. The filter in the control voltage serves to reduce clock jitter.

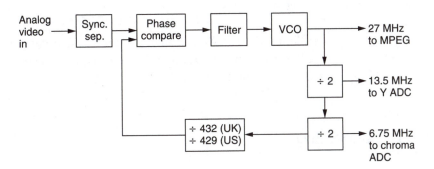

Figure 2.24 Using a phase-locked loop, the H-sync pulses of input video can be used to derive the 27 MHz master clock of MPEG and the 13.5 MHz and 6.75 MHz sampling clocks of 4:2:2 video.

is driven by a phase error measured between the output and some reference. The error changes the control voltage in such a way that the error is reduced, so that the output eventually has the same frequency as the reference. A low-pass filter is fitted in the control voltage path to prevent the loop becoming unstable. If a divider is placed between the VCO and the phase comparator, as in the figure, the VCO frequency can be made to be a multiple of the reference. This also has the effect of making the loop more heavily damped, so that it is less likely to change frequency if the input is irregular.

In digital video, the frequency multiplication of a phase-locked loop is extremely useful. Figure 2.24 shows how the 13.5 MHz clock of component digital video and the 27 MHz master clock of MPEG are obtained from the sync pulses of an analog reference by such a multiplication process.

The numerically locked loop is a digital relative of the phase-locked loop. Figure 2.25 shows that the input is an intermittently transmitted value from a counter. The input count is compared with the value of a local count and the difference is used to control the frequency of a local

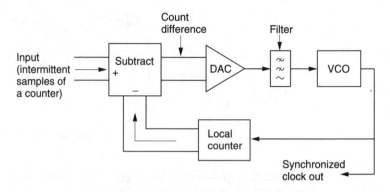

Figure 2.25 In the numerically locked loop, the state of a master counter is intermittently sent. A local oscillator is synchronized to the master oscillator by comparing the states of the local and master counters.

oscillator. Once lock is achieved, the local oscillator and the remote oscillator will run at exactly the same frequency even though there is no continuous link between them.

2.11 Quantizing

Quantizing is the process of expressing some infinitely variable quantity by discrete or stepped values. Quantizing turns up in a remarkable number of everyday guises. Figure 2.26 shows that an inclined ramp enables infinitely variable height to be achieved, whereas a stepladder allows only discrete heights to be had. A stepladder quantizes height. When accountants round off sums of money to the nearest pound or dollar they are quantizing.

In audio the values to be quantized are infinitely variable voltages from an analog source. Strict quantizing is a process which is restricted to the voltage domain only. For the purpose of studying the quantizing of a single sample, time is assumed to stand still. This is achieved in practice either by the use of a track/hold circuit or the adoption of a quantizer technology which operates before the sampling stage.

Figure 2.27(a) shows that the process of quantizing divides the voltage range up into quantizing intervals Q. In applications such as telephony these may be of differing size, but for digital audio and video the quantizing intervals are made as identical as possible. If this is done, the binary numbers which result are truly proportional to the original analog voltage, and the digital equivalents of filtering and gain changing can be performed by adding and multiplying sample values. If the quantizing intervals are unequal this cannot be done. When all quantizing intervals are the same, the term uniform quantizing is used. The term linear

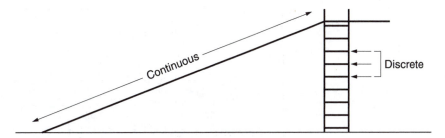

Figure 2.26 An analog parameter is continuous whereas a quantized parameter is restricted to certain values. Here the sloping side of a ramp can be used to obtain any height whereas a ladder only allows discrete heights.

quantizing will be found, but this is, like military intelligence, a contradiction in terms.

The term LSB (least significant bit) will also be found in place of quantizing interval in some treatments, but this is a poor term because quantizing is not always used to create binary values and because a bit can only have two values. In studying quantizing we wish to discuss values smaller than a quantizing interval, but a fraction of an LSB is a contradiction in terms.

Whatever the exact voltage of the input signal, the quantizer will determine the quantizing interval in which it lies. In what may be considered a separate step, the quantizing interval is then allocated a code value which is typically some form of binary number. The information sent is the number of the quantizing interval in which the input voltage lay. Exactly where that voltage lay within the interval is not conveyed, and this mechanism puts a limit on the accuracy of the quantizer. When the number of the quantizing interval is converted back to the analog domain, it will result in a voltage at the centre of the quantizing interval as this minimizes the magnitude of the error between input and output. The number range is limited by the wordlength of the binary numbers used. In a sixteen-bit system commonly used for audio, 65 536 different quantizing intervals exist, whereas video systems typically have eight-bit systems having 256 quantizing intervals.

2.12 Quantizing error

It is possible to draw a transfer function for such an ideal quantizer followed by an ideal DAC, and this is shown in Figure 2.27(b). A transfer function is simply a graph of the output with respect to the input. When the term linearity is used, this generally means the straightness of the transfer function. Linearity is a goal in audio and video, yet it will be seen that an ideal quantizer is anything but. Quantizing causes a voltage error in the sample which cannot exceed $\pm\frac{1}{2}Q$ unless the input is so large that

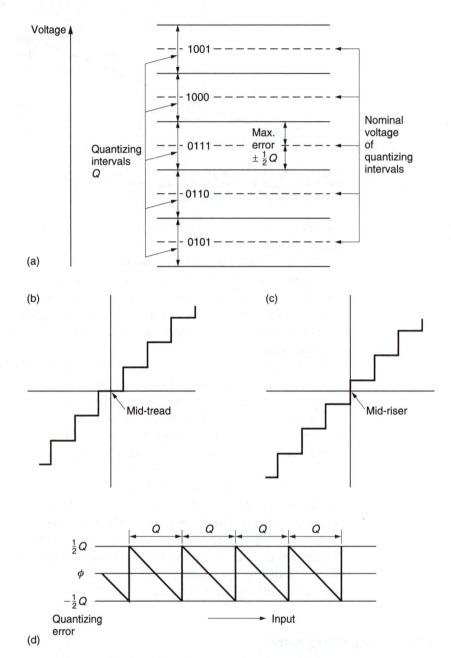

Figure 2.27 Quantizing assigns discrete numbers to variable voltages. All voltages within the same quantizing interval are assigned the same number which causes a DAC to produce the voltage at the centre of the intervals shown by the dashed lines in (a). This is the characteristic of the mid-tread quantizer shown in (b). An alternative system is the mid-riser system shown in (c). Here 0 volts analog fails between two codes and there is no code for zero. Such quantizing cannot be used prior to signal processing because the number is no longer proportional to the voltage. Quantizing error cannot exceed $\pm\frac{1}{2}Q$ as shown in (d).

clipping occurs. Figure 2.27(b) shows the transfer function is somewhat like a staircase, and the voltage corresponding to audio muting or video blanking is half-way up a quantizing interval, or on the centre of a tread. This is the so-called mid-tread quantizer which is universally used in audio and video. Figure 2.27(c) shows the alternative mid-riser transfer function which causes difficulty because it does not have a code value at muting/blanking level and as a result the code value is not proportional to the signal voltage.

In studying the transfer function it is better to avoid complicating matters with the aperture effect of the DAC. For this reason it is assumed here that output samples are of negligible duration. Then impulses from the DAC can be compared with the original analog waveform and the difference will be impulses representing the quantizing error waveform. As can be seen in Figure 2.28, the quantizing error waveform can be thought of as an unwanted signal which the quantizing process adds to the perfect original. As the transfer function is non-linear, ideal quantizing can cause distortion. As a result practical digital audio devices use non-ideal quantizers to achieve linearity. The quantizing error of an ideal quantizer is a complex function, and it has been researched in great depth.[12]

As the magnitude of the quantizing error is limited, its effect can be minimized by making the signal larger. This will require more quantizing intervals and more bits to express them. The number of quantizing intervals multiplied by their size gives the quantizing range of the convertor. A signal outside the range will be clipped. Clearly if clipping is avoided, the larger the signal, the less will be the effect of the quantizing error.

Consider first the case where the input signal exercises the whole quantizing range and has a complex waveform. In audio this might be orchestral music; in video a bright, detailed contrasty scene. In these cases successive samples will have widely varying numerical values and the quantizing error on a given sample will be independent of that on others. In this case the size of the quantizing error will be distributed with equal probability between the limits.

Figure 2.28(c) shows the resultant uniform probability density. In this case the unwanted signal added by quantizing is an additive broadband noise uncorrelated with the signal, and it is appropriate in this case to call it quantizing noise. This is not quite the same as thermal noise which has a Gaussian probability shown in Figure 2.28(d). The subjective difference is slight.

Treatments which then assume that quantizing error is *always* noise give results which are at variance with reality. Such approaches only work if the probability density of the quantizing error is uniform. Unfortunately at low levels, and particularly with pure or simple

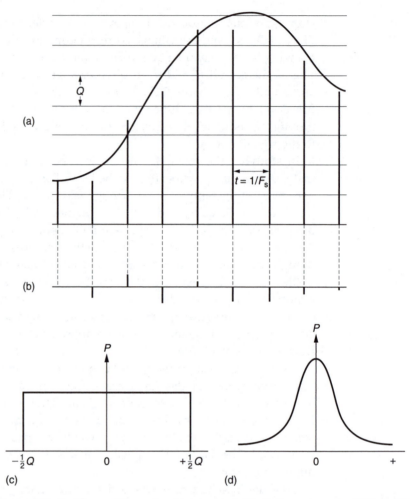

Figure 2.28 In (a) an arbitrary signal is represented to finite accuracy by PAM needles whose peaks are at the centre of the quantizing intervals. The errors caused can be thought of as an unwanted signal (b) added to the original. In (c) the amplitude of a quantizing error needle will be from $-\frac{1}{2}Q$ to $+\frac{1}{2}Q$ with equal probability. Note, however, that white noise in analog circuits generally has Gaussian amplitude distribution, shown in (d).

waveforms, this is simply not true. At low levels, quantizing error ceases to be random, and becomes a function of the input waveform and the quantizing structure. Once an unwanted signal becomes a deterministic function of the wanted signal, it has to be classed as a distortion rather than a noise. We predicted a distortion because of the non-linearity or staircase nature of the transfer function. With a large signal, there are so many steps involved that we must stand well back, and a staircase with many steps appears to be a slope. With a small signal there are few steps and they can no longer be ignored.

The non-linearity of the transfer function results in distortion, which produces harmonics. Unfortunately these harmonics are

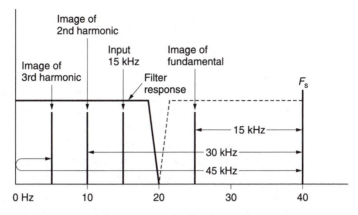

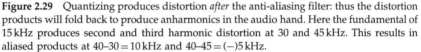

Figure 2.29 Quantizing produces distortion *after* the anti-aliasing filter: thus the distortion products will fold back to produce anharmonics in the audio hand. Here the fundamental of 15 kHz produces second and third harmonic distortion at 30 and 45 kHz. This results in aliased products at 40–30 = 10 kHz and 40–45 = (–)5 kHz.

generated *after* the anti-aliasing filter, and so any which exceed half the sampling rate will alias. Figure 2.29 shows how this results in anharmonic distortion in audio. These anharmonics result in spurious tones known as birdsinging.

When the sampling rate is a multiple of the input frequency the result is harmonic distortion. Where more than one frequency is present in the input, intermodulation distortion occurs, which is known as granulation.

As the input signal is further reduced in level, it may remain within one quantizing interval. The output will be silent because the signal is now the quantizing error. In this condition, low-frequency signals such as air-conditioning rumble can shift the input in and out of a quantizing interval so that the quantizing distortion comes and goes, resulting in noise modulation.

In video, quantizing error in luminance results in visible contouring on low-key scenes or flat fields. Slowly changing brightness across the screen is replaced by areas of constant brightness separated by sudden steps. In colour difference signals, contouring results in an effect known as posterization where subtle variations in colour are removed and large areas are rendered by the same colour as if they had been painted by numbers.

2.13 Dither

At high signal level, quantizing error is effectively noise. As the level falls, the quantizing error of an ideal quantizer becomes more strongly correlated with the signal and the result is distortion. If the quantizing error can be decorrelated from the input in some way, the system can remain linear. Dither performs the job of decorrelation by making the action of the quantizer unpredictable.

The first documented use of dither was in picture coding.[12] In this system, the noise added prior to quantizing was subtracted after reconversion to analog. This is known as subtractive dither. Although subsequent subtraction has some slight advantages[13] it suffers from practical drawbacks, since the original noise waveform must accompany the samples or must be synchronously re-created at the DAC. This is virtually impossible in a system where the signal may have been edited. Practical systems use non-subtractive dither where the dither signal is added prior to quantization and no subsequent attempt is made to remove it. The introduction of dither inevitably causes a slight reduction in the signal-to-noise ratio attainable, but this reduction is a small price to pay for the elimination of non-linearities. As linearity is an essential requirement for digital audio and video, the use of dither is equally essential.

The ideal (noiseless) quantizer of Figure 2.28 has fixed quantizing intervals and must always produce the same quantizing error from the same signal. In Figure 2.30 it can be seen that an ideal quantizer can be

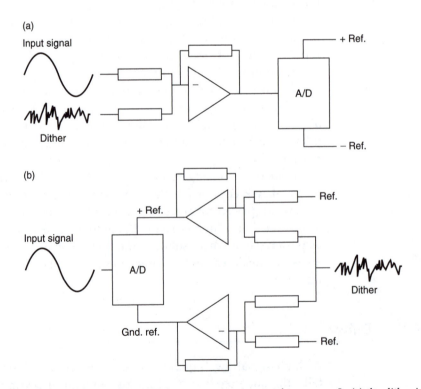

Figure 2.30 Dither can be applied to a quantizer in one of two ways. In (a) the dither is linearly added to the analog input signal, whereas in (b) it is added to the reference voltages of the quantizer.

dithered by linearly adding a controlled level of noise either to the input signal or to the reference voltage which is used to derive the quantizing intervals. There are several ways of considering how dither works, all of which are valid.

The addition of dither means that successive samples effectively find the quantizing intervals in different places on the voltage scale. The quantizing error becomes a function of the dither, rather than just a function of the input signal. The quantizing error is not eliminated, but the subjectively unacceptable distortion is converted into broadband noise which is more benign. An alternative way of looking at dither is to consider the situation where a low-level input signal is changing slowly within a quantizing interval. Without dither, the same numerical code results, and the variations within the interval are lost. Dither has the effect of forcing the quantizer to switch between two or more states. The higher the voltage of the input signal within the interval, the more probable it becomes that the output code will take on a higher value. The lower the input voltage within the interval, the more probable it is that the output code will take the lower value. The dither has resulted in a form of duty cycle modulation, and the resolution of the system has been extended indefinitely instead of being limited by the size of the steps.

Dither can also be understood by considering the effect it has on the transfer function of the quantizer. This is normally a perfect staircase, but in the presence of dither it is smeared horizontally until with a certain minimum amplitude the average transfer function becomes straight.

The characteristics of the noise used are rather important for optimal performance, although many suboptimal but nevertheless effective systems are in use. The main parameters of interest are the peak-to-peak amplitude, and the probability distribution of the amplitude. Triangular probability works best and this can be obtained by summing the output of two uniform probability processes.

The use of dither invalidates the conventional calculations of signal-to-noise ratio available for a given wordlength. This is of little consequence as the rule of thumb that multiplying the number of bits in the wordlength by 6 dB gives the SNR a result that will be close enough for all practical purposes.

It has only been possible to introduce the principles of conversion of audio and video signals here. For more details of the operation of convertors the reader is referred elsewhere.[2,14]

2.14   Introduction to digital processing

However complex a digital process, it can be broken down into smaller stages until finally one finds that there are really only two basic types of

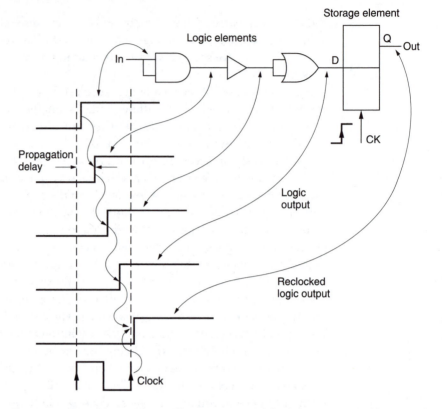

Figure 2.31 Logic elements have a finite propagation delay between input and output and cascading them delays the signal an arbitrary amount. Storage elements sample the input on a clock edge and can return a signal to near coincidence with the system clock. This is known as reclocking. Reclocking eliminates variations in propagation delay in logic elements.

element in use, and these can be combined in some way and supplied with a clock to implement virtually any process. Figure 2.31 shows that the first type is a *logic* element. This produces an output which is a logical function of the input with minimal delay. The second type is a *storage* element which samples the state of the input(s) when clocked and holds or delays that state.

The strength of binary logic is that the signal has only two states, and considerable noise and distortion of the binary waveform can be tolerated before the state becomes uncertain. At every logical element, the signal is compared with a threshold, and can thus can pass through any number of stages without being degraded. In addition, the use of a storage element at regular locations throughout logic circuits eliminates time variations or jitter. Figure 2.31 shows that if the inputs to a logic element change, the output will not change until the *propagation delay* of the element has elapsed. However, if the output of the logic element forms the input to a storage element, the output of that element will not change until the input is sampled *at the next clock edge*. In this way the signal edge is aligned to the system clock and the propagation delay of the logic becomes irrelevant. The process is known as reclocking.

2.15 Logic elements

The two states of the signal when measured with an oscilloscope are simply two voltages, usually referred to as high and low. The actual voltage levels will depend on the type of logic family in use, and on the supply voltage used. Supply voltages have tended to fall as designers seek to reduce power consumption. Within logic, the exact levels are not of much consequence, and it is only necessary to know them when interfacing between different logic families or when driving external devices. The pure logic designer is not interested at all in these voltages, only in their meaning.

Just as the electrical waveform from a microphone represents sound velocity, so the waveform in a logic circuit represents the truth of some statement. As there are only two states, there can only be *true* or *false* meanings. The true state of the signal can be assigned by the designer to either voltage state. When a high voltage represents a true logic condition and a low voltage represents a false condition, the system is known as *positive logic*, or *high true* logic. This is the usual system, but sometimes the low voltage represents the true condition and the high voltage represents the false condition. This is known as *negative logic* or *low true* logic. Provided that everyone is aware of the logic convention in use, both work equally well.

In logic systems, all logical functions, however complex, can be configured from combinations of a few fundamental logic elements or *gates*. It is not profitable to spend too much time debating which are the truly fundamental ones, since most can be made from combinations of others. Figure 2.32 shows the important simple gates and their derivatives, and introduces the logical expressions to describe them, which can be compared with the truth-table notation. The figure also shows the important fact that when negative logic is used, the OR gate function interchanges with that of the AND gate.

If numerical quantities need to be conveyed down the two-state signal paths described here, then the only appropriate numbering system is binary, which has only two symbols, 0 and 1. Just as positive or negative logic could be used for the truth of a logical binary signal, it can also be used for a numerical binary signal. Normally, a high voltage level will represent a binary 1 and a low voltage will represent a binary 0, described as a 'high for a one' system. Clearly a 'low for a one' system is

Positive logic name	Boolean expression	Positive logic symbol	Positive logic truth table	Plain English
Inverter or NOT gate	$Q = \overline{A}$	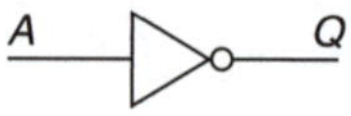 (symbol)	A | Q 0 | 1 1 | 0	Output is opposite of input
AND gate	$Q = A \cdot B$	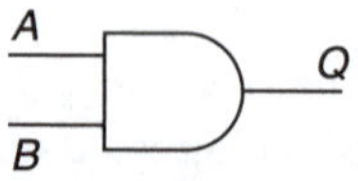 (symbol)	A B | Q 0 0 | 0 0 1 | 0 1 0 | 0 1 1 | 1	Output true when both inputs are true only
NAND (Not AND) gate	$Q = \overline{A \cdot B}$ $= \overline{A} + \overline{B}$	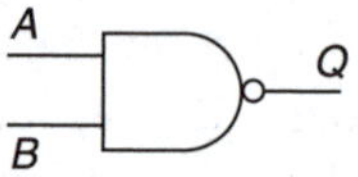 (symbol)	A B | Q 0 0 | 1 0 1 | 1 1 0 | 1 1 1 | 0	Output false when both inputs are true only
OR gate	$Q = A + B$	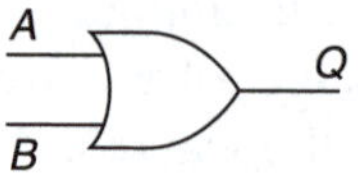 (symbol)	A B | Q 0 0 | 0 0 1 | 1 1 0 | 1 1 1 | 1	Output true if either or both inputs true
NOR (Not OR) gate	$Q = \overline{A + B}$ $= \overline{A} \cdot \overline{B}$	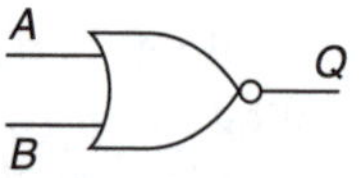 (symbol)	A B | Q 0 0 | 1 0 1 | 0 1 0 | 0 1 1 | 0	Output false if either or both inputs true
Exclusive OR (XOR) gate	$Q = A \oplus B$	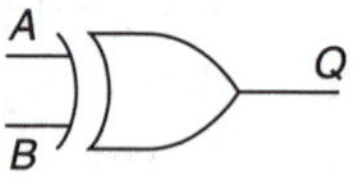 (symbol)	A B | Q 0 0 | 0 0 1 | 1 1 0 | 1 1 1 | 0	Output true if inputs are different

Figure 2.32 The basic logic gates compared.

just as feasible. Decimal numbers have several columns, each of which represents a different power of ten; in binary the column position specifies the power of two.

Several binary digits or bits are needed to express the value of a binary sample. These bits can be conveyed at the same time by several signals to form a parallel system, which is most convenient inside equipment or for short distances because it is inexpensive, or one at a time down a single signal path, which is more complex, but convenient for cables between pieces of equipment because the connectors require fewer pins. When a binary system is used to convey numbers in this way, it can be called a digital system.

2.16 Storage elements

The basic memory element in logic circuits is the latch, which is constructed from two gates as shown in Figure 2.33(a), and which can be set or reset. A more useful variant is the D-type latch shown at (b) which remembers the state of the input at the time a separate clock either changes state, for an edge-triggered device, or after it goes false, for a level-triggered device. A shift register can be made from a series of latches by connecting the Q output of one latch to the D input of the next and connecting all the clock inputs in parallel. Data are delayed by the number of stages in the register. Shift registers are also useful for converting between serial and parallel data formats.

Where large numbers of bits are to be stored, cross-coupled latches are less suitable because they are more complicated to fabricate inside integrated circuits than dynamic memory, and consume more current.

In large random access memories (RAMs), the data bits are stored as the presence or absence of charge in a tiny capacitor as shown in Figure 2.33(c). The capacitor is formed by a metal electrode, insulated by a layer of silicon dioxide from a semiconductor substrate, hence the term MOS (metal oxide semiconductor). The charge will suffer leakage, and the value would become indeterminate after a few milliseconds. Where the delay needed is less than this, decay is of no consequence, as data will be read out before they have had a chance to decay. Where longer delays are necessary, such memories must be refreshed periodically by reading the bit value and writing it back to the same place. Most modern MOS RAM chips have suitable circuitry built in. Large RAMs store many megabits, and it is clearly impractical to have a connection to each one. Instead, the desired bit has to be addressed before it can be read or written. The size of the chip package restricts the number of pins available, so that large memories use the same address pins more than once. The bits are arranged internally as rows and columns, and the row address and the column address are specified sequentially on the same pins.

Just like recording devices, electronic data storage devices come in many varieties. The basic volatile RAM will lose data if power is interrupted. However, there are also non-volatile RAMS or NVRAMs which retain the data in the absence of power. A type of memory which is written once is called a *read-only-memory* or ROM. Some of these are programmed by using a high current which permanently vaporizes conductors in each location so that the data are fixed. Other types can be written electrically, but cannot be erased electrically. These need to be erased by exposure to ultraviolet light and are called UVROMS. Once erased they can be reprogrammed with new data. Another type of ROM

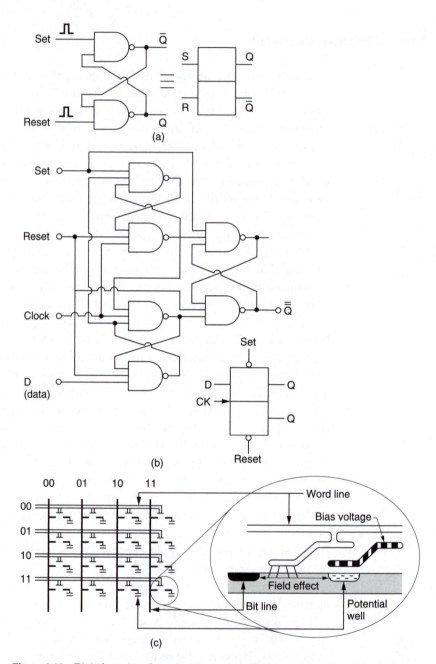

Figure 2.33 Digital semiconductor memory types. In (a), one data bit can be stored in a simple set-reset latch, which has little application because the D-type latch in (b) can store the state of the single data input when the clock occurs. These devices can be implemented with bipolar transistors of FETs, and are called static memories because they can store indefinitely. They consume a lot of power. In (c), a bit is stored as the charge in a potential well in the substrate of a chip. It is accessed by connecting the bit line with the field effect from the word line. The single well where the two lines cross can then be written or read. These devices are called dynamic RAMs because the charge decays, and they must be read and rewritten (refreshed) periodically.

can be rewritten electrically a limited number of times. These are known as *electric alterable* ROMs or EAROMS.

2.17 Binary coding

In many cases a binary code is used to represent a sample of an audio or video waveform. Practical digital hardware places a limit on the wordlength which in turn limits the range of values available. In the eight-bit samples used in much digital video equipment, there are 256 different numbers, whereas in the sixteen-bit codes common in digital audio, there are 65 536 different numbers.

Figure 2.34(a) shows the result of counting upwards in binary with a fixed wordlength. When the largest possible value of all ones is reached, adding a further one to the LSB causes it to become zero with a carry-out. This carry is added to the next bit which becomes zero with a carry-out and so on. The carry will ripple up the word until the MSB becomes zero and produces a carry-out. This carry-out represents the setting of a bit to the left of the MSB, which is not present in the hardware and is thus lost. Consequently when the highest value is reached, further counting causes the value to reset to zero and begin again. This is known as an *overflow*. Counting downwards will achieve the reverse. When zero is reached, subtracting one will cause an *underflow* where a borrow should be taken from a bit to the left of the MSB, which does not exist, the result being that the bits which do exist take the value of all ones, being the highest possible code value.

Storage devices such as latches can be configured so that they count pulses. Figure 2.34(b) shows such an arrangement. The pulses to be counted are fed to the clock input of a D-type latch, whose input is connected to its complemented output. This configuration will change state at every input pulse, so that it will be in a true state after every other pulse. This is a divide-by-two counter. If the output is connected to the clock input of another stage, this will divide by four. A series of divide-by-two stages can be cascaded indefinitely in this way to count up to arbitrarily high numbers. Note that when the largest possible number is reached, when all latches are in the high state, the next pulse will result in all latches going to a low state, corresponding to the count of zero. This is the overflow condition described above.

Counters often include reset inputs which can be used to force the count to zero. Some are presettable so that a specific value can be loaded into each latch before counting begins.

As a result of the fixed wordlength, underflow and overflow, the infinite range of real numbers is mapped onto the limited range of a

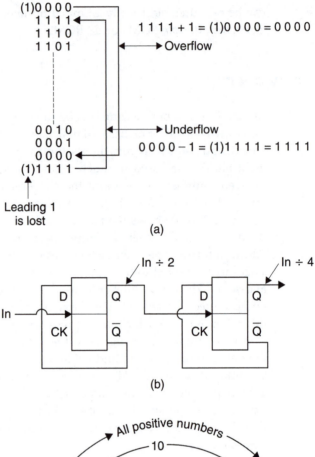

(a)

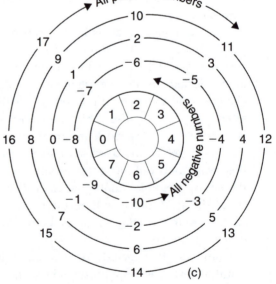

(b)

(c)

Figure 2.34 Counting up in a fixed wordlength system leads to overflow (a) where the high-order bit is lost. A binary counter can be made by cascading divide-by-two stages. Overflow results in wraparound as shown in (c).

binary code of finite wordlength. Figure 2.34(c) shows that the overflow makes the number scale circular and it is as if the real number scale were rolled around it so that a binary code could represent any of a large possible number of real values, positive or negative. This is why the term *wraparound* is sometimes used to describe the result of an overflow condition.

Mathematically the pure binary mapping of Figure 2.34(c) from an infinite scale to a finite scale is known as *modulo* arithmetic. The four-bit example shown expresses real numbers as Modulo-16 codes.

In a practical ADC, each number represents a different analog signal voltage, and the hardware is arranged such that voltages outside the finite range do not overflow but instead result in one or other limit codes being output. This is the equivalent of clipping in analog systems. In Figure 2.35(a) it will be seen that in an eight-bit pure binary system, the number range goes from 00 hex, which represents the smallest voltage

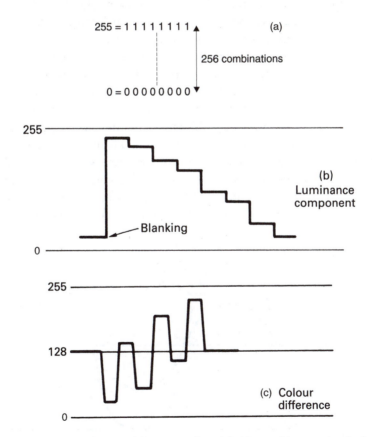

Figure 2.35 The unipolar quantizing range of an eight-bit pure binary system is shown at (a). The analog input must be shifted to fit into the quantizing range. In component, sync pulses are not digitized, so the quantizing intervals can be smaller as at (b). An offset of half scale is used for colour difference signals (c).

and all those voltages below it, through to FF hex, which represents the largest positive voltage and all voltages above it.

In some computer graphics systems these extremes represent black and peak white respectively. In television systems the traditional analog video waveform must be accommodated within this number range. Figure 2.35(b) shows how this is done for a broadcast standard luminance signal. As digital systems only handle the active line, the quantizing range is optimized to suit the gamut of the unblanked luminance and the sync pulses go off the bottom of the scale. There is a small offset in order to handle slightly misadjusted inputs. Additionally the codes at the extremes of the range are reserved for synchronizing and are not available to video values.

Colour difference video signals are bipolar and so blanking is in the centre of the signal range. In order to accommodate colour difference signals in the quantizing range, the blanking voltage level of the analog waveform has been shifted as in Figure 2.35(c) so that the positive and negative voltages in a real signal can be expressed by binary numbers which are only positive. This approach is called offset binary and has the advantage that the codes of all ones and all zeros are still at the ends of the scale and can continue to be used for synchronizing.

Figure 2.36 shows that analog audio signal voltages are referred to midrange. The level of the signal is measured by how far the waveform deviates from midrange, and attenuation, gain and mixing all take place around that level. Digital audio mixing is achieved by adding sample values from two or more different sources, but unless all the quantizing intervals are of the same size and there is no offset, the sum of two sample values will not represent the sum of the two original analog voltages. Thus sample values which have been obtained by non-uniform

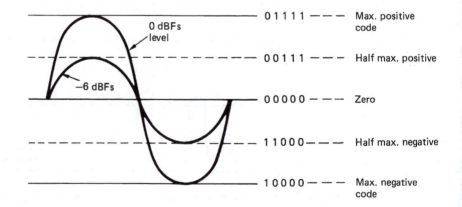

Figure 2.36 0 dBFs is defined as the level of the largest sinusoid which will fit into the quantizing range without clipping.

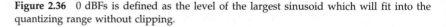

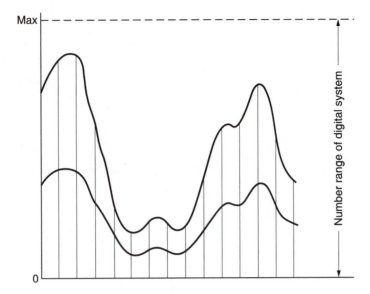

Figure 2.37 The result of an attempted attenuation in pure binary code is an offset. Pure binary cannot be used for digital audio processing.

or offset quantizing cannot readily be processed because the binary numbers are not proportional to the signal voltage.

If two offset binary sample streams are added together in an attempt to perform digital mixing, the result will be that the offsets are also added and this may lead to an overflow. Similarly, if an attempt is made to attenuate by, say, 6.02 dB by dividing all the sample values by two, Figure 2.37 shows that the offset is also divided and the waveform suffers a shifted baseline. This problem can be overcome with digital luminance signals simply by subtracting the offset from each sample before processing as this results in positive-only numbers truly proportional to the luminance voltage. This approach is not suitable for audio or colour difference signals because negative numbers would result when the analog voltage goes below blanking and pure binary coding cannot handle them.

The problem with offset binary is that it works with reference to one end of the range. What is needed is a numbering system which operates symmetrically with reference to the centre of the range.

In the two's complement system, the mapping of real numbers onto the finite range of a binary word is modified. Instead of the mapping of Figure 2.38(a) in which only positive numbers are mapped, in (b) the upper half of the pure binary number range has been redefined to represent negative quantities. In two's complement, the range represented by the circle of numbers does not start at zero, but starts on the diametrically opposite side of the circle such that zero is now in the centre of the number range. All numbers clockwise from zero are positive

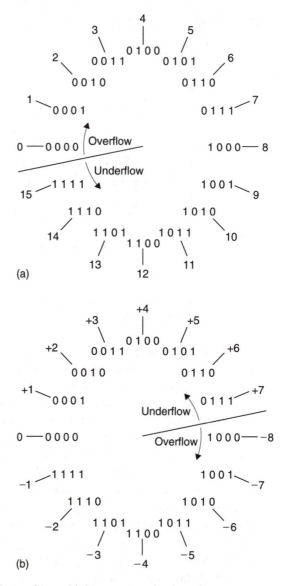

Figure 2.38 In pure binary (a) this mapping of real numbers is used. In two's complement an alternative mapping (b) is used. See text.

and have the MSB reset. All numbers anticlockwise from zero are negative and have the MSB set. The MSB is thus the equivalent of a sign bit where 1 = minus. Two's complement notation differs from pure binary in that the most significant bit is inverted in order to achieve the half circle rotation.

Figure 2.39 shows how a real ADC is configured to produce two's complement output. At (a) an analog offset voltage equal to one half the quantizing range is added to the bipolar analog signal in order to

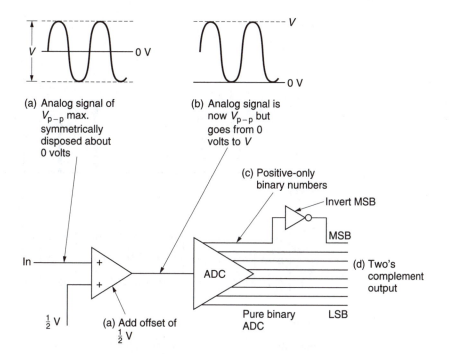

Figure 2.39 A two's complement ADC. In (a) an analog offset voltage equal to one-half the quantizing range is added to the bipolar analog signal in order to make it unipolar as in (b). The ADC produces positive-only numbers in (c), but the MSB is then inverted in (d) to give a two's complement output.

make it unipolar as at (b). The ADC produces positive-only numbers at (c) which are proportional to the input voltage. This is actually an offset binary code. The MSB is then inverted at (d) so that the all-zeros code moves to the centre of the quantizing range. The analog offset is often incorporated into the ADC as is the MSB inversion. Some convertors are designed to be used in either pure binary or two's complement mode. In this case the designer must arrange the appropriate DC conditions at the input. The MSB inversion may be selectable by an external logic level. In the broadcast digital video interface standards the colour difference signals use offset binary because the codes of all zeros and all ones are at the end of the range and can be reserved for synchronizing. A digital vision mixer simply inverts the MSB of each colour difference sample to convert it to two's complement.

The two's complement system allows two sample values to be added, or mixed in audio and video parlance, and the result will be referred to the system midrange; this is analogous to adding analog signals in an operational amplifier.

Figure 2.40 illustrates how adding two's complement samples simulates a bipolar mixing process. The waveform of input A is

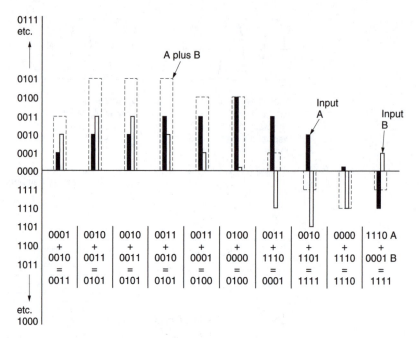

Figure 2.40 Using two's complement arithmetic, single values from two waveforms are added together with respect to midrange to give a correct mixing function.

depicted by solid black samples, and that of B by samples with a solid outline. The result of mixing is the linear sum of the two waveforms obtained by adding pairs of sample values. The dashed lines depict the output values. Beneath each set of samples is the calculation which will be seen to give the correct result. Note that the calculations are pure binary. No special arithmetic is needed to handle two's complement numbers.

It is interesting to see why the two's complement adding process works. Effectively both two's complement numbers to be added contain an offset of half full scale. When they are added, the two offsets add to produce a sum offset which has a value of full scale. As adding full scale to a code consists of moving one full rotation round the circle of numbers, the offset has no effect and is effectively eliminated.

It is sometimes necessary to phase reverse or invert a digital signal. The process of inversion in two's complement is simple. All bits of the sample value are inverted to form the one's complement, and one is added. This can be checked by mentally inverting some of the values in Figure 2.38(b). The inversion is transparent and performing a second inversion gives the original sample values. Using inversion, signal subtraction can be performed using only adding logic.

Two's complement numbers can have a radix point and bits below it just as pure binary numbers can. It should, however, be noted that in two's complement, if a radix point exists, numbers to the right of it are added. For example, 1100.1 is not -4.5, it is $-4 + 0.5 = -3.5$.

The circuitry necessary for adding pure binary or two's complement binary numbers is shown in Figure 2.41. Addition in binary requires two bits to be taken at a time from the same position in each word, starting at the least significant bit. Should both be ones, the output is zero, and there is a *carry-out* generated. Such a circuit is called a half adder, shown in Figure 2.41(a) and is suitable for the least significant bit of the calculation. All higher stages will require a circuit which can accept a carry input as well as two data inputs. This is known as a full adder (Figure 2.41(b)).

Such a device is also convenient for inverting a two's complement number, in conjunction with a set of invertors. The adder has one set of inputs taken to a false state, and the carry-in permanently held true, such that it adds one to the one's complement number from the invertor.

When mixing by adding sample values, care has to be taken to ensure that if the sum of the two sample values exceeds the number range the result will be clipping rather than overflow. In two's complement, the action necessary depends on the polarities of the two signals. Clearly if one positive and one negative number are added, the result cannot exceed the number range. If two positive numbers are added, the symptom of positive overflow is that the most significant bit sets, causing an erroneous negative result, whereas a negative overflow results in the most significant bit clearing. The overflow control circuit will be designed to detect these two conditions, and override the adder output. If the MSB of both inputs is zero, the numbers are both positive, thus if the sum has the MSB set, the output is replaced with the maximum positive code (0111 ...). If the MSB of both inputs is set, the numbers are both negative, and if the sum has no MSB set, the output is replaced with the maximum negative code (1000 ...). These conditions can also be connected to warning indicators. Figure 2.41(c) shows this system in hardware. The resultant clipping on overload is sudden, and sometimes a PROM is included which translates values around and beyond maximum to soft-clipped values below or equal to maximum.

A storage element can be combined with an adder to obtain a number of useful functional blocks which will crop up frequently in digital signal processing. Figure 2.42(a) shows that a latch is connected in a feedback loop around an adder. The latch contents are added to the input each time it is clocked. The configuration is known as an accumulator in computation because it adds up or

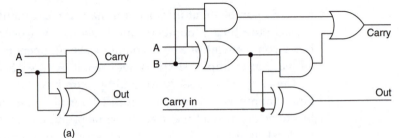

(a)

Data A	Bits B	Carry in	Out	Carry out
0	0	0	0	0
0	0	1	1	0
0	1	0	1	0
0	1	1	0	1
1	0	0	1	0
1	0	1	0	1
1	1	0	0	1
1	1	1	1	1

(b)

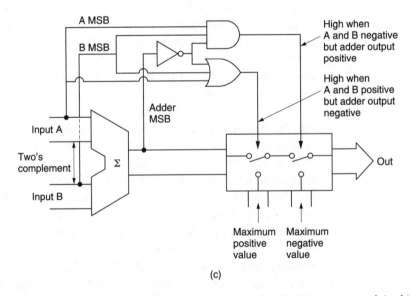

(c)

Figure 2.41 (a) Half adder; (b) full-adder circuit and truth table; (c) comparison of sign bits prevents wraparound on adder overflow by substituting clipping level.

accumulates values fed into it. In filtering, it is known as a discrete time integrator. If the input is held at some constant value, the output increases by that amount on each clock. The output is thus a sampled ramp.

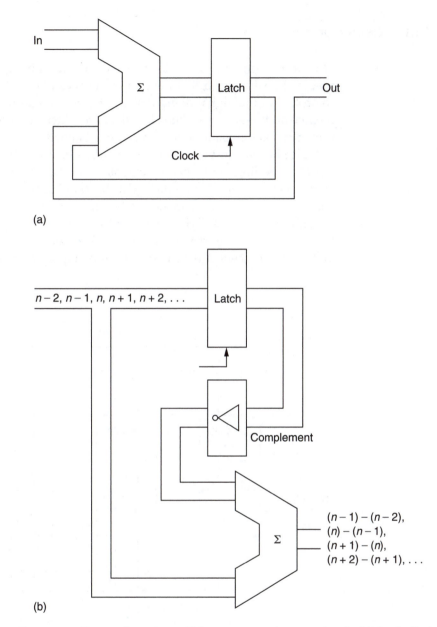

Figure 2.42 Two configurations which are common in processing. In (a) the feedback around the adder adds the previous sum to each input to perform accumulation or digital integration. In (b) an invertor allows the difference between successive inputs to be computed. This is differentiation.

Figure 2.42(b) shows that the addition of an invertor allows the difference between successive inputs to be obtained. This is digital differentiation. The output is proportional to the slope of the input.

2.18 Gain control

When processing digital audio or image data the gain of the system will need to be variable so that mixes and fades can be performed. Gain is controlled in the digital domain by multiplying each sample value by a coefficient. If that coefficient is less than one, attenuation will result; if it is greater than one, amplification can be obtained.

Multiplication in binary circuits is difficult. It can be performed by repeated adding, but this is too slow to be of any use. In fast multiplication, one of the inputs will be simultaneously multiplied by one, two, four, etc., by hard-wired bit shifting. Figure 2.43 shows that the other input bits will determine which of these powers will be added to produce the final sum, and which will be neglected. If multiplying by five, the process is the same as multiplying by four, multiplying by

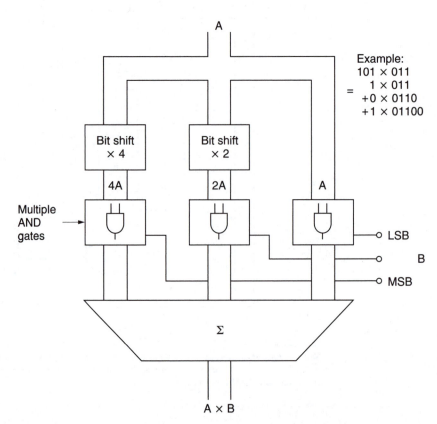

Figure 2.43 Structure of fast multiplier: the input A is multiplied by 1, 2, 4, 8, etc., by bit shifting. The digits of the B input then determine which multiples of A should be added together by enabling AND gates between the shifters and the adder. For long wordlengths, the number of gates required becomes enormous, and the device is best implemented in a chip.

one, and adding the two products. This is achieved by adding the input to itself shifted two places. As the wordlength of such a device increases, the complexity increases exponentially.

In a given application, all that matters is that the output has the correct numerical value. It does not matter if this is achieved using dedicated hardware or using software in a general-purpose processor. It should be clear that if it is wished to simulate analog gain control in the digital domain by multiplication, the samples to be multiplied must have been uniformly quantized. If the quantizing is non-uniform the binary numbers are no longer proportional to the original parameter and multiplication will not give the correct result.

In audio, uniform quantizing is universal in production systems. However, in video it is not owing to the widespread use of gamma which will be discussed in Chapter 6. Strictly speaking, video signals with gamma should be returned to the uniformly quantized domain before processing but this is seldom done in practice.

2.19 Floating-point coding

Computers operate on data words of fixed length and if binary or two's complement coding is used, this limits the range of the numbers. For this reason many computers use *floating-point coding* which allows a much greater range of numbers with a penalty of reduced accuracy.

Figure 2.44(a) shows that in pure binary, numbers which are significantly below the full scale value have a number of high-order

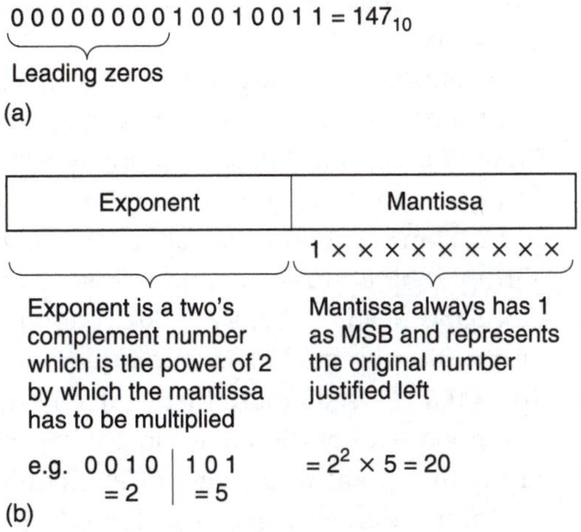

Figure 2.44 Small numbers in a long wordlength system have inefficient leading zeros (a). Floating-point coding (b) is more efficient, but can lead to inaccuracy.

bits which are all zero. Instead of handling these bits individually, as they are all zero it is good enough simply to count them. Figure 2.44(b) shows that every time a leading zero is removed, the remaining bits are shifted left one place and this has the effect in binary of multiplying by two. Two shifts multiply by four, three shifts by eight and so on. In order to recreate the number with the right magnitude, the power of two by which the number was multiplied must also be sent. This value is known as the *exponent*.

In order to convert a binary number of arbitrary value with an arbitrarily located radix point into floating-point notation, the position of the most significant or leading one and the position of the radix point are noted. The number is then multiplied or divided by powers of two until the radix point is immediately to the right of the leading one. This results in a value known as the *mantissa* (plural: mantissae) which always has the form 1.XXX . . . where X is 1 or 0 (known in logic as 'don't care').

The exponent is a two's complement code which determines whether the mantissa has to be multiplied by positive powers of two which will shift it left and make it bigger, or whether it has to be multiplied by negative powers of two which will shift it right and make it smaller.

In floating-point notation, the range of the numbers and the precision are independent. The range is determined by the wordlength of the exponent. For example, a six-bit exponent having 64 values allows a range from $1.XX \times 2^{31}$ to $1.XX \times 2^{-32}$. The precision is determined by the length of the mantissa. As the mantissa is always in the format 1.XXX it is not necessary to store the leading one so the actual stored value is in the form .XXX. Thus a ten-bit mantissa has eleven-bit precision. It is possible to pack a ten-bit mantissa and a six-bit exponent in one sixteen-bit word.

Although floating-point operation extends the number range of a computer, the user must constantly be aware that floating point has limited precision. Floating point is the computer's equivalent of lossy compression. In trying to get more for less, there is always a penalty.

In some signal-processing applications, floating-point coding is simply not accurate enough. For example, in an audio filter, if the stopband needs to be, say, 100 dB down, this can only be achieved if the entire filtering arithmetic has adequate precision. 100 dB is one part in 100 000 and needs more than sixteen bits of resolution. The poor quality of a good deal of digital audio equipment is due to the unwise adoption of floating-point processing of inadequate precision.

Computers of finite wordlength can operate on larger numbers without the inaccuracy of floating-point coding by using techniques such as *double precision*. For example, thirty-two-bit precision data words can be stored in two adjacent memory locations in a sixteen-bit machine, and the processor can manipulate them by operating on the two halves at different times. This takes longer, or needs a faster processor.

2.20   Multiplexing principles

Multiplexing is used where several signals are to be transmitted down the same channel. The channel bit rate must be the same as or greater than the sum of the source bit rates. Figure 2.45 shows that when multiplexing is used, the data from each source has to be time compressed. This is done by buffering source data in a memory at the multiplexer. It is written into the memory in real time as it arrives, but will be read from the memory with a clock which has a much higher rate. This means that the readout occurs in a smaller timespan. If, for example, the clock frequency is raised by a factor of ten, the data for a given signal will be transmitted in a tenth of the normal time, leaving time in the multiplex for nine more such signals.

In the demultiplexer another buffer memory will be required. Only the data for the selected signal will be written into this memory at the bit rate of the multiplex. When the memory is read at the correct speed, the data will emerge with its original timebase.

In practice it is essential to have mechanisms to identify the separate signals to prevent them being mixed up and to convey the original signal clock frequency to the demultiplexer. In time-division multiplexing the timebase of the transmission is broken into equal slots, one for each signal. This makes it easy for the demultiplexer, but forces a rigid structure on all the signals such that they must all be locked to one another and have an unchanging bit rate. Packet multiplexing overcomes these limitations.

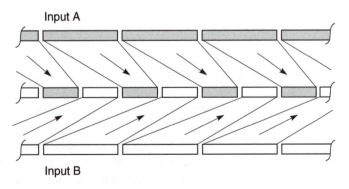

Figure 2.45   Multiplexing requires time compression on each input.

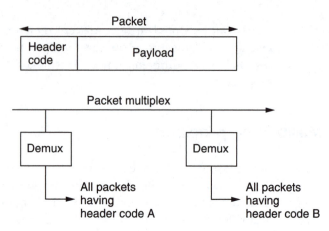

Figure 2.46 Packet multiplexing relies on headers to identify the packets.

2.21 Packets

The multiplexer must switch between different time-compressed signals to create the bitstream and this is much easier to organize if each signal is in the form of data packets of constant size. Figure 2.46 shows a packet multiplexing system.

Each packet consists of two components: the header, which identifies the packet, and the payload, which is the data to be transmitted. The header will contain at least an identification code (ID) which is unique for each signal in the multiplex. The demultiplexer checks the ID codes of all incoming packets and discards those which do not have the wanted ID.

In complex systems it is common to have a mechanism to check that packets are not lost or repeated. This is the purpose of the packet continuity count which is carried in the header. For packets carrying the same ID, the count should increase by one from one packet to the next. Upon reaching the maximum binary value, the count overflows and recommences.

2.22 Statistical multiplexing

Packet multiplexing has advantages over time-division multiplexing because it does not set the bit rate of each signal. A demultiplexer simply checks packet IDs and selects all packets with the wanted code. It will do this however frequently such packets arrive. Consequently it is practicable to have variable bit rate signals in a packet multiplex. The multiplexer has to ensure that the total bit rate does not exceed the rate of the channel, but that rate can be allocated arbitrarily between the various signals.

As a practical matter it is usually necessary to keep the bit rate of the multiplex constant. With variable-rate inputs this is done by creating null packets which are generally called *stuffing* or *packing*. The headers of these packets contain an unique ID which the demulti-plexer does not recognize and so these packets are discarded on arrival.

In an MPEG environment, statistical multiplexing can be extremely useful because it allows for the varying difficulty of real program material. In a multiplex of several television programs, it is unlikely that all the programs will encounter difficult material simultaneously. When one program encounters a detailed scene or frequent cuts which are hard to compress, more data rate can be allocated at the allowable expense of the remaining programs which are handling easy material.

2.23 Timebase correction

One of the strengths of digital technology is the ease with which delay can be provided. Accurate control of delay is the essence of timebase correction, necessary whenever the instantaneous time of arrival or rate from a data source does not match the destination. In digital video and audio, the destination will almost always have perfectly regular timing, namely the sampling rate clock of the final DAC. Timebase correction consists of aligning irregular data from storage media, transmission channels or compression decoders with that stable reference.

When compression is used, the amount of data resulting from equal units of time will vary. Figure 2.47 shows that if these data have to be sent at a constant bit rate, a buffer memory will be needed between the encoder and the channel. The result will be that effectively the picture period varies. Similar buffering will be needed at the decoder. Timebase correction is used to recover a constant picture rate.

Section 2.16 showed the principles of digital storage elements which can be used for delay purposes. The shift-register approach and the RAM approach to delay are very similar, as a shift register can be thought of as a memory whose address increases automatically when clocked. The data rate and the maximum delay determine the capacity of the RAM required. Figure 2.48 shows that the addressing of the RAM is by a counter that overflows endlessly from the end of the memory back to the beginning, giving the memory a ring-like structure. The write address is

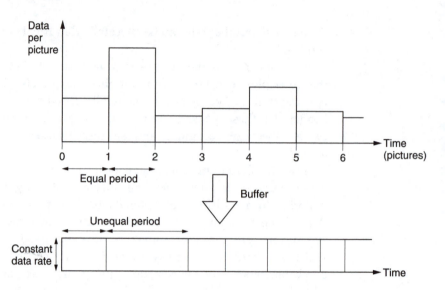

Figure 2.47 Compression results in a variable amount of data for each picture. To send this at a constant bit rate requires a buffer at encoder and decoder. The result is that the time taken to send each picture varies.

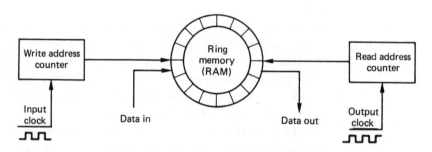

Figure 2.48 If the memory address is arranged to come from a counter which overflows, the memory can be made to appear circular. The write address then rotates endlessly, overwriting previous data once per revolution. The read address can follow the write address by a variable distance (not exceeding one revolution) and so a variable delay takes place between reading and writing.

determined by the incoming data, and the read address is determined by the outgoing data. This means that the RAM has to be able to read and write at the same time.

In an MPEG decoder, the exact time of arrival of the data corresponding to a picture can vary, along with the time taken to decode it. In practice the decoded picture is placed in memory and read out according to a locally re-created picture rate clock. If the phase of the picture clock is too early, decoding may not be completed before the memory has to be read. Conversely if the picture clock phase is too late, the memory may overflow. During lock-up, a decoder has to set the picture phase in such a way that the buffer memories are an average of half-full so that equal correcting power is available in both directions.

References

1. Watkinson, J.R., *Television Fundamentals*. Oxford: Focal Press (1998)
2. Watkinson, J.R., *The Art of Digital Audio*, third edition. Oxford: Focal Press (2001)
3. Nyquist, H., Certain topics in telegraph transmission theory. *AIEE Trans.*, 617–644 (1928)
4. Shannon, C.E., A mathematical theory of communication. *Bell Syst. Tech. J.*, **27**, 379 (1948)
5. Jerri, A.J., The Shannon sampling theorem – its various extensions and applications: a tutorial review. *Proc. IEEE*, **65**, 1565–1596 (1977)
6. Whittaker, E.T., On the functions which are represented by the expansions of the interpolation theory. *Proc. R. Soc. Edinburgh*, 181–194 (1915)
7. Porat, B., *A Course in Digital Signal Processing*. New York: John Wiley (1996)
8. Betts, J.A., *Signal Processing Modulation and Noise*, Ch. 6. Sevenoaks: Hodder and Stoughton (1970)
9. Ishida, Y. *et al.*, A PCM digital audio processor for home use VTRs. Presented at 64th AES Convention (New York, 1979), Preprint 1528
10. Rumsey, F.J. and Watkinson, J.R., *The Digital Interface Handbook*. Oxford: Focal Press (1995)
11. Anon., AES recommended practice for professional digital audio applications employing pulse code modulation: preferred sampling frequencies. AES5–1984 (ANSI S4.28–1984). *J. Audio Eng. Soc.*, **32**, 781–785 (1984)
12. Roberts, L.G., Picture coding using pseudo-random noise. *IRE Trans. Inform. Theory*, **IT-8**, 145–154 (1962)
13. Lipshitz, S.P., Wannamaker, R.A. and Vanderkooy, J., Quantization and dither: a theoretical survey. *J. Audio Eng. Soc.*, **40**, 355–375 (1992)
14. Watkinson, J.R., *The Art of Digital Video*, second edition. Oxford: Focal Press (1994)

3

Processing for compression

Virtually all compression systems rely on some combination of the basic processes outlined in this chapter. In order to understand compression a good grasp of filtering and transforms is essential along with motion estimation for video applications. These processes only express the information in the best way for the actual compression stage, which almost exclusively begins by using requantizing to shorten the wordlength. In this chapter the principles of filters and transforms will be explored, along with motion estimation and requantizing. These principles will be useful background for the subsequent chapters.

3.1   Introduction

In compression systems it is very important to remember that the valuable commodity is information. For practical reasons the way information is represented may have to be changed a number of times during its journey. If accuracy or realism is a goal these changes must be well engineered. In the course of this book we shall explore changes between the continuous domain of real sounds and images, the discrete domain of sampled data and the discrete spatial and temporal frequency domains. A proper understanding of these processes requires familiarity with the principles of filters and transforms.

Figure 3.1 shows an optical system of finite resolution. If an object containing an infinitely sharp line is presented to this system, the image will be an intensity function known in optics as a *point spread function*. Such functions are almost invariably symmetrical in optics. There is no movement or change here, the phenomenon is purely spatial. A point spread function is a spatial impulse response. All images passing through the optical system are convolved with it.

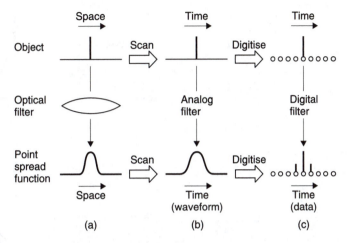

Figure 3.1 In optical systems an infinitely sharp line is reproduced as a point spread function (a) which is the impulse response of the optical path. Scanning either object or image produces an analog time-variant waveform (b). The scanned object waveform can be converted to the scanned image waveform with an electrical filter having an impulse response which is an analog of the point spread function. (c) The object and image may also be sampled or the object samples can be converted to the image samples by a filter with an analogous discrete impulse response.

Figure 3.1(b) shows that the object may be scanned by an analog system to produce a waveform. The image may also be scanned in this way. These waveforms are now temporal. However, the second waveform may be obtained in another way, using an analog filter in series with the first scanned waveform which has an equivalent impulse response. This filter must have linear phase, i.e. its impulse response must be symmetrical.

Figure 3.1(c) shows that the object may also be sampled in which case all samples but one will have a value of zero. The image may also be sampled, and owing to the point spread function, there will now be a number of non-zero sample values. However, the image samples may also be obtained by passing the input sample into a digital filter having the appropriate impulse response. Note that it is possible to obtain the same result as (c) by passing the scanned waveform of (b) into an ADC and storing the samples in a memory.

Clearly there are a number of equivalent routes leading to the same result. One consequence is that optical systems and sampled systems can simulate one another. This gives us considerable freedom to perform processing in the most advantageous domain which gives the required result. There are many parallels between analog, digital and optical filters, which this chapter treats as a common subject.

It should be clear from Figure 3.1 why video signal paths need to have linear phase. In general, analog circuitry and filters tend not to have linear phase because they must be *causal* which means that the output

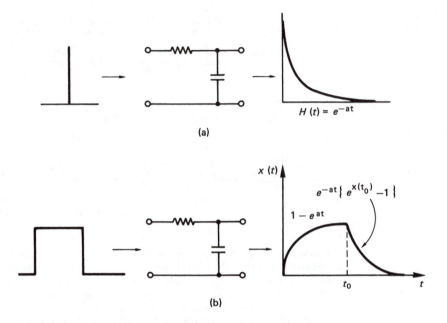

Figure 3.2 (a) The impulse response of a simple RC network is an exponential decay. This can be used to calculate the response to a square wave, as in (b).

can only occur after the input. Figure 3.2(a) shows a simple RC network and its impulse response. This is the familiar exponential decay due to the capacitor discharging through the resistor (in series with the source impedance which is assumed here to be negligible). The figure also shows the response to a squarewave at (b). With other waveforms the process is inevitably more complex.

Filtering is unavoidable. Sometimes a process has a filtering effect which is undesirable, for example the limited frequency response of an audio amplifier or loss of resolution in a lens, and we try to minimize it. On other occasions a filtering effect is specifically required. Analog or digital filters, and sometimes both, are required in ADCs, DACs, in the data channels of digital recorders and transmission systems and in DSP. Optical filters may also be necessary in imaging systems to convert between sampled and continuous images. Optical systems used in displays and in laser recorders also act as spatial filters.[1]

Figure 3.3 shows that impulse response testing tells a great deal about a filter. In a perfect filter, all frequencies should experience the same time delay. If some groups of frequencies experience a different delay from others, there is a group-delay error. As an impulse contains an infinite spectrum, a filter suffering from group-delay error will separate the different frequencies of an impulse along the time axis.

A pure delay will cause a phase shift proportional to frequency, and a filter with this characteristic is said to be phase-linear. The impulse

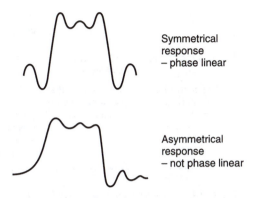

Symmetrical
response
– phase linear

Asymmetrical
response
– not phase linear

Figure 3.3 If a filter is not phase-linear, different frequencies will emerge at different times if an impulse is input. This is undesirable in video circuitry.

response of a phase-linear filter is symmetrical. If a filter suffers from group-delay error it cannot be phase-linear. It is almost impossible to make a perfectly phase-linear analog filter, and many filters have a group-delay equalization stage following them which is often as complex as the filter itself. In the digital domain it is straightforward to make a phase-linear filter, and phase equalization becomes unnecessary.

Because of the sampled nature of the signal, whatever the response at low frequencies may be, all PCM channels (and sampled analog channels) act as low-pass filters because they cannot contain frequencies above the Nyquist limit of half the sampling frequency.

3.2   Transforms

Transforms are a useful subject because they can help to understand processes which cause undesirable filtering or to design filters. The information itself may be subject to a transform. Transforming converts the information into another analog. The information is still there, but expressed with respect to temporal or spatial frequency rather than time or space. Instead of binary numbers representing the magnitude of samples, there are binary numbers representing the magnitude of frequency coefficients. The close relationship of transforms to compression technology makes any description somewhat circular as Figure 3.4 shows. The solution adopted in this chapter is to introduce a number of filtering-related topics, and to interpret these using transforms whenever a useful point can be illustrated.

Transforms are only a different representation of the same information. As a result what happens in the frequency domain must always be consistent with what happens in the time or space domains. A filter may modify the frequency response of a system, and/or the phase response,

DVB			
Image sampling	DCT-based compression	Randomizing	OFDM modulation
Transforms help explain Nyquist rate and resolution	Transform makes video data easier to compress	Transforms explain why randomizing optimizes transmitter spectrum	Modulator performs an inverse transform

Figure 3.4 Transforms are extensively found in convergent systems. They may be used to explain the operation of a process, or a process may actually create a transform. Here the relationship between transforms and DVB is shown.

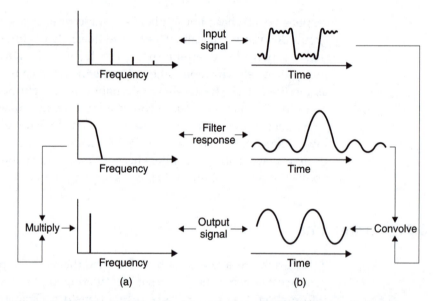

(a) (b)

Figure 3.5 If a signal having a given spectrum is passed into a filter, multiplying the two spectra will give the output spectrum at (a). Equally transforming the filter frequency response will yield the impulse response of the filter. If this is convolved with the time domain waveform, the result will be the output waveform, whose transform is the output spectrum (b).

but every combination of frequency and phase response has a corresponding impulse response in the time domain.

Figure 3.5 shows the relationship between the domains. On the left is the frequency domain. Here an input signal having a given spectrum is input to a filter having a given frequency response. The output spectrum will be the product of the two functions. If the functions are expressed logarithmically in deciBels, the product can be obtained by simple addition.

On the right, the time-domain output waveform represents the convolution of the impulse response with the input waveform. However, if the frequency transform of the output waveform is taken, it must be the same as the result obtained from the frequency response and the input spectrum. This is a useful result because it means that when image or audio sampling is considered, it will be possible to explain the process in both domains. In fact if this is not possible the phenomenon is incompletely understood.

3.3   Convolution

When a waveform is input to a system, the output waveform will be the convolution of the input waveform and the impulse response of the system. Convolution can be followed by reference to a graphic example in Figure 3.6. Where the impulse response is asymmetrical, the decaying tail occurs *after* the input. As a result it is necessary to reverse the impulse response in time so that it is mirrored prior to sweeping it through the input waveform. The output voltage is proportional to the shaded area shown where the two impulses overlap. If the impulse response is symmetrical, as would be the case with a linear phase filter, or in an optical system, the mirroring process is superfluous.

The same process can be performed in the sampled or discrete time domain as shown in Figure 3.7. The impulse and the input are now a set of discrete samples which clearly must have the same sample spacing. The impulse response only has value where impulses coincide. Elsewhere it is zero. The impulse response is therefore stepped through the input one sample period at a time. At each step, the area is still proportional to the output, but as the time steps are of uniform width, the area is proportional to the impulse height and so the output is obtained by adding up the lengths of overlap. In mathematical terms, the output samples represent the convolution of the input and the impulse response by summing the coincident cross-products.

In digital-to-analog convertors, the impulse response of the reconstruction filter is convolved with the sample pulses to create a continuous output waveform. In a wavelet decoder the output is reconstructed by convolving the wavelet function with a pulse whose amplitude is determined by a coefficient.

3.4   FIR and IIR filters

Filters can be described in two main classes, as shown in Figure 3.8, according to the nature of the impulse response. Finite-impulse response

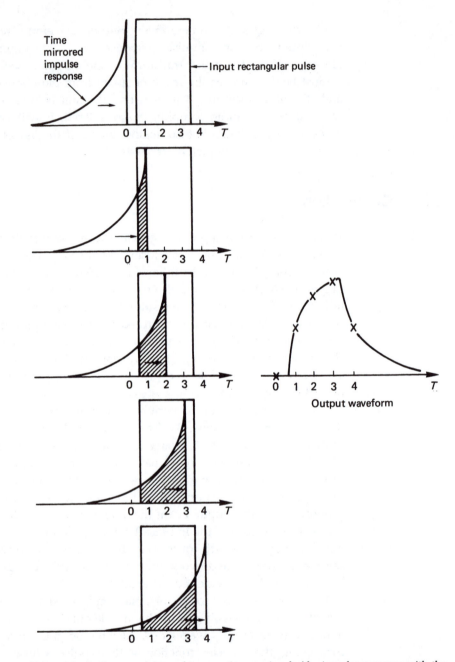

Figure 3.6 In the convolution of two continuous signals (the impulse response with the input), the impulse must be time reversed or mirrored. This is necessary because the impulse will be moved from left to right, and mirroring gives the impulse the correct time-domain response when it is moved past a fixed point. As the impulse response slides continuously through the input waveform, the area where the two overlap determines the instantaneous output amplitude. This is shown for five different times by the crosses on the output waveform.

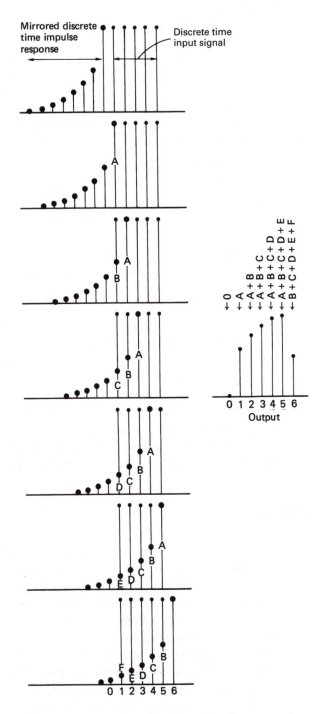

Figure 3.7 In discrete time convolution, the mirrored impulse response is stepped through the input one sample period at a time. At each step, the sum of the cross-products is used to form an output value. As the input in this example is a constant height pulse, the output is simply proportional to the sum of the coincident impulse response samples. This figure should be compared with Figure 3.6.

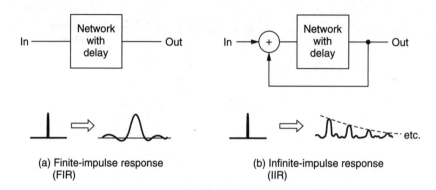

(a) Finite-impulse response
(FIR)

(b) Infinite-impulse response
(IIR)

Figure 3.8 An FIR filter (a) responds only once to an input, whereas the output of an IIR filter (b) continues indefinitely rather like a decaying echo.

(FIR) filters are always stable and, as their name suggests, respond to an impulse once, as they have only a forward path. In the temporal domain, the time for which the filter responds to an input is finite, fixed and readily established. The same is therefore true about the distance over which an FIR filter responds in the spatial domain. FIR filters can be made perfectly phase linear if a significant processing delay is accepted. Most filters used for image processing, sampling rate conversion and oversampling fall into this category.

Infinite-impulse response (IIR) filters respond to an impulse indefinitely and are not necessarily stable, as they have a return path from the output to the input. For this reason they are also called recursive filters. As the impulse response in not symmetrical, IIR filters are not phase linear. Audio equalizers often employ recursive filters.

3.5 FIR filters

An FIR filter performs convolution of the input waveform with its own impulse response. It does this by graphically constructing the impulse response for every input sample and superimposing all these responses. It is first necessary to establish the correct impulse response. Figure 3.9(a) shows an example of a low-pass filter which cuts off at $\frac{1}{4}$ of the sampling rate. The impulse response of an ideal low-pass filter is a $\sin x/x$ curve, where the time between the two central zero crossings is the reciprocal of the cut-off frequency. According to the mathematics, the waveform has always existed, and carries on for ever.

The peak value of the output coincides with the input impulse. This means that the filter cannot be causal, because the output has changed before the input is known. Thus in all practical applications it is necessary to truncate the extreme ends of the impulse response, which causes an aperture effect, and to introduce a time delay in the filter equal

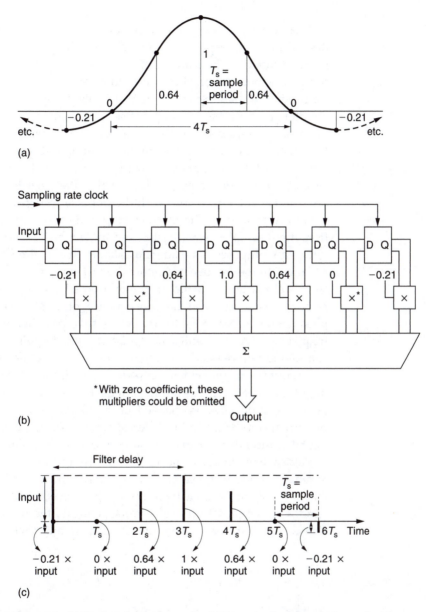

Figure 3.9 (a) The impulse response of an LPF is a $\sin x/x$ curve which stretches from $-\infty$ to $+\infty$ in time. The ends of the response must be neglected, and a delay introduced to make the filter causal. (b) The structure of an FIR LPF. Input samples shift across the register and at each point are multiplied by different coefficients. (c) When a single unit sample shifts across the circuit of Figure 3.9(b), the impulse response is created at the output as the impulse is multiplied by each coefficient in turn.

to half the duration of the truncated impulse in order to make the filter causal. As an input impulse is shifted through the series of registers in Figure 3.9(b), the impulse response is created, because at each point it is multiplied by a coefficient as in Figure 3.9(c).

These coefficients are simply the result of sampling and quantizing the desired impulse response. Clearly the sampling rate used to sample the impulse must be the same as the sampling rate for which the filter is being designed. In practice the coefficients are calculated, rather than attempting to sample an actual impulse response. The coefficient wordlength will be a compromise between cost and performance. Because the input sample shifts across the system registers to create the shape of the impulse response, the configuration is also known as a transversal filter. In operation with real sample streams, there will be several consecutive sample values in the filter registers at any time in order to convolve the input with the impulse response.

Simply truncating the impulse response causes an abrupt transition from input samples which matter and those which do not. Truncating the filter superimposes a rectangular shape on the time-domain impulse response. In the frequency domain the rectangular shape transforms to a $\sin x/x$ characteristic which is superimposed on the desired frequency response as a ripple. One consequence of this is known as Gibb's phenomenon; a tendency for the response to peak just before the cut-off frequency.[2,3] As a result, the length of the impulse which must be considered will depend not only on the frequency response but also on the amount of ripple which can be tolerated. If the relevant period of the impulse is measured in sample periods, the result will be the number of points or multiplications needed in the filter. Figure 3.10 compares the performance of filters with different numbers of points. A high-quality digital audio FIR filter may need in excess of 100 points.

Rather than simply truncate the impulse response in time, it is better to make a smooth transition from samples which do not count to those that do. This can be done by multiplying the coefficients in the filter by a window function which peaks in the centre of the impulse. Figure 3.11 shows some different window functions and their responses. The

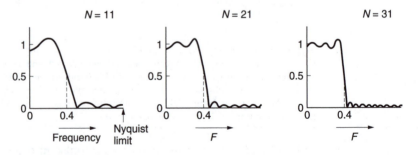

Figure 3.10 The truncation of the impulse in an FIR filter caused by the use of a finite number of points (*N*) results in ripple in the response. Shown here are three different numbers of points for the same impulse response. The filter is an LPF which rolls off at 0.4 of the fundamental interval. (Courtesy *Philips Technical Review*)

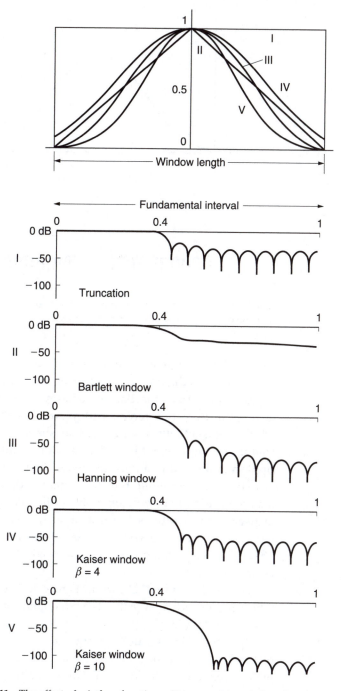

Figure 3.11 The effect of window functions. At top, various window functions are shown in continuous form. Once the number of samples in the window is established, the continuous functions shown here are sampled at the appropriate spacing to obtain window coefficients. These are multiplied by the truncated impulse response coefficients to obtain the actual coefficients used by the filter. The amplitude responses I–V correspond to the window functions illustrated. (Responses courtesy *Philips Technical Review*)

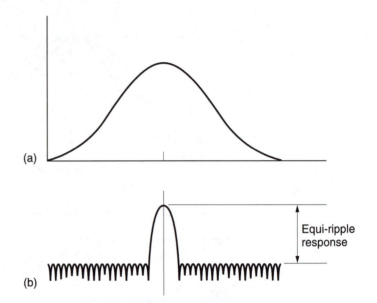

Figure 3.12 The Dolph window shape is shown at (a). The frequency response is at (b). Note the constant height of the response ripples.

rectangular window is the case of truncation, and the response is shown at I. A linear reduction in weight from the centre of the window to the edges characterizes the Bartlett window II, which trades ripple for an increase in transition-region width. At III is shown the Hann window, which is essentially a raised cosine shape. Not shown is the similar Hamming window, which offers a slightly different trade-off between ripple and the width of the main lobe. The Blackman window introduces an extra cosine term into the Hamming window at half the period of the main cosine period, reducing Gibb's phenomenon and ripple level, but increasing the width of the transition region. The Kaiser window is a family of windows based on the Bessel function, allowing various trade-offs between ripple ratio and main lobe width. Two of these are shown in IV and V.

The Dolph window[4] shown in Figure 3.12 results in an *equiripple filter* which has the advantage that the attenuation in the stopband never falls below a certain level.

Filter coefficients can be optimized by computer simulation. One of the best-known techniques used is the Remez exchange algorithm, which converges on the optimum coefficients after a number of iterations.

In the example of Figure 3.13, a low-pass FIR filter is shown which is intended to allow downsampling by a factor of two. The key feature is that the stopband must have begun before one half of the output sampling rate. This is most readily achieved using a Hamming window

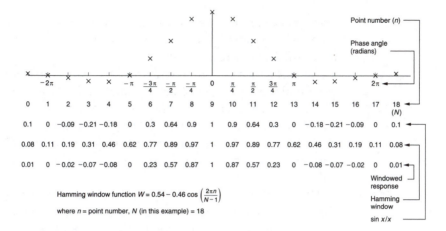

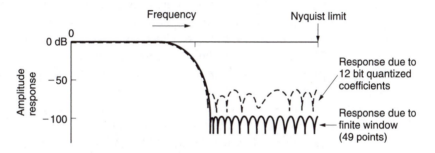

Figure 3.13 A downsampling filter using the Hamming window.

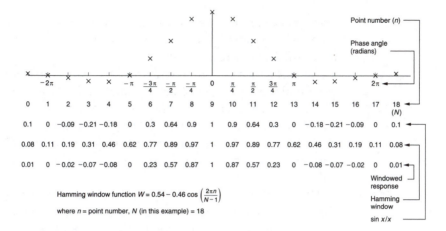

Figure 3.14 Frequency response of a 49-point transversal filter with infinite precision (solid line) shows ripple due to finite window size. Quantizing coefficients to twelve bits reduces attenuation in the stopband. (Responses courtesy *Philips Technical Review*)

because it was designed empirically to have a flat stopband so that good aliasing attenuation is possible. The width of the transition band determines the number of significant sample periods embraced by the impulse. The Hamming window doubles the width of the transition band. This determines in turn both the number of points in the filter, and the filter delay. For the purposes of illustration, the number of points is much smaller than would normally be the case in an audio application.

As the impulse is symmetrical, the delay will be half the impulse period. The impulse response is a $\sin x/x$ function, and this has been calculated in the figure. The equation for the Hamming window function is shown with the window values which result. The $\sin x/x$ response is next multiplied by the Hamming window function to give the windowed impulse response shown. If the coefficients are not quantized finely enough, it will be as if they had been calculated inaccurately, and the performance of the filter will be less than expected. Figure 3.14 shows an example of quantizing coefficients. Conversely, raising the wordlength of the coefficients increases cost.

The FIR structure is inherently phase linear because it is easy to make the impulse response absolutely symmetrical. The individual samples in a digital system do not know in isolation what frequency they represent, and they can only pass through the filter at a rate determined by the clock. Because of this inherent phase-linearity, an FIR filter can be designed for a specific impulse response, and the frequency response will follow.

The frequency response of the filter can be changed at will by changing the coefficients. A programmable filter only requires a series of PROMs to supply the coefficients; the address supplied to the PROMs will select the response. The frequency response of a digital filter will also change if the clock rate is changed, so it is often less ambiguous to specify a frequency of interest in a digital filter in terms of a fraction of the fundamental interval rather than in absolute terms. The configuration shown in Figure 3.9 serves to illustrate the principle. The units used on the diagrams are sample periods and the response is proportional to these periods or spacings, and so it is not necessary to use actual figures.

Where the impulse response is symmetrical, it is often possible to reduce the number of multiplications, because the same product can be used twice, at equal distances before and after the centre of the window. This is known as folding the filter. A folded filter is shown in Figure 3.15.

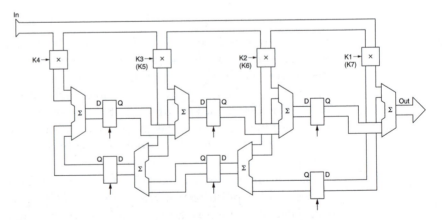

Figure 3.15 A seven-point folded filter for a symmetrical impulse response. In this case K1 and K7 will be identical, and the input sample can be multipled once, and the product fed into the output shift system in two different places. The centre coefficient K4 appears once. In an even-numbered filter the centre coefficient would also be used twice.

3.6   Interpolation

Interpolation is an important enabling technology on which a large number of practical digital video devices are based. Some of the applications of interpolation are set out below:

1 Digital video standards often differ from the sampling standard used in MPEG, particularly with respect to the disposition of colour samples. Interpolation is needed to format video into the standard MPEG expects and to return the signal to its original format after decoding. In low-bit rate applications such as Internet video, the picture resolution may be reduced by downsampling. For display the number of pixels may have to be increased again.

2 In digital audio, different sampling rates exist today for different purposes. Rate conversion allows material to be exchanged freely between such formats. Low-bit rate compressed channels may require a reduced sampling rate as an input format.

3 In scaleable compression, a number of different pixel array sizes can be decoded, depending on how much of the compressed bitstream is decoded. Decoding at high resolution involves upsampling the lower-resolution image before adding detail to it.

4 Changing between sampling formats may be necessary in order to view an incoming image on an available display. This technique is generally known as *resizing* and is essentially a two-dimensional sampling rate conversion, the rate in this case being the spatial frequency of the pixels.

5 In MPEG-4 a compression tool known as warping is introduced. This allows the changes in perspective as objects turn to be coded as a few vectors instead of a large picture change. The warping process is a two-dimensional interpolation.

There are three basic but related categories of interpolation, as shown in Figure 3.16. The most straightforward (a) changes the sampling rate by an integer ratio, up or down. The timing of the system is thus simplified because all samples (input and output) are present on edges of the higher-rate sampling clock. Such a system is generally adopted for oversampling convertors; the exact sampling rate immediately adjacent to the analog domain is not critical, and will be chosen to make the filters easier to implement.

Next in order of difficulty is the category shown at (b) where the rate is changed by the ratio of two small integers. Samples in the input periodically time-align with the output. Such devices can be used for converting between the various rates of ITU-601.

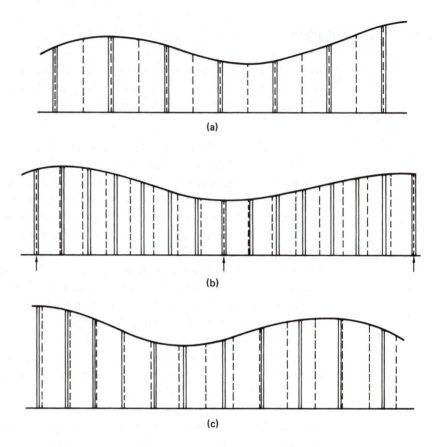

Figure 3.16 Categories of rate conversion. (a) Integer-ratio conversion, where the lower-rate samples are always coincident with those of the higher rate. There are a small number of phases needed. (b) Fractional-ratio conversion, where sample coincidence is periodic. A larger number of phases is required. Example here is conversion from 50.4 kHz to 44.1 kHz (8/7). (c) Variable-ratio conversion, where there is no fixed relationship, and a large number of phases are required.

The most complex rate-conversion category is where there is no simple relationship between input and output sampling rates, and in fact they may vary. This situation, shown at (c), is known as variable-ratio conversion. The temporal or spatial relationship of input and output samples is arbitrary. This problem will be met in effects machines which zoom or rotate images and in MPEG-4 warping.

The technique of integer-ratio conversion is used in conjunction with oversampling convertors in digital video and audio and in motion estimation and scaleable compression systems where sub-sampled or reduced-resolution versions of an input image are required.

Figure 3.17(a) shows the spectrum of a typical sampled system where the sampling rate is a little more than twice the analog bandwidth. Attempts to reduce the sampling rate by simply omitting samples, a

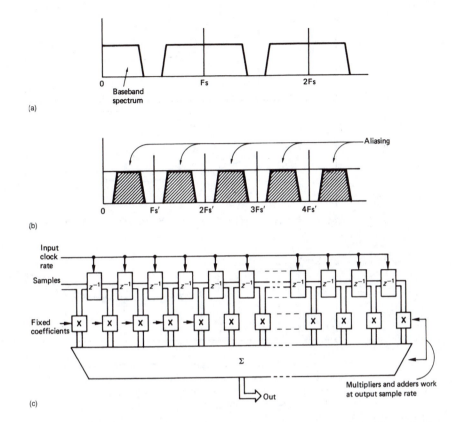

Figure 3.17 The spectrum of a typical digital sample stream at (a) will be subject to aliasing as in (b) if the baseband width is not reduced by an LPF. At (c) an FIR low-pass filter prevents aliasing. Samples are clocked transversely across the filter at the input rate, but the filter only computes at the output sample rate. Clearly this will only work if the two are related by an integer factor.

process known as decimation, will result in aliasing, as shown in Figure 3.17(b). Intuitively it is obvious that omitting samples is the same as if the original sampling rate was lower. In order to prevent aliasing, it is necessary to incorporate low-pass filtering into the system where the cut-off frequency reflects the new, lower, sampling rate. An FIR type low-pass filter could be installed, as described earlier in this chapter, immediately prior to the stage where samples are omitted, but this would be wasteful, because for much of its time the FIR filter would be calculating sample values which are to be discarded. The more effective method is to combine the low-pass filter with the decimator so that the filter only calculates values to be retained in the output sample stream. Figure 3.17(c) shows how this is done. The filter makes one accumulation for every output sample, but that accumulation is the result of multiplying all relevant input samples in the filter window by an appropriate coefficient. The number of points in the filter is determined

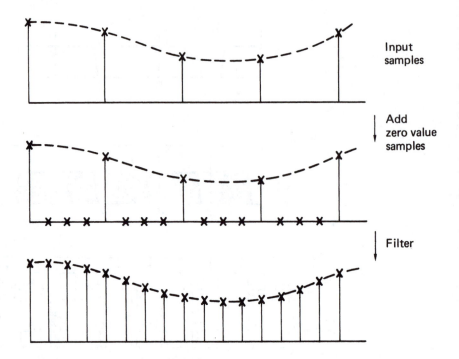

Figure 3.18 In integer-ratio sampling, rate increase can be obtained in two stages. First, zero-value samples are inserted to increase the rate, and then filtering is used to give the extra samples real values. The filter necessary will be an LPF with a response which cuts off at the Nyquist frequency of the input samples.

by the number of *input* samples in the period of the filter window, but the number of multiplications per second is obtained by multiplying that figure by the *output* rate. If the filter is not integrated with the decimator, the number of points has to be multiplied by the input rate. The larger the rate-reduction factor, the more advantageous the decimating filter ought to be, but this is not quite the case, as the greater the reduction in rate, the longer the filter window will need to be to accommodate the broader impulse response.

When the sampling rate is to be increased by an integer factor, additional samples must be created at even spacing between the existing ones. There is no need for the bandwidth of the input samples to be reduced since, if the original sampling rate was adequate, a higher one must also be adequate.

Figure 3.18 shows that the process of sampling-rate increase can be thought of in two stages. First, the correct rate is achieved by inserting samples of zero value at the correct instant, and then the additional samples are given meaningful values by passing the sample stream through a low-pass filter which cuts off at the Nyquist frequency of the original sampling rate. This filter is known as an interpolator, and one of its tasks is to prevent images of the lower input-sampling spectrum from appearing in the extended baseband of the higher-rate output spectrum.

All sampled systems have finite bandwidth and need a reconstruction filter to remove the frequencies above the baseband due to sampling. After reconstruction, one infinitely short digital sample ideally represents a $\sin x/x$ pulse whose central peak width is determined by the response of the reconstruction filter, and whose amplitude is proportional to the sample value. This implies that, in reality, one sample value has meaning over a considerable timespan, rather than just at the sample instant. Were this not true, it would be impossible to build an interpolator.

Performing interpolation steps separately is inefficient. The bandwidth of the information is unchanged when the sampling rate is increased; therefore the original input samples will pass through the filter unchanged, and it is superfluous to compute them. The combination of the two processes into an interpolating filter minimizes the amount of computation.

As the purpose of the system is purely to increase the sampling rate, the filter must be as transparent as possible, and this implies that a linear-phase configuration is mandatory, suggesting the use of an FIR structure. Figure 3.19 shows that the theoretical impulse response of such a filter is

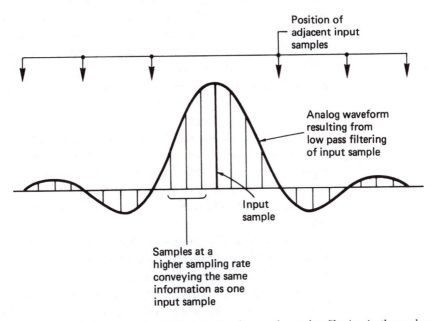

Figure 3.19 A single sample results in a $\sin x/x$ waveform after filtering in the analog domain. At a new, higher, sampling rate, the same waveform after filtering will be obtained if the numerous samples of differing size shown here are used. It follows that the values of these new samples can be calculated from the input samples in the digital domain in an FIR filter.

a $\sin x/x$ curve which has zero value at the position of adjacent input samples. In practice this impulse cannot be implemented because it is infinite. The impulse response used will be truncated and windowed as described earlier.

To simplify this discussion, assume that a $\sin x/x$ impulse is to be used. There is a strong parallel with the operation of a DAC where the analog voltage is returned to the time-continuous state by summing the analog impulses due to each sample. In a digital interpolating filter, this process is duplicated.[5]

If the sampling rate is to be doubled, new samples must be interpolated exactly halfway between existing samples. The necessary impulse response is shown in Figure 3.20; it can be sampled at the *output* sample period and quantized to form coefficients. If a single input sample is multiplied by each of these coefficients in turn, the impulse response of that sample at the new sampling rate will be obtained. Note that every other coefficient is zero, which confirms that no computation is necessary on the existing samples; they are just transferred to the output. The intermediate sample is computed by adding together the impulse responses of every input sample in the window. The figure shows how this mechanism operates. If the sampling rate is to be increased by a factor of four, three sample values must be interpolated between existing input samples. Figure 3.21 shows that it is only necessary to sample the impulse response at one-quarter the period of input samples to obtain three sets of coefficients which will be used in turn. In hardware-implemented filters, the input sample which is passed straight to the output is transferred by using a fourth filter phase where all coefficients are zero except the central one, which is unity.

Fractional ratio conversion allows interchange between different images having different pixel array sizes. Fractional ratios also occur in the vertical axis of standards convertors. Figure 3.16 showed that when the two sampling rates have a simple fractional relationship m/n, there is a periodicity in the relationship between samples in the two streams. It is possible to have a system clock running at the least-common multiple frequency which will divide by different integers to give each sampling rate.[6]

The existence of a common clock frequency means that a fractional-ratio convertor could be made by arranging two integer-ratio convertors in series. This configuration is shown in Figure 3.22(a). The input-sampling rate is multiplied by m in an interpolator, and the result is divided by n in a decimator. Although this system would work, it would be grossly inefficient, because only one in n of the interpolator's outputs would be used. A decimator followed by an interpolator would also offer the correct sampling rate at the output, but the intermediate sampling rate would be so low that the system bandwidth would be quite unacceptable.

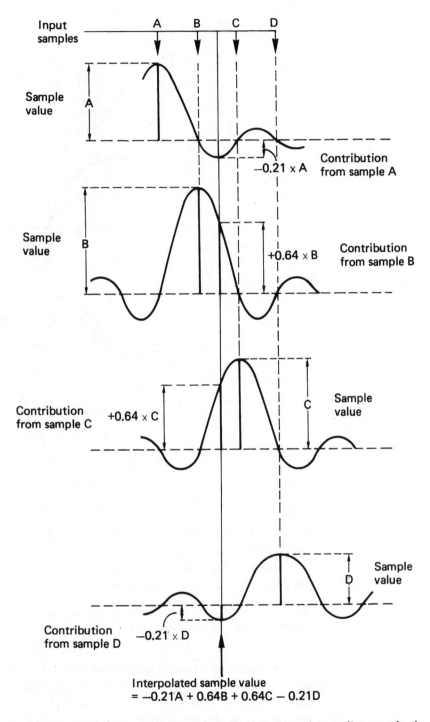

Figure 3.20 A 2 × oversampling interpolator. To compute an intermediate sample, the input samples are imagined to be sin x/x impulses, and the contributions from each at the point of interest can be calculated. In practice, rather more samples on either side need to be taken into account.

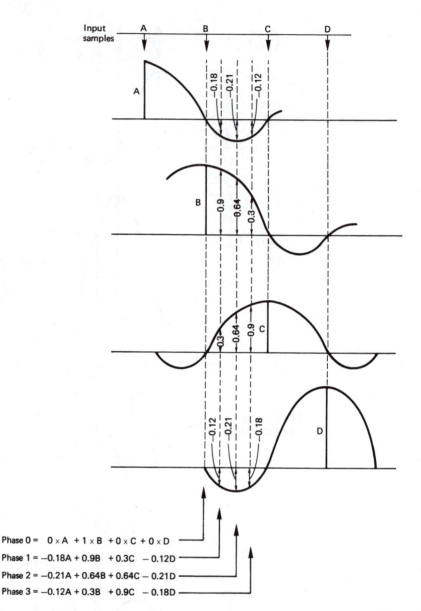

Phase 0 = 0 × A + 1 × B + 0 × C + 0 × D

Phase 1 = −0.18A + 0.9B + 0.3C − 0.12D

Phase 2 = −0.21A + 0.64B + 0.64C − 0.21D

Phase 3 = −0.12A + 0.3B + 0.9C − 0.18D

Figure 3.21   In 4 × oversampling, for each set of input samples, four phases of coefficients are necessary, each of which produces one of the oversampled values.

As has been seen, a more efficient structure results from combining the processes. The result is exactly the same structure as an integer-ratio interpolator, and requires an FIR filter. The impulse response of the filter is determined by the lower of the two sampling rates, and, as before, it prevents aliasing when the rate is being reduced, and prevents images when the rate is being increased. The interpolator has sufficient coefficient phases to interpolate *m* output samples for every input

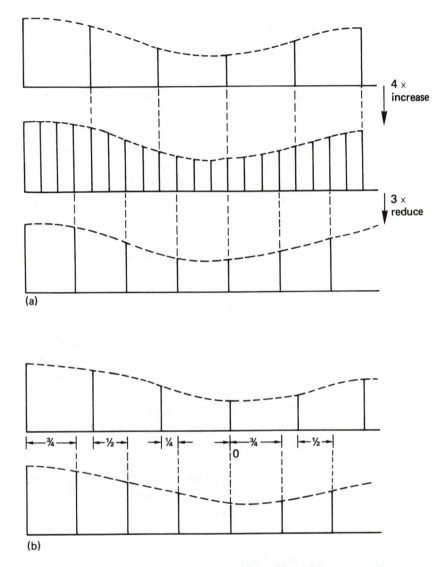

Figure 3.22 At (a), fractional-ratio conversion of 3/4 in this example is by increasing to 4 × input prior to reducing by 3 ×. The inefficiency due to discarding previously computed values is clear. At (b), efficiency is raised since only needed values will be computed. Note how the interpolation phase changes for each output. Fixed coefficients can no longer be used.

sample, but not all of these values are computed; only interpolations which coincide with an output sample are performed. It will be seen in Figure 3.22(b) that input samples shift across the transversal filter at the input sampling rate, but interpolations are only performed at the output sample rate. This is possible because a different filter phase will be used at each interpolation.

In the previous examples, the sample rate or spacing of the filter output had a constant relationship to the input, which meant that the two rates had to be phase-locked. This is an undesirable constraint in some applications, including warping processors. In a variable-ratio inter-polator, values will exist for the points at which input samples were made, but it is necessary to compute what the sample values would have been at absolutely any point in two dimensions between available samples. The general concept of the interpolator is the same as for the fractional-ratio convertor, except that an infinite number of filter phases is ideally necessary. Since a realizable filter will have a finite number of phases, it is necessary to study the degradation this causes. The desired continuous temporal or spatial axis of the interpolator is quantized by the phase spacing, and a sample value needed at a particular point will be replaced by a value for the nearest available filter phase. The number of phases in the filter therefore determines the accuracy of the interpolation.

The effects of calculating a value for the wrong point are identical to those of sampling with clock jitter, in that an error occurs proportional to the slope of the signal. The result is program-modulated noise. The higher the noise specification, the greater the desired time accuracy and the greater the number of phases required. The number of phases is equal to the number of sets of coefficients available, and should not be confused with the number of points in the filter, which is equal to the number of coefficients in a set (and the number of multiplications needed to calculate one output value).

The sampling jitter accuracy necessary for eight-bit working is measured in picoseconds. This implies that something like 32 filter phases will be required for adequate performance in an eight-bit sampling-rate convertor.

3.7   Downsampling filters

In compression pre-processing, it is often necessary to downsample the input picture. This may be needed to obtain the desired picture size, e.g. 360 pixels across, from a standard definition picture which is 720 pixels across. 4:2:2 inputs will need vertical filtering to produce 4:2:0 which most of the MPEG-2 profiles use.

Figure 3.23 shows that when a filter is used for downsampling, the stopband rejection is important because poor performance here results in aliasing. In an MPEG environment aliasing is particularly undesirable on an input signal as after the DCT stage aliasing will result in spurious coefficients which will require a higher bit rate to convey. If this bit rate is not available the picture quality will be impaired. Consequently the

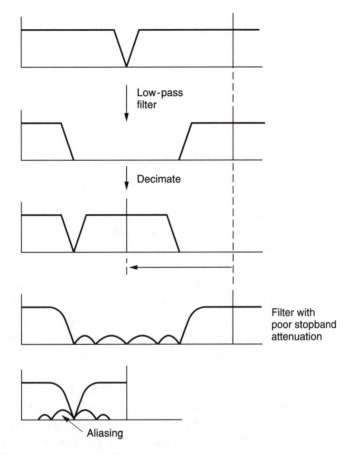

Figure 3.23 Downsampling filters for MPEG prefiltering must have good stopband rejection to avoid aliasing when the sampling rate is reduced. Stopband performance is critical for a pre-processing filter.

performance criteria for MPEG downsampling filters is more stringent than for general use and filters will generally require more points than in other applications.

3.8   The quadrature mirror filter

Audio compression often uses a process known as band splitting which splits up the audio spectrum into a series of frequency ranges. Band splitting is complex and requires a lot of computation. One band-splitting method which is useful is quadrature mirror filtering.[7] The QMF is is a kind of twin FIR filter which converts a PCM sample stream into two sample streams of half the input sampling rate, so that the output data rate equals the input data rate. The frequencies in the lower half of the audio spectrum are carried in one sample stream, and the

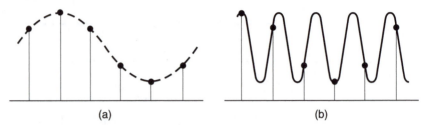

(a)   (b)

Figure 3.24 The sample stream shown would ordinarily represent the waveform shown in (a), but if it is known that the original signal could exist only between two frequencies then the waveform in (b) must be the correct one. A suitable bandpass reconstruction filter, or synthesis filter, will produce the waveform in (b).

frequencies in the upper half of the spectrum are carried in the other. Whilst the lower frequency output is a PCM band-limited representation of the input waveform, the upper frequency output is not. A moment's thought will reveal that it could not be because the sampling rate is not high enough. In fact the upper half of the input spectrum has been heterodyned down to the same frequency band as the lower half by the clever use of aliasing. The waveform is unrecognizable, but when heterodyned back to its correct place in the spectrum in an inverse step, the correct waveform will result once more. Figure 3.24 shows how the idea works.

Sampling theory states that the sampling rate needed must be at least twice the bandwidth in the signal to be sampled. If the signal is band limited, the sampling rate need only be more than twice the signal *bandwidth* not the signal *frequency*. Downsampled signals of this kind can be reconstructed by a reconstruction or *synthesis* filter having a bandpass response rather than a low pass response. As only signals within the passband can be output, it is clear from Figure 3.24 that the waveform which will result is the original as the intermediate aliased waveform lies outside the passband.

Figure 3.25 shows the operation of a simple QMF. At (a) the input spectrum of the PCM audio is shown, having an audio baseband extending up to half the sampling rate and the usual lower sideband extending down from there up to the sampling frequency. The input is passed through an FIR low-pass filter which cuts off at one-quarter of the sampling rate to give the spectrum shown at (b). The input also passes in parallel through a second FIR filter which is physically identical, but the coefficients are different. The impulse response of the FIR LPF is multiplied by a cosinusoidal waveform which amplitude modulates it. The resultant impulse gives the filter a frequency response shown at (c). This is a mirror image of the LPF response. If certain criteria are met, the overall frequency response of the two filters is flat. The spectra of both (b) and (c) show that both are oversampled by a factor of 2 because they are half-empty. As a result both can be decimated by a factor of 2, which is

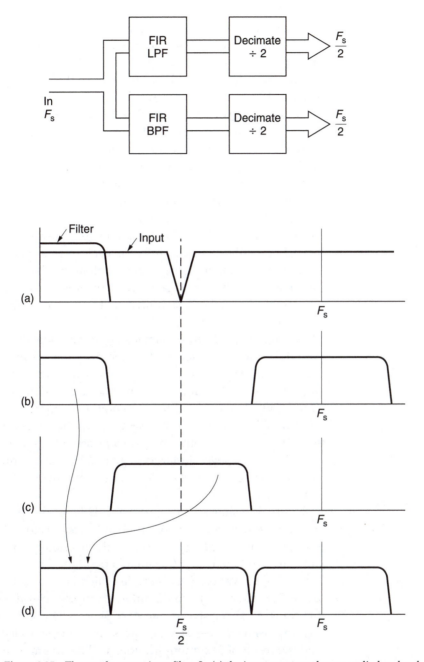

Figure 3.25 The quadrature mirror filter. In (a) the input spectrum has an audio baseband extending up to half the sampling rate. The input is passed through an FIR low-pass filter which cuts off at one-quarter of the sampling rate to give the spectrum shown in (b). The input also passes in parallel through a second FIR filter whose impulse response has been multiplied by a cosinusoidal waveform in order to amplitude-modulate it. The resultant impulse gives the filter a mirror image frequency response shown in (c). The spectra of both (b) and (c) show that both are oversampled by a factor of two because they are half empty. As a result both can be decimated by a factor of two, resulting in (d) in two identical Nyquist-sampled frequency bands of half the original width.

the equivalent of dropping every other sample. In the case of the lower half of the spectrum, nothing remarkable happens. In the case of the upper half, it has been resampled at half the original frequency as shown at (d). The result is that the upper half of the audio spectrum aliases or heterodynes to the lower half.

An inverse QMF will recombine the bands into the original broadband signal. It is a feature of a QMF/inverse QMF pair that any energy near the band edge which appears in both bands due to inadequate selectivity in the filtering reappears at the correct frequency in the inverse filtering process provided that there is uniform quantizing in all the sub-bands. In practical coders, this criterion is not met, but any residual artifacts are sufficiently small to be masked.

The audio band can be split into as many bands as required by cascading QMFs in a tree. However, each stage can only divide the input spectrum in half. In some coders certain sub-bands will have passed through one splitting stage more than others and will have half their bandwidth.[8] A delay is required in the wider sub-band data for time alignment.

A simple quadrature mirror is computationally intensive because sample values are calculated which are later decimated or discarded, and an alternative is to use polyphase pseudo-QMF filters[9] or wave filters[10] in which the filtering and decimation process is combined. Only wanted sample values are computed. In a polyphase filter a set of samples is shifted into position in the transversal register and then these are multiplied by different sets of coefficients and accumulated in each of several phases to give the value of a number of different samples between input samples. In a polyphase QMF, the same approach is used.

Figure 3.26 shows an example of a 32-band polyphase QMF having a 512-sample window. With 32 sub-bands, each band will be decimated to $\frac{1}{32}$ of the input sampling rate. Thus only one sample in 32 will be retained after the combined filter/decimate operation. The polyphase QMF only computes the value of the sample which is to be retained in each sub-band. The filter works in 32 different phases with the same samples in the transversal register. In the first phase, the coefficients will describe the impulse response of a low-pass filter, the so-called prototype filter, and the result of 512 multiplications will be accumulated to give a single sample in the first band. In the second phase the coefficients will be obtained by multiplying the impulse response of the prototype filter by a cosinusoid at the centre frequency of the second band. Once more 512 multiply accumulates will be required to obtain a single sample in the second band. This is repeated for each of the 32 bands, and in each case a different centre frequency is obtained by multiplying the prototype impulse by a different modulating frequency. Following 32 such

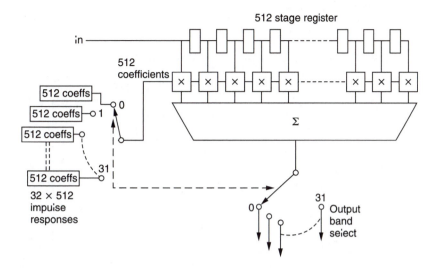

Figure 3.26 In polyphase QMF the same input samples are subject to computation using coefficient sets in many different time-multiplexed phases. The decimation is combined with the filtering so only wanted values are computed.

computations, 32 output samples, one in each band, will have been computed. The transversal register then shifts 32 samples and the process repeats.

The principle of the polyphase QMF is not so different from the techniques used to compute a frequency transform and effectively blurs the distinction between sub-band coding and transform coding.

3.9 Filtering for video noise reduction

The basic principle of all video noise reducers is that there is a certain amount of correlation between the video content of successive frames, whereas there is no correlation between the noise content.

A basic recursive device is shown in Figure 3.27. There is a frame store which acts as a delay, and the output of the delay can be fed back to the input through an attenuator, which in the digital domain will be a multiplier. In the case of a still picture, successive frames will be identical, and the recursion will be large. This means that the output video will actually be the average of many frames. If there is movement of the image, it will be necessary to reduce the amount of recursion to prevent the generation of trails or smears. Probably the most famous examples of recursion smear are the television pictures sent back of astronauts walking on the moon. The received pictures were very noisy and needed a lot of averaging to make them viewable. This was fine until

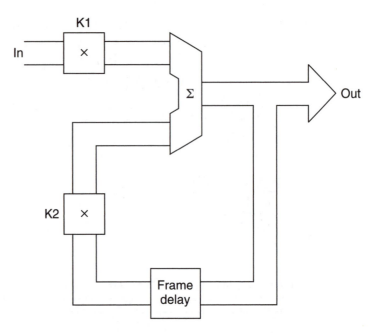

Figure 3.27 A basic recursive device feeds back the output to the input via a frame store which acts as a delay. The characteristics of the device are controlled totally by the values of the two coefficients K1 and K2 which control the multipliers.

the astronaut moved. The technology of the day did not permit motion sensing.

The noise reduction increases with the number of frames over which the noise is integrated, but image motion prevents simple combining of frames. It will be seen in section 3.14 that if motion estimation is available, the image of a moving object in a particular frame can be integrated from the images in several frames which have been super-imposed on the same part of the screen by displacements derived from the motion measurement. The result is that greater reduction of noise becomes possible.[11]

In a median filter, sample values adjacent to the one under examination are considered. These may be in the same place in previous or subsequent images, or nearby in the same image. A median filter computes the distribution of values on all its input points. If the value of the centre point lies centrally within the distribution then it is considered to be valid and is passed to the output without change. In this case the median filter has no effect whatsoever. However, if the value of the centre point is at the edge of the distribution it is considered to be in error due to impulsive noise and a different input point, nearest the mean, is selected as the output pixel. Effectively a pixel value from nearby is used to conceal the error. The median filter is very effective against dropouts, film dirt and bit errors.

3.10 Warping

Warping is a technique which allows the texture of an object correctly to be mapped onto its surface. The concept is simple, whereas the implementation is not. Figure 3.28 shows a simple example. A flag is stretched absolutely flat so that the true shape of the pattern can be seen. However, when the flag blows in the wind, the pattern which can be seen is not the same because the flag is no longer flat. Warping is a technique which, *inter alia*, allows the appearance of a flag correctly to be computed from a knowledge of what the flag looked like when it was flat.

Figure 3.29 shows another example. Here a simple rectangular object such as a bus is turning a corner. In one picture, the outline of the bus may be a rectangle, whereas in the next it has become a trapezoid. In MPEG-2 it would be necessary to send a considerable amount of data to convert the first picture into the second. In MPEG-4 the facility exists to transmit warping codes so that the texture of the side of the bus is warped in the decoder to the new shape. This requires fewer data to be transmitted.

The principle of warping is the same as the technique used by cartographers for centuries. Cartographers are faced with the problem that the earth is round, and paper is flat. In order to produce flat maps, it is necessary to project the features of the round original onto a flat surface. There are a number of different ways of projecting maps, and all of them must by definition produce distortion. The effect of this

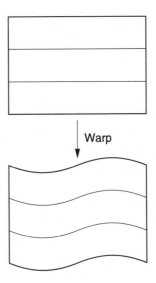

Figure 3.28 Warping is a process which allows the appearance of a non-flat surface to be computed.

Figure 3.29 An example of warping in compression. The change in perspective as the vehicle turns would require a large residual in MPEG-2, but with MPEG-4 much of the new shape can be obtained by warping the pixels from an earlier picture.

distortion is that distances measured near the extremities of the map appear further than they actually are. Another effect is that *great circle routes* (the shortest or longest path between two places on a planet) appear curved on a projected map. The type of projection used is usually printed somewhere on the map, a very common system being that due to Mercator. Clearly the process of mapping involves some three-dimensional geometry in order to simulate the paths of light rays from the map so that they appear to have come from the curved surface. Video effects machines work in exactly the same way. It is an interesting demonstration of the evolving power of microelectronics that the circuitry developed for DVEs costing hundreds of thousands of dollars in the 1980s is now just part of an MPEG-4 decoder chip.

The distortion of maps means that things are not where they seem. In timesharing computers, every user appears to have his own identical address space in which his program resides, despite the fact that many different programs are simultaneously in the memory. In order to resolve this contradiction, memory management units are constructed which add a constant value to the address which the user thinks he has (the *virtual address*) in order to produce the *physical address*. As long as the unit gives each user a different constant, they can all program in the same

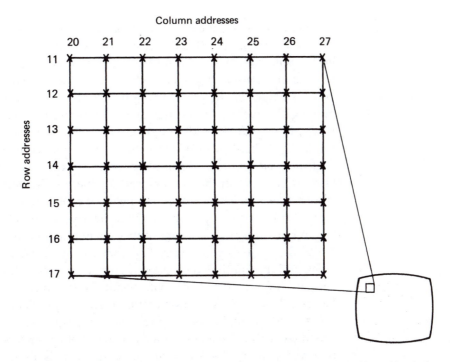

Figure 3.30 The entire TV picture can be broken down into uniquely addressable pixels.

virtual address space without one corrupting another's programs. Because the program is no longer where it seems to be, the term mapping was introduced. The address space of a computer is one dimensional, but a video frame expressed as rows and columns of pixels can be considered to have a two-dimensional address as in Figure 3.30. Video manipulators work by mapping the pixel addresses in two dimensions.

Every pixel in the frame array has an address. The address is two dimensional, because in order to uniquely specify one pixel, the column address and the row address must be supplied. It is possible to transform a picture by simultaneously addressing in rows and columns. It was discovered some time ago in connection with computer graphics that the two-dimensional problem can sometimes be converted into two one-dimensional problems.[12] Essentially if a horizontal transform affecting whole rows of pixels independently of other rows is performed on the array, followed by or preceded by a vertical transform which affects entire columns independently of other columns, the effect will be the same as if a two-dimensional transform had been performed. This is the principle of separability.

There are many different manipulations needed in warping, and the approach here will be to begin with the simplest, which require the least processing, and to graduate to the most complex, introducing the necessary processes at each stage. Initially the examples given will be one dimensional. Figure 3.31 shows a single row of pixels which are held in a buffer where each can be addressed individually and transferred to another. If a constant is added to the read address, the selected pixel will be to the right of the place where it will be put. This has the effect of moving the picture to the left. If the buffer represented a column of pixels, the picture would be moved vertically. As these two transforms can be controlled independently, the picture could be moved diagonally.

If the read address is multiplied by a constant, say 2, the effect is to bring samples from the input closer together on the output, so that the picture size is reduced. Again independent control of the horizontal and vertical transforms is possible, so that the aspect ratio of the picture can be modified. Clearly the secret of these manipulations is in the constants fed to the address generators. The added constant represents displacement, and the multiplied constant represents magnification. A multiplier constant of less than one will result in the picture getting larger. Figure 3.31 also shows, however, that there is a problem. If a constant of 0.5 is used, to make the picture twice as large, half of the addresses generated are not integers. A memory does not understand an address of two and a half! If an arbitrary magnification is used, nearly all the addresses generated are non-integer. A similar problem crops up if a constant of less than one is added to the address in an attempt to move the picture less than the pixel spacing. The solution to the problem is to use the interpolation techniques described earlier in this chapter. Because the input image is spatially sampled, those samples contain enough information to represent the brightness and colour all over the screen.

When the address generator produces an address of 2.5, it actually means that what is wanted is the value of the signal interpolated half-way between pixel 2 and pixel 3. The output of the address generator will thus be split into two parts. The integer part will become the memory address, and the fractional part is the phase of the necessary interpolation. In order to interpolate pixel values a digital filter is necessary.

In order to follow the operation of warping, some knowledge of perspective is necessary. Stated briefly, the phenomenon of perspective is due to the angle subtended to the eye by objects being a function not only of their size but also of their distance. Figure 3.32 shows that the size of an image on the rear wall of a pinhole camera can be increased either by making the object larger or bringing it closer. In the absence of stereoscopic vision, it is not possible to tell which has happened. The pinhole camera is very useful for study of perspective, and has indeed been used by artists for that purpose. The clinically precise perspective of Canaletto paintings was achieved through the use of the camera obscura ('darkened room' in Italian).[13]

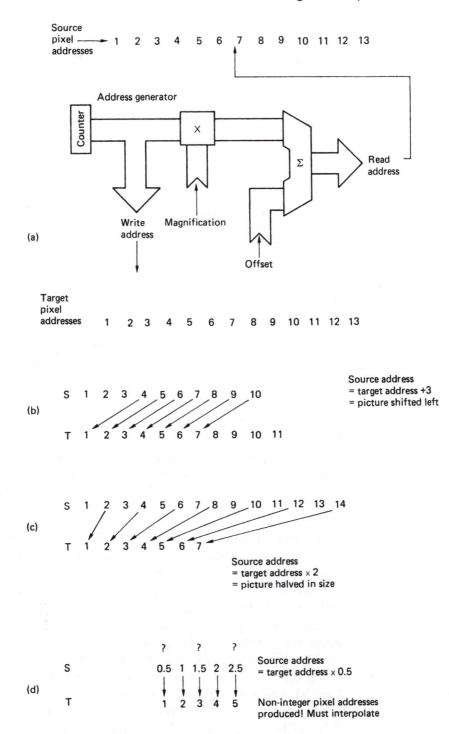

Figure 3.31 Address generation is the fundamental process behind transforms.

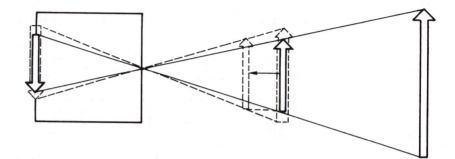

Figure 3.32 The image on the rear of the pinhole camera is identical for the two solid objects shown because the size of the object is proportional to distance, and the subtended angle remains the same. The image can be made larger (dashed) by making the object larger or moving it closer.

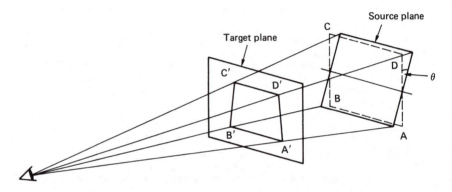

Figure 3.33 In a planar rotation effect the source plane ABCD is the rectangular input picture. If it is rotated through the angle θ, ray tracing to a single eye at left will produce a trapezoidal image A 'B' C 'D' on the target. Magnification will now vary with position on the picture.

Warping processors work by producing the correct subtended angles which the brain perceives as a three-dimensional effect. Figure 3.33 shows that to a single eye, there is no difference between a three-dimensional scene and a two-dimensional image formed where rays traced from features to the eye intersect an imaginary plane.

Figure 3.33 also shows that when a plane input picture is rotated about a horizontal axis, the distance from the top of the picture to the eye is no longer the same as the distance from the bottom of the picture to the eye. The result is that the top and bottom edges of the picture subtend different angles to the eye, and where the rays cross the target plane, the image has become trapezoidal. There is now no such thing as the magnification of the picture. The magnification changes continuously from top to bottom of the picture, and if a uniform grid is input, after a perspective rotation it will appear non-linear as the diagram shows.

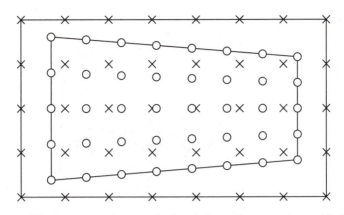

Figure 3.34 When a picture is warped, the pixels no longer register with the standard locations. Interpolation in two dimensions is used to create pixels on the standard grid.

Figure 3.34 shows that when a picture is warped, this causes the pixels in the picture to fail to register with the standard pixel spacing. The solution is two-dimensional interpolation. One pixel value actually represents the peak brightness of a two-dimensional intensity function, which is the effect of the modulation transfer function of the system on an infinitely small point. In order to compute an interpolated value, it is necessary to add together the contribution from all relevant samples, at the point of interest. Each contribution can be obtained by looking up the value of a unity impulse curve at the distance from the input pixel to the output pixel to obtain a coefficient, and multiplying the input pixel value by that coefficient.

The process of taking several pixel values, multiplying each by a different coefficient and summing the products can be performed by the FIR (finite impulse response) configuration described earlier. The impulse response of the filter necessary depends on the magnification. Where the picture is being enlarged, the impulse response can be the same as at normal size, but as the size is reduced, the impulse response has to become broader (corresponding to a reduced spatial frequency response) so that more input samples are averaged together to prevent aliasing. The coefficient store will need a three-dimensional structure, such that the magnification and the interpolation phase in each axis must both be supplied to obtain a set of coefficients. The magnification can easily be obtained by comparing successive outputs from the address generator. Alternatively, the coefficients could be computed dynamically.

3.11 Transforms and duality

The duality of transforms provides an interesting insight into what is happening in common processes. Fourier analysis holds that any

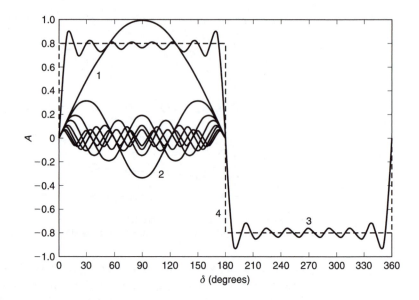

Figure 3.35 Fourier analysis of a square wave into fundamental and harmonics. *A*, amplitude; δ, phase of fundamental wave in degrees; 1, first harmonic (fundamental); 2, odd harmonics 3–15; 3, sum of harmonics 1–15; 4, ideal square wave.

periodic waveform can be reproduced by adding together an arbitrary number of harmonically related sinusoids of various amplitudes and phases. Figure 3.35 shows how a square wave can be built up of harmonics. The spectrum can be drawn by plotting the amplitude of the harmonics against frequency. It will be seen that this gives a spectrum which is a decaying wave. It passes through zero at all even multiples of the fundamental. The shape of the spectrum is a $\sin x/x$ curve. If a square wave has a $\sin x/x$ spectrum, it follows that a filter with a rectangular impulse response will have a $\sin x/x$ spectrum.

A low-pass filter has a rectangular spectrum, and this has a $\sin x/x$ impulse response. These characteristics are known as a transform pair. In transform pairs, if one domain has one shape of the pair, the other domain will have the other shape. Figure 3.36 shows a number of transform pairs.

At (a) a square wave has a $\sin x/x$ spectrum and a $\sin x/x$ impulse has a square spectrum. In general the product of equivalent parameters on either side of a transform remains constant, so that if one increases, the other must fall. If (a) shows a filter with a wider bandwidth, having a narrow impulse response, then (b) shows a filter of narrower bandwidth which has a wide impulse response. This is duality in action. The limiting case of this behaviour is where one parameter becomes zero, the other goes to infinity. At (c) a time-domain pulse of infinitely short duration has a flat spectrum. Thus a flat waveform, i.e. DC, has only zero in its spectrum. The impulse response of the optics of a laser disk (d) has a

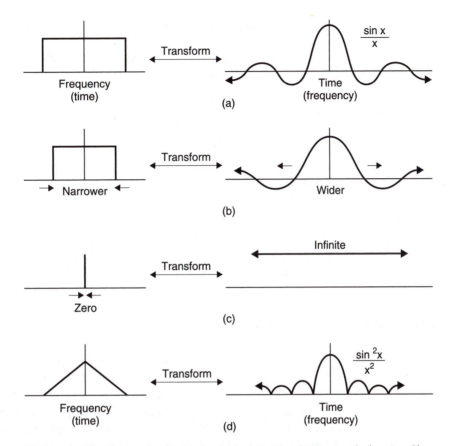

Figure 3.36 Transform pairs. At (a) the dual of a rectangle is a $\sin x/x$ function. If one is time domain, the other is frequency domain. At (b), narrowing one domain widens the other. The limiting case of this is (c). Transform of the $\sin x/x$ squared function is triangular (d).

$\sin^2 x/x^2$ intensity function, and this is responsible for the triangular falling frequency response of the pickup. The lens is a rectangular aperture, but as there is no such thing as negative light, a $\sin x/x$ impulse response is impossible. The squaring process is consistent with a positive-only impulse response. Interestingly the transform of a Gaussian response in still Gaussian.

Duality also holds for sampled systems. A sampling process is periodic in the time domain. This results in a spectrum which is periodic in the frequency domain. If the time between the samples is reduced, the bandwidth of the system rises. Figure 3.37(a) shows that a continuous time signal has a continuous spectrum whereas at (b) the frequency transform of a sampled signal is also discrete. In other words sampled signals can only be analysed into a finite number of frequencies. The more accurate the frequency analysis has to be, the more samples are needed in the block. Making the block longer reduces the ability to locate

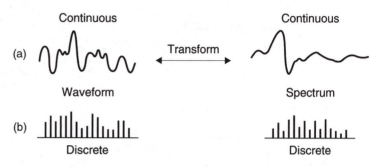

Figure 3.37 Continuous time signal (a) has continuous spectrum. Discrete time signal (b) has discrete spectrum.

a transient in time. This is the Heisenberg inequality which is the limiting case of duality, because when infinite accuracy is achieved in one domain, there is no accuracy at all in the other.

3.12 The Fourier transform

Figure 3.35 showed that if the amplitude and phase of each frequency component is known, linearly adding the resultant components in an inverse transform results in the original waveform. The ideal Fourier transform operates over an infinite time. In practice the time span has to be constrained, resulting in a short-term Fourier transform (STFT). In digital systems the waveform is expressed as a (finite) number of discrete samples. As a result the Fourier transform analyses the signal into an equal number of discrete frequencies. This is known as a discrete Fourier transform or DFT in which the number of frequency coefficients is equal to the number of input samples. The fast Fourier transform is no more than an efficient way of computing the DFT.[14]

It will be evident from Figure 3.35 that the knowledge of the phase of the frequency component is vital, as changing the phase of any component will seriously alter the reconstructed waveform. Thus the DFT must accurately analyse the phase of the signal components.

There are a number of ways of expressing phase. Figure 3.38 shows a point which is rotating about a fixed axis at constant speed. Looked at from the side, the point oscillates up and down at constant frequency. The waveform of that motion is a sine wave, and that is what we would see if the rotating point were to translate along its axis whilst we continued to look from the side.

One way of defining the phase of a waveform is to specify the angle through which the point has rotated at time zero ($T = 0$). If a second point is made to revolve at 90° to the first, it would produce a cosine wave when translated. It is possible to produce a waveform having arbitrary

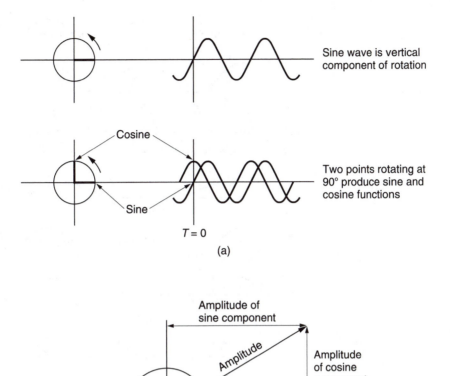

Figure 3.38 The origin of sine and cosine waves is to take a particular viewpoint of a rotation. Any phase can be synthesized by adding proportions of sine and cosine waves.

phase by adding together the sine and cosine wave in various proportions and polarities. For example, adding the sine and cosine waves in equal proportion results in a waveform lagging the sine wave by 45°.

Figure 3.38 shows that the proportions necessary are respectively the sine and the cosine of the phase angle. Thus the two methods of describing phase can be readily interchanged.

The discrete Fourier transform spectrum-analyses a string of samples by searching separately for each discrete target frequency. It does this by multiplying the input waveform by a sine wave, known as the basis function, having the target frequency and adding up or integrating the products. Figure 3.39(a) shows that multiplying by basis functions

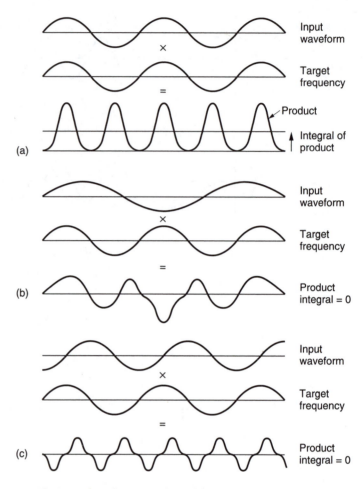

Figure 3.39 The input waveform is multiplied by the target frequency and the result is averaged or integrated. In (a) the target frequency is present and a large integral results. With another input frequency the integral is zero as in (b). The correct frequency will also result in a zero integral shown in (c) if it is at 90° to the phase of the search frequency. This is overcome by making two searches in quadrature.

gives a non-zero integral when the input frequency is the same, whereas Figure 3.39(b) shows that with a different input frequency (in fact all other different frequencies) the integral is zero showing that no component of the target frequency exists. Thus from a real waveform containing many frequencies all frequencies except the target frequency are excluded. The magnitude of the integral is proportional to the amplitude of the target component.

Figure 3.39(c) shows that the target frequency will not be detected if it is phase shifted 90° as the product of quadrature waveforms is always zero. Thus the discrete Fourier transform must make a further search for the target frequency using a cosine basis function. It follows from the arguments above that the relative proportions of the sine and cosine integrals reveals the phase of the input component. Thus each discrete frequency in the spectrum must be the result of a pair of quadrature searches.

Searching for one frequency at a time as above will result in a DFT, but only after considerable computation. However, a lot of the calculations are repeated many times over in different searches. The fast Fourier transform gives the same result with less computation by logically gathering together all the places where the same calculation is needed and making the calculation once.

The amount of computation can be reduced by performing the sine and cosine component searches together. Another saving is obtained by noting that every 180° the sine and cosine have the same magnitude but are simply inverted in sign. Instead of performing four multiplications on two samples 180° apart and adding the pairs of products it is more economical to subtract the sample values and multiply twice, once by a sine value and once by a cosine value.

The first coefficient is the arithmetic mean which is the sum of all the sample values in the block divided by the number of samples. Figure 3.40 shows how the search for the lowest frequency in a block is performed. Pairs of samples are subtracted as shown, and each difference is then multiplied by the sine and the cosine of the search frequency. The process shifts one sample period, and a new sample pair is subtracted and multiplied by new sine and cosine factors. This is repeated until all the sample pairs have been multiplied. The sine and cosine products are then added to give the value of the sine and cosine coefficients respectively.

It is possible to combine the calculation of the DC component which requires the sum of samples and the calculation of the fundamental which requires sample differences by combining stages shown in Figure 3.41(a) which take a pair of samples and add and subtract them. Such a stage is called a butterfly because of the shape of the schematic. Figure 3.41(b) shows how the first two components are calculated. The phase rotation boxes attribute the input to the sine or cosine component outputs according to the phase angle. As shown, the box labelled 90° attributes nothing to the sine output, but unity gain to the cosine output. The 45° box attributes the input equally to both components.

Figure 3.41(c) shows a numerical example. If a sine wave input is considered where zero degrees coincides with the first sample, this will produce a zero sine coefficient and non-zero cosine coefficient. Figure 3.41(d) shows the same input waveform shifted by 90°. Note how the coefficients change over.

Figure 3.41(e) shows how the next frequency coefficient is computed. Note that exactly the same first-stage butterfly outputs are used, reducing the computation needed.

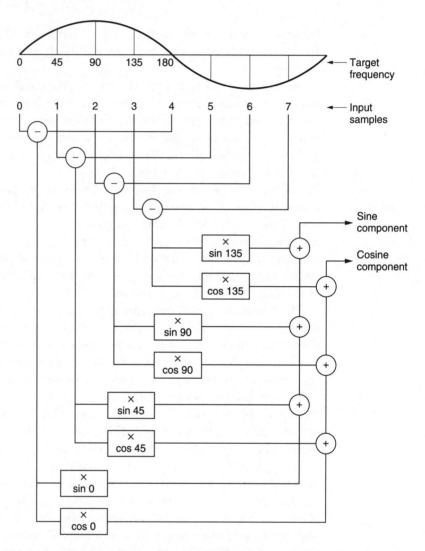

Figure 3.40 An example of a filtering search. Pairs of samples are subtracted and multiplied by sampled sine and cosine waves. The products are added to give the sine and cosine components of the search frequency.

A similar process may be followed to obtain the sine and cosine coefficients of the remaining frequencies. The full FFT diagram for eight samples is shown in Figure 3.42(a) on page 141. The spectrum this calculates is shown in Figure 3.42(b) on page 141. Note that only half of the coefficients are useful in a real band-limited system because the remaining coefficients represent frequencies above one half of the sampling rate.

In STFTs the overlapping input sample blocks must be multiplied by window functions. The principle is the same as for the application

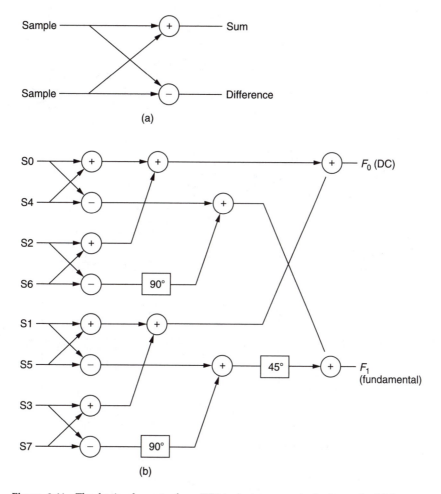

Figure 3.41 The basic element of an FFT is known as a butterfly as in (a) because of the shape of the signal paths in a sum and difference system. The use of butterflies to compute the first two coefficients is shown in (b). An actual example is given in (c) which should be compared with the result of (d) with a quadrature input. In (e) the butterflies for the first two coefficients form the basis of the computation of the third coefficient. (See pages 138–140 for parts (c)–(e).)

in FIR filters shown in section 3.5. Figure 3.43 (page 142) shows that multiplying the search frequency by the window has exactly the same result except that this need be done only once and much computation is saved. Thus in the STFT the basis function is a windowed sine or cosine wave.

The FFT is used extensively in such applications as phase correlation, where the accuracy with which the phase of signal components can be analysed is essential. It also forms the foundation of the discrete cosine transform.

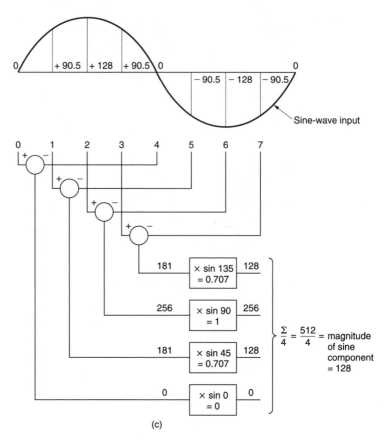

(c)

Figure 3.41   Continued.

3.13   The discrete cosine transform (DCT)

The DCT is a special case of a discrete Fourier transform in which the sine components of the coefficients have been eliminated leaving a single number. This is actually quite easy. Figure 3.44(a) (page 142) shows a block of input samples to a transform process. By repeating the samples in a time-reversed order and performing a discrete Fourier transform on the double-length sample set a DCT is obtained. The effect of mirroring the input waveform is to turn it into an even function whose sine coefficients are all zero. The result can be understood by considering the effect of individually transforming the input block and the reversed block.

Figure 3.44(b) (page 142) shows that the phase of all the components of one block is in the opposite sense to those in the other. This means that when the components are added to give the transform of the double length block all the sine components cancel out, leaving only the cosine coefficients, hence the name of the transform.[15] In practice the sine

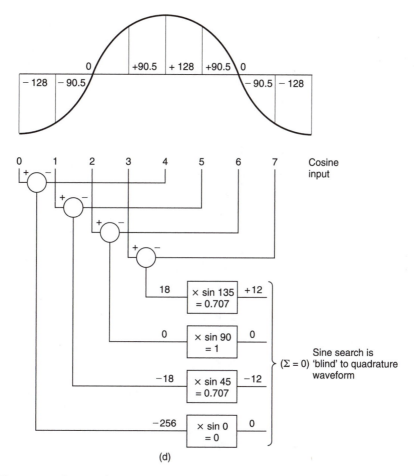

Figure 3.41 Continued.

component calculation is eliminated. Another advantage is that doubling the block length by mirroring doubles the frequency resolution, so that twice as many useful coefficients are produced. In fact a DCT produces as many useful coefficients as input samples.

For image processing two-dimensional transforms are needed. In this case for every horizontal frequency, a search is made for all possible vertical frequencies. A two-dimensional DCT is shown in Figure 3.45 on page 143. The DCT is separable in that the two-dimensional DCT can be obtained by computing in each dimension separately. Fast DCT algorithms are available.[16]

Figure 3.45 shows how a two-dimensional DCT is calculated by multiplying each pixel in the input block by terms which represent sampled cosine waves of various spatial frequencies. A given DCT coefficient is obtained when the result of multiplying every input pixel in the block is summed. Although most compression systems, including

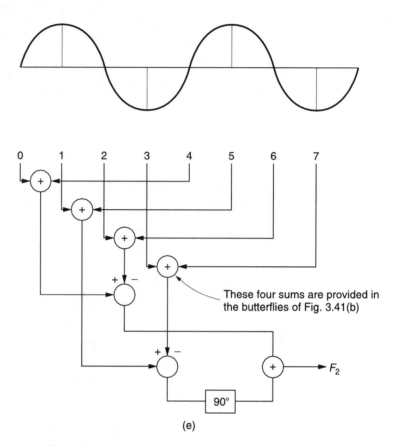

Figure 3.41 Continued.

JPEG and MPEG, use square DCT blocks, this is not a necessity and rectangular DCT blocks are possible and are used in, for example, Digital Betacam and DVC.

The DCT is primarily used in MPEG because it converts the input waveform into a form where redundancy can be easily detected and removed. More details of the DCT can be found in Chapter 5.

3.14 The wavelet transform

The wavelet transform was not discovered by any one individual, but has evolved via a number of similar ideas and was only given a strong mathematical foundation relatively recently.[17,18] Much of the early work was performed in France, where the term *ondelette* was coined. Wavelet is an anglicized equivalent. The Fourier transform is based on periodic signals and endless basis functions and requires windowing to a short-term transform in practical use. The wavelet transform is fundamentally

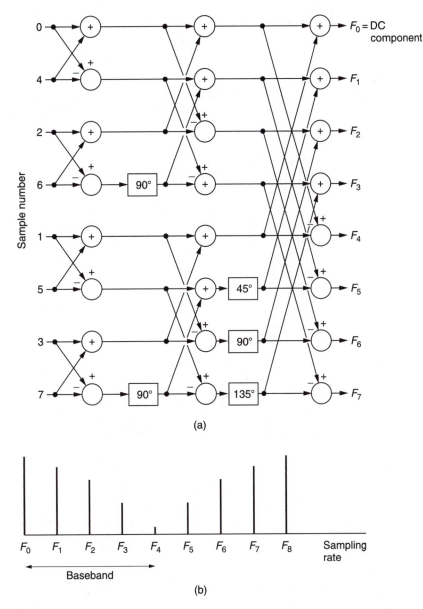

Figure 3.42 In (a) is the full butterfly diagram for an FFT. The spectrum this computes is shown in (b).

windowed and there is no assumption of periodic signals. The basis functions employed are not endless sine waves, but are finite on the time axis. Wavelet transforms do not use a fixed window, but instead the window period is inversely proportional to the frequency being analysed.

As a result a useful combination of time and frequency resolutions is obtained. High frequencies corresponding to transients in audio or edges

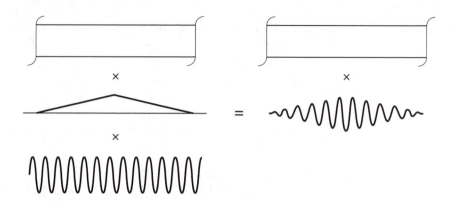

Figure 3.43 Multiplication of a windowed block by a sine wave basis function is the same as multiplying the raw data by a windowed basis function but requires less multiplication as the basis function is constant and can be pre-computed.

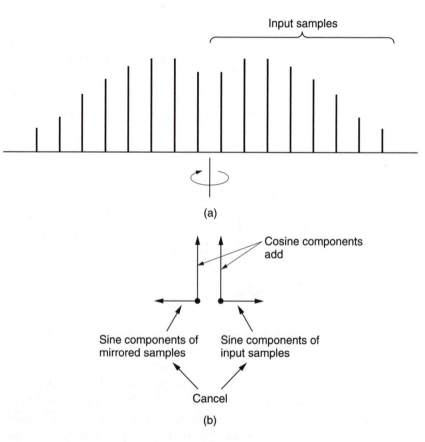

Figure 3.44 The DCT is obtained by mirroring the input block as shown in (a) prior to an FFT. The mirroring cancels out the sine components as in (b), leaving only cosine coefficients.

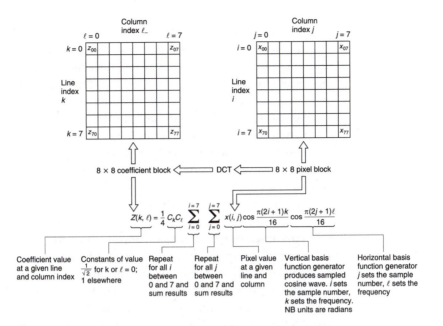

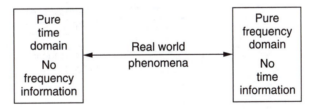

Figure 3.45 A two-dimensional DCT is calculated as shown here. Starting with an input pixel block one calculation is necessary to find a value for each coefficient. After 64 calculations using different basis functions the coefficient block is complete.

Pure time domain No frequency information	←— Real world phenomena —→	Pure frequency domain No time information

Figure 3.46 When in the pure time domain, nothing is known about frequency and vice versa. These pure domains are academic and require infinitely large and small quantities to implement. Wavelets operate in the real world where time and frequency information is simultaneously present.

in video are transformed with short basis functions and therefore are accurately located. Low frequencies are transformed with long basis functions which have good frequency resolution.[19,20] Figure 3.46 shows that in the pure time (or space in imaging) domain, there are only samples or pixels. These are taken at vanishingly small instants and so cannot contain any frequency information. At the other extreme is the Fourier domain. Here there are only coefficients representing the amplitude of endless sinusoids which cannot carry any time/space information.

The Heisenberg uncertainty principle simply observes that at any position on the continuum between extremes a certain combination of time and frequency accuracy can be obtained. Clearly the human senses operate with a combination of both. Wavelets are transforms which operate in the time/frequency domain as shown in the figure. There are pixels at one end of the scale and coefficients at the other. Wavelet parameters fall somewhere in between the pure pixel and the pure coefficient. In addition to describing the amount of energy at a certain frequency, they may also describe *where* that energy existed. There seems to be no elegant contraction of coefficient and pixel to produce an English term for a wavelet parameter, but the Franglais terms pixelette and ondel have a certain charm.

The fundamental component of a wavelet transform is the filter decimator shown in Figure 3.47(a). This is a complementary high- and low-pass filter which divides the input bandwidth in half. The high-pass filter impulse response is a wavelet. If a block of samples or pixels of a certain size is input, each output is decimated by a factor of two so that the same number of samples is present on the output. There is a strong parallel with the quadrature mirror filter here. The low-pass output is a reduced resolution signal and the high-pass output represents the detail which must be added to make the original signal. The high-pass process is a form of differentiation. Figure 3.48 shows that these two sample

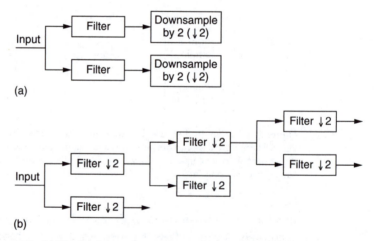

(a)

(b)

Figure 3.47 (a) The fundamental component of a wavelet transform is a filter decimator. (b) These stages can be cascaded.

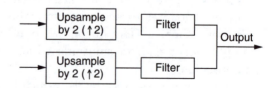

Figure 3.48 This wavelet decoder can perfectly recover the transformed data of Figure 3.47.

streams can be recombined. Each one is upsampled by a factor of two by an appropriate form of interpolator and then the two sample streams are added.

Provided that the decoding filters have responses which are appropriate to the responses of the encoding filters, the output sample stream will be identical to the original. This is known as *perfect reconstruction* and the practical use of wavelets relies upon finding sets of four filters which combine to display this characteristic.

Figure 3.47(b) shows that stages are cascaded in such a way that the low-pass process iterates. At each stage the number of samples representing the original block has halved, but exactly the same filter pair is employed. As a result the wavelet at each stage appears to have become twice as long with respect to the input block.

As a result of this cascading, wavelets are naturally and fundamentally scaleable. At the end of a cascade is a heavily band-limited signal. Adding coefficients from the next frequency band doubles the resolution available. Adding coefficients from the next band further doubles it.

The wavelet transform outputs the same amount of data as is input. Figure 3.49(a) shows a one-dimensional example of a four-stage cascade into which sixteen samples are fed. At the first stage eight difference values are created. At the next, four difference values are created. At the

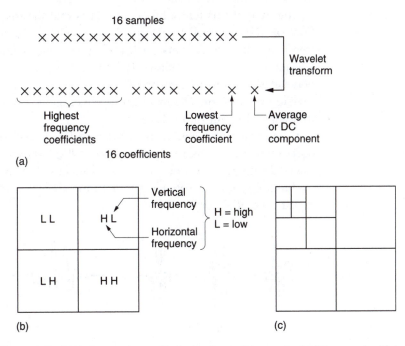

(a)

(b)

(c)

Figure 3.49 (a) A four-stage one-dimensional wavelet cascade. (b) When used with two-dimensional pixel arrays, each wavelet stage divides the data into one quarter and three quarters. (c) Cascading the process of (b).

next there are two. Finally a single difference value is created along with a single output value from the sequence of four low-pass filters which represents the average brightness of the sixteen pixels. The number of output values is then:

$$8 + 4 + 2 + 1 \text{ differences} + 1 \text{ average} = 16$$

Like other transforms, the wavelet itself does not result in any compression. However, what it does do is to represent the original information in such a way that redundancy is easy to identify.

Figure 3.50 shows that that a set of wavelets or basis functions can be obtained simply by *dilating* (scaling) a single wavelet on the time or space axis by a factor of two each time. Each wavelet contains the same number of cycles such that as the frequency reduces, the wavelet gets longer. In a block of fixed size, a large number of short wavelets are required to describe the highest frequency, whereas the number of wavelets at the next resolution down would be halved. The desirable result is that as frequency rises, the spatial or temporal resolution increases. Figure 3.51(a) shows the fixed time/frequency characteristic of the Fourier transform. This can be improved by using window sizes which are a function of frequency as in (b). The wavelet transform in (c) has better temporal resolution as frequency increases due to the dilation of the basis function.

The dual of this temporal behaviour is that the frequency discrimination of the wavelet transform is a constant fraction of the signal frequency. In a filter bank such a characteristic would be described as 'constant Q'. Figure 3.52 shows the division of the frequency domain by a wavelet transform is logarithmic whereas in the Fourier transform the division is uniform. The logarithmic coverage is effectively dividing the frequency domain into octaves.

When using wavelets with two-dimensional pixel arrays, vertical and horizontal filtering is required. Figure 3.49(b) shows that after a single stage, decimation by two in two axes means that the low-pass output contains one quarter of the original data, whereas the difference data require the other three quarters.

Fourier transform   Wavelet transform

Figure 3.50 Unlike discrete Fourier transforms, wavelet basis functions are scaled so that they contain the same number of cycles irrespective of frequency. As a result their frequency discrimination ability is a constant proportion of the centre frequency.

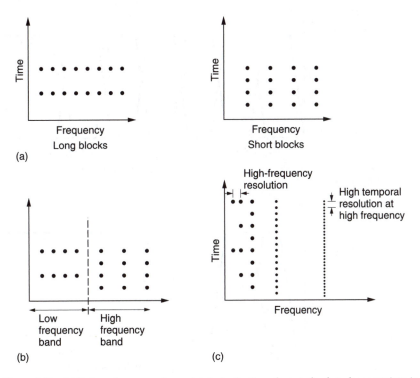

Figure 3.51 (a) In transforms greater certainty in the time domain leads to less certainty in the frequency domain and vice versa. Some transform coders split the spectrum as in (b) and use different window lengths in the two bands. In the recently developed wavelet transform the window length is inversely proportional to the frequency, giving the advantageous time/frequency characteristic shown in (c).

Figure 3.49(c) shows that cascading this process results in an ever smaller low-pass pixel block which eventually converges to a single average brightness code.

3.15 The importance of motion compensation

The optic flow axis is the locus of some point on a moving object which will be in a different place in successive pictures. Any device which computes with respect to the optic flow axis is said to be *motion compensated*. Until recently the amount of computation required in motion compensation was too expensive, but as this is no longer the case the technology has become very important in moving image portrayal systems.

Figure 3.53(a) shows an example of a moving object which is in a different place in each of three pictures. The optic flow axis is shown. The object is not moving with respect to the optic flow axis and if this axis can

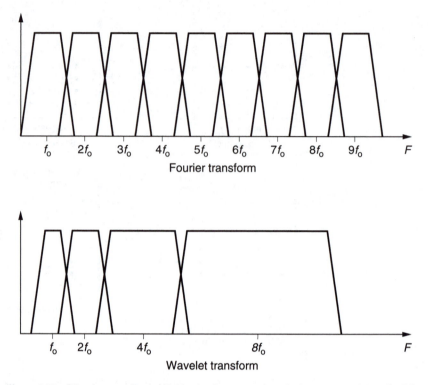

Figure 3.52 Wavelet transforms divide the frequency domain into octaves instead of the equal bands of the Fourier transform.

be found some very useful results are obtained. The process of finding the optic flow axis is called *motion estimation*. Motion estimation is literally a process which analyses successive pictures and determines how objects move from one to the next. It is an important enabling technology because of the way it parallels the action of the human eye.

Figure 3.53(b) shows that if the object does not change its appearance as it moves, it can be portrayed in two of the pictures by using data from one picture only, simply by shifting part of the picture to a new location. This can be done using vectors as shown. Instead of transmitting a lot of pixel data, a few vectors are sent instead. This is the basis of motion-compensated compression which is used extensively in MPEG as will be seen in Chapter 5.

Figure 3.53(c) shows that if a high-quality standards conversion is required between two different frame rates, the output frames can be synthesized by moving image data, not through time, but along the optic flow axis. This locates objects where they would have been if frames had been sensed at those times, and the result is a judder-free conversion. This process can be extended to drive image displays at a frame rate higher than the input rate so that flicker and background strobing are reduced. This technology is available in certain high-quality consumer

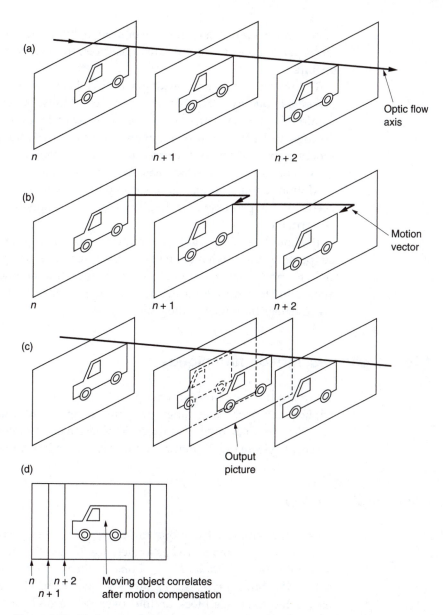

Figure 3.53 Motion compensation is an important technology. (a) The optic flow axis is found for a moving object. (b) The object in picture $(n+1)$ and $(n+2)$ can be re-created by shifting the object of picture n using motion vectors. MPEG uses this process for compression. (c) A standards convertor creates a picture on a new timebase by shifting object data along the optic flow axis. (d) With motion compensation a moving object can still correlate from one picture to the next so that noise reduction is possible.

television sets. This approach may also be used with 24 Hz film to eliminate judder in telecine machines.

Figure 3.53(d) shows that noise reduction relies on averaging two or more images so that the images add but the noise cancels. Conventional noise reducers fail in the presence of motion, but if the averaging process takes place along the optic flow axis, noise reduction can continue to operate.

The way in which eye tracking avoides aliasing is fundamental to the perceived quality of television pictures. Many processes need to manipulate moving images in the same way in order to avoid the obvious difficulty of processing with respect to a fixed frame of reference. Processes of this kind are referred to as *motion compensated* and rely on a quite separate process which has measured the motion.

Motion compensation is also important where interlaced video needs to be processed as it allows the best possible de-interlacing performance.

It should be clear that any motion-compensated process must be adaptive in order to handle edits or cuts which effectively terminate one set of optic flow axes and replace them with another. In general, attempting to code a cut using motion compensation will be significantly less efficient than using other tools.

3.16   Motion-estimation techniques

There are three motion-estimation tools that are to be found in various applications: block matching, gradient matching and phase correlation. Each has its their own characteristic strengths and weaknesses so that practical systems will often combine these tools in some way.

3.16.1   Block matching

This is the simplest technique to follow. In a given picture, a block of pixels is selected and stored as a reference. If the selected block is part of a moving object, a similar block of pixels will exist in the next picture, but not in the same place. As Figure 3.54 shows, block matching simply moves the reference block around over the second picture looking for matching pixel values. When a match is found, the displacement needed to obtain it is used as a basis for a motion vector.

If there is a match over the whole of the block, the moving area must be bigger than the block. On the other hand, the edge of the moving area may cut through the block. In this case correlation will only be obtained over that part of the block which is moving.

Whilst simple in concept, block matching requires an enormous amount of computation because every possible motion must be tested over the assumed range. Thus if the object is assumed to have moved over a sixteen-pixel range, then it will be necessary to test sixteen

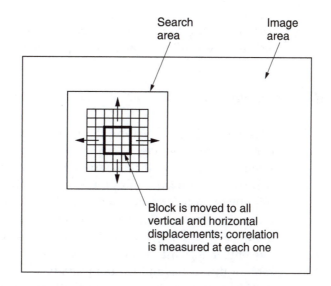

Figure 3.54 In block matching the search block has to be positioned at all possible relative motions within the search area and a correlation measured at each one.

different horizontal displacements in each of sixteen vertical positions; in excess of 65 000 positions. At each position every pixel in the block must be compared with every pixel in the second picture. In typical video, displacements of twice the figure quoted here may be found, particularly in sporting events, and the computation then required becomes enormous.

One way of reducing the amount of computation is to perform the matching in stages where the first stage is inaccurate but covers a large motion range but the last stage is accurate but covers a small range.[16] The first matching stage is performed on a heavily filtered and subsampled picture, which contains far fewer pixels. When a match is found, the displacement is used as a basis for a second stage which is performed with a less heavily filtered picture. Eventually the last stage takes place to any desired accuracy. This hierarchical approach does reduce the computation required, but it suffers from the problem that the filtering of the first stage may make small objects disappear and they can never be found by subsequent stages if they are moving with respect to their background. Many televised sports events contain small, fast-moving objects. As the matching process depends upon finding similar luminance values, this can be confused by objects moving into shade or fades.

The simple block-matching systems described above can only measure motion to the nearest pixel. If more accuracy is required, interpolators will be needed to shift the image by sub-pixel distances before attempting a match. The complexity rises once more. In compression systems an accuracy of half a pixel is accurate enough for most purposes, although AVC offers quarter-pixel precision.

3.16.2 Gradient matching

At some point in a picture, the function of brightness with respect to distance across the screen will have a certain slope, known as the spatial luminance gradient. If the associated picture area is moving, the slope will traverse a fixed point on the screen and the result will be that the brightness now changes with respect to time. This is a temporal luminance gradient. Figure 3.55 shows the principle. For a given spatial gradient, the temporal gradient becomes steeper as the speed of movement increases. Thus motion speed can be estimated from the ratio of the spatial and temporal gradients.[21]

The method only works well if the gradient remains essentially constant over the displacement distance; a characteristic which is not necessarily present in real video. In practice there are numerous processes which can change the luminance gradient. When an object moves so as to obscure or reveal the background, the spatial gradient will change from field to field even if the motion is constant. Variations in illumination, such as when an object moves into shade, also cause difficulty.

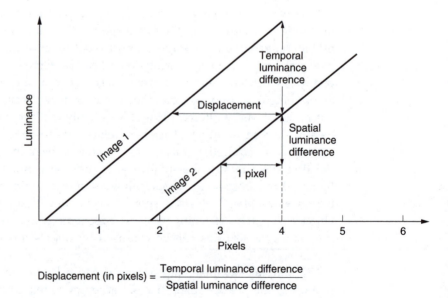

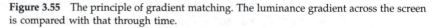

$$\text{Displacement (in pixels)} = \frac{\text{Temporal luminance difference}}{\text{Spatial luminance difference}}$$

Figure 3.55 The principle of gradient matching. The luminance gradient across the screen is compared with that through time.

Block and gradient matching processes can be assisted in various ways that cut down computation by eliminating in advance searches that will not result in correlations. One such method is to project motion in previous pictures forwards to the present picture to act as a basis for the calculation. One of the most powerful ways of steering a block matcher is phase correlation.

3.16.3 Phase correlation

Phase correlation works by performing a discrete Fourier transform on two successive fields and then subtracting all the phases of the spectral components. The phase differences are then subject to a reverse transform which directly reveals peaks whose positions correspond to motions between the fields.[22,23] The nature of the transform domain means that if the distance and direction of the motion is measured accurately, the area of the screen in which it took place is not. This may or may not be a consequence of Heisenberg's uncertainty theorem. Thus in practical systems the phase-correlation stage is followed by a matching stage not dissimilar to the block-matching process. However, the matching process is steered by the motions from the phase correlation, and so there is no need to attempt to match at all possible motions. By attempting matching on measured motion the overall process is made much more efficient.

One way of considering phase correlation is that by using the Fourier transform to break the picture into its constituent spatial frequencies the hierarchical structure of block matching at various resolutions is in fact performed in parallel. In this way small objects are not missed because they will generate high-frequency components in the transform.

Although the matching process is simplified by adopting phase correlation, the Fourier transforms themselves require complex calculations. The high performance of phase correlation would remain academic if it were too complex to put into practice. However, if realistic values are used for the motion speeds which can be handled, the computation required by block matching actually exceeds that required for phase correlation.

The elimination of amplitude information from the phase-correlation process ensures that motion estimation continues to work in the case of fades, objects moving into shade or flashguns firing.

The details of the Fourier transform have been described in section 3.5. A one-dimensional example of phase correlation will be given here by way of introduction. A line of luminance, which in the digital domain consists of a series of samples, is a function of brightness with respect to distance across the screen. The Fourier transform converts this function

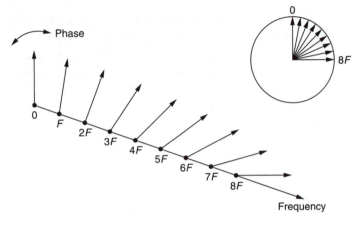

Figure 3.56 The definition of phase linearity is that phase shift is proportional to frequency. In phase-linear systems the waveform is preserved, and simply moves in time or space.

into a spectrum of spatial frequencies (units of cycles per picture width) and phases.

All television signals must be handled in linear-phase systems. A linear-phase system is one in which the delay experienced is the same for all frequencies. If video signals pass through a device which does not exhibit linear phase, the various frequency components of edges become displaced across the screen. Figure 3.56 shows what phase linearity means. If the left-hand end of the frequency axis (DC) is considered to be firmly anchored, but the right-hand end can be rotated to represent a change of position across the screen, it will be seen that as the axis twists evenly the result is phase-shift proportional to frequency. A system having this characteristic is said to display linear phase.

In the spatial domain, a phase shift corresponds to a physical movement. Figure 3.57 shows that if between fields a waveform moves along the line, the lowest frequency in the Fourier transform will suffer a given phase shift, twice that frequency will suffer twice that phase shift and so on. Thus it is potentially possible to measure movement between two successive fields if the phase differences between the Fourier spectra are analysed. This is the basis of phase correlation.

Figure 3.58 shows how a one-dimensional phase correlator works. The Fourier transforms of two lines from successive fields are computed and expressed in polar (amplitude and phase) notation (see section 3.5). The phases of one transform are all subtracted from the phases of the same frequencies in the other transform. Any frequency component having significant amplitude is then normalized, or boosted to full amplitude.

The result is a set of frequency components which all have the same amplitude, but have phases corresponding to the difference between two fields. These coefficients form the input to an inverse transform.

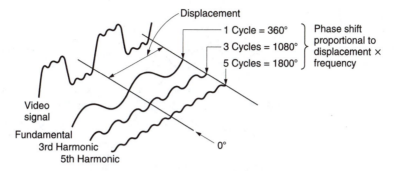

Figure 3.57 In a phase-linear system, shifting the video waveform across the screen causes phase shifts in each component proportional to frequency.

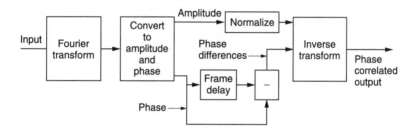

Figure 3.58 The basic components of a phase correlator.

Figure 3.59(a) shows what happens. If the two fields are the same, there are no phase differences between the two, and so all the frequency components are added with zero degree phase to produce a single peak in the centre of the inverse transform. If, however, there was motion between the two fields, such as a pan, all the components will have phase differences, and this results in a peak shown in Figure 3.59(b) which is displaced from the centre of the inverse transform by the distance moved. Phase correlation thus actually measures the movement between fields.

In the case where the line of video in question intersects objects moving at different speeds, Figure 3.59(c) shows that the inverse transform would contain one peak corresponding to the distance moved by each object.

Whilst this explanation has used one dimension for simplicity, in practice the entire process is two dimensional. A two-dimensional Fourier transform of each field is computed, the phases are subtracted, and an inverse two-dimensional transform is computed, the output of which is a flat plane out of which three-dimensional peaks rise. This is known as a correlation surface.

Figure 3.60(a) shows some examples of a correlation surface. At (a) there has been no motion between fields and so there is a single central peak. At (b) there has been a pan and the peak moves across the

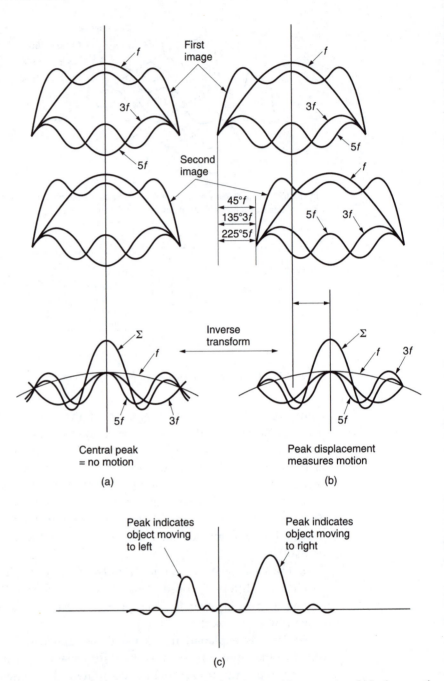

Figure 3.59 (a) The peak in the inverse transform is central for no motion. (b) In the case of motion the peak shifts by the distance moved. (c) If there are several motions, each one results in a peak.

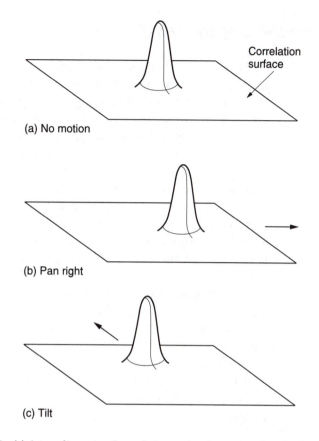

Figure 3.60 (a) A two-dimensional correlation surface has a central peak when there is no motion. (b) In the case of a pan, the peak moves laterally. (c) A camera tilt moves the peak at right angles to the pan.

surface. At (c) the camera has been depressed and the peak moves upwards.

Where more complex motions are involved, perhaps with several objects moving in different directions and/or at different speeds, one peak will appear in the correlation surface for each object.

It is a fundamental strength of phase correlation that it actually measures the direction and speed of moving objects rather than estimating, extrapolating or searching for them. The motion can be measured to sub-pixel accuracy without excessive complexity.

However, the consequences of uncertainty are that accuracy in the transform domain is incompatible with accuracy in the spatial domain. Although phase correlation accurately measures motion speeds and directions, it cannot specify where in the picture these motions are taking place. It is necessary to look for them in a further matching process. The efficiency of this process is dramatically improved by the inputs from the phase-correlation stage.

3.17 Motion-compensated displays

MPEG coding is frequently used with film-originated material in DVD and in DVB. When this is done the pictures are coded at their native rate of 24 (or sometimes 25) Hertz. Figure 3.61(a) shows the time axis of film, where entire frames are simultaneously exposed, or sampled, at typically 24 Hz. The result is that the image is effectively at right angles to the time axis. During filming, some of the frame period is required to transport the film, and the shutter is closed whilst this takes place. The temporal aperture or exposure is thus somewhat shorter than the frame period.

When 25 Hz film is displayed with a simple MPEG decoder each frame of a film is generally output twice to produce a flicker frequency of 50 Hz. The result with a moving object is that the motion is not properly portrayed and there is judder. Figure 3.61(b) shows the origin of the judder.

In 60 Hz areas the film frames are decoded at 24 Hz, but odd frames are output as three fields, even frames result in two fields. This is the well-known 3/2 pulldown system used to convert film rate to 60 Hz video.

Motion portrayal (or lack of it) in this case is even worse.

In fact the 24/25 Hz frame rate output of an MPEG decoder is a perfect application for motion compensation. As Figure 3.62 shows, a motion-compensated standards conversion process is used to output whatever

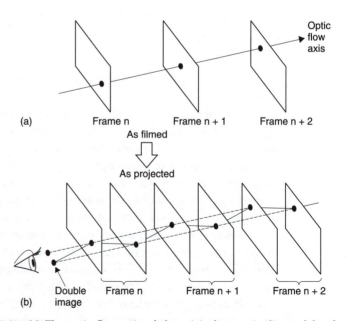

Figure 3.61 (a) The optic flow axis of the original scene is distorted by the double projection of each frame. (b) A tracking eye sees a double image in the presence of motion.

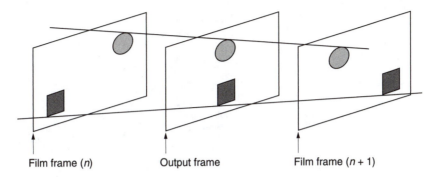

Film frame (*n*)   Output frame   Film frame (*n* + 1)

Figure 3.62 A film with a frame rate of 24 Hz cannot be displayed directly because of flicker. Using a motion-compensated standards conversion process extra frames can be synthesized in which moving objects are correctly positioned. Any television picture rate can then be obtained from film.

frame rate is required without judder, leading to much-improved subjective quality.

3.18 Camera-shake compensation

As video cameras become smaller and lighter, it becomes increasingly difficult to move them smoothly and the result is camera shake. This is irritating to watch, as well as requiring a higher bit rate in compression systems. There are two solutions to the problem, one which is contained within the camera, and one which can be used at some later time on the video data.

Figure 3.63 shows that image-stabilizing cameras contain miniature gyroscopes which produce an electrical output proportional to their rate of turn about a specified axis. A pair of these, mounted orthogonally, can produce vectors describing the camera shake. This can be used to oppose the shake by shifting the image. In one approach, the shifting is done optically. Figure 3.64 shows a pair of glass plates with the intervening spaced filled with transparent liquid. By tilting the plates a variable-angle prism can be obtained and this is fitted in the optical system before the sensor. If the prism plates are suitably driven by servos from the gyroscopic sensors, the optical axis along which the camera is looking can remain constant despite shake. Shift is also possible by displacing some of the lens elements.

Alternatively, the camera can contain a DVE where the vectors from the gyroscopes cause the CCD camera output to be shifted horizontally or vertically so that the image remains stable. This approach is commonly used in consumer camcorders.

A great number of video recordings and films already exist in which there is camera shake. Film also suffers from weave in the telecine

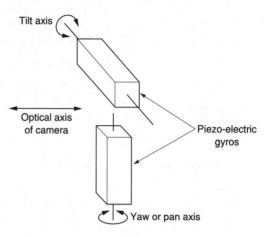

Figure 3.63 Image-stabilizing cameras sense shake using a pair of orthogonal gyros which sense movement of the optical axis.

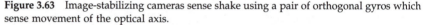

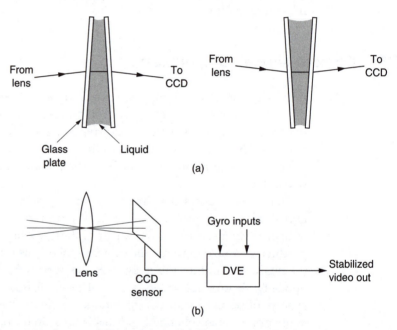

Figure 3.64 Image-stabilizing cameras. (a) The image is stabilized optically prior to the CCD sensors. (b) The CCD output contains image shake, but this is opposed by the action of a DVE configured to shift the image under control of the gyro inputs.

machine. In this case the above solutions are inappropriate and a suitable signal processor is required. Figure 3.65 shows that motion compensation can be used. If a motion estimator is arranged to find the motion between a series of pictures, camera shake will add a fixed component in each picture to the genuine object motions. This can be used to compute the optic flow axis of the camera, independently of the objects portrayed.

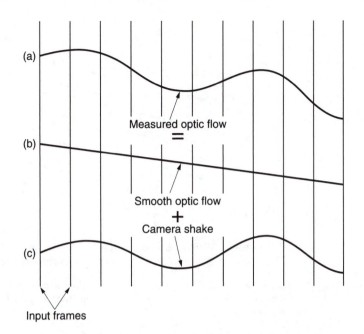

Figure 3.65 In digital image stabilizing the optic flow axis of objects in the input video is measured as in (a). This motion is smoothed to obtain a close approximation to the original motion (b). If this is subtracted from (a) the result is the camera shake motion (c) which is used to drive the image stabilizer.

Operating over several pictures, the trend in camera movement can be separated from the shake by filtering, to produce a position error for each picture. Each picture is then shifted in a DVE in order to cancel the position error. The result is that the camera shake is gone and the camera movements appear smooth. In order to prevent the edges of the frame moving visibly, the DVE also performs a slight magnification so that the edge motion is always outside the output frame.

3.19 Motion-compensated de-interlacing

The most efficient way of de-interlacing is to use motion compensation. Figure 3.66 shows that when an object moves in an interlaced system, the interlace breaks down with respect to the optic flow axis. If the motion is known, two or more fields can be shifted so that a moving object is in the same place in both. Pixels from both fields can then be used to describe the object with better resolution than would be possible from one field alone. It will be seen from Figure 3.67 that the combination of two fields in this way will result in pixels having a highly irregular spacing and a special type of filter is needed to convert this back to a progressive frame with regular pixel spacing. At some critical vertical speeds there will be

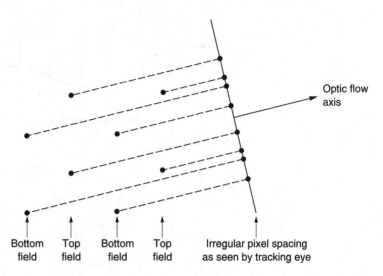

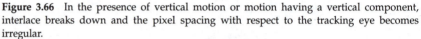

Optic flow
axis

Bottom field   Top field   Bottom field   Top field   Irregular pixel spacing as seen by tracking eye

Figure 3.66 In the presence of vertical motion or motion having a vertical component, interlace breaks down and the pixel spacing with respect to the tracking eye becomes irregular.

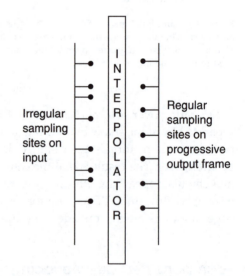

Irregular sampling sites on input

Regular sampling sites on progressive output frame

Figure 3.67 A de-interlacer needs an interpolator which can operate with input samples which are positioned arbitrarily rather than regularly.

alignment between pixels in adjacent fields and no improvement is possible, but at other speeds the process will always give better results.

3.20 Compression and requantizing

In compression systems the goal is to achieve coding gain by using fewer bits to represent the same information. The band-splitting filters and transform techniques decribed earlier in this chapter *do not* achieve any coding gain. Their job is to express the information in a form in which redundancy can be identified. Paradoxically the output of a transform or a filter actually has a longer wordlength than the input because the integer input samples are multiplied by fractions. These processes have actually increased the redundancy in the signal. This section is concerned with the subsequent stage where the compression actually takes place.

Coding gain is obtained in one simple way: by shortening the wordlength of data words so that fewer bits are needed. These data words may be waveform samples in a sub-band-based system or coefficients in a transform-based system. In both cases positive and negative values must be handled. Figure 3.68(a) shows various signal

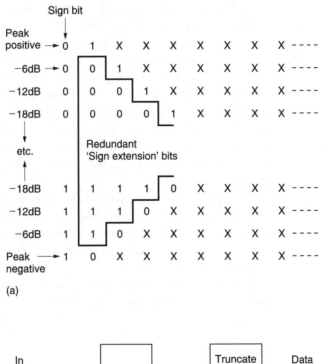

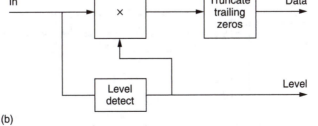

Figure 3.68 In two's complement coding, sign extension takes place as the level falls. These sign-extended bits are redundant and can be eliminated by multiplying by a level-dependent factor and neglecting the trailing zeros as shown in (b).

levels in two's complement coding. As the level falls a phenomenon called *sign extension* takes place where more and more bits at the most significant end of the word simply copy the sign bit (which is the MSB). Coding gain can be obtained by eliminating the redundant sign extension bits as Figure 3.68(b) shows.

Taking bits out of the middle of a word is not straightforward and in practice the solution is to multiply by a level-dependent factor to eliminate the sign extension bits. If this is a power of 2 the useful bits will simply shift left up to the sign bit. The right-hand zeros are simply omitted from the transmission. On decoding a compensating division must be performed. The multiplication factor must be transmitted along with the compressed data so this can be done. Clearly if only the sign extension bits are eliminated this process is lossless because exactly the same data values are available at the decoder.

The reason for sub-band filtering and transform coding now becomes clear because in real signals the levels in most sub-bands and the value of most coefficients are considerably less than the highest level.

In many cases the coding gain obtained in this way will not be enough and the wordlength has to be shortened even more. Following the multiplication, a larger number of bits are rounded off from the least significant end of the word. The result is that the same signal range is retained but it is expressed with less accuracy. It is as if the original analog signal had been converted using fewer quantizing steps, hence the term requantizing.

During the decoding process an *inverse quantizer* will be employed to convert the compressed value back to its original form. Figure 3.69 shows a requantizer and an inverse quantizer. The inverse quantizer must divide by the same gain factor as was used in the compressor and reinsert trailing zeros up to the required wordlength.

A non-uniform quantization process may be used in which the quantizing steps become larger as the signal amplitude increases. As the quantizing steps are made larger, more noise will be suffered, but

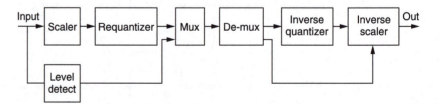

Figure 3.69 Coding gain is obtained by shortening the sample or coefficient wordlength so fewer bits are needed. The input values are scaled or amplified to near maximum amplitude prior to rounding off the low-order bits. The scale factor must be transmitted to allow the process to be reversed at the decoder.

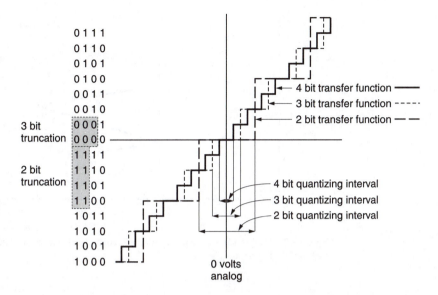

Figure 3.70 Shortening the wordlength of a sample reduces the number of codes which can describe the voltage of the waveform. This makes the quantizing steps bigger, hence the term requantizing. It can be seen that simple truncation or omission of low-order bits does not give analogous behaviour. Rounding is necessary to give the same result as if the larger steps had been used in the original conversion.

the noise is arranged to be generated at frequencies where it will not be perceived, or on signal values which occur relatively infrequently.

Shortening the wordlength of a sample from the LSB end reduces the number of quantizing intervals available without changing the signal amplitude. As Figure 3.70 shows, the quantizing intervals become larger and the original signal is *requantized* with the new interval structure. It will be seen that truncation does not meet the above requirement as it results in signal-dependent offsets because it always rounds in the same direction. Proper numerical rounding is essential for accuracy. Rounding in two's complement is a little more complex than in pure binary.

If the parameter to be requantized is a transform coefficient the result after decoding is that the frequency which is reproduced has an incorrect amplitude due to quantizing error. If all the coefficients describing a signal are requantized to roughly the same degree then the error will be uniformly present at all frequencies and will be noise-like.

However, if the data are time-domain samples, as in, for example, an audio sub-band coder, the result will be different. Although the original audio conversion would have been correctly dithered, the linearizing random element in the low-order bits will be some way below the end of the shortened word. If the word is simply rounded to the nearest integer the linearizing effect of the original dither will be lost and the

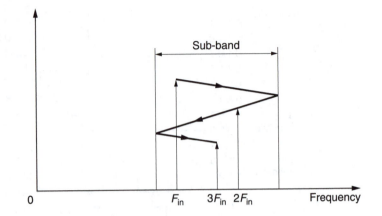

Figure 3.71 Requantizing a band-limited signal causes harmonics which will always alias back within the band.

result will be quantizing distortion. As the distortion takes place in a band-limited system the harmonics generated will alias back within the band. Where the requantizing process takes place in a sub-band, the distortion products will be confined to that sub-band as shown in Figure 3.71.

In practice, the wordlength of samples should be shortened in such a way that the requantizing error is converted to noise rather than distortion. One technique which meets this requirement is to use digital dithering[24] prior to rounding.

Digital dither is a pseudo-random sequence of numbers. If it is required to simulate the analog dither signal of Figure 2.30, then it is obvious that the noise must be bipolar so that it can have an average voltage of zero. Two's complement coding must be used for the dither values.

Figure 3.72 shows a simple digital dithering system for shortening sample wordlength. The output of a two's complement pseudo-random sequence generator of appropriate wordlength is added to input samples prior to rounding. The most significant of the bits to be discarded is examined in order to determine whether the bits to be removed sum to more or less than half a quantizing interval. The dithered sample is either rounded down, i.e. the unwanted bits are simply discarded, or rounded up, i.e. the unwanted bits are discarded but one is added to the value of the new short word. The rounding process is no longer deterministic because of the added dither which provides a linearizing random component.

The probability density of the pseudo-random sequence is important. Lipshitz *et al.*[25] found that uniform probability density produced noise modulation, in which the amplitude of the random

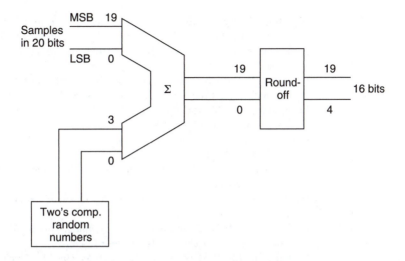

Figure 3.72   In a simple digital dithering system, two's complement values from a random number generator are added to low-order hits of the input. The dithered values are then rounded up or down according to the value of the bits to be removed. The dither linearizes the requantizing.

component varies as a function of the amplitude of the samples. A triangular probability density function obtained by adding together two pseudo-random sequences eliminated the noise modulation to yield a signal-independent white-noise component in the least significant bit.

References

1. Ray, S.F., *Applied Photographic Optics*, Ch. 17. Oxford: Focal Press (1988)
2. van den Enden, A.W.M. and Verhoeckx, N.A.M., Digital signal processing: theoretical background. *Philips Tech. Rev.*, **42**, 110–144 (1985)
3. McClellan, J.H., Parks, T.W. and Rabiner, L.R., A computer program for designing optimum FIR linear-phase digital filters. *IEEE Trans. Audio and Electroacoustics*, **AU-21**, 506–526 (1973)
4. Dolph, C.L., A current distribution for broadside arrays which optimises the relationship between beam width and side-lobe level. *Proc. IRE*, **34**, 335–348 (1946)
5. Crochiere, R.E. and Rabiner, L.R., Interpolation and decimation of digital signals – a tutorial review. *Proc. IEEE*, **69**, 300–331 (1981)
6. Rabiner, L.R., Digital techniques for changing the sampling rate of a signal. In *Digital Audio*, edited by B. Blesser, B. Locanthi and T.G. Stockham Jr, pp. 79–89, New York: Audio Engineering Society (1982)
7. Jayant, N.S. and Noll, P., *Digital Coding of Waveforms: Principles and applications to speech and video*. Englewood Cliffs, NJ: Prentice Hall (1984)
8. Theile, G., Stoll, G. and Link, M., Low bit rate coding of high quality audio signals: an introduction to the MASCAM system. *EBU Tech. Review*, No. 230, 158–181 (1988)

9. Chu, P.L., Quadrature mirror filter design for an arbitrary number of equal bandwidth channels. *IEEE Trans. ASSP*, **ASSP-33**, 203–218 (1985)

10. Fettweis, A., Wave digital filters: theory and practice. *Proc. IEEE*, **74**, 270–327 (1986)

11. Weiss, P. and Christensson, J., Real time implementation of sub-pixel motion estimation for broadcast applications. *IEE Digest*, 1990/128

12. Newman, W.M. and Sproull, R.F., *Principles of Interactive Computer Graphics*. Tokyo: McGraw-Hill (1979)

13. Gernsheim, H., *A Concise History of Photography*. London: Thames and Hudson, 9–15 (1971)

14. Kraniauskas, P., *Transforms in Signals and Systems*. Ch. 6. Wokingham: Addison-Wesley (1992)

15. Ahmed, N., Natarajan, T. and Rao, K., Discrete cosine transform. *IEEE Trans. Computers*, **C-23**, 90–93 (1974)

16. De With, P.H.N., *Data Compression Techniques for Digital Video Recording*. PhD Thesis, Technical University of Delft (1992)

17. Goupillaud, P., Grossman, A. and Morlet, J., Cycle-octave and related transforms in seismic signal analysis. *Geoexploration*, **23**, 85–102, Elsevier Science (1984/5)

18. Daubechies, I., The wavelet transform, time–frequency localisation and signal analysis. *IEEE Trans. Info. Theory*, **36**, No. 5, 961–1005 (1990)

19. Rioul, O. and Vetterli, M., Wavelets and signal processing. *IEEE Signal Process. Mag.*, 14–38 (Oct. 1991)

20. Strang, G. and Nguyen, T., *Wavelets and Filter Banks*. Wellesly, MA: Wellesley-Cambridge Press (1996)

21. Limb, J.O. and Murphy, J.A., Measuring the speed of moving objects from television signals. *IEEE Trans. Commun.*, 474–478 (1975)

22. Thomas, G.A., Television motion measurement for DATV and other applications. *BBC Res. Dept. Rept*, RD 1987/11 (1987)

23. Pearson, J.J. *et al.*, Video rate image correlation processor. *SPIE*, Vol. 119, Application of digital image processing, IOCC (1977)

24. Vanderkooy, J. and Lipshitz, S.P., Digital dither. Presented at the 81st Audio Engineering Society Convention (Los Angeles, 1986), Preprint 2412 (C-8)

25. Lipshitz, S.P., Wannamaker, R.A. and Vanderkooy, J., Quantization and dither: a theoretical survey. *J. Audio Eng. Soc.*, **40**, 355–375 (1992)

4

Audio compression

4.1 Introduction

Physics can tell us the mechanism by which disturbances propagate through the air. If this is our definition of sound, we have the problem that in physics there are no limits to the frequencies and levels which must be considered. Biology can tell that the ear only responds to a certain range of frequencies provided a threshold level is exceeded. This is a better definition of sound; reproduction is easier because it is only necessary to reproduce that range of levels and frequencies which the ear can detect.

Psychoacoustics can describe how our hearing has finite resolution in time, frequency and spatial domains such that what we perceive is an inexact impression. Some aspects of the original disturbance are inaudible to us and are said to be masked. If our goal is the highest quality, we can design our imperfect equipment so that the shortcomings are masked. Conversely if our goal is minimal bit rate we can use heavy compression and hope that masking will disguise the inaccuracies it causes.

By definition, the sound quality of a perceptive coder can only be assessed by human hearing. Equally, a useful perceptive coder can only be designed with a good knowledge of the human hearing mechanism.[1] The acuity of the human ear is astonishing. The frequency range is extremely wide, covering some ten octaves (an octave is a doubling of pitch or frequency) without interruption. It can detect tiny amounts of distortion, and will accept an enormous dynamic range. If the ear detects a different degree of impairment between two codecs having the same bit rate in properly conducted tests, we can say that one of them is superior.

Quality is completely subjective and can only be checked by listening tests, although these are meaningless if the loudspeakers are not of sufficient quality. This topic will be considered in section 4.25.

However, any characteristic of a signal which can be heard can in principle also be measured by a suitable instrument. Subjective tests can tell us how sensitive the instrument should be. Then the objective readings from the instrument give an indication of how acceptable a signal is in respect of that characteristic. Instruments and loudspeakers suitable for assessing the performance of codecs are currently extremely rare and there remains much work to be done.

4.2   The deciBel

The first audio signals to be transmitted were on analog telephone lines. Where the wiring is long compared to the electrical wavelength (not to be confused with the acoustic wavelength) of the signal, a transmission line exists in which the distributed series inductance and the parallel capacitance interact to give the line a characteristic impedance. In telephones this turned out to be about 600 Ω. In transmission lines the best power delivery occurs when the source and the load impedance are the same; this is the process of matching. It was often required to measure the power in a telephone system, and 1 milliWatt was chosen as a suitable unit. Thus the reference against which signals could be compared was the dissipation of one milliWatt in 60 Ω. Figure 4.1 shows that the dissipation of 1 mW in 60 Ω will be due to an applied voltage of 0.775 V rms. This voltage is the reference against which all audio levels are compared.

The deciBel is a logarithmic measuring system and has its origins in telephony[2] where the loss in a cable is a logarithmic function of the length. Human hearing also has a logarithmic response with respect to sound pressure level (SPL). In order to relate to the subjective response audio signal level measurements have also to be logarithmic and so the deciBel was adopted for audio.

Figure 4.2 shows the principle of the logarithm. To give an example, if it is clear that 10^2 is 100 and 10^3 is 1000, then there must be a power between 2 and 3 to which 10 can be raised to give any value between 100 and 1000. That power is the logarithm to base 10 of the value, e.g. $\log_{10} 300 = 2.5$ approx. Note that 10^0 is 1.

Logarithms were developed by mathematicians before the availability of calculators or computers to ease calculations such as multiplication, squaring, division and extracting roots. The advantage is that armed with a set of log tables, multiplication can be performed by adding, division by subtracting. Figure 4.2 shows some examples. It will be clear that squaring a number is performed by adding two identical logs and the same result will be obtained by multiplying the log by 2.

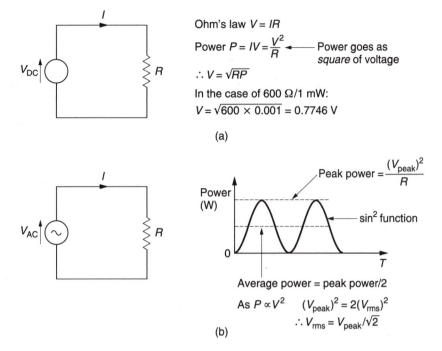

Figure 4.1 (a) Ohm's law: the power developed in a resistor is proportional to the square of the voltage. Consequently, 1 mW in 600 Ω requires 0.775 V. With a sinusoidal alternating input (b), the power is a sine square function which can be averaged over one cycle. A DC voltage which would deliver the same power has a value which is the square root of the mean of the square of the sinusoidal input.

The slide rule is an early calculator which consists of two logarithmically engraved scales in which the length along the scale is proportional to the log of the engraved number. By sliding the moving scale two lengths can easily be added or subtracted and as a result multiplication and division are readily obtained.

The logarithmic unit of measurement in telephones was called the Bel after Alexander Graham Bell, the inventor. Figure 4.3(a) shows that the Bel was defined as the log of the *power* ratio between the power to be measured and some reference power. Clearly the reference power must have a level of 0 Bels since $\log_{10} 1$ is 0.

The Bel was found to be an excessively large unit for many purposes and so it was divided into 10 deciBels, abbreviated to dB with a small d and a large B and pronounced 'deebee'. Consequently the number of dBs is ten times the log of the power ratio. A device such as an amplifier can have a fixed power gain which is independent of signal level and this can be measured in dB. However, when measuring the power of a signal, it must be appreciated that the dB is a ratio and to quote the number of dBs without stating the reference is about as senseless as describing the height of a mountain as 2000 without specifying whether this is feet or

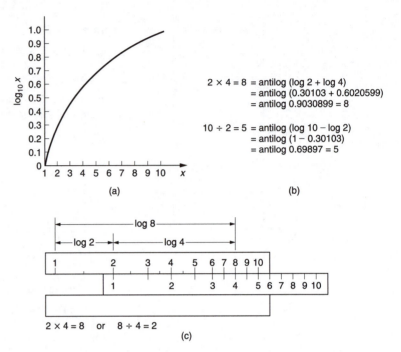

$$2 \times 4 = 8 = \text{antilog (log 2 + log 4)}$$
$$= \text{antilog } (0.30103 + 0.6020599)$$
$$= \text{antilog } 0.9030899 = 8$$

$$10 \div 2 = 5 = \text{antilog (log 10 } - \text{ log 2)}$$
$$= \text{antilog } (1 - 0.30103)$$
$$= \text{antilog } 0.69897 = 5$$

(a)   (b)

$2 \times 4 = 8$ or $8 \div 4 = 2$

(c)

Figure 4.2   (a) The logarithm of a number is the power to which the base (in this case 10) must be raised to obtain the number. (b) Multiplication is obtained by adding logs, division by subtracting. (c) The slide rule has two logarithmic scales whose length can easily be added or subtracted.

$$1 \text{ Bel } = \log_{10} \frac{P_1}{P_2} \qquad 1 \text{ deciBel } = 1/10 \text{ Bel}$$

$$\text{Power ratio (dB) } = 10 \times \log_{10} \frac{P_1}{P_2}$$

(a)

As power α V^2, when using voltages:

$$\text{Power ratio (dB) } = 10 \log \frac{V_1^2}{V_2^2}$$

$$= 10 \times \log \frac{V_1}{V_2} \times 2$$

$$= 20 \log \frac{V_1}{V_2}$$

(b)

Figure 4.3   (a) The Bel is the log of the ratio between two powers, that to be measured and the reference. The Bel is too large so the deciBel is used in practice. (b) As the dB is defined as a power ratio, voltage ratios have to be squared. This is conveniently done by doubling the logs so the ratio is now multiplied by 20.

metres. To show that the reference is one milliWatt into 600 Ω, the units will be dB(m). In radio engineering, the dB(W) will be found which is power relative to one Watt.

Although the dB(m) is defined as a power ratio, level measurements in audio are often done by measuring the signal voltage using 0.775 V as a reference in a circuit whose impedance is not necessarily 600 Ω. Figure 4.3(b) shows that as the power is proportional to the square of the voltage, the power ratio will be obtained by squaring the voltage ratio. As squaring in logs is performed by doubling, the squared term of the voltages can be replaced by multiplying the log by a factor of two. To give a result in deciBels, the log of the voltage ratio now has to be multiplied by 20.

Whilst 600 Ω matched-impedance working is essential for the long distances encountered with telephones, it is quite inappropriate for analog audio wiring in the studio or the home. The wavelength of audio in wires at 20 kHz is 15 km. Most studios are built on a smaller scale than this and clearly analog audio cables are *not* transmission lines and their characteristic impedance is swamped by the devices connected at each end. Consequently the reader is cautioned that anyone who attempts to sell exotic analog audio cables by stressing their transmission line characteristics is more of a salesman than a physicist.

In professional analog audio systems impedance matching is not only unnecessary it is also undesirable. Figure 4.4(a) shows that when

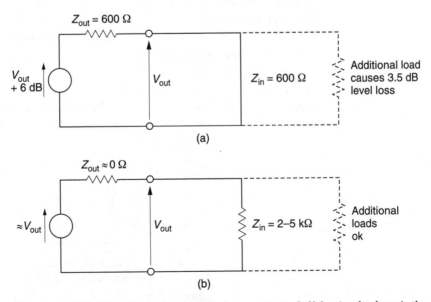

Figure 4.4 (a) Traditional impedance matched source wastes half the signal voltage in the potential divider due to the source impedance and the cable. (b) Modern practice is to use low-output impedance sources with high-impedance loads.

impedance matching is required the output impedance of a signal source must be artificially raised so that a potential divider is formed with the load. The actual drive voltage must be twice that needed on the cable as the potential divider effect wastes 6 dB of signal level and requires unnecessarily high power supply rail voltages in equipment. A further problem is that cable capacitance can cause an undesirable HF roll-off in conjunction with the high source impedance. In modern professional analog audio equipment, shown in Figure 4.4(b) the source has the lowest output impedance practicable. This means that any ambient interference is attempting to drive what amounts to a short circuit and can only develop very small voltages. Furthermore, shunt capacitance in the cable has very little effect. The destination has a somewhat higher impedance (generally a few kΩ) to avoid excessive currents flowing and to allow several loads to be placed across one driver.

In the absence of a fixed impedance it is now meaningless to consider power. Consequently only signal voltages are measured. The reference remains at 0.775 V, but power and impedance are irrelevant. Voltages measured in this way are expressed in dB(u); the commonest unit of level in modern systems. Most installations boost the signals on interface cables by 4 dB. As the gain of receiving devices is reduced by 4 dB, the result is a useful noise advantage without risking distortion due to the drivers having to produce high voltages. In order to make the difference between dB(m) and dB(u) clear, consider the lossless matching tansformer shown in Figure 4.5. The turns ratio is 2:1 therefore the impedance matching ratio is 4:1. As there is no loss in the transformer, the power in is the same as the power out so that the transformer shows a gain of 0 dB(m). However, the turns ratio of 2:1 provides a voltage gain of 6 dB(u). The doubled output voltage will develop the same power into the quadrupled load impedance.

In a complex system signals may pass through a large number of processes, each of which may have a different gain. Figure 4.6 shows that if one stays in the linear domain and measures the input level in volts

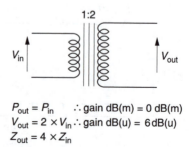

$$P_{out} = P_{in} \quad \therefore \text{gain dB(m)} = 0 \text{ dB(m)}$$
$$V_{out} = 2 \times V_{in} \therefore \text{gain dB(u)} = 6 \text{dB(u)}$$
$$Z_{out} = 4 \times Z_{in}$$

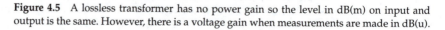

Figure 4.5 A lossless transformer has no power gain so the level in dB(m) on input and output is the same. However, there is a voltage gain when measurements are made in dB(u).

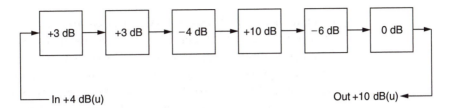

Figure 4.6 In complex systems each stage may have voltage gain measured in dB. By adding all of these gains together and adding to the input level in dB(u), the output level in dB(u) can be obtained.

rms, the output level will be obtained by multiplying by the gains of all the stages involved. This is a complex calculation.

The difference between the signal level with and without the presence of a device in a chain is called the *insertion loss* measured in dB. However, if the input is measured in dB(u), the output level of the first stage can be obtained by adding the insertion loss in dB. The output level of the second stage can be obtained by further adding the loss of the second stage in dB and so on. The final result is obtained by adding together all the insertion losses in dB and adding them to the input level in dB(u) to give the output level in dB(u). As the dB is a pure ratio it can multiply anything (by addition of logs) without changing the units. Thus dB(u) of level added to dB of gain are still dB(u).

In acoustic measurements, the sound pressure level (SPL) is measured in deciBels relative to a reference pressure of 2×10^{-5} Pascals (Pa) rms. In order to make the reference clear the units are dB(SPL). In measurements which are intended to convey an impression of subjective loudness, a weighting filter is used prior to the level measurement which reproduces the frequency response of human hearing which is most sensitive in the midrange. The most common standard frequency response is the so-called A-weighting filter, hence the term dB(A) used when a weighted level is being measured. At high or low frequencies, a lower reading will be obtained in dB(A) than in dB(SPL).

4.3 Audio level metering

There are two main reasons for having level meters in audio equipment: to line up or adjust the gain of equipment, and to assess the amplitude of the program material. Gain line-up is especially important in digital systems where an incorrect analog level can result in ADC clipping.

Line-up is often done using a 1 kHz sine wave generated at an agreed level such as 0 dB(u). If a receiving device does not display the same level, then its input sensitivity must be adjusted. Tape recorders and other devices which pass signals through are usually lined up so that their input and output levels are identical, i.e. their insertion loss is 0 dB. Line-up is important in large systems because it ensures that inadvertent level changes do not occur. In measuring the level of a sine wave for the purposes of line-up, the dynamics of the meter are of no consequence, whereas on program material the dynamics matter a great deal. The simplest (and cheapest) level meter is essentially an AC voltmeter with a logarithmic response. As the ear is logarithmic, the deflection of the meter is roughly proportional to the perceived volume, hence the term Volume Unit (VU) meter.

In audio recording and broadcasting, the worst sin is to overmodulate the tape, the ADC or the transmitter by allowing a signal of excessive amplitude to pass. Real audio signals are rich in short transients which pass before the sluggish VU meter responds. Consequently the VU meter is also called the virtually useless meter in professional circles.

Broadcasters developed the Peak Program Meter (PPM) that is also logarithmic, but which is designed to respond to peaks as quickly as the ear responds to distortion. Consequently the attack time of the PPM is carefully specified. If a peak is so short that the PPM fails to indicate its true level, the resulting overload will also be so brief that the human auditory system (HAS) will not hear it. A further feature of the PPM is that the decay time of the meter is very slow, so that any peaks are visible for much longer and the meter is easier to read because the meter movement is less violent. The original PPM as developed by the BBC was sparsely calibrated, but other users have adopted the same dynamics and added dB scales, Figure 4.7 shows some of the scales in use.

In broadcasting, the use of level metering and line-up procedures ensures that the level experienced by the viewer/listener does not change significantly from program to program. Consequently in a transmission suite, the goal would be to broadcast tapes at a level identical to that which was obtained during production. However, when making a recording prior to any production process, the goal would be to modulate the tape as fully as possible without clipping as this would then give the best signal-to-noise ratio. The level would then be reduced if necessary in the production process.

Unlike analog recorders, digital systems do not have headroom, as there is no progressive onset of distortion until convertor clipping, the equivalent of saturation, occurs at 0 dBFs. Accordingly many digital recorders have level meters which read in dBFs. The scales are marked with 0 at the clipping level and all operating levels are below that. This causes no difficulty provided the user is aware of the consequences.

However, in the situation where a digital copy of an analog tape is to be made, it is very easy to set the input gain of the digital recorder so that line-up tone from the analog tape reads 0 dB. This lines up digital

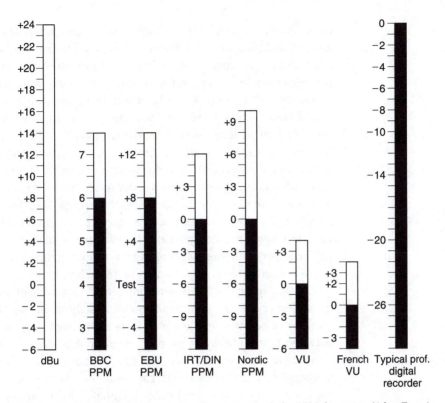

Figure 4.7 Some of the scales used in conjunction with the PPM dynamics. (After Francis Rumsey, with permission)

clipping with the analog operating level. When the tape is dubbed, all signals in the headroom suffer convertor clipping.

In order to prevent such problems, manufacturers and broadcasters have introduced artificial headroom on digital level meters, simply by calibrating the scale and changing the analog input sensitivity so that 0 dB analog is some way below clipping. Unfortunately there has been little agreement on how much artificial headroom should be provided, and machines which have it are seldom labelled with the amount. There is an argument which suggests that the amount of headroom should be a function of the sample wordlength, but this causes difficulties when transferring from one wordlength to another. In sixteen-bit working, 12 dB of headroom is a useful figure, but now that eighteen- and twenty-bit convertors are available, 18 dB may be more appropriate.

4.4 The ear

The human auditory system (HAS), the sense called hearing, is based on two obvious tranducers at the side of the head, and a number of less obvious mental processes which give us an impression of the world around us based on disturbances to the equilibrium of the air which we call sound. It is only possible briefly to introduce the subject here. The interested reader is referred to Moore[3] for an excellent treatment.

The HAS can tell us, without aid from any other senses, where a sound source is, how big it is, whether we are in an enclosed space and how big that is. If the sound source is musical, we can further establish information such as pitch and timbre, attack, sustain and decay. In order to do this, the auditory system must work in the time, frequency and space domains. A sound reproduction system which is inadequate in one of these domains will be unrealistic however well the other two are satisfied. Chapter 3 introduced the concept of uncertainty between the time and frequency domains and the ear cannot analyse both at once. The HAS circumvents this by changing its characteristics dynamically so that it can concentrate on one domain or the other.

The acuity of the HAS is astonishing. It can detect tiny amounts of distortion, and will accept an enormous dynamic range over a wide number of octaves. If the ear detects a different degree of impairment between two audio systems and an original or 'live' sound in properly conducted tests, we can say that one of them is superior. Thus quality is completely subjective and can only be checked by listening tests. However, any characteristic of a signal which can be heard can in principle also be measured by a suitable instrument, although in general the availability of such instruments lags the requirement and the use of such instruments lags the availability. The subjective tests will tell us how sensitive the instrument should be. Then the objective readings from the instrument give an indication of how acceptable a signal is in respect of that characteristic.

Figure 4.8 shows that the structure of the ear is traditionally divided into the outer, middle and inner ears. The outer ear works at low impedance, the inner ear works at high impedance, and the middle ear is

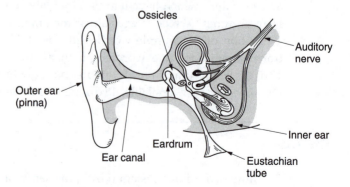

Figure 4.8 The structure of the human ear. See text for details.

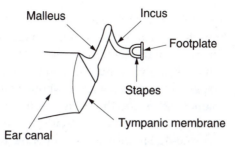

Figure 4.9 The malleus tensions the tympanic membrane into a conical shape. The ossicles provide an impedance-transforming lever system between the tympanic membrane and the oval.

an impedance-matching device. The visible part of the outer ear is called the pinna which plays a subtle role in determining the direction of arrival of sound at high frequencies. It is too small to have any effect at low frequencies. Incident sound enters the auditory canal or meatus. The pipe-like meatus causes a small resonance at around 4 kHz. Sound vibrates the eardrum or tympanic membrane which seals the outer ear from the middle ear. The inner ear or cochlea works by sound travelling though a fluid. Sound enters the cochlea via a membrane called the oval window. If airborne sound were to be incident on the oval window directly, the serious impedance mismatch would cause most of the sound to be reflected. The middle ear remedies that mismatch by providing a mechanical advantage.

The tympanic membrane is linked to the oval window by three bones known as ossicles which act as a lever system such that a large displacement of the tympanic membrane results in a smaller displacement of the oval window but with greater force. Figure 4.9 shows that the malleus applies a tension to the tympanic membrane rendering it conical in shape. The malleus and the incus are firmly joined together to form a lever. The incus acts upon the stapes through a spherical joint. As the area of the tympanic membrane is greater than that of the oval window, there is a further multiplication of the available force. Consequently small pressures over the large area of the tympanic membrane are converted to high pressures over the small area of the oval window. The middle ear evolved to operate at natural sound levels and causes distortion at the high levels which can be generated with artificial amplification.

The middle ear is normally sealed, but ambient pressure changes will cause static pressure on the tympanic membrane which is painful. The pressure is relieved by the Eustachian tube which opens involuntarily whilst swallowing. Some of the discomfort of the common cold is due to these tubes becoming blocked. The Eustachian tubes open into the cavities of the head and must normally be closed to avoid one's own speech appearing deafeningly loud. The ossicles are located by minute muscles which are normally relaxed. However, the middle ear reflex is an involuntary tightening of the *tensor tympani* and *stapedius* muscles which heavily damp the ability of the tympanic membrane and the stapes to transmit sound by about 12 dB at frequencies below 1 kHz. The main function of this reflex is to reduce the audibility of one's own speech. However, loud sounds will also trigger this reflex which takes some 60–120 milliseconds to operate; too late to protect against transients such as gunfire.

4.5   The cochlea

The cochlea is the transducer proper, converting pressure variations in the fluid into nerve impulses. However, unlike a microphone, the nerve impulses are not an analog of the incoming waveform. Instead the cochlea has some analysis capability which is combined with a number of mental processes to make a complete analysis. As shown in Figure 4.10(a), the cochlea is a fluid-filled tapering spiral cavity within bony walls. The widest part, near the oval window, is called the *base* and the distant end is the *apex*. Figure 4.10(b) shows that the cochlea is divided lengthwise into three volumes by Reissner's membrane and the basilar membrane. The *scala vestibuli* and the *scala tympani* are connected by a small aperture at the apex of the cochlea known as the *helicotrema*. Vibrations from the stapes are transferred to the oval window and become fluid pressure variations which are relieved by the flexing of the round window. Effectively the basilar membrane is in series with the fluid motion and is driven by it except at very low

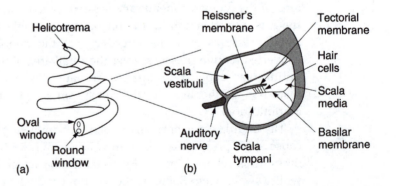

(a)   (b)

Figure 4.10   (a) The cochlea is a tapering spiral cavity. (b) The cross-section of the cavity is divided by Reissner's membrane and the basilar membrane.

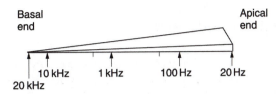

Figure 4.11 The basilar membrane tapers so its resonant frequency changes along its length.

frequencies where the fluid flows through the helicotrema, decoupling the basilar membrane.

To assist in its frequency domain operation, the basilar membrane is not uniform. Figure 4.11 shows that it tapers in width and varies in thickness in the opposite sense to the taper of the cochlea. The part of the basilar membrane which resonates as a result of an applied sound is a function of the frequency. High frequencies cause resonance near to the oval window, whereas low frequencies cause resonances further away. More precisely the distance from the apex where the maximum resonance occurs is a logarithmic function of the frequency. Consequently tones spaced apart in octave steps will excite evenly spaced resonances in the basilar membrane. The prediction of resonance at a particular location on the membrane is called *place theory*. Among other things, the basilar membrane is a mechanical frequency analyser. A knowledge of the way it operates is essential to an understanding of musical phenomena such as pitch discrimination, timbre, consonance and dissonance and to auditory phenomena such as critical bands, masking and the precedence effect.

The vibration of the basilar membrane is sensed by the organ of Corti which runs along the centre of the cochlea. The organ of Corti is active in that it contains elements which can generate vibration as well as sense it. These are connected in a regenerative fashion so that the Q factor, or frequency selectivity, of the ear is higher than it would otherwise be. The deflection of hair cells in the organ of Corti triggers nerve firings and these signals are conducted to the brain by the auditory nerve.

Nerve firings are not a perfect analog of the basilar membrane motion. A nerve firing appears to occur at a constant phase relationship to the basilar vibration, a phenomenon called phase locking, but firings do not necessarily occur on every cycle. At higher frequencies firings are intermittent, yet each is in the same phase relationship.

The resonant behaviour of the basilar membrane is not observed at the lowest audible frequencies below 50 Hz. The pattern of vibration does not appear to change with frequency and it is possible that the frequency is low enough to be measured directly from the rate of nerve firings.

4.6 Level and loudness

At its best, the HAS can detect a sound pressure variation of only 2×10^{-5} Pascals rms and so this figure is used as the reference against which sound pressure level (SPL) is measured. The sensation of loudness is a logarithmic function of SPL hence the use of the deciBel explained in section 4.2. The dynamic range of the HAS exceeds 130 dB, but at the extremes of this range, the ear is either straining to hear or is in pain.

The frequency response of the HAS is not at all uniform and it also changes with SPL. The subjective response to level is called loudness and is measured in *phons*. The phon scale and the SPL scale coincide at 1 kHz, but at other frequencies the phon scale deviates because it displays the actual SPLs judged by a human subject to be equally loud as a given level at 1 kHz. Figure 4.12 shows the so-called equal loudness contours which were originally measured by Fletcher and Munson and subsequently by Robinson and Dadson. Note the irregularities caused by resonances in the meatus at about 4 kHz and 13 kHz.

Usually, people's ears are at their most sensitive between about 2 kHz and 5 kHz, and although some people can detect 20 kHz at high level, there is much evidence to suggest that most listeners cannot tell if the

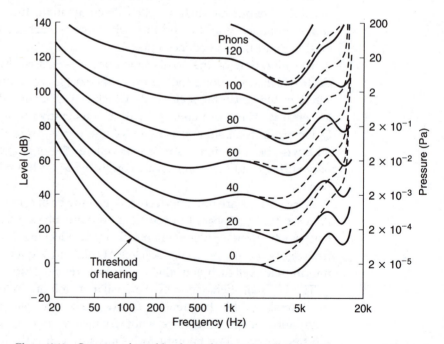

Figure 4.12 Contours of equal loudness showing that the frequency response of the ear is highly level dependent (solid line, age 20; dashed line, age 60).

upper frequency limit of sound is 20 kHz or 16 kHz.[4,5] For a long time it was thought that frequencies below about 40 Hz were unimportant, but it is now clear that reproduction of frequencies down to 20 Hz improves reality and ambience.[6] The generally accepted frequency range for high-quality audio is 20 Hz to 20 000 Hz, although for broadcasting an upper limit of 15 000 Hz is often applied.

The most dramatic effect of the curves of Figure 4.12 is that the bass content of reproduced sound is disproportionately reduced as the level is turned down. This would suggest that if a powerful yet high-quality reproduction system is available the correct tonal balance when playing a good recording can be obtained simply by setting the volume control to the correct level. This is indeed the case. A further consideration is that many musical instruments and the human voice change timbre with level and there is only one level which sounds correct for the timbre.

Oddly, there is as yet no standard linking the signal level in a transmission or recording system with the SPL at the microphone, although with the advent of digital microphones this useful information could easily be sent as metadata. Loudness is a subjective reaction and is almost impossible to measure. In addition to the level-dependent frequency response problem, the listener uses the sound not for its own sake but to draw some conclusion about the source. For example, most people hearing a distant motorcycle will describe it as being loud. Clearly at the source, it *is* loud, but the listener has compensated for the distance. Paradoxically the same listener may then use a motor mower without hearing protection.

The best that can be done is to make some compensation for the level-dependent response using *weighting curves*. Ideally there should be many, but in practice the A, B and C weightings were chosen where the A curve is based on the 40-phon response. The measured level after such a filter is in units of dBA. The A curve is almost always used because it most nearly relates to the annoyance factor of distant noise sources. The use of A weighting at higher levels is highly questionable.

4.7   Frequency discrimination

Figure 4.13 shows an uncoiled basilar membrane with the apex on the left so that the usual logarithmic frequency scale can be applied. The envelope of displacement of the basilar membrane is shown for a single frequency at (a). The vibration of the membrane in sympathy with a single frequency cannot be localized to an infinitely small area, and nearby areas are forced to vibrate at the same frequency with an amplitude that decreases with distance. Note that the envelope is asymmetrical because the membrane is tapering and because of

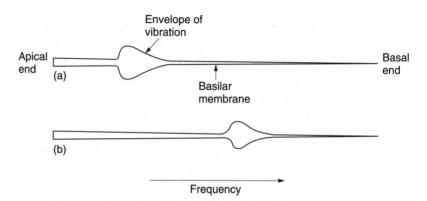

Figure 4.13 The basilar membrane symbolically uncoiled. (a) Single frequency causes the vibration envelope shown. (b) Changing the frequency moves the peak of the envelope.

frequency-dependent losses in the propagation of vibrational energy down the cochlea. If the frequency is changed, as in (b), the position of maximum displacement will also change. As the basilar membrane is continuous, the position of maximum displacement is infinitely variable allowing extremely good pitch discrimination of about one twelfth of a semitone which is determined by the spacing of hair cells.

In the presence of a complex spectrum, the finite width of the vibration envelope means that the ear fails to register energy in some bands when there is more energy in a nearby band. Within those areas, other frequencies are mechanically excluded because their amplitude is insufficient to dominate the local vibration of the membrane. Thus the Q factor of the membrane is responsible for the degree of auditory masking, defined as the decreased audibility of one sound in the presence of another.

4.8   Critical bands

The term used in psychoacoustics to describe the finite width of the vibration envelope is *critical bandwidth*. Critical bands were first described by Fletcher.[7] The envelope of basilar vibration is a complicated function. It is clear from the mechanism that the area of the membrane involved will increase as the sound level rises. Figure 4.14 shows the bandwidth as a function of level.

As was shown in Chapter 3, the Heisenberg inequality teaches that the higher the frequency resolution of a transform, the worse the time accuracy. As the basilar membrane has finite frequency resolution measured in the width of a critical band, it follows that it must have finite time resolution. This also follows from the fact that the membrane

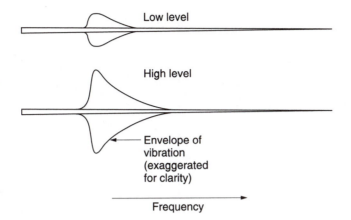

Figure 4.14 The critical bandwidth changes with SPL.

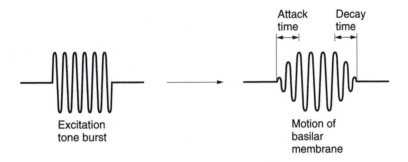

Figure 4.15 Impulse response of the ear showing slow attack and decay due to resonant behaviour.

is resonant, taking time to start and stop vibrating in response to a stimulus. There are many examples of this. Figure 4.15 shows the impulse response. Figure 4.16 shows the perceived loudness of a tone burst increases with duration up to about 200 ms due to the finite response time.

The HAS has evolved to offer intelligibility in reverberant environments which it does by averaging all received energy over a period of about 30 milliseconds. Reflected sound arriving within this time is integrated to produce a louder sensation, whereas reflected sound which arrives after that time can be temporally discriminated and is perceived as an echo. Microphones have no such ability, hence the need for acoustic treatment in areas where microphones are used.

A further example of the finite time discrimination of the HAS is the fact that short interruptions to a continuous tone are difficult to detect. Finite time resolution means that masking can take place even when the masking tone begins after and ceases before the masked sound. This is referred to as forward and backward masking.[8]

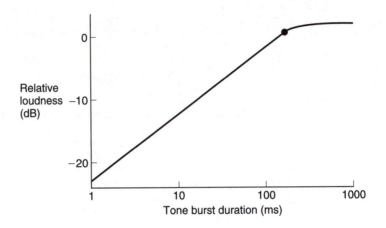

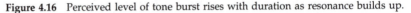

Figure 4.16 Perceived level of tone burst rises with duration as resonance builds up.

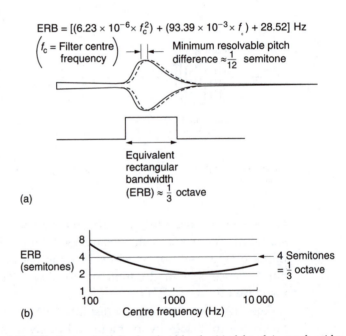

Figure 4.17 Effective rectangular bandwidth of critical band is much wider than the resolution of the pitch discrimination mechanism.

As the vibration envelope is such a complicated shape, Moore and Glasberg have proposed the concept of equivalent rectangular bandwidth (ERB) to simplify matters. The ERB is the bandwidth of a rectangular filter which passes the same power as a critical band. Figure 4.17(a) shows the expression they have derived linking the ERB with frequency. This is plotted in (b) where it will be seen that one third of an octave is a good approximation. This is about thirty times broader than the pitch discrimination also shown in (b).

4.9   Beats

Figure 4.18 shows an electrical signal (a) in which two equal sine waves of nearly the same frequency have been linearly added together. Note that the envelope of the signal varies as the two waves move in and out of phase. Clearly the frequency transform calculated to infinite accuracy is that shown at (b). The two amplitudes are constant and there is no evidence of the envelope modulation. However, such a measurement requires an infinite time. When a shorter time is available, the frequency discrimination of the transform falls and the bands in which energy is detected become broader.

When the frequency discrimination is too wide to distinguish the two tones as in (c), the result is that they are registered as a single tone. The amplitude of the single tone will change from one measurement to the next because the envelope is being measured. The rate at which the

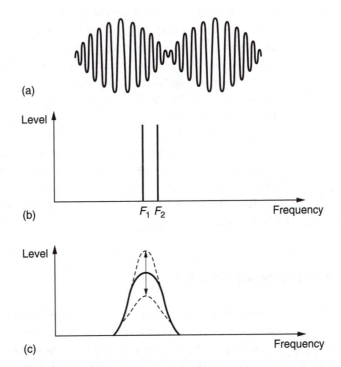

(a)

(b)

(c)

Figure 4.18   (a) Result of adding two sine waves of similar frequency. (b) Spectrum of (a) to infinite accuracy. (c) With finite accuracy only a single frequency is distinguished whose amplitude changes with the envelope of (a) giving rise to beats.

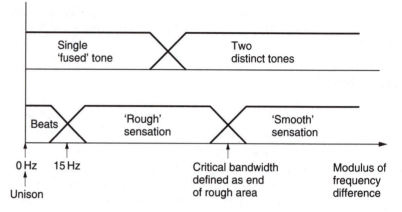

Figure 4.19 Perception of two-tone signal as frequency difference changes.

envelope amplitude changes is called a *beat* frequency which is not actually present in the input signal. Beats are an artifact of finite frequency resolution transforms. The fact that the HAS produces beats from pairs of tones proves that it has finite resolution.

Measurement of when beats occur allows measurement of critical bandwidth. Figure 4.19 shows the results of human perception of a two-tone signal as the frequency **dF** difference changes. When **dF** is zero, described musically as *unison*, only a single note is heard. As **dF** increases, beats are heard, yet only a single note is perceived. The limited frequency resolution of the basilar membrane has *fused* the two tones together. As **dF** increases further, the sensation of beats ceases at 12–15 Hz and is replaced by a sensation of roughness or *dissonance*. The roughness is due to parts of the basilar membrane being unable to decide the frequency at which to vibrate. The regenerative effect may well become confused under such conditions. The roughness which persists until **dF** has reached the critical bandwidth beyond which two separate tones will be heard because there are now two discrete basilar resonances. In fact this is the definition of critical bandwidth.

4.10 Codec level calibration

Perceptive coding relies on the principle of auditory masking. Masking causes the ear/brain combination to be less sensitive to sound at one frequency in the presence of another at a nearby frequency. If a first tone is present in the input, then it will mask signals of lower level at nearby frequencies. The quantizing of the first tone and of further tones at those frequencies can be made coarser. Fewer bits are needed and a coding

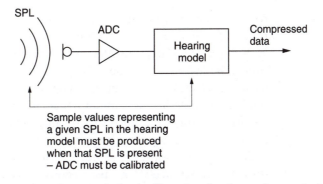

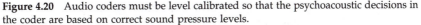

Figure 4.20 Audio coders must be level calibrated so that the psychoacoustic decisions in the coder are based on correct sound pressure levels.

gain results. The increased quantizing distortion is allowable if it is masked by the presence of the first tone.

The functioning of the ear is noticeably level dependent and perceptive coders take this into account. However, all signal processing takes place in the electrical or digital domain with respect to electrical or numerical levels whereas the hearing mechanism operates with respect to true sound pressure level. Figure 4.20 shows that in an ideal system the overall gain of the microphones and ADCs is such that the PCM codes have a relationship with sound pressure which is the same as that assumed by the model in the codec. Equally the overall gain of the DAC and loudspeaker system should be such that the sound pressure levels which the codec assumes are those actually heard. Clearly the gain control of the microphone and the volume control of the reproduction system must be calibrated if the hearing model is to function properly. If, for example, the microphone gain was too low and this was compensated by advancing the loudspeaker gain, the overall gain would be the same but the codec would be fooled into thinking that the sound pressure level was less than it really was and the masking model would not then be appropriate.

The above should come as no surprise as analog audio codecs such as the various Dolby systems have required and implemented line-up procedures and suitable tones. However obvious the need to calibrate coders may be, the degree to which this is recognized in the industry is almost negligible to date and this can only result in sub-optimal performance.

4.11 Quality measurement

As has been seen, one way in which coding gain is obtained is to requantize sample values to reduce the wordlength. Since the resultant requantizing error is a distortion mechanism it results in energy moving from one frequency to another. The masking model is essential to estimate how audible the effect of this will be. The greater the degree of compression required, the more precise the model must be. If the masking model is inaccurate, then equipment based upon it may produce audible artifacts under some circumstances. Artifacts may also result if the model is not properly implemented. As a result, development of audio compression units requires careful listening tests with a wide range of source material[9,10] and precision loudspeakers. The presence of artifacts at a given compression factor indicates only that performance is below expectations; it does not distinguish between the implementation and the model. If the implementation is verified, then a more detailed model must be sought.

Naturally comparative listening tests are only valid if all the codecs have been level calibrated and if the loudspeakers cause less loss of information than any of the codecs, a requirement which is frequently overlooked. Properly conducted listening tests are expensive and time consuming, and alternative methods have been developed which can be used objectively to evaluate the performance of different techniques. The noise-to-masking ratio (NMR) is one such measurement.[11] Figure 4.21 shows how NMR is measured. Input audio signals are fed simultaneously to a data reduction coder and decoder in tandem and to a compensating delay whose length must be adjusted to match the codec delay. At the output of the delay, the coding error is obtained by subtracting the codec output from the original. The original signal is spectrum-analysed into critical bands in order to derive the masking threshold of the input audio, and this is compared with the critical band spectrum of the error. The NMR in each critical band is the ratio between the masking threshold and the quantizing error due to the codec. An average NMR for all bands can be

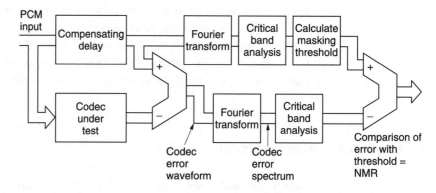

Figure 4.21 The noise-to-masking ratio is derived as shown here.

computed. A positive NMR in any band indicates that artifacts are potentially audible. Plotting the average NMR against time is a powerful technique, as with an ideal codec the NMR should be stable with different types of program material. If this is not the case the codec could perform quite differently as a function of the source material. NMR excursions can be correlated with the waveform of the audio input to analyse how the extra noise was caused and to redesign the codec to eliminate it.

Practical systems should have a finite NMR in order to give a degree of protection against difficult signals which have not been anticipated and against the use of post-codec equalization or several tandem codecs which could change the masking threshold. There is a strong argument that devices used for audio production should have a greater NMR than consumer or program delivery devices.

4.12 The limits

There are, of course, limits to all technologies. Eventually artifacts will be heard as the amount of compression is increased which no amount of detailed modelling will remove. The ear is only able to perceive a certain proportion of the information in a given sound. This could be called the perceptual entropy,[12] and all additional sound is redundant or irrelevant. Data reduction works by removing the redundancy, and clearly an ideal system would remove all of it, leaving only the entropy. Once this has been done, the masking capacity of the ear has been reached and the NMR has reached zero over the whole band. Reducing the data rate further must reduce the entropy, because raising noise further at any frequency will render it audible. In practice the audio bandwidth will have to be reduced in order to keep the noise level acceptable. In MPEG-1 pre-filtering allows data from higher sub-bands to be neglected. MPEG-2 has introduced some low sampling rate options for this purpose. Thus there is a limit to the degree of data reduction which can be achieved even with an ideal coder. Systems which go beyond that limit are not appropriate for high-quality music, but are relevant in news gathering and communications where intelligibility of speech is the criterion. Interestingly, the data rate out of a coder is virtually independent of the input sampling rate unless the sampling rate is very low. This is because the entropy of the sound is in the waveform, not in the number of samples carrying it.

The compression factor of a coder is only part of the story. All codecs cause delay, and in general the greater the compression the longer the delay. In some applications, such as telephony, a short delay is required.[13] In many applications, the compressed channel will have a constant bit rate, and so a constant compression factor is required. In real program material, the entropy varies and so the NMR will fluctuate. If greater delay can be accepted, as in a recording application, memory buffering can be used to allow the coder to operate at constant NMR and instantaneously variable data rate. The memory absorbs the instantaneous data rate differences of the coder and allows a constant rate in the channel. A higher effective compression factor will then be obtained. Near-constant quality can also be achieved using statistical multiplexing.

4.13 Compression applications

One of the fundamental concepts of PCM audio is that the signal-to-noise ratio of the channel can be determined by selecting a suitable wordlength. In conjunction with the sampling rate, the resulting data rate is then determined. In many cases the full data rate can be transmitted or recorded. A high-quality digital audio channel requires around one megabit per second, whereas a standard definition component digital video channel needs two hundred times as much. With mild video compression the video bit rate is still so much in excess of the audio rate that audio compression is not worth while. Only when high video compression factors are used does it become necessary to apply compression to the audio.

Professional equipment traditionally has operated with higher sound quality than consumer equipment in order to allow for some inevitable quality loss in production, and so there will be less pressure to use data reduction. In fact there is even pressure against the use of audio compression in critical applications because of the loss of quality, particularly in stereo and surround sound.

With the rising density and falling cost of digital recording media, the use of compression in professional audio storage applications is hard to justify. However, where there is a practical or economic restriction on channel bandwidth compression becomes essential. Now that the technology exists to broadcast television pictures using compressed digital coding, it is obvious that the associated audio should be conveyed in the same way.

4.14 Audio compression tools

There are many different techniques available for audio compression, each having advantages and disadvantages. Real compressors will

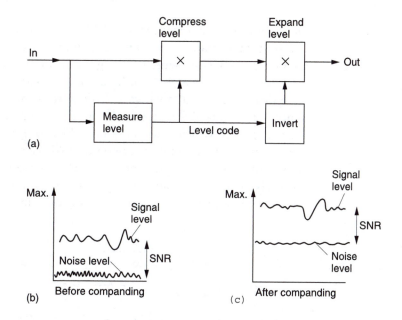

Figure 4.22 Digital companding. In (a) the encoder amplifies the input to maximum level and the decoder attenuates by the same amount. (b) In a companded system, the signal is kept as far as possible above the noise caused by shortening the sample wordlength (c).

combine several techniques or tools in various ways to achieve different combinations of cost and complexity. Here it is intended to examine the tools separately before seeing how they are used in actual compression systems.

The simplest coding tool is companding: a digital parallel of the noise reducers used in analog tape recording. Figure 4.22(a) shows that in companding the input signal level is monitored. Whenever the input level falls below maximum, it is amplified at the coder. The gain which was applied at the coder is added to the data stream so that the decoder can apply an equal attenuation. The advantage of companding is that the signal is kept as far away from the noise floor as possible. In analog noise reduction this is used to maximize the SNR of a tape recorder, whereas in digital compression it is used to keep the signal level as far as possible above the distortion introduced by various coding steps.

One common way of obtaining coding gain is to shorten the wordlength of samples so that fewer bits need to be transmitted. Figure 4.22(b) shows that when this is done, the distortion will rise by 6 dB for (c) every bit removed. This is because removing a bit halves the number of quantizing intervals which then must be twice as large, doubling the error amplitude.

Clearly if this step follows the compander of (a), the audibility of the distortion will be minimized. As an alternative to shortening the wordlength, the uniform quantized PCM signal can be converted to a non-uniform format. In non-uniform coding, shown at (c), the size of the quantizing step rises with the magnitude of the sample so that the distortion level is greater when higher levels exist.

Companding is a relative of floating-point coding shown in Figure 4.23 where the sample value is expressed as a mantissa and a binary exponent which determines how the mantissa needs to be shifted to have its correct absolute value on a PCM scale. The exponent is the equivalent of the gain setting or scale factor of a compander.

Clearly in floating-point the signal-to-noise ratio is defined by the number of bits in the mantissa, and as shown in Figure 4.24, this will

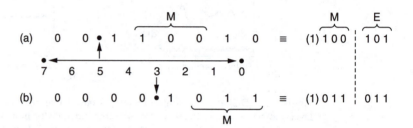

Figure 4.23 In this example of floating-point notation, the radix point can have eight positions determined by the exponent E. The point is placed to the left of the first '1', and the next four bits to the right form the mantissa M. As the MSB of the mantissa is always 1, it need not always be stored.

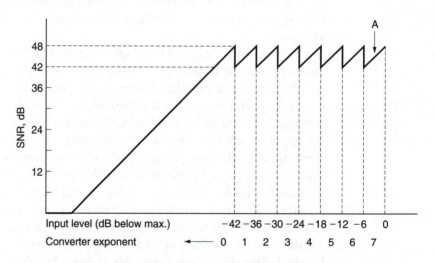

Figure 4.24 In this example of an eight-bit mantissa, three-bit exponent system, the maximum SNR is 6 dB × 8 = 48 dB with maximum input of 0 dB. As input level falls by 6 dB, the convertor noise remains the same, so SNR falls to 42 dB. Further reduction in signal level causes the convertor to shift range (point A in the diagram) by increasing the input analog gain by 6 dB. The SNR is restored, and the exponent changes from 7 to 6 in order to cause the same gain change at the receiver. The noise modulation would be audible in this simple system. A longer mantissa word is needed in practice.

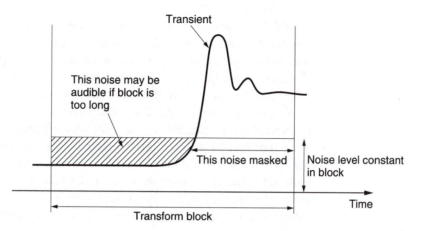

Figure 4.25 If a transient occurs towards the end of a transform block, the quantizing noise will still be present at the beginning of the block and may result in a pre-echo where the noise is audible before the transient.

vary as a sawtooth function of signal level, as the best value, obtained when the mantissa is near overflow, is replaced by the worst value when the mantissa overflows and the exponent is incremented. Floating-point notation is used within DSP chips as it eases the computational problems involved in handling long wordlengths. For example, when multiplying floating-point numbers, only the mantissae need to be multiplied. The exponents are simply added.

A floating-point system requires one exponent to be carried with each mantissa and this is wasteful because in real audio material the level does not change so rapidly and there is redundancy in the exponents. A better alternative is floating-point block coding, also known as near-instantaneous companding, where the magnitude of the largest sample in a block is used to determine the value of an exponent which is valid for the whole block. Sending one exponent per block requires a lower data rate than in true floating-point.[14]

In block coding the requantizing in the coder raises the quantizing error, but it does so over the entire duration of the block. Figure 4.25 shows that if a transient occurs towards the end of a block, the decoder will reproduce the waveform correctly, but the quantizing noise will start at the beginning of the block and may result in a burst of distortion products (also called pre-noise or pre-echo) which is audible before the transient. Temporal masking may be used to make this inaudible. With a 1 ms block, the artifacts are too brief to be heard.

Another solution is to use a variable time window according to the transient content of the audio waveform. When musical transients occur, short blocks are necessary and the coding gain will be low.[15] At other times the blocks become longer allowing a greater coding gain.

Whilst the above systems used alone do allow coding gain, the compression factor has to be limited because little benefit is obtained from masking. This is because the techniques above produce distortion which may be found anywhere over the entire audio band. If the audio input spectrum is narrow, this noise will not be masked.

Sub-band coding[16] splits the audio spectrum up into many different frequency bands. Once this has been done, each band can be individually processed. In real audio signals many bands will contain lower level signals than the loudest one. Individual companding of each band will be more effective than broadband companding. Sub-band coding also allows the level of distortion products to be raised selectively so that distortion is only created at frequencies where spectral masking will be effective.

It should be noted that the result of reducing the wordlength of samples in a sub-band coder is often referred to as noise. Strictly, noise is an unwanted signal which is decorrelated from the wanted signal. This is not generally what happens in audio compression. Although the original audio conversion would have been correctly dithered, the linearizing random element in the low-order bits will be some way below the end of the shortened word. If the word is simply rounded to the nearest integer the linearizing effect of the original dither will be lost and the result will be quantizing distortion. As the distortion takes place in a band-limited system the harmonics generated will alias back within the band. Where the requantizing process takes place in a sub-band, the distortion products will be confined to that sub-band as shown in Figure 3.71. Such distortion is anharmonic.

Following any perceptive coding steps, the resulting data may be further subject to lossless binary compression tools such as prediction, Huffman coding or a combination of both.

Audio is usually considered to be a time-domain waveform as this is what emerges from a microphone. As has been seen in Chapter 3, spectral analysis allows any periodic waveform to be represented by a set of harmonically related components of suitable amplitude and phase. In theory it is perfectly possible to decompose a periodic input waveform into its constituent frequencies and phases, and to record or transmit the transform. The transform can then be inverted and the original waveform will be precisely re-created.

Although one can think of exceptions, the transform of a typical audio waveform changes relatively slowly much of the time. The slow speech of an organ pipe or a violin string, or the slow decay of most musical sounds allows the rate at which the transform is sampled to be reduced, and a coding gain results. At some frequencies the level will be below maximum and a shorter wordlength can be used to describe the coefficient. Further coding gain will be achieved if the coefficients

Figure 4.26 Transform coding can only be practically performed on short blocks. These are overlapped using window functions in order to handle continuous waveforms.

describing frequencies which will experience masking are quantized more coarsely.

In practice there are some difficulties, real sounds are not periodic, but contain transients which transformation cannot accurately locate in time. The solution to this difficulty is to cut the waveform into short segments and then to transform each individually. The delay is reduced, as is the computational task, but there is a possibility of artifacts arising because of the truncation of the waveform into rectangular time windows. A solution is to use window functions, and to overlap the segments as shown in Figure 4.26. Thus every input sample appears in just two transforms, but with variable weighting depending upon its position along the time axis.

The DFT (discrete frequency transform) does not produce a continuous spectrum, but instead produces coefficients at discrete frequencies. The frequency resolution (i.e. the number of different frequency coefficients) is equal to the number of samples in the window. If overlapped windows are used, twice as many coefficients are produced as are theoretically necessary. In addition the DFT requires intensive computation, owing to the requirement to use complex arithmetic to render the phase of the components as well as the amplitude. An alternative is to use discrete cosine transforms (DCT) or the modified discrete cosine transform (MDCT) which has the ability to eliminate the overhead of coefficients due to overlapping the windows and return to the critically sampled domain.[17] Critical sampling is a term which means that the number of coefficients does not exceed the number which would be obtained with non-overlapping windows.

4.15   Sub-band coding

Sub-band coding takes advantage of the fact that real sounds do not have uniform spectral energy. The wordlength of PCM audio is based on the dynamic range required and this is generally constant with frequency although any pre-emphasis will affect the situation. When a signal with an uneven spectrum is conveyed by PCM, the whole dynamic range is occupied only by the loudest spectral component, and all of the other components are coded with excessive headroom. In its simplest form, sub-band coding works by splitting the

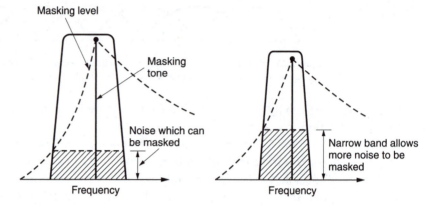

Figure 4.27 In sub-band coding the worst case occurs when the masking tone is at the top edge of the sub-band. The narrower the band, the higher the noise level which can be masked.

audio signal into a number of frequency bands and companding each band according to its own level. Bands in which there is little energy result in small amplitudes which can be transmitted with short wordlength. Thus each band results in variable-length samples, but the sum of all the sample wordlengths is less than that of PCM and so a coding gain can be obtained. Sub-band coding is not restricted to the digital domain; the analog Dolby noise-reduction systems use it extensively.

The number of sub-bands to be used depends upon what other compression tools are to be combined with the sub-band coding. If it is intended to optimize compression based on auditory masking, the sub-bands should preferably be narrower than the critical bands of the ear, and therefore a large number will be required. This requirement is frequently not met: ISO/MPEG Layers I and II use only 32 sub-bands. Figure 4.27 shows the critical condition where the masking tone is at the top edge of the sub-band. It will be seen that the narrower the sub-band, the higher the requantizing 'noise' that can be masked. The use of an excessive number of sub-bands will, however, raise complexity and the coding delay, as well as risking pre-ringing on transients which may exceed the temporal masking.

The bandsplitting process is complex and requires a lot of computation. One bandsplitting method which is useful is quadrature mirror filtering described in Chapter 3.

4.16 Audio compression formats

There are numerous formats intended for audio compression and these can be divided into international standards and proprietary designs

The ISO (International Standards Organization) and the IEC (International Electrotechnical Commission) recognized that compression would have an important part to play and in 1988 established the ISO/IEC/MPEG (Moving Picture Experts Group) to compare and assess various coding schemes in order to arrive at an international standard for compressing video. The terms of reference were extended the same year to include audio and the MPEG/Audio group was formed. MPEG audio coding is used for DAB (digital audio broadcasting) and for the audio content of digital television broadcasts to the DVB standard.

In the USA, it has been proposed to use an alternative compression technique for the audio content of ATSC (advanced television systems committee) digital television broadcasts. This is the AC-3[18] system developed by Dolby Laboratories. The MPEG transport stream structure has also been standardized to allow it to carry AC-3 coded audio. The Digital Video Disk can also carry AC-3 or MPEG audio coding. Other popular proprietary codes include apt-X which is a mild compression factor/short delay codec and ATRAC which is the codec used in MiniDisc.

4.17   MPEG audio compression

The subject of audio compression was well advanced when the MPEG/Audio group was formed. As a result it was not necessary for the group to produce *ab initio* codecs because existing work was considered suitable. As part of the Eureka 147 project, a system known as MUSICAM[19] (Masking pattern adapted Universal Sub-band Integrated Coding And Multiplexing) was developed jointly by CCETT in France, IRT in Germany and Philips in the Netherlands. MUSICAM was designed to be suitable for DAB (digital audio broadcasting). As a parallel development, the ASPEC[20] (Adaptive Spectral Perceptual Entropy Coding) system was developed from a number of earlier systems as a joint proposal by AT&T Bell Labs, Thomson, the Fraunhofer Society and CNET. ASPEC was designed for use at high compression factors to allow audio transmission on ISDN.

These two systems were both fully implemented by July 1990 when comprehensive subjective testing took place at the Swedish Broadcasting Corporation.[21,22] As a result of these tests, the MPEG/Audio group combined the attributes of both ASPEC and MUSICAM into a standard[23,24] having three levels of complexity and performance.

These three different levels, which are known as *layers*, are needed because of the number of possible applications. Audio coders can be operated at various compression factors with different quality expectations. Stereophonic classical music requires different quality criteria from monophonic speech. The complexity of the coder will be reduced with a smaller compression factor. For moderate compression, a simple codec will be more cost effective. On the other hand, as the compression factor is increased, it will be necessary to employ a more complex coder to maintain quality.

MPEG Layer I is a simplified version of MUSICAM which is appropriate for the mild compression applications at low cost. Layer II is identical to MUSICAM and is used for DAB and for the audio content of DVB digital television broadcasts. Layer III is a combination of the best features of ASPEC and MUSICAM and is mainly applicable to telecommunications where high compression factors are required.

At each layer, MPEG Audio coding allows input sampling rates of 32, 44.1 and 48 kHz and supports output bit rates of 32, 48, 56, 64, 96, 112, 128, 192, 256 and 384 kbits/s. The transmission can be mono, dual channel (e.g. bilingual), or stereo. Another possibility is the use of joint stereo mode in which the audio becomes mono above a certain frequency. This allows a lower bit rate with the obvious penalty of reduced stereo fidelity.

The layers of MPEG Audio coding (I, II and III) should not be confused with the MPEG-1 and MPEG-2 television coding standards. MPEG-1 and MPEG-2 flexibly define a range of systems for video and audio coding, whereas the layers define types of audio coding.

The earlier MPEG-1 standard compresses audio and video into about 1.5 Mbits/s. The audio coding of MPEG-1 may be used on its own to encode one or two channels at bit rates up to 448 kbits/s. MPEG-2 allows the number of channels to increase to five: Left, Right, Centre, Left surround and Right surround. In order to retain reverse compatibility with MPEG-1, the MPEG-2 coding converts the five-channel input to a compatible two-channel signal, L_0, R_0, by matrixing[25] as shown in Figure 4.28. The data from these two channels are encoded in a standard

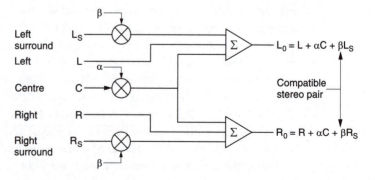

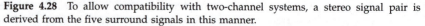

Figure 4.28 To allow compatibility with two-channel systems, a stereo signal pair is derived from the five surround signals in this manner.

L	R	C
L	R_S	C
L_S	R	C
L_S	R_S	C
L	R	L_S
L	R	R_S
L_S	R	R_S
L	R_S	L_S

Figure 4.29 In addition to sending the stereo compatible pair, one of the above combinations of signals can be sent. In all cases a suitable inverse matrix can recover the original five channels.

MPEG-1 audio frame, and this is followed in MPEG-2 by an ancillary data frame which an MPEG-1 decoder will ignore. The ancillary frame contains data for another three audio channels. Figure 4.29 shows that there are eight modes in which these three channels can be obtained. The encoder will select the mode which gives the least data rate for the prevailing distribution of energy in the input channels. An MPEG-2 decoder will extract those three channels in addition to the MPEG-1 frame and then recover all five original channels by an inverse matrix which is steered by mode select bits in the bitstream.

The requirement for MPEG-2 audio to be backward compatible with MPEG-1 audio coding was essential for some markets, but did compromise the performance because certain useful coding tools could not be used. Consequently the MPEG Audio group evolved a multi-channel standard which was not backward compatible because it incorporated additional coding tools in order to achieve higher performance. This came to be known as MPEG-2 AAC (advanced audio coding).

4.18 MPEG Layer I audio coding

Figure 4.30 shows a block diagram of a Layer I coder which is a simplified version of that used in the MUSICAM system. A polyphase filter divides the audio spectrum into 32 equal sub-bands. The output of the filter bank is critically sampled. In other words the output data rate is no higher than the input rate because each band has been heterodyned to a frequency range from zero upwards. Sub-band compression takes advantage of the fact that real sounds do not have uniform spectral energy. The wordlength of PCM audio is based on the dynamic range

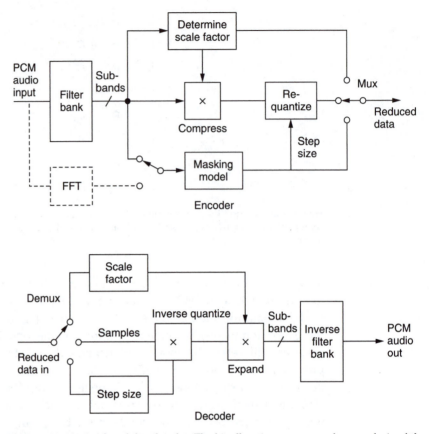

Figure 4.30 A simple sub-band coder. The bit allocation may come from analysis of the sub-band energy, or, for greater reduction, from a spectral analysis in a side chain.

required and this is generally constant with frequency although any pre-emphasis will affect the situation. When a signal with an uneven spectrum is conveyed by PCM, the whole dynamic range is occupied only by the loudest spectral component, and all the other components are coded with excessive headroom. In its simplest form, sub-band coding works by splitting the audio signal into a number of frequency bands and companding each band according to its own level. Bands in which there is little energy result in small amplitudes which can be transmitted with short wordlength. Thus each band results in variable-length samples, but the sum of all the sample wordlengths is less than that of the PCM input and so a degree of coding gain can be obtained.

A Layer I-compliant encoder, i.e. one whose output can be understood by a standard decoder, can be made which does no more than this. Provided the syntax of the bitstream is correct, the decoder is not concerned with how the coding decisions were made. However, higher compression factors require the distortion level to be increased and this should only be done if it is known that the distortion products will be masked. Ideally the sub-bands should be narrower than the critical bands of the ear. Figure 4.27 showed the critical condition where the masking tone is at the top edge of the sub-band. The use of an excessive number of sub-bands will, however, raise complexity and the coding delay. The use of 32 equal sub-bands in MPEG Layers I and II is a compromise.

Efficient polyphase bandsplitting filters can only operate with equal-width sub-bands and the result, in an octave-based hearing model, is that sub-bands are too wide at low frequencies and too narrow at high frequencies.

To offset the lack of accuracy in the sub-band filter a parallel fast Fourier transform is used to drive the masking model. The standard suggests masking models, but compliant bitstreams can result from other models. In Layer I a 512-point FFT is used. The output of the FFT is employed to determine the masking threshold which is the sum of all masking sources. Masking sources include at least the threshold of hearing which may locally be raised by the frequency content of the input audio. The degree to which the threshold is raised depends on whether the input audio is sinusoidal or atonal (broadband, or noise-like). In the case of a sine wave, the magnitude and phase of the FFT at each frequency will be similar from one window to the next, whereas if the sound is atonal the magnitude and phase information will be chaotic.

The masking threshold is effectively a graph of just noticeable noise as a function of frequency. Figure 4.31(a) shows an example. The masking threshold is calculated by convolving the FFT spectrum with the cochlea spreading function with corrections for tonality. The level of the masking threshold cannot fall below the absolute masking threshold which is the threshold of hearing. The masking threshold is then

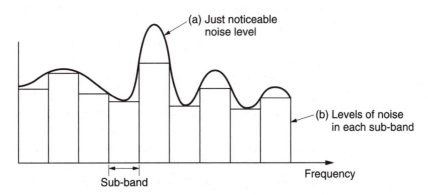

Figure 4.31 A continuous curve (a) of the just-noticeable noise level is calculated by the masking model. The level of noise in each sub-band (b) must be set so as not to exceed the level of the curve.

superimposed on the actual frequencies of each sub-band so that the allowable level of distortion in each can be established. This is shown in Figure 4.31(b).

Constant size input blocks are used, containing 384 samples. At 48 kHz, 384 samples correspond to a period of 8 ms. After the sub-band filter each band contains 12 samples per block. The block size is too long to avoid the pre-masking phenomenon of Figure 4.27. Consequently the masking model must ensure that heavy requantizing is not used in a block which contains a large transient following a period of quiet. This can be done by comparing parameters of the current block with those of the previous block as a significant difference will indicate transient activity.

The samples in each sub-band block or *bin* are companded according to the peak value in the bin. A six-bit scale factor is used for each sub-band which applies to all 12 samples. The gain step is 2 dB and so with a six-bit code over 120 dB of dynamic range is available.

A fixed output bit rate is employed, and as there is no buffering the size of the coded output block will be fixed. The wordlengths in each bin will have to be such that the sum of the bits from all the sub-bands equals the size of the coded block. Thus some sub-bands can have long wordlength coding if others have short wordlength coding. The process of determining the requantization step size, and hence the wordlength in each sub-band, is known as bit allocation. In Layer I all sub-bands are treated in the same way and fourteen different requantization classes are used. Each one has an odd number of quantizing intervals so that all codes are referenced to a precise zero level. Where masking takes place, the signal is quantized more coarsely until the distortion level is raised to just below the masking level. The coarse quantization requires shorter wordlengths and allows a coding gain. The bit allocation may be iterative as adjustments are made to obtain an equal NMR across all sub-bands. If the allowable data rate is adequate, a positive NMR will result and the decoded quality will be optimal. However, at lower bit rates and in the absence of buffering a temporary increase in bit rate is not possible. The coding distortion cannot be masked and the best the encoder can do is to make the (negative) NMR equal across the spectrum so that artifacts are not emphasized unduly in any one sub-band. It is possible that in some sub-bands there will be no data at all, either because such frequencies were absent in the program material or because the encoder has discarded them to meet a low bit rate.

The samples of differing wordlengths in each bin are then assembled into the output coded block. Unlike a PCM block, which contains samples of fixed wordlength, a coded block contains many different wordlengths and which may vary from one sub-band to the next. In order to deserialize the block into samples of various wordlength and

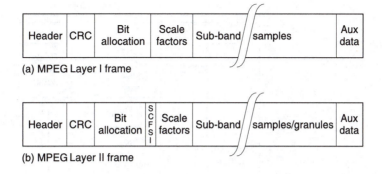

Figure 4.32 (a) The MPEG Layer I data frame has a simple structure. (b) In the Layer II frame, the compression of the scale factors requires the additional SCFSI code described in the text (see page 207).

demultiplex the samples into the appropriate frequency bins, the decoder has to be told what bit allocations were used when it was packed, and some synchronizing means is needed to allow the beginning of the block to be identified.

The compression factor is determined by the bit-allocation system. It is trivial to change the output block size parameter to obtain a different compression factor. If a larger block is specified, the bit allocator simply iterates until the new block size is filled. Similarly, the decoder need only deserialize the larger block correctly into coded samples and then the expansion process is identical except for the fact that expanded words contain less noise. Thus codecs with varying degrees of compression are available which can perform different bandwidth/performance tasks with the same hardware.

Figure 4.32(a) shows the format of the Layer I elementary stream. The frame begins with a sync pattern to reset the phase of deserialization, and a header which describes the sampling rate and any use of pre-emphasis. Following this is a block of 32 four-bit allocation codes. These specify the wordlength used in each sub-band and allow the decoder to deserialize the sub-band sample block. This is followed by a block of 32 six-bit scale factor indices, which specify the gain given to each band during companding. The last block contains 32 sets of 12 samples. These samples vary in wordlength from one block to the next, and can be from 0 to 15 bits long. The deserializer has to use the 32 allocation information codes to work out how to deserialize the sample block into individual samples of variable length.

The Layer I MPEG decoder is shown in Figure 4.33. The elementary stream is deserialized using the sync pattern and the variable-length samples are assembled using the allocation codes. The variable-length samples are returned to fifteen-bit wordlength by adding zeros. The scale factor indices are then used to determine multiplication factors used to

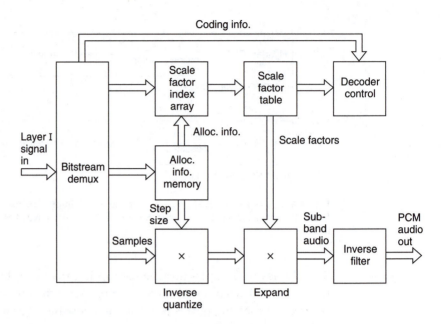

Figure 4.33 The Layer I decoder. See text for details.

return the waveform in each sub-band to its original amplitude. The 32 sub-band signals are then merged into one spectrum by the synthesis filter. This is a set of bandpass filters which heterodynes every sub-band to the correct place in the audio spectrum and then adds them to produce the audio output.

4.19 MPEG Layer II audio coding

MPEG Layer II audio coding is identical to MUSICAM. The same 32-band filterbank and the same block companding scheme as Layer I is used. In order to give the masking model better spectral resolution, the side-chain FFT has 1024 points. The FFT drives the masking model which may be the same as is suggested for Layer I. The block length is increased to 1152 samples. This is three times the block length of Layer I, corresponding to 24 ms at 48 kHz.

Figure 4.32(b) shows the Layer II elementary stream structure. Following the sync pattern the bit-allocation data are sent. The requantizing process of Layer II is more complex than in Layer I. The sub-bands are categorized into three frequency ranges, low, medium and high, and the requantizing in each range is different. Low-frequency samples can be quantized into 15 different wordlengths, mid-frequencies into seven different wordlengths and high frequencies into only three different wordlengths. Accordingly the bit-allocation data use words of four, three and two bits depending on the sub-band concerned. This reduces the amount of allocation data to be sent. In each case one extra combination exists in the allocation code. This is used to indicate that no data are being sent for that sub-band.

The 1152 sample block of Layer II is divided into three blocks of 384 samples so that the same companding structure as Layer I can be used. The 2 dB step size in the scale factors is retained. However, not all the scale factors are transmitted, because they contain a degree of redundancy. In real program material, the difference between scale factors in successive blocks in the same band exceeds 2 dB less than 10 per cent of the time. Layer II coders analyse the set of three successive scale factors in each sub-band. On a stationary program, these will be the same and only one scale factor out of three is sent. As the transient content increases in a given sub-band, two or three scale factors will be sent. A two-bit code known as SCFSI (scale factor select information) must be sent to allow the decoder to determine which of the three possible scale factors have been sent for each sub-band. This technique effectively halves the scale factor bit rate.

As for Layer I, the requantizing process always uses an odd number of steps to allow a true centre zero step. In long-wordlength codes this is not a problem, but when three, five or nine quantizing intervals are used, binary is inefficient because some combinations are not used. For example, five intervals need a three-bit code having eight combinations leaving three unused. The solution is that when three-, five- or nine-level coding is used in a sub-band, sets of three samples are encoded into a *granule*. Figure 4.34 shows how granules work. Continuing the example of five quantizing intervals, each sample could have five different values,

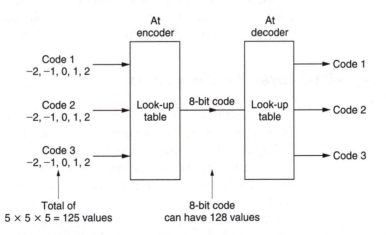

Figure 4.34 Codes having ranges smaller than a power of two are inefficient. Here three codes with a range of five values which would ordinarily need 3 × 3 bits can be carried in a single eight-bit word.

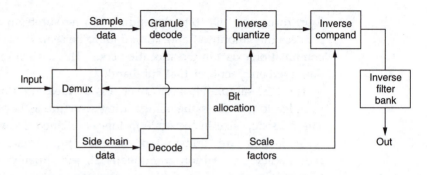

Figure 4.35 A Layer II decoder is slightly more complex than the Layer I decoder because of the need to decode granules and scale factors.

therefore all combinations of three samples could have 125 different values. As 128 values can be sent with a seven-bit code, it will be seen that this is more efficient than coding the samples separately as three five-level codes would need nine bits. The three requantized samples are used to address a look-up table which outputs the granule code. The decoder can establish that granule coding has been used by examining the bit-allocation data.

The requantized samples/granules in each sub-band, bit-allocation data, scale factors and scale factor select codes are multiplexed into the output bitstream.

The Layer II decoder is shown in Figure 4.35. This is not much more complex than the Layer I decoder. The demultiplexing will separate the sample data from the side information. The bit-allocation data will specify the wordlength or granule size used so that the sample block can be deserialized and the granules decoded. The scale factor select information will be used to decode the compressed scale factors to produce one scale factor per block of 384 samples. Inverse quantizing and inverse sub-band filtering takes place as for Layer I.

4.20 MPEG Layer III audio coding

Layer III is the most complex layer, and is only really necessary when the most severe data rate constraints must be met. It is also known as MP3 in its application of music delivery over the Internet. It is a transform code based on the ASPEC system with certain modifications to give a degree of commonality with Layer II. The original ASPEC coder used a direct MDCT on the input samples. In Layer III this was modified to use a hybrid transform incorporating the existing polyphase 32 band QMF of Layers I and II and retaining the block size of 1152 samples. In Layer III, the 32 sub-bands from the QMF are further processed by a critically sampled MDCT.

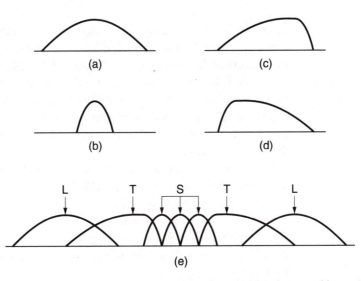

Figure 4.36 The window functions of Layer III coding. At (a) is the normal long window, whereas (b) shows the short window used to handle transients. Switching between window sizes requires transition windows (c) and (d). An example of switching using transition windows is shown in (e).

The windows overlap by two to one. Two window sizes are used to reduce pre-echo on transients. The long window works with 36 sub-band samples corresponding to 24 milliseconds only at 48 kHz and resolves 18 different frequencies, making 576 frequencies altogether. Coding products are spread over this period which is acceptable in stationary material but not in the vicinity of transients. In this case the window length is reduced to 8 ms. Twelve sub-band samples are resolved into six different frequencies making a total of 192 frequencies. This is the Heisenberg inequality: by increasing the time resolution by a factor of three, the frequency resolution has fallen by the same factor.

Figure 4.36 shows the available window types. In addition to the long and short symmetrical windows there is a pair of transition windows, known as start and stop windows, which allow a smooth transition between the two window sizes. In order to use critical sampling, MDCTs must resolve into a set of frequencies which is a multiple of four. Switching between 576 and 192 frequencies allows this criterion to be met. Note that an 8 ms window is still too long to eliminate pre-echo. Pre-echo is eliminated using buffering. The use of a short window minimizes the size of the buffer needed.

Layer III provides a suggested (but not compulsory) pychoacoustic model which is more complex than that suggested for Layers I and II, primarily because of the need for window switching. Pre-echo is associated with the entropy in the audio rising above the average value and this can be used to switch the window size. The perceptive model is used to take advantage of the high-frequency resolution available from the DCT which allows the noise floor to be shaped much more accurately than with the 32 sub-bands of Layers I and II. Although the MDCT has high-frequency resolution, it does not carry the phase of the waveform in an identifiable form and so is not useful for discriminating between tonal and atonal inputs. As a result a side FFT which gives conventional amplitude and phase data is still required to drive the masking model.

Non-uniform quantizing is used, in which the quantizing step size becomes larger as the magnitude of the coefficient increases. The quantized coefficients are then subject to Huffman coding. This is a technique where the most common code values are allocated the shortest wordlength. Layer III also has a certain amount of buffer memory so that pre-echo can be avoided during entropy peaks despite a constant output bit rate.

Figure 4.37 shows a Layer III encoder. The output from the sub-band filter is 32 continuous band-limited sample streams. These are subject to 32 parallel MDCTs. The window size can be switched individually in each sub-band as required by the characteristics of the input audio. The parallel FFT drives the masking model which decides on window sizes as well as producing the masking threshold for the coefficient quantizer. The distortion control loop iterates until the available output data capacity is reached with the most uniform NMR. The available output capacity can vary owing to the presence of the buffer.

Figure 4.38 shows that the buffer occupancy is fed back to the quantizer. During stationary program material, the buffer contents are deliberately run down by slight coarsening of the quantizing. The buffer empties because the output rate is fixed but the input rate has been reduced. When a transient arrives, the large coefficients which result can be handled by filling the buffer, avoiding raising the output bit rate

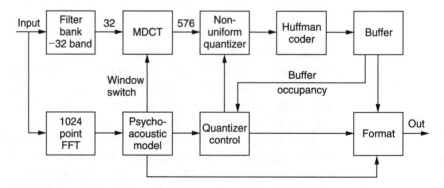

Figure 4.37 The Layer III coder. Note the connection between the buffer and the quantizer which allows different frames to contain different amounts of data.

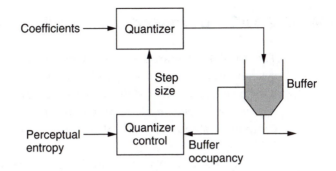

Figure 4.38 The variable rate coding of Layer III. An approaching transient via the perceptual entropy signal causes the coder to quantize more heavily in order to empty the buffer. When the transient arrives, the quantizing can be made more accurate and the increased data can be accepted by the buffer.

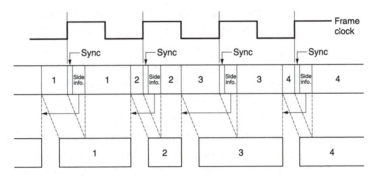

Figure 4.39 In Layer III, the logical frame rate is constant and is transmitted by equally spaced sync patterns. The data blocks do not need to coincide with sync. A pointer after each sync pattern specifies where the data block starts. In this example block 2 is smaller whereas 1 and 3 have enlarged.

whilst also avoiding the pre-echo which would result if the coefficients were heavily quantized.

In order to maintain synchronism between encoder and decoder in the presence of buffering, headers and side information are sent synchronously at frame rate. However, the position of boundaries between the main data blocks which carry the coefficients can vary with respect to the position of the headers in order to allow a variable frame size. Figure 4.39 shows that the frame begins with an unique sync pattern which is followed by the side information. The side information contains a parameter called *main data begin* which specifies where the main data for the present frame began in the transmission. This parameter allows the decoder to find the coefficient block in the decoder buffer. As the frame headers are at fixed locations, the main data blocks may be interrupted by the headers.

4.21　MPEG-2 AAC – advanced audio coding

The MPEG standards system subsequently developed an enhanced system known as advanced audio coding (AAC).[26,27] This was intended to be a standard which delivered the highest possible performance using newly developed tools that could not be used in any backward-compatible standard. AAC also forms the core of the audio coding of MPEG-4.

AAC supports up to 48 audio channels with default support of monophonic, stereo and 5.1 channel (3/2) audio. The AAC concept is based on a number of coding tools known as *modules* which can be combined in different ways to produce bitstreams at three different profiles.

The main profile requires the most complex encoder which makes use of all the coding tools. The low-complexity (LC) profile omits certain tools and restricts the power of others to reduce processing and memory requirements. The remaining tools in LC profile coding are identical to those in main profile such that a main profile decoder can decode LC profile bitstreams. The scaleable sampling rate (SSR) profile splits the input audio into four equal frequency bands each of which results in a self-contained bitstream. A simple decoder can decode only one, two or three of these bitstreams to produce a reduced bandwidth output. Not all the AAC tools are available to SSR profile.

The increased complexity of AAC allows the introduction of loss-less coding tools. These allow a lower bit rate for the same or improved quality at a given bit rate where the reliance on lossy coding is reduced. There is greater attention given to the interplay between time-domain and frequency-domain precision in the human hearing system.

Figure 4.40 shows a block diagram of an AAC main profile encoder. The audio signal path is straight through the centre. The formatter assembles any side chain data along with the coded audio data to produce a compliant bitstream. The input signal passes to the filter bank and the perceptual model in parallel. The filter bank consists of a 50 per cent overlapped critically sampled MDCT which can be switched between block lengths of 2048 and 256 samples. At 48 kHz the filter allows resolutions of 23 Hz and 21 ms or 187 Hz and 2.6 ms. As AAC is a multichannel coding system, block length switching cannot be done indiscriminately as this would result in loss of block phase between channels. Consequently if short blocks are selected, the coder will remain in short block mode for integer multiples of eight blocks. This is shown in Figure 4.41 which also shows the use of transition windows between the block sizes as was done in Layer III.

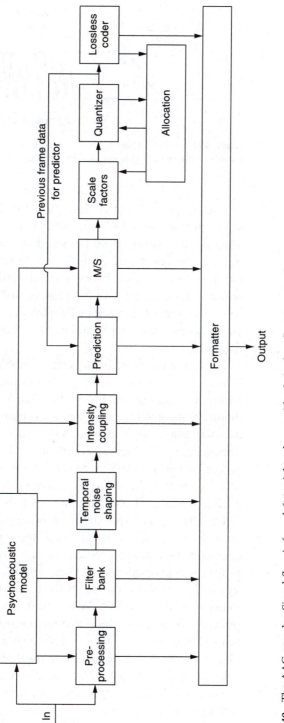

Figure 4.40 The AAC encoder. Signal flow is from left to right whereas side-chain data flow is vertical.

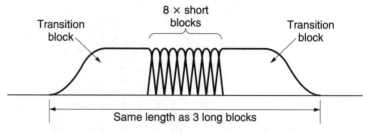

Figure 4.41 In AAC short blocks must be used in multiples of 8 so that the long block phase is undisturbed. This keeps block synchronism in multichannel systems.

The shape of the window function interferes with the frequency selectivity of the MDCT. In AAC it is possible to select either a sine window or a Kaiser–Bessel-derived (KBD) window as a function of the input audio spectrum. As was seen in Chapter 3, filter windows allow different compromises between bandwidth and rate of roll-off. The KBD window rolls off later but is steeper and thus gives better rejection of frequencies more than about 200 Hz apart whereas the sine window rolls off earlier but less steeply and so gives better rejection of frequencies less than 70 Hz.

Following the filter bank is the intra-block predictive coding module. When enabled this module finds redundancy between the coefficients within one transform block. In Chapter 3 the concept of transform duality was introduced, in which a certain characteristic in the frequency domain would be accompanied by a dual characteristic in the time domain and vice versa. Figure 4.42 shows that in the time domain, predictive coding works well on stationary signals but fails on transients. The dual of this characteristic is that in the frequency domain, predictive coding works well on transients but fails on stationary signals.

Equally, a predictive coder working in the time domain produces an error spectrum which is related to the input spectrum. The dual of this characteristic is that a predictive coder working in the frequency domain produces a prediction error which is related to the input time domain signal. This explains the use of the term *temporal noise shaping* (TNS) used in the AAC documents.[28] When used during transients, the TNS module produces distortion which is time-aligned with the input such that pre-echo is avoided. The use of TNS also allows the coder to use longer blocks more of the time. This module is responsible for a significant amount of the increased performance of AAC.

Figure 4.43 shows that the coefficients in the transform block are serialized by a commutator. This can run from the lowest frequency to the highest or in reverse. The prediction method is a conventional forward predictor structure in which the result of filtering a number of earlier coefficients (20 in main profile) is used to predict the current one.

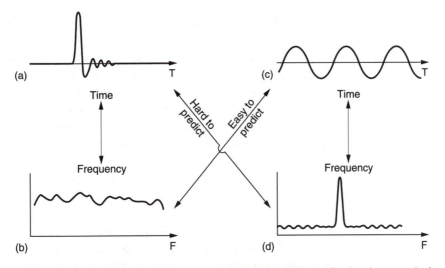

Figure 4.42 Transform duality suggests that predictability will also have a dual characteristic. A time predictor will not anticipate the transient in (a), whereas the broad spectrum of signal (a), shown in (b), will be easy for a predictor advancing down the frequency axis. In contrast, the stationary signal (c) is easy for a time predictor, whereas in the spectrum of (c) shown at (d) the spectral spike will not be predicted.

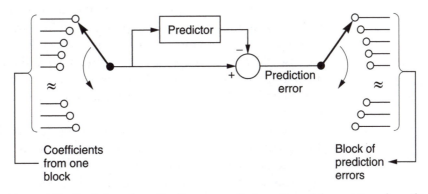

Figure 4.43 Predicting along the frequency axis is performed by running along the coefficients in a block and attempting to predict the value of the current coefficient from the values of some earlier ones. The prediction error is transmitted.

The prediction is subtracted from the actual value to produce a prediction error or residual which is transmitted. At the decoder, an identical predictor produces the same prediction from earlier coefficient values and the error in this is cancelled by adding the residual.

Following the intra-block prediction, an optional module known as the intensity/coupling stage is found. This is used for very low bit rates where spatial information in stereo and surround formats are discarded to keep down the level of distortion. Effectively over at least part of the spectrum a mono signal is transmitted along with amplitude codes which allow the signal to be panned in the spatial domain at the decoder.

The next stage is the inter-block prediction module. Whereas the intra-block predictor is most useful on transients, the inter-block predictor module explores the redundancy between successive blocks on stationary signals.[29] This prediction only operates on coefficients below 16 kHz. For each DCT coefficient in a given block, the predictor uses the quantized coefficients from the same locations in two previous blocks to estimate the present value. As before the prediction is subtracted to produce a residual which is transmitted. Note that the use of quantized coefficients to drive the predictor is necessary because this is what the decoder will have to do. The predictor is adaptive and calculates its own coefficients from the signal history. The decoder uses the same algorithm so that the two predictors always track. The predictors run all the time whether prediction is enabled or not in order to keep the prediction coefficients adapted to the signal.

Audio coefficients are associated into sets known as *scale factor bands* for later companding. Within each scale factor band inter-block prediction can be turned on or off depending on whether a coding gain results.

Protracted use of prediction makes the decoder prone to bit errors and drift and removes decoding entry points from the bitstream. Consequently the prediction process is reset cyclically. The predictors are assembled into groups of 30 and after a certain number of frames a different group is reset until all have been reset. Predictor reset codes are transmitted in the side data. Reset will also occur if short frames are selected.

In stereo and 3/2 surround formats there is less redundancy because the signals also carry spatial information. The effecting of masking may be up to 20 dB less when distortion products are at a different location in the stereo image from the masking sounds. As a result, stereo signals require much higher bit rate than two mono channels, particularly on transient material which is rich in spatial clues.

In some cases a better result can be obtained by converting the signal to a mid-side (M/S) or sum/difference format before quantizing. In surround sound the M/S coding can be applied to the front L/R pair and the rear L/R pair of signals.

The M/S format can be selected on a block-by-block basis for each scale factor band.

Next comes the lossy stage of the coder where distortion is selectively introduced as a function of frequency as determined by the masking threshold. This is done by a combination of amplification and requantizing. As mentioned, coefficients (or residuals) are grouped into scale factor bands. As Figure 4.44 shows, the number of coefficients

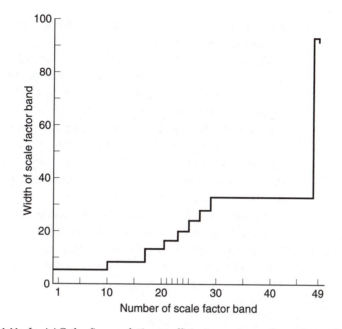

Figure 4.44 In AAC the fine-resolution coefficients are grouped together to form scale factor bands. The size of these varies to loosely mimic the width of critical bands.

varies in order to divide the coefficients into approximate critical bands. Within each scale factor band, all coefficients will be multiplied by the same scale factor prior to requantizing.

Coefficients which have been multiplied by a large scale factor will suffer less distortion by the requantizer whereas those which have been multiplied by a small scale factor will have more distortion. Using scale factors, the psychoacoustic model can shape the distortion as a function of frequency so that it remains masked. The scale factors allow gain control in 1.5 dB steps over a dynamic range equivalent to twenty-four-bit PCM and are transmitted as part of the side data so that the decoder can re-create the correct magnitudes. The scale factors are differentially coded with respect to the first one in the block and the differences are then Huffman coded.

The requantizer uses non-uniform steps which give better coding gain and has a range of ±8191. The global step size (which applies to all scale factor bands) can be adjusted in 1.5 dB steps. Following requantizing the coefficients are Huffman coded.

There are many ways in which the coder can be controlled and any which results in a compliant bitstream is acceptable although the highest performance may not be reached. The requantizing and scale factor stages will need to be controlled in order to make best use of the available bit rate and the buffering. This is non-trivial because the use of Huffman coding after the requantizer makes it impossible to predict the exact amount of data which will result from a given step size. This means that the process must iterate.

Whatever bit rate is selected, a good encoder will produce consistent quality by selecting window sizes, intra- or inter-frame prediction and using the buffer to handle entropy peaks. This suggests a connection between buffer occupancy and the control system. The psychoacoustic model will analyse the incoming audio entropy and during periods of average entropy it will empty the buffer by slightly raising the quantizer step size so that the bit rate entering the buffer falls. By running the buffer down, the coder can temporarily support a higher bit rate to handle transients or difficult material.

Simply stated, the scale factor process is controlled so that the distortion spectrum has the same shape as the masking threshold and the quantizing step size is controlled to make the level of the distortion spectrum as low as possible within the allowed bit rate. If the bit rate allowed is high enough, the distortion products will be masked.

4.22   Dolby AC-3

Dolby AC-3[18] is in fact a family of transform coders based on time-domain aliasing cancellation (TDAC) which allows various compromises between coding delay and bit rate to be used. In the modified discrete cosine transform (MDCT), windows with 50 per cent overlap are used. Thus twice as many coefficients as necessary are produced. These are sub-sampled by a factor of two to give a critically sampled transform, which results in potential aliasing in the frequency domain. However, by making a slight change to the transform, the alias products in the second half of a given window are equal in size but of opposite polarity to the alias products in the first half of the next window, and so will be cancelled on reconstruction. This is the principle of TDAC.

Figure 4.45 shows the generic block diagram of the AC-3 coder. Input audio is divided into 50 per cent overlapped blocks of 512 samples. These are subject to a TDAC transform which uses alternate modified sine and cosine transforms. The transforms produce 512 coefficients per block, but these are redundant and after the redundancy has been removed there are 256 coefficients per block. The input waveform is constantly analysed for the presence of transients and if these are present the block length will be halved to prevent pre-noise. This halves the frequency resolution but doubles the temporal resolution.

The coefficients have high-frequency resolution and are selectively combined in sub-bands which approximate the critical bands.

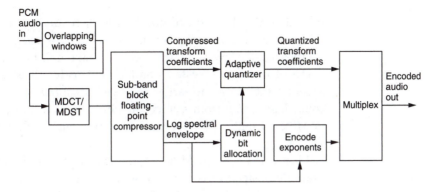

Figure 4.45 Block diagram of the Dolby AC-3 coder. See text for details. The exponents are then used to return the coefficients to fixed-point notation. Inverse transforms are then computed, followed by a weighted overlapping of the windows to obtain PCM data.

Coefficients in each sub-band are normalized and expressed in floating-point block notation with common exponent. The exponents in fact represent the logarithmic spectral envelope of the signal and can be used to drive the perceptive model which operates the bit allocation. The mantissae of the transform coefficients are then requantized according to the bit allocation.

The output bitstream consists of the requantized coefficients and the log spectral envelope in the shape of the exponents. There is a great deal of redundancy in the exponents. In any block, only the first exponent, corresponding to the lowest frequency, is transmitted absolutely. Remaining coefficients are transmitted differentially. Where the input has a smooth spectrum the exponents in several bands will be the same and the differences will then be zero. In this case exponents can be grouped using flags.

Further use is made of temporal redundancy. An AC-3 sync frame contains six blocks. The first block of the frame contains absolute exponent data, but where stationary audio is encountered, successive blocks in the frame can use the same exponents.

The receiver uses the log spectral envelope to deserialize the mantissae of the coefficients into the correct wordlengths. The highly redundant exponents are decoded starting with the lowest frequency coefficient in the first block of the frame and adding differences to create the remainder.

4.23   MPEG-4 audio

The audio coding options of MPEG-4 parallel the video coding in complexity. In the same way that the video coding in MPEG-4 has moved in the direction of graphics with rendering taking place in the decoder, MPEG-4 audio introduces *structured audio* in which audio synthesis takes place in the decoder, taking MPEG-4 audio into the realm of interactive systems and virtual reality. It is now necessary to describe the audio of earlier formats as *natural sound*, i.e. that which could have come from a microphone. Natural sound is well supported in MPEG-4 with a development of AAC which is described in the next section.

Like video coding, MPEG-4 audio coding may be object based. For example, instead of coding the waveforms of a stereo mix, each sound source in the mix may become a sound object which is individually coded. At the decoder each sound object is then supplied to the composition stage where it will be panned and mixed with other objects. At the moment techniques do not exist to create audio objects from a natural stereo signal pair, but where the audio source is a synthetic, or a mixdown of multiple natural tracks, object coding can be used with a saving in data rate.

It is also possible to define virtual instruments at the decoder and then to make each of these play by transmitting a score.

Speech coding is also well supported. Natural speech may be coded at very low bit rates where the goal is intelligibility of the message rather than fidelity. This can be done with one of two tools: HVXC (Harmonic Vector eXcitation Coding) or CELP (Code Excited Linear Prediction). Synthetic speech capability allows applications such as text-to-speech (TTS). MPEG-4 has standardized transmission of speech information in IPA (International Phonetic Alphabet) or as text.

4.24 MPEG-4 AAC

The MPEG-2 AAC coding tools described in section 4.21 are extended in MPEG-4. The additions are perceptual noise substitution (PNS) and vector quantization. All coding schemes find noise difficult because it contains no redundancy. Real audio program material may contain a certain proportion of noise from time to time, traditionally requiring a high bit rate to transmit without artifacts.

However, experiments have shown that under certain conditions, the listener is unable to distinguish between the original noise-like waveform and noise locally generated in the decoder. This is the basis for PNS. Instead of attempting to code a difficult noise sequence, the PNS process will transmit the amplitude of the noise which the decoder will then create.

At the encoder, PNS will be selected if, over a certain range of frequencies, there is no dominant tone and the time-domain waveform remains stable, i.e. there are no transients. On a scale factor band and group basis the Huffman-coded symbols describing the frequency coefficients will be replaced by the PNS flag. At the decoder the missing coefficients will be derived from random vectors. The amplitude of the noise is encoded in 1.5 dB steps with noise energy parameters for each group and scale factor band.

In stereo applications, where PNS is used at the same time and frequency in both channels, the random processes in each channel will be different in order to avoid creating a mid-stage noise object. PNS cannot be used with M/S audio coding.

In MPEG-2 AAC, the frequency coefficients (or their residuals) are quantized according to the adaptive bit-allocation system and then Huffman coded. At low bit rates the heavy requantizing necessary will result in some coefficients being in error. At bit rates below 16 kbits/s/channel an alternative coding scheme known as TwinVQ (Transform Domain Weighted Interleaved Vector Quantization) may be used. Vector quantization, also known as block quantization,[30] works on blocks of coefficients rather than the individual coefficients used by the Huffman code. In vector quantizing, one transmitted symbol represents the state of a number of coefficients. In a lossless system, this symbol would need as many bits as the sum of the coefficients to be coded. In practice the symbol has fewer bits because the coefficients are quantized (and thereby contain errors). The encoder will select a symbol which minimizes the errors over the whole block.

Error minimization is assisted by interleaving at the encoder. After interleaving, adjacent coefficients in frequency space are in different blocks. After the symbol look-up process in the decoder, de-interleaving is necessary to return the coefficients to their correct frequencies. In TwinVQ the transmitted symbols have constant wordlength because the vector table has a fixed size for a given bit rate. Constant size symbols have an advantage in the presence of bit errors because it is easier to maintain synchronization.

4.25 Compression in stereo and surround sound

Once hardware became economic, the move to digital audio was extremely rapid. One of these reasons was the sheer sound quality available. When well engineered, the PCM digital domain does so little damage to the sound quality that the problems of the remaining analog parts usually dominate. The one serious exception to this is lossy compression which does not preserve the original waveform and must therefore be carefully assessed before being used in high-quality applications.

In a monophonic system, all the sound is emitted from a single point and psychoacoustic masking operates to its fullest extent. Audio compression techniques of the kind described above work well in mono. However, in stereophonic (which in this context also includes surround sound) applications different criteria apply. In addition to the timbral information describing the nature of the sound sources, stereophonic systems also contain spatial information describing their location.

The greatest cause for concern is that in stereophonic systems, masking is not as effective. When two sound sources are in physically different locations, the degree of masking is not as great as when they are co-sited. Unfortunately all the psychoacoustic masking models used in today's compressors assume co-siting. When used in stereo or surround systems, the artifacts of the compression process can be revealed. This was first pointed out by the late Michael Gerzon who introduced the term *unmasking* to describe the phenomenon.

The hearing mechanism has an ability to concentrate on one of many simultaneous sound sources based on direction. The brain appears to be able to insert a controllable time delay in the nerve signals from one ear with respect to the other so that when sound arrives from a given direction the nerve signals from both ears are coherent causing the binaural threshold of hearing to be 3–6 dB better than monaural at around 4 kHz. Sounds arriving from other directions are incoherent and are heard less well. This is known as *attentional selectivity*, or more colloquially as the *cocktail party effect*.[31]

Human hearing can locate a number of different sound sources simultaneously by constantly comparing excitation patterns from the two ears with different delays. Strong correlation will be found where the delay corresponds to the interaural delay for a given source. This delay varying mechanism will take time and the ear is slow to react to changes in source direction. Oscillating sources can only be tracked up to 2–3 Hz and the ability to locate bursts of noise improves with burst duration up to about 700 milliseconds.

Monophonic systems prevent the use of either of these effects completely because the first version of all sounds reaching the listener come from the same loudspeaker. Stereophonic systems allow attentional selectivity to function in that the listener can concentrate on specific sound sources in a reproduced stereophonic image with the same facility as in the original sound. When two sound sources are spatially separated, if the listener uses attentional selectivity to concentrate on one of them, the contributions from both ears will correlate. This means that the contributions from the other sound will be decorrelated, reducing its masking ability significantly. Experiments showed long ago that even technically poor stereo was always preferred to pristine mono. This is because we are accustomed to sounds and reverberation coming from all different directions in real life and having them all superimposed in a mono speaker convinces no one, however accurate the waveform.

We live in a reverberant world which is filled with sound reflections. If we could separately distinguish every different reflection in a reverberant room we would hear a confusing cacophony. In practice we hear very well in reverberant surroundings, far better than microphones can, because of the transform nature of the ear and the way in which the brain processes nerve signals. Because the ear has finite frequency discrimination ability in the form of critical bands, it must also have finite temporal discrimination. When two or more versions of a sound arrive at the ear, provided they fall within a time span of about 30 ms, they will not be treated as separate sounds, but will be fused into one sound. Only when the time separation reaches 50–60 ms do the delayed sounds appear as echoes from different directions. As we have evolved to function in reverberant surroundings, most reflections do not impair our ability to locate the source of a sound.

Clearly the first version of a transient sound to reach the ears must be the one which has travelled by the shortest path and this must be the direct sound rather than a reflection. Consequently the ear has evolved to attribute source direction from the time of arrival difference at the two ears of the first version of a transient. This phenomenon is known as the precedence effect. Intensity stereo, the type of signal format obtained with coincident microphones or panpots, works purely by amplitude differences at the two loudspeakers. The two signals should be exactly in phase. As both ears hear both speakers the result is that the space between the speakers and the ears turns the intensity differences into time of arrival differences. These give the illusion of virtual sound sources.

A virtual sound source from a panpot has zero width and on ideal loudspeakers would appear as a virtual point source. Figure 4.46(a) shows how a panpotted dry mix should appear spatially on ideal speakers whereas (b) shows what happens when artificial stereo reverb is added. Figure 4.46(b) is also what is obtained with real sources using a coincident pair of high-quality mikes. In this case the sources are the real sources and the sound between is reverb/ ambience.

When listening on high-quality loudspeakers, audio compressors change the characteristic of Figure 4.46(b) to that shown in (c). Even at high bit rates, corresponding to the smallest amount of compression, there is an audible difference between the original and the compressed result. The dominant sound sources are reproduced fairly accurately,

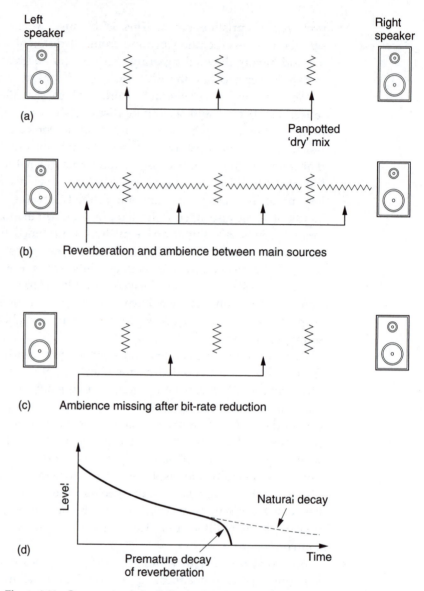

Figure 4.46 Compression is less effective in stereo. In (a) is shown the spatial result of a 'dry' panpotted mix. (b) shows the result after artificial reverberation which can also be obtained in an acoustic recording with coincident mikes. After compression (c) the ambience and reverberation may be reduced or absent. (d) Reverberation may also decay prematurely.

but what is most striking is that the ambience and reverb between is dramatically reduced or absent, making the decoded sound much drier than the original. It will also be found that the rate of decay of reverberation is accelerated as shown in (d).

These effects are heard because the reverberation exists at a relatively low level. The coder will assume that it is inaudible due to masking and remove or attenuate it. The effect is apparent to the same extent with both MPEG Layer II and Dolby AC-3 coders even though their internal workings are quite different. This is not surprising because both are probably based on the same psychoacoustic masking model.

MPEG Layer III fares quite badly in stereo because the bit rate is lower. Transient material has a peculiar effect whereby the ambience would come and go according to the entropy of the dominant source. A percussive note would narrow the sound stage and appear dry but afterwards the reverb level would come back up.

The effects are not subtle and do not require 'golden ears' or special source material. The author has successfully demonstrated these effects under conference conditions.

All these effects disappear when the signals to the speakers are added to make mono as this prevents attentional selectivity and unmasking cannot occur. The above compression artifacts are less obvious or even absent when poor-quality loudspeakers are used. Loudspeakers are part of the communication channel and have an information capacity, both timbral and spatial. If the quality of the loudspeaker is poor, it may remove more information from the signal than the preceding compressor and coding artifacts will not be revealed. The precedence effect allows the listener to locate the source of a sound by concentrating on the first version of the sound and rejecting later versions. Versions which may arrive from elsewhere simply add to the perceived loudness but do not change the perceived location of the source. The precedence effect can only reject reverberant sounds which arrive after the inter-aural delay. When reflections arrive within the inter-aural delay of about 700 μs the precedence effect breaks down and the perceived direction can be pulled away from that of the first arriving source by an increase in level. Figure 4.47 shows that this area is known as the time–intensity trading region. Once the maximum inter-aural delay is exceeded, the hearing mechanism knows that the time difference must be due to reverberation and the trading ceases to change with level.

Unfortunately reflections with delays of the order of 700 μs are exactly what are provided by the traditional rectangular loudspeaker with flat sides and sharp corners. The discontinuities between the panels cause impedance changes which act as acoustic reflectors. The loudspeaker becomes a multiple source producing an array of signals within the time intensity trading region and instead of acting as a point source the loudspeaker becomes a distributed source.

Figure 4.48 shows that when a loudspeaker is a distributed source, it cannot create a point image. Instead the image is also distributed, an effect known as smear. Note that the point sources have spread so that there are almost no gaps between them, effectively masking the

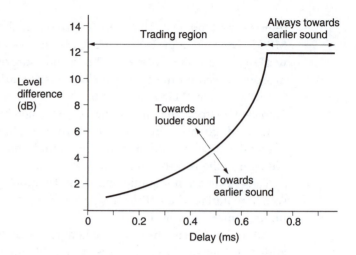

Figure 4.47 Time–intensity trading occurs within the inter-aural delay period.

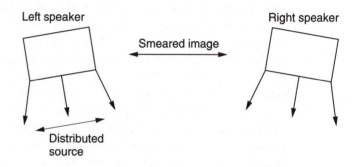

Figure 4.48 A loudspeaker which is a distributed source cannot produce a point stereo image; only a spatially spread or smeared image.

ambience. If a compressor removes it the effect cannot be heard. It may erroneously be assumed that the compressor is transparent when in fact it is not.

For the above reasons, the conclusions of many of the listening tests carried out on audio compressors are simply invalid. The author has read descriptions of many such tests, and in almost all cases little is said about the loudspeakers used or about what steps were taken to measure their spatial accuracy. This is simply unscientific and has led to the use of compression being more widespread than is appropriate.

A type of flat panel loudspeaker which uses chaotic bending modes of the diaphragm has recently been introduced. It should be noted that these speakers are distributed sources and so are quite unsuitable for assessing compression quality.

Whilst compression may be adequate to deliver post-produced audio to a consumer with mediocre loudspeakers, these results underline that it

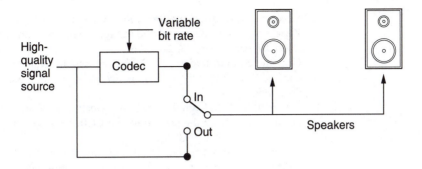

Figure 4.49 Using compression to test loudspeakers. The better the loudspeaker, the less compression can be used before it becomes audible.

has no place in a high-quality production environment. When assessing codecs, loudspeakers having poor diffraction design will conceal artifacts. When mixing for a compressed delivery system, it will be necessary to include the codec in the monitor feeds so that the results can be compensated. Where high-quality stereo is required, either full bit rate PCM or lossless (packing) techniques must be used.

An interesting corollary of the above is that compressors can be used to test stereo loudspeakers. The arrangement of Figure 4.49 is used. Starting with the highest bit rate possible, the speakers are switched between the source material and the output of the codec. The compression factor is increased until the effects noted above are heard. When the effects are just audible, the bit rate of the compressor is at the information capacity of the loudspeakers. Domestic bookshelf loudspeakers measure approximately 100 kbits/s. Traditional square box hi-fi speakers measure around 200 kbits/s but a pair of state-of-the-art speakers will go above 500 kbits/s.

References

1. Johnston, J.D., Transform coding of audio signals using perceptual noise criteria. *IEEE J. Selected Areas in Comms.*, **JSAC-6**, 314–323 (1988)
2. Martin, W.H., Decibel – the new name for the transmission unit. *Bell System Tech. J.* (Jan. 1929)
3. Moore, B.C., *An Introduction to the Psychology of Hearing*, section 6.12. London: Academic Press (1989)
4. Muraoka, T., Iwahara, M. and Yamada, Y., Examination of audio bandwidth requirements for optimum sound signal transmission. *J. Audio Eng. Soc.*, **29**, 2–9 (1982)
5. Muraoka, T., Yamada, Y. and Yamazaki, M., Sampling frequency considerations in digital audio. *J. Audio Eng. Soc.*, **26**, 252–256 (1978)
6. Fincham, L.R., The subjective importance of uniform group delay at low frequencies. Presented at the 74th Audio Engineering Society Convention (New York, 1983), Preprint 2056(H-1)

7. Fletcher, H., Auditory patterns. *Rev. Modern Physics*, **12**, 47–65 (1940)

8. Zwicker, E., Subdivision of the audible frequency range into critical bands. *J. Acoust. Soc. Amer.*, **33**, 248 (1961)

9. Grewin, C. and Ryden, T., Subjective assessments on low bit-rate audio codecs. *Proc. 10th. Int. Audio Eng. Soc. Conf.*, 91–102, New York: Audio Eng. Soc. (1991)

10. Gilchrist, N.H.C., Digital sound: the selection of critical programme material and preparation of the recordings for CCIR tests on low bit rate codecs. *BBC Res. Dept. Rep.* RD 1993/1

11. Colomes, C. and Faucon, G., A perceptual objective measurement system (POM) for the quality assessment of perceptual codecs. Presented at 96th Audio Eng. Soc. Conv. Amsterdam (1994), Preprint No. 3801 (P4.2)

12. Johnston, J., Estimation of perceptual entropy using noise masking criteria. *Proc. ICASSP*, 2524–2527 (1988)

13. Gilchrist, N.H.C., Delay in broadcasting operations. Presented at 90th Audio Eng. Soc. Conv. (1991), Preprint 3033

14. Caine, C.R., English, A.R. and O'Clarey, J.W.H., NICAM-3: near-instantaneous companded digital transmission for high-quality sound programmes. *J. IERE*, **50**, 519–530 (1980)

15. Davidson, G.A. and Bosi, M., AC-2: high quality audio coding for broadcast and storage. *Proc. 46th Ann. Broadcast Eng. Conf.*, Las Vegas, 98–105 (1992)

16. Crochiere, R.E., Sub-band coding. *Bell System Tech. J.*, **60**, 1633–1653 (1981)

17. Princen, J.P., Johnson, A. and Bradley, A.B., Sub-band/transform coding using filter bank designs based on time domain aliasing cancellation. *Proc. ICASSP*, 2161–2164 (1987)

18. Davis, M.F., The AC-3 multichannel coder. Presented at 95th AES Conv., Preprint 2774.

19. Wiese, D., MUSICAM: flexible bitrate reduction standard for high quality audio. Presented at Digital Audio Broadcasting Conference (London, March 1992)

20. Brandenburg, K., ASPEC coding. *Proc. 10th. Audio Eng. Soc. Int. Conf.*, 81–90, New York: Audio Eng. Soc. (1991)

21. ISO/IEC JTC1/SC2/WG11 N0030: MPEG/AUDIO test report. Stockholm (1990)

22. ISO/IEC JTC1/SC2/WG11 MPEG 91/010 The SR report on: The MPEG/AUDIO subjective listening test. Stockholm (1991)

23. ISO/IEC JTC1/SC29/WG11 MPEG, International standard ISO 11172–3 Coding of moving pictures and associated audio for digital storage media up to 1.5 Mbits/s, Part 3: Audio (1992)

24. Brandenburg, K. and Stoll, G., ISO-MPEG-1 Audio: a generic standard for coding of high quality audio. *JAES*, **42**, 780–792 (1994)

25. Bonicel, P. *et al.*, A real time ISO/MPEG2 Multichannel decoder. Presented at 96th Audio Eng. Soc. Conv. (1994), Preprint No. 3798 (P3.7)4.30

26. ISO/IEC 13818-7, Information Technology – Generic coding of moving pictures and associated audio, Part 7: Advanced audio coding (1997)

27. Bosi, M. *et al.*, ISO/IEC MPEG-2 Advanced Audio Coding. *JAES*, **45**, 789–814 (1997)

28. Herre, J. and Johnston, J.D., Enhancing the performance of perceptual audio coders by using temporal noise shaping (TNS). Presented at 101st AES Conv., Preprint 4384 (1996)

29. Fuchs, H., Improving MPEG audio coding by backward adaptive linear stereo prediction. Presented at 99th AES Conv., Preprint 4086 (1995)
30. Gersho, A., Asymptotically optimal block quantization. *IEEE Trans. Info. Theory,* **IT-25**, No. 4, 373–380 (1979)
31. Cao, Y., Sridharan, S. and Moody, M., Co-talker separation using the cocktail party effect. *J. Audio Eng. Soc.,* **44**, No. 12, 1084–1096 (1996)

5

MPEG video compression

In this chapter the principles of video compression are explored, leading to descriptions of MPEG-1, MPEG-2 MPEG-4. MPEG-4 Part 10, also known as H.264 or AVC, is also covered, and for simplicity it will be referred to throughout as AVC.

MPEG-1 supports only progressively scanned images, whereas MPEG-2 and MPEG-4 support both progressive and interlaced scan. MPEG uses the term 'picture' to mean a full-screen image of any kind at one point on the time axis. This could be a field or a frame in interlaced systems but only a frame in non-interlaced systems. The terms field and frame will be used only when the distinction is important. MPEG-4 introduces object coding that can handle entities that may not fill the screen. In MPEG-4 the picture becomes a plane in which one or more video objects can be displayed, hence the term video object plane (VOP).

5.1   The eye

All imaging signals ultimately excite some response in the eye and the viewer can only describe the result subjectively. Familiarity with the functioning and limitations of the eye is essential to an understanding of image compression. The simple representation of Figure 5.1 shows that the eyeball is nearly spherical and is swivelled by muscles. The space between the cornea and the lens is filled with transparent fluid known as *aqueous humour*. The remainder of the eyeball is filled with a transparent jelly known as *vitreous humour*. Light enters the cornea, and the amount of light admitted is controlled by the pupil in the iris. Light entering is involuntarily focused on the retina by the lens in a process called *visual accommodation*. The lens is the only part of the eye which is not nourished by the bloodstream and its centre is technically dead. In a young person

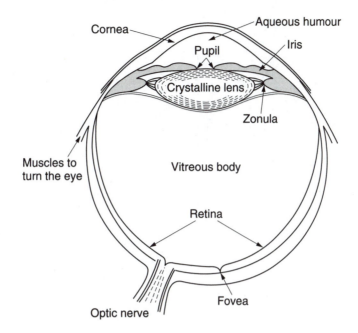

Figure 5.1 The eyeball is in effect a living camera except for the lens that receives no blood supply and is technically dead.

the lens is flexible and muscles distort it to perform the focusing action. In old age the lens loses some flexibility and causes *presbyopia* or limited accommodation. In some people the length of the eyeball is incorrect resulting in *myopia* (short-sightedness) or *hypermetropia* (long-sightedness). The cornea should have the same curvature in all meridia, and if this is not the case, *astigmatism* results.

The retina is responsible for light sensing and contains a number of layers. The surface of the retina is covered with arteries, veins and nerve fibres and light has to penetrate these in order to reach the sensitive layer. This contains two types of discrete receptors known as *rods* and *cones* from their shape. The distribution and characteristics of these two receptors are quite different. Rods dominate the periphery of the retina whereas cones dominate a central area known as the *fovea* outside which their density drops off. Vision using the rods is monochromatic and has poor resolution but remains effective at very low light levels, whereas the cones provide high resolution and colour vision but require more light. Figure 5.2 shows how the sensitivity of the retina slowly increases in response to entering darkness. The first part of the curve is the adaptation of the cone or *photopic* vision. This is followed by the greater adaptation of the rods in *scotopic* vision. At such low light levels the fovea is essentially blind and small objects which can be seen in the peripheral rod vision disappear when stared at.

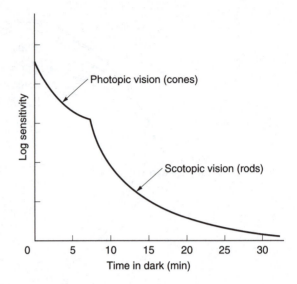

Figure 5.2 Vision adapts to darkness in two stages known as photopic and scotopic vision.

The cones in the fovea are densely packed and directly connected to the nervous system allowing the highest resolution. Resolution then falls off away from the fovea. As a result the eye must move to scan large areas of detail. The image perceived is not just a function of the retinal response, but is also affected by processing of the nerve signals. The overall acuity of the eye can be displayed as a graph of the response plotted against the degree of detail being viewed. Detail is generally measured in lines per millimetre or cycles per picture height, but this takes no account of the distance from the eye. A better unit for eye resolution is one based upon the subtended angle of detail as this will be independent of distance. Units of cycles per degree are then appropriate. Figure 5.3 shows the response of the eye to static detail. Note that the response to very low frequencies is also attenuated. An extension of this characteristic allows the vision system to ignore the fixed pattern of shadow on the retina due to the nerves and arteries.

The retina does not respond instantly to light, but requires between 0.15 and 0.3 second before the brain perceives an image. The resolution of the eye is primarily a spatio-temporal compromise. The eye is a spatial sampling device; the spacing of the rods and cones on the retina represents a spatial sampling frequency.

The measured acuity of the eye exceeds the value calculated from the sample site spacing because a form of oversampling is used. The eye is in a continuous state of subconscious vibration called saccadic motion. This causes the sampling sites to exist in more than one location, effectively increasing the spatial sampling rate provided there is a temporal filter which is able to integrate the information from the various different positions of the retina. This temporal filtering is responsible for 'persistence of vision'. Flashing lights are perceived to flicker only until the critical flicker frequency (CFF) is reached; the light appears continuous for higher frequencies. The CFF is not constant but changes with brightness (see Figure 5.4). Note that the field rate of European television at 50 fields per second is marginal with bright images.

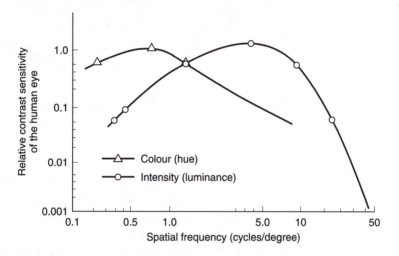

Figure 5.3 The response of the eye to static detail falls off at both low and high spatial frequencies.

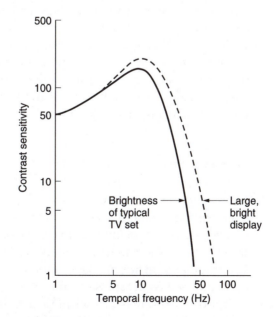

Figure 5.4 The critical flicker frequency is not constant but rises as brightness increases.

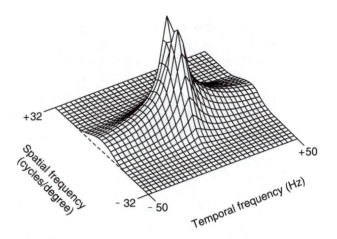

Figure 5.5 The response of the eye shown with respect to temporal and spatial frequencies. Note that even slow relative movement causes a serious loss of resolution. The eye tracks moving objects to prevent this loss.

Figure 5.5 shows the two-dimensional or spatio-temporal response of the eye. If the eye were static, a detailed object moving past it would give rise to temporal frequencies, as Figure 5.6(a) shows. The temporal frequency is given by the detail in the object, in lines per millimetre, multiplied by the speed. Clearly a highly detailed object can reach high temporal frequencies even at slow speeds, yet Figure 5.5 shows that the eye cannot respond to high temporal frequencies.

However, the human viewer has an interactive visual system which causes the eyes to track the movement of any object of interest. Figure 5.6(b) shows that when eye tracking is considered, a moving object is rendered stationary with respect to the retina so that temporal frequencies fall to zero and much the same acuity to detail is available despite motion. This is known as dynamic resolution and it describes how humans judge the detail in real moving pictures.

5.2   Dynamic resolution

As the eye uses involuntary tracking at all times, the criterion for measuring the definition of moving-image portrayal systems has to be *dynamic resolution*, defined as the apparent resolution perceived by the viewer in an object moving within the limits of accurate eye tracking. The traditional metric of static resolution in film and television has to be abandoned as unrepresentative of the subjective results.

Figure 5.7(a) shows that when the moving eye tracks an object on the screen, the viewer is watching with respect to the optic flow axis, not the

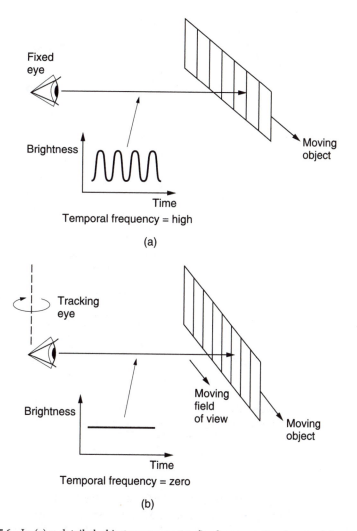

Figure 5.6 In (a) a detailed object moves past a fixed eye, causing temporal frequencies beyond the response of the eye. This is the cause of motion blur. In (b) the eye tracks the motion and the temporal frequency becomes zero. Motion blur cannot then occur.

time axis, and these are not parallel when there is motion. The optic flow axis is defined as an imaginary axis in the spatio-temporal volume which joins the same points on objects in successive frames. Clearly when many objects move independently there will be one optic flow axis for each.

The optic flow axis is identified by motion-compensated standards convertors to eliminate judder and also by MPEG compressors because the greatest similarity from one picture to the next is along that axis. The success of these devices is testimony to the importance of the theory.

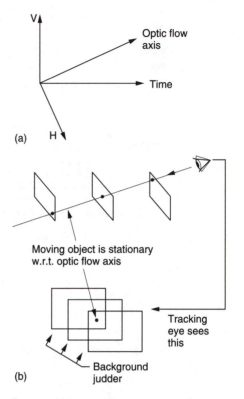

Figure 5.7 The optic flow axis (a) joins points on a moving object in successive pictures. (b) When a tracking eye follows a moving object on a screen, that screen will be seen in a different place at each picture. This is the origin of background strobing.

According to sampling theory, a sampling system cannot properly convey frequencies beyond half the sampling rate. If the sampling rate is considered to be the picture rate, then no temporal frequency of more than 25 or 30 Hz can be handled (12 Hz for film). With a stationary camera and scene, temporal frequencies can only result from the brightness of lighting changing, but this will not approach the limit. However, when there is relative movement between camera and scene, detailed areas develop high temporal frequencies, just as was shown in Figure 5.6(a) for the eye. This is because relative motion results in a given point on the camera sensor effectively scanning across the scene. The temporal frequencies generated are beyond the limit set by sampling theory, and aliasing should take place.

However, when the resultant pictures are viewed by a human eye, this aliasing is not perceived because, once more, the eye tracks the motion of the scene.[1]

Figure 5.8 shows what happens when the eye follows correctly. Although the camera sensor and display are both moving through the

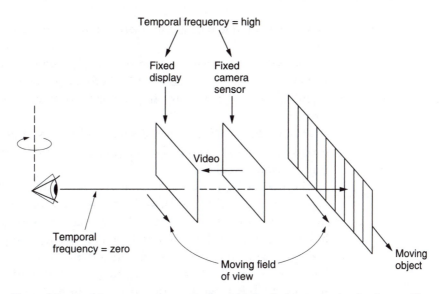

Figure 5.8 An object moves past a camera, and is tracked on a monitor by the eye. The high temporal frequencies cause aliasing in the TV signal, but these are not perceived by the tracking eye as this reduces the temporal frequency to zero.

field of view, the original scene and the retina are now stationary with respect to one another. As a result the temporal frequency at the eye due to the object being followed is brought to zero and no aliasing is perceived by the viewer due to sampling in the image-portrayal system.

Whilst this result is highly desirable, it does not circumvent sampling theory because the effect only works if several assumptions are made, including the requirement for the motion to be smooth.

Figure 5.7(b) shows that when the eye is tracking, successive pictures appear in different places with respect to the retina. In other words if an object is moving down the screen and followed by the eye, the raster is actually moving up with respect to the retina. Although the tracked object is stationary with respect to the retina and temporal frequencies are zero, the object is moving with respect to the sensor and the display and in those units high temporal frequencies will exist. If the motion of the object on the sensor is not correctly portrayed, dynamic resolution will suffer. Dynamic resolution analysis confirms that both interlaced television and conventionally projected cinema film are both seriously sub-optimal. In contrast, progressively scanned television systems have no such defects.

In real-life eye tracking, the motion of the background will be smooth, but in an image-portrayal system based on periodic presentation of frames, the background will be presented to the retina in a different position in each frame. The retina separately perceives each impression of the background leading to an effect called *background strobing*.

The criterion for the selection of a display frame rate in an imaging system is sufficient reduction of background strobing. It is a complete myth that the display rate simply needs to exceed the critical flicker frequency.

Manufacturers of graphics displays which use frame rates well in excess of those used in film and television are doing so for a valid reason: it gives better results!

The traditional reason against high picture rates is that they require excessive bandwidth. In PCM form this may be true, but there are major exceptions. First, in the MPEG domain, it is the information that has to be sent, not the individual picture. Raising the picture rate does not raise the MPEG bit rate in proportion. This is because pictures which are closer together in time have more redundancy and smaller motion distances. Second, the display rate and the transmission rate need not be the same in an advanced system. Motion-compensated up-conversion at the display can correctly render the background at intermediate positions to those transmitted.

5.3 Contrast

The contrast sensitivity of the eye is defined as the smallest brightness difference which is visible. In fact the contrast sensitivity is not constant, but increases proportionally to brightness. Thus whatever the brightness of an object, if that brightness changes by about 1 per cent it will be equally detectable.

The true brightness of a television picture can be affected by electrical noise on the video signal. As contrast sensitivity is proportional to brightness, noise is more visible in dark picture areas than in bright areas. In practice the gamma characteristic of the CRT is put to good use in making video noise less visible. Instead of having linear video signals which are subjected to an inverse gamma function immediately prior to driving the CRT, the inverse gamma correction is performed at the camera. In this way the video signal is non-linear for most of its journey.

Figure 5.9 shows a reverse gamma function. As a true power function requires infinite gain near black, a linear segment is substituted. It will be seen that contrast variations near black result in larger signal amplitude than variations near white. The result is that noise picked up by the video signal has less effect on dark areas than on bright areas. After the gamma of the CRT has acted, noise near black is compressed with respect to noise near white. Thus a video transmission system using gamma

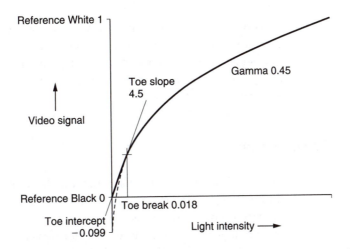

Figure 5.9 CCIR Rec. 709 reverse gamma function used at camera has a straight line approximation at the lower part of the curve to avoid boosting camera noise. Note that the output amplitude is greater for modulation near black.

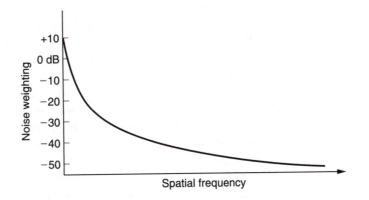

Figure 5.10 The sensitivity of the eye to noise is greatest at low frequencies and drops rapidly with increasing frequency. This can be used to mask quantizing noise caused by the compression process.

correction at source has a better perceived noise level than if the gamma correction is performed near the display.

In practice the system is not rendered perfectly linear by gamma correction and a slight overall exponential effect is usually retained in order further to reduce the effect of noise in darker parts of the picture. A gamma correction factor of 0.45 may be used to achieve this effect. If another type of display is to be used with signals designed for CRTs, the gamma characteristic of that display will probably be different and some gamma conversion will be required.

Sensitivity to noise is also a function of spatial frequency. Figure 5.10 shows that the sensitivity of the eye to noise falls with frequency from a maximum at zero. Thus it is vital that the average brightness should be correctly conveyed by a compression system, whereas higher spatial frequencies can be subject to more requantizing noise. Transforming the image into the frequency domain allows this characteristic to be explored.

5.4   Colour vision

Colour vision is due to the cones on the retina which occur in three different types, responding to different colours. Figure 5.11 shows that human vision is restricted to a range of light wavelengths from 400 nanometres to 700 nanometres. Shorter wavelengths are called ultraviolet and longer wavelengths are called infra-red. Note that the response is not uniform, but peaks in the area of green. The response to blue is very poor and makes a nonsense of the use of blue lights on emergency vehicles which owe much to tradition and little to psycho-optics.

Figure 5.11 shows an approximate response for each of the three types of cone. If light of a single wavelength is observed, the relative responses of the three sensors allow us to discern what we call the colour of the light. Note that at both ends of the visible spectrum there are areas in which only one receptor responds; all colours in those areas look the same. There is a great deal of variation in receptor response from one individual to the next and the curves used in television are the average of a great many tests. In a surprising number of people the single receptor zones are extended and discrimination between, for example, red and orange is difficult.

The triple receptor characteristic of the eye is extremely fortunate as it means that we can generate a range of colours by adding together light sources having just three different wavelengths in various proportions. This process is known as *additive colour matching* which should be clearly distinguished from the subtractive colour matching that occurs with paints and inks. Subtractive matching begins with white light and selectively removes parts of the spectrum by filtering. Additive matching uses coloured light sources which are combined.

5.5   Colour difference signals

An effective colour television system can be made in which only three pure or single wavelength colours or *primaries* can be generated. The primaries need to be similar in wavelength to the peaks of the three receptor responses, but need not be identical. Figure 5.12 shows a

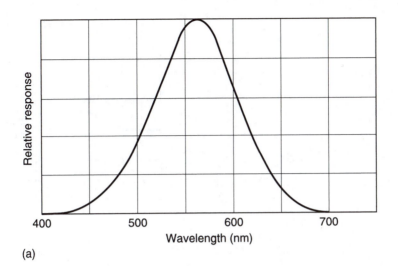

(a)

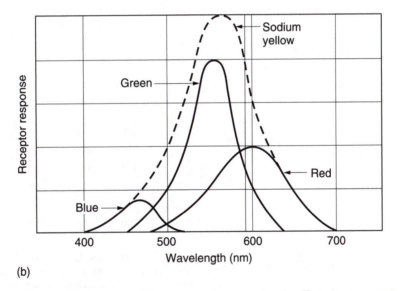

(b)

Figure 5.11 (a) The response of the eye to various wavelengths. There is a pronounced peak in the green region. (b) The different types of cone in the eye have the approximate responses shown here which allow colour vision.

rudimentary colour television system. Note that the colour camera is in fact three cameras in one, where each is fitted with a different coloured filter. Three signals, R, G and B, must be transmitted to the display which produces three images that must be superimposed to obtain a colour picture.

A monochrome camera produces a single luminance signal Y whereas a colour camera produces three signals, or *components*, R, G and B which

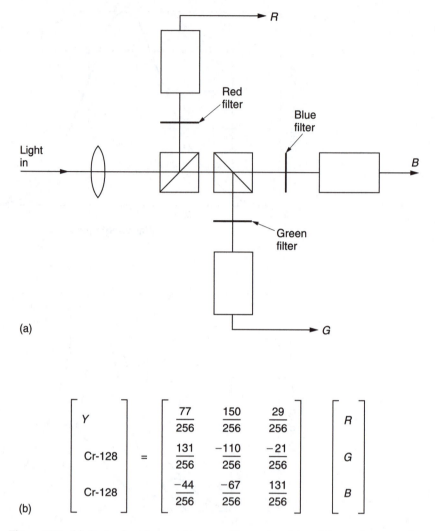

$$
\begin{bmatrix} Y \\ Cr-128 \\ Cr-128 \end{bmatrix} = \begin{bmatrix} \dfrac{77}{256} & \dfrac{150}{256} & \dfrac{29}{256} \\ \dfrac{131}{256} & \dfrac{-110}{256} & \dfrac{-21}{256} \\ \dfrac{-44}{256} & \dfrac{-67}{256} & \dfrac{131}{256} \end{bmatrix} \begin{bmatrix} R \\ G \\ B \end{bmatrix}
$$

(b)

Figure 5.12 (a) A simple colour system uses three primaries and transmits a complete picture for each. This is incompatible with monochrome and uses too much bandwidth. Practical systems use colour difference and luminance signals which are obtained by a weighted calculation as shown in (b).

are essentially monochrome video signals representing an image in each primary colour. *RGB* and *Y* signals are incompatible, yet when colour television was introduced it was a practical necessity that it should be possible to display colour signals on a monochrome display and vice versa. Creating or *transcoding* a luminance signal from *R, G* and *B* is relatively easy. Figure 5.11 showed the spectral response of the eye which has a peak in the green region. Green objects will produce a larger stimulus than red objects of the same brightness, with blue objects producing the least stimulus. A luminance signal can be obtained by adding R, G and B together, not in equal amounts, but in a sum which is *weighted* by the relative response of the eye. Thus:

$$Y = 0.3R + 0.59G + 0.11B$$

If Y is derived in this way, a monochrome display will show nearly the same result as if a monochrome camera had been used in the first place. The results are not identical because of the non-linearities introduced by gamma correction.

As colour pictures require three signals, it should be possible to send Y and two other signals which a colour display could arithmetically convert back to R, G and B. There are two important factors which restrict the form which the other two signals may take. One is to achieve reverse compatibility. If the source is a monochrome camera, it can only produce Y and the other two signals will be completely absent. A colour display should be able to operate on the Y signal only and show a monochrome picture. The other is the requirement to conserve bandwidth for economic reasons.

These requirements are met by sending two *colour difference signals* along with Y. There are three possible colour difference signals, R–Y, B–Y and G–Y. As the green signal makes the greatest contribution to Y, then the amplitude of G–Y would be the smallest and would be most susceptible to noise. Thus R–Y and B–Y are used in practice as Figure 5.13 shows.

R and B are readily obtained by adding Y to the two colour difference signals. G is obtained by rearranging the expression for Y above such that:

$$G = \frac{Y - 0.3R - 0.11B}{0.59}$$

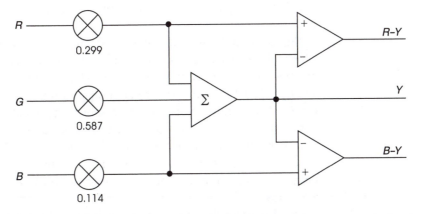

Figure 5.13 Colour components are converted to colour difference signals by the transcoding shown here.

If a colour CRT is being driven, it is possible to apply inverted luminance to the cathodes and the $R-Y$ and $B-Y$ signals directly to two of the grids so that the tube performs some of the matrixing. It is then only necessary to obtain $G-Y$ for the third grid, using the expression:

$$G-Y = 0.51(R-Y) - 0.186(B-Y)$$

If a monochrome source having only a Y output is supplied to a colour display, $R-Y$ and $B-Y$ will be zero. It is reasonably obvious that if there are no colour difference signals the colour signals cannot be different from one another and $R=G=B$. As a result the colour display can produce only a neutral picture.

The use of colour difference signals is essential for compatibility in both directions between colour and monochrome, but it has a further advantage that follows from the way in which the eye works. In order to produce the highest resolution in the fovea, the eye will use signals from all types of cone, regardless of colour. In order to determine colour the stimuli from three cones must be compared. There is evidence that the nervous system uses some form of colour difference processing to make this possible. As a result the full acuity of the human eye is only available in monochrome. Differences in colour cannot be resolved so well. A further factor is that the lens in the human eye is not achromatic and this means that the ends of the spectrum are not well focused. This is particularly noticeable on blue.

If the eye cannot resolve colour very well there is no point is expending valuable bandwidth sending high-resolution colour signals. Colour difference working allows the luminance to be sent separately at a bit rate which determines the subjective sharpness of the picture. The colour difference signals can be sent with considerably reduced bit rate, as little as one quarter that of luminance, and the human eye is unable to tell.

The overwhelming advantages obtained by using downsampled colour difference signals mean that in broadcast and production facilities their use has become almost universal. The technique is equally attractive for compression applications and is retained in MPEG. The outputs from the *RGB* sensors in most cameras are converted directly to Y, $R-Y$ and $B-Y$ in the camera control unit and output in that form. Whilst signals such as Y, R, G and B are *unipolar* or positive only, it should be stressed that colour difference signals are *bipolar* and may meaningfully take on levels below zero volts.

The downsampled colour formats used in MPEG were described in section 2.9.

5.6   Progressive or interlaced scan?

Analog video samples in the time domain and vertically down the screen so a two-dimensional vertical/temporal sampling spectrum will result. In a progressively scanned system there is a rectangular matrix of sampling sites vertically and temporally. The rectangular sampling structure of progressive scan is *separable* which means that, for example, a vertical manipulation can be performed on frame data without affecting the time axis. The sampling spectrum will be obtained according to section 2.6 and consists of the baseband spectrum repeated as sidebands above and below harmonics of the two-dimensional sampling frequencies. The corresponding spectrum is shown in Figure 5.14. The baseband spectrum is in the centre of the diagram, and the repeating sampling sideband spectrum extends vertically and horizontally. The vertical aspects of the star-shaped spectrum result from vertical spatial frequencies in the image. The horizontal aspect is due to image movement. Note that the star shape is rather hypothetical; the actual shape depends heavily on the source material. On a still picture the horizontal dimensions collapse to a line structure. In order to return a progressive scan video signal to a continuous moving picture, a two-dimensional low-pass filter having a rectangular response is required. This is quite feasible as persistence of vision acts as a temporal filter and by sitting far enough away from the screen the finite acuity of the eye acts as a spatial reconstruction filter.

Interlace is actually a primitive form of compression in which the system bandwidth is typically halved by sending only half the frame

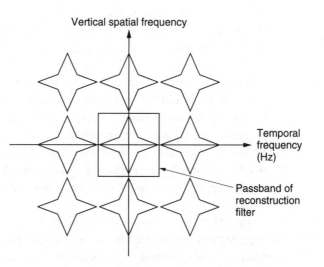

Figure 5.14   The vertical/temporal spectrum of a non-interlaced video signal.

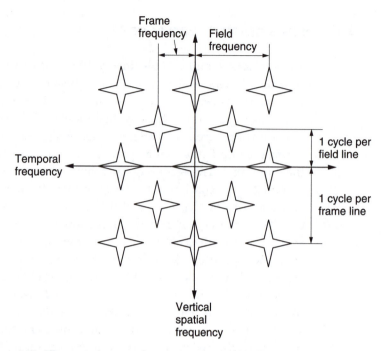

Figure 5.15 The vertical temporal spectrum of monochrome video due to interlace.

lines in the first field, with the remaining lines being sent in the second field. The use of interlace has a profound effect on the vertical/temporal spectrum. Figure 5.15 shows that the lowest sampling frequency on the time axis is the frame rate, and the lowest sampling frequency on the vertical axis is the number of lines in a field. The arrangement is called a quincunx pattern because of the similarity to the five of dice. The triangular passband has exactly half the area of the rectangular passband of Figure 5.14 illustrating that half the information rate is available.

As a consequence of the triangular passband of an interlaced signal, if the best vertical frequency response is to be obtained, no motion is allowed. It should be clear from Figure 5.16 that a high vertical spatial frequency resulting from a sharp horizontal edge in the picture is only repeated at frame rate, resulting in an artifact known as *interlace twitter*. Conversely, to obtain the best temporal response, the vertical resolution must be impaired. Thus interlaced systems have poor resolution on moving images, in other words their *dynamic resolution* is poor.

In order to return to a continuous signal, a quincuncial spectrum requires a triangular spatio-temporal low-pass filter. In practice no such filter can be realized. Consequently the sampling sidebands are not filtered out and are visible, particularly the frame rate component. This

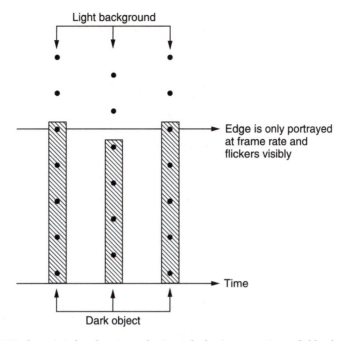

Figure 5.16 In an interlaced system, a horizontal edge is present in *one* field only and so is presented to the viewer at frame rate not field rate. This is below the critical flicker frequency and is visible as *twitter*.

artifact is visible on an interlaced display even at distances so great that resolution cannot be assessed.

Figure 5.17(a) shows a dynamic resolution analysis of interlaced scanning. When there is no motion, the optic flow axis and the time axis are parallel and the apparent vertical sampling rate is the number of lines in a frame. However, when there is vertical motion, (b), the optic flow axis turns. In the case shown, the sampling structure due to interlace results in the vertical sampling rate falling to one half of its stationary value.

Consequently interlace does exactly what would be expected from a half-bandwidth filter. It halves the vertical resolution when any motion with a vertical component occurs. In a practical television system, there is no anti-aliasing filter in the vertical axis and so when the vertical sampling rate of an interlaced system is halved by motion, high spatial frequencies will alias or heterodyne causing annoying artifacts in the picture. This is easily demonstrated.

Figure 5.17(c) shows how a vertical spatial frequency well within the static resolution of the system aliases when motion occurs. In a progressive scan system this effect is absent and the dynamic resolution due to scanning can be the same as the static case.

This analysis also illustrates why interlaced television systems must have horizontal raster lines. This is because in real life, horizontal motion

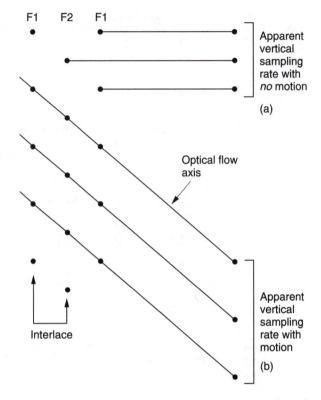

Figure 5.17 When an interlaced picture is stationary, viewing takes place along the time axis as shown in (a). When a vertical component of motion exists, viewing takes place along the optic flow axis. (b) The vertical sampling rate falls to one half its stationary values. (c) The halving in sampling rate causes high spatial frequencies to alias.

is more common than vertical. It is easy to calculate the vertical image motion velocity needed to obtain the half-bandwidth speed of interlace, because it amounts to one raster line per field. In 525/60 (NTSC) there are about 500 active lines, so motion as slow as one picture height in 8 seconds will halve the dynamic resolution. In 625/50 (PAL) there are about 600 lines, so the half-bandwidth speed falls to one picture height in 12 seconds. This is why NTSC, with fewer lines and lower bandwidth, doesn't look as soft as it should compared to PAL, because it actually has better dynamic resolution.

The situation deteriorates rapidly if an attempt is made to use interlaced scanning in systems with a lot of lines. In 1250/50, the resolution is halved at a vertical speed of just one picture height in 24 seconds. In other words on real moving video a 1250/50 interlaced system has the same dynamic resolution as a 625/50 progressive system. By the same argument a 1080 I system has the same performance as a 480 P system.

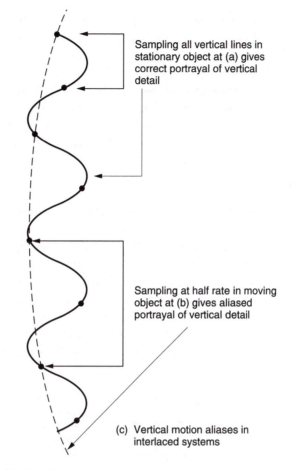

Sampling all vertical lines in stationary object at (a) gives correct portrayal of vertical detail

Sampling at half rate in moving object at (b) gives aliased portrayal of vertical detail

(c) Vertical motion aliases in interlaced systems

Figure 5.17 Continued.

Interlaced signals are not separable and so processes that are straightforward in progressively scanned systems become more complex in interlaced systems. Compression systems should not be cascaded indiscriminately, especially if they are different. As digital compression techniques based on transforms are now available, it makes no sense to use an interlaced, i.e. compressed, video signal as an input.

Interlaced signals are harder for MPEG to compress.[2] The confusion of temporal and spatial information makes accurate motion estimation more difficult and this reflects in a higher bit rate being required for a given quality. In short, how can a motion estimator accurately measure motion from one field to another when differences between the fields can equally be due to motion, vertical detail or vertical aliasing?

Computer-generated images and film are not interlaced, but consist of discrete frames spaced on a time axis. As digital technology is bringing computers and television closer the use of interlaced transmission is an embarrassing source of incompatibility. The future will bring image delivery systems based on computer technology and oversampling cameras and displays which can operate at resolutions much closer to the theoretical limits.

Interlace was the best that could be managed with thermionic valve technology sixty years ago, and we should respect the achievement of its developers at a time when things were so much harder. However, we must also recognize that the context in which interlace made sense has disappeared.

5.7 Spatial and temporal redundancy in MPEG

Chapter 1 introduced these concepts in a general sense and now they will be treated with specific reference to MPEG. Figure 5.18(a) shows that spatial redundancy is redundancy within a single picture or object, for example repeated pixel values in a large area of blue sky. Temporal redundancy (b) exists between successive pictures or objects.

In MPEG, where temporal compression is used, the current picture/object is not sent in its entirety; instead the difference between the current

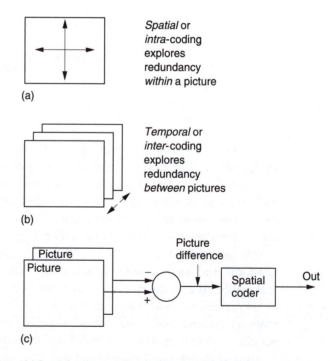

Figure 5.18 (a) Spatial or intra-coding works on individual images. (b) Temporal or inter-coding works on successive images. (c) In MPEG inter-coding is used to create difference images. These are then compressed spatially.

picture/object and the previous one is sent. The decoder already has the previous picture/object, and so it can add the difference, or residual image, to make the current picture/object. A residual image is created by subtracting every pixel in one picture/object from the corresponding pixel in another. This is trivially easy when pictures are restricted to progressive scan, as in MPEG-1, but MPEG-2 had to develop greater complexity (continued in MPEG-4) so that this can also be done with interlaced pictures. The handling of interlace in MPEG will be detailed later.

A residual is an image of a kind, although not a viewable one, and so should contain some kind of spatial redundancy. Figure 5.18(c) shows that MPEG takes advantage of both forms of redundancy. Residual images are spatially compressed prior to transmission. At the decoder the spatial compression is decoded to re-create the residual, then this is added to the previous picture/object to complete the decoding process.

Whenever objects move they will be in a different place in successive pictures. This will result in large amounts of difference data. MPEG overcomes the problem using motion compensation. The encoder contains a motion estimator which measures the direction and distance of any motion between pictures and outputs this as vectors which are sent to the decoder. When the decoder receives the vectors it uses them to shift data in a previous picture to more closely resemble the current picture. Effectively the vectors are describing the optic flow axis of some moving screen area, along which axis the image is highly redundant. Vectors are bipolar codes which determine the amount of horizontal and vertical shift required. The shifts may be in whole pixels or some binary fraction of a pixel. Whole pixel shifts are simply achieved by changing memory addresses, whereas sub-pixel shifts require interpolation. Chapter 3 showed how interpolation of this kind can be performed.

In real images, moving objects do not necessarily maintain their appearance as they move. For example, objects may move into shade or light. Consequently motion compensation can never be ideal and it is still necessary to send a residual to make up for any shortcomings in the motion compensation.

Figure 5.19 shows how this works in MPEG. In addition to the motion-encoding system, the coder also contains a motion decoder. When the encoder outputs motion vectors, it also uses them locally in the same way that a real decoder will, and is able to produce a *predicted picture* based solely on the previous picture shifted by motion vectors. This is then subtracted from the *actual* current picture to produce a *prediction error* or *residual* which is an image of a kind that can be spatially compressed. The decoder takes the previous picture, shifts it with the vectors to re-create the predicted picture and then decodes and adds the prediction error to

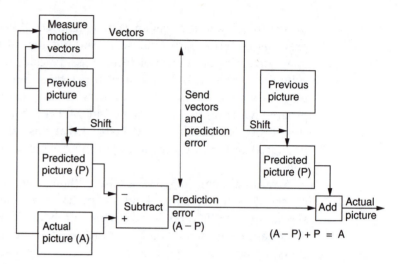

Figure 5.19 A motion-compensated compression system. The coder calculates motion vectors which are transmitted as well as being used locally to create a predicted picture. The difference between the predicted picture and the actual picture is transmitted as a prediction error.

produce the actual picture. Picture data sent as vectors plus prediction error are said to be *P* coded.

The concept of sending a prediction error is a useful approach because it allows both the motion estimation and compensation to be imperfect. An ideal motion compensation system will send just the right amount of vector data. With insufficient vector data, the prediction error will be large, but transmission of excess vector data will also cause the bit rate to rise. There will be an optimum balance which minimizes the sum of the prediction error data and the vector data.

In MPEG-1 and MPEG-2 the balance is obtained by dividing the screen into areas called *macroblocks* which are 16 luminance pixels square. Each macroblock is associated with a vector. The vector has horizontal and vertical components so that, used in combination, pixel data may be shifted in any direction. The location of the boundaries of a macroblock are fixed with respect to the display screen and so clearly the vector cannot move the macroblock. Instead the vector tells the decoder where to look in another picture to find pixel data which will be fetched *to* the macroblock. Figure 5.20(a) shows this concept. MPEG-2 vectors have half-pixel resolution.

MPEG-1 and MPEG-2 also use a simple compression scheme on the vectors. Figure 5.21 shows that in the case of a large moving object, all the vectors within the object will be identical or nearly so. A horizontal run of macroblocks can be associated to form a structure called a *slice* (see section 5.14). The first vector of a slice is sent as an absolute value, but

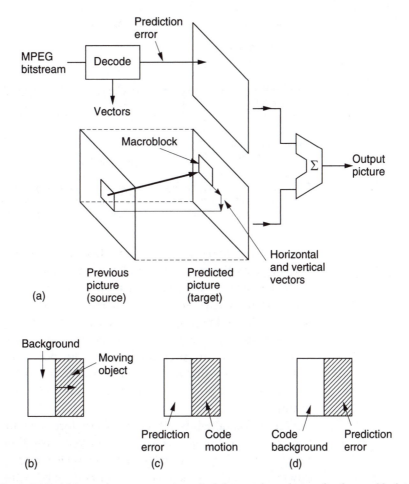

Figure 5.20 (a) In motion compensation, pixel data are brought to a fixed macroblock in the target picture from a variety of places in another picture. (b) Where only part of a macroblock is moving, motion compensation is non-ideal. The motion can be coded (c), causing a prediction error in the background, or the background can be coded (d) causing a prediction error in the moving object.

subsequent vectors will be sent as differences. No advantage is taken of vertical vector redundancy.

Real moving objects will not coincide with macroblocks and so the motion compensation will not be ideal but the prediction error makes up for any shortcomings. Figure 5.20(b) shows the case where the boundary of a moving object bisects a macroblock. If the system measures the moving part of the macroblock and sends a vector, the decoder will shift the entire block making the stationary part wrong. If no vector is sent, the moving part will be wrong. Both approaches are legal in MPEG-1 and MPEG-2 because the prediction error compensates for the incorrect values. An intelligent coder might try both approaches to see which required the least prediction error data.

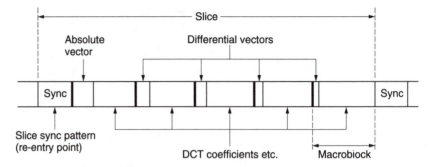

Figure 5.21 In a slice, the first vector is sent as an absolute value, whereas subsequent vectors are sent as differences. When a large moving object is to be coded, several macroblocks may have the same velocity and this is efficiently coded in a slice.

The prediction error concept also allows the use of simple but inaccurate motion estimators in low-cost systems. The greater prediction error data are handled using a higher bit rate. On the other hand if a precision motion estimator is available, a very high compression factor may be achieved because the prediction error data are minimized. MPEG does not specify how motion is to be measured; it simply defines how a decoder will interpret the vectors. Encoder designers are free to use any motion-estimation system provided that the right vector protocol is created. Chapter 3 contrasted a number of motion estimation techniques.

Figure 5.22(a) shows that a macroblock contains both luminance and colour difference data at different resolutions. Most of the MPEG-2 Profiles use a 4:2:0 structure which means that the colour is downsampled by a factor of two in both axes. Thus in a 16×16 pixel block, there are only 8×8 colour difference sampling sites. MPEG-2 is based upon the 8×8 DCT (see section 3.7) and so the 16×16 block is the screen area which contains an 8×8 colour difference sampling block. Thus in 4:2:0 in each macroblock there are four luminance DCT blocks, one $R-Y$ DCT block and one $B-Y$ DCT block, all steered by the same vector. In the 4:2:2 Profile of MPEG-2, shown in Figure 5.22(b), the chroma is not downsampled vertically, and so there is twice as much chroma data in each macroblock which is otherwise substantially the same.

In MPEG-4 a number of refinements are made to motion compensation in addition to the MPEG-2 tools which are still available. One of these tools is a more complex form of vector compression which will be described in section 5.21. This cuts down the bit rate needed for a given set of vector data and has a number of benefits. If the existing macroblock size is retained, a higher compression factor results from the reduced vector data. However, the opportunity also arises to increase the vector density. Optionally, MPEG-4 allows one vector to be associated with an

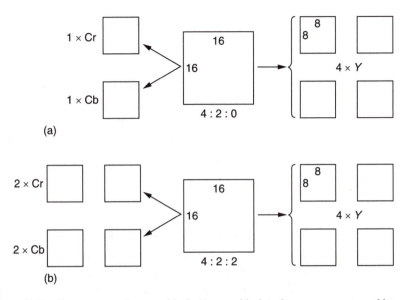

Figure 5.22 The structure of a macroblock. (A macroblock is the screen area steered by *one* vector.) (a) In 4:2:0, there are two chroma DCT blocks per macroblock whereas in 4:2:2 (b) there are four, 4:2:2 needs 33 per cent more data than 4:2:0.

8×8 DCT block rather than with a 16×16 macroblock. This allows much more precise prediction of complex motion, especially near the edge of objects, and will result in a reduced residual bit rate. On a macroblock-by-macroblock basis an MPEG-4 coder can decide whether to code four vectors per macroblock or only one. When the compressed vector data and residual are combined, one of these approaches will result in the least data. In AVC the vector density may be even higher still.

5.8   *I* and *P* coding

Predictive (*P*) coding cannot be used indefinitely, as it is prone to error propagation. A further problem is that it becomes impossible to decode the transmission if reception begins part-way through. In real video signals, cuts or edits can be present across which there is little redundancy and which make motion estimators throw up their hands.

In the absence of redundancy over a cut, there is nothing to be done but to send the new picture information in absolute form. This is called *I* coding where *I* is an abbreviation of *intra*-coding. As *I* coding needs no previous picture for decoding, then decoding and/or error recovery can begin at *I* coded information.

MPEG is effectively a toolkit. The bigger the MPEG-number, the more tools are available. However, there is no compulsion to use all the tools available. Thus an encoder may choose whether to use *I* or *P* coding,

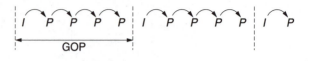

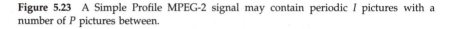

I = Intra-coded picture
P = Predicted picture
⌒◂ = Picture difference
(vectors plus prediction error)

Figure 5.23 A Simple Profile MPEG-2 signal may contain periodic *I* pictures with a number of *P* pictures between.

either once and for all or dynamically on a macroblock-by-macroblock basis. For practical reasons, an entire frame should be encoded as *I* macroblocks periodically. This creates a place where the bitstream might be edited or where decoding could begin.

Figure 5.23 shows a typical application of the Simple Profile of MPEG-2. Periodically an *I* picture is created. Between *I* pictures are *P* pictures which are based on the picture before. These *P* pictures predominantly contain macroblocks having vectors and prediction errors. However, it is perfectly legal for *P* pictures to contain *I* macroblocks. This might be useful where, for example, a camera pan introduces new material at the edge of the screen which cannot be created from an earlier picture.

Note that although what is sent is called a *P* picture, it is not a picture at all. It is a set of instructions to convert the previous picture into the current picture. If the previous picture is lost, decoding is impossible. An *I* picture together with all of the pictures before the next *I* picture form a *group of pictures* (GOP). There is no requirement for GOPs to be of constant size and indeed the size may vary dynamically.

5.9   Bidirectional coding

Motion-compensated predictive coding is a useful compression technique, but it does have the drawback that it can only take data from a previous picture.

Where moving objects reveal a background this is completely unknown in previous pictures and forward prediction fails. However, more of the background is visible in later pictures. Figure 5.24 shows the concept. In the centre of the diagram, a moving object has revealed some background. The previous picture can contribute nothing, whereas the next picture contains all that is required.

Bidirectional coding is shown in Figure 5.25. A bidirectional or *B* macroblock can be created using a combination of motion compensation

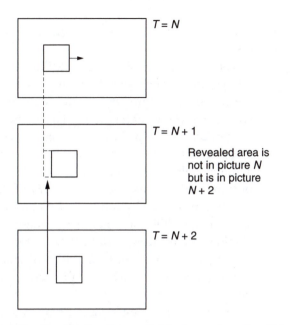

Figure 5.24 In bidirectional coding the revealed background can be efficiently coded by bringing data back from a future picture.

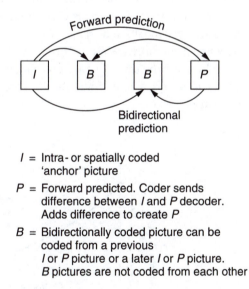

Figure 5.25 In bidirectional coding, a number of *B* pictures can be inserted between periodic forward predicted pictures. See text.

and the addition of a prediction error. This can be done by forward prediction from a previous picture or backward prediction from a subsequent picture. It is also possible to use an average of both forward and backward prediction. On noisy material this may result in some reduction in bit rate. The technique is also a useful way of portraying a dissolve.

The averaging process in MPEG-1 and -2 is a simple linear interpolation which works well when only one *B* picture exists between the reference pictures before and after. A larger number of *B* pictures would require weighted interpolation but only AVC supports this.

Typically two *B* pictures are inserted between *P* pictures or between *I* and *P* pictures. As can be seen, *B* pictures are never predicted from one another, only from *I* or *P* pictures. A typical GOP for broadcasting purposes might have the structure *IBBPBBPBBPBB*. Note that the last *B* pictures in the GOP require the *I* picture in the next GOP for decoding and so the GOPs are not truly independent. Independence can be obtained by creating a *closed GOP* which may contain *B* pictures but which ends with a *P* picture. It is also legal to have a *B* picture in which every macroblock is forward predicted, needing no future picture for decoding.

In AVC, bidirectional coding may take picture data from more than one picture either side of the target picture.

Bidirectional coding is very powerful. Figure 5.26 is a constant quality curve showing how the bit rate changes with the type of coding. On the left, only *I* or spatial coding is used, whereas on the right a *IBBP* structure is used. This means that there are two bidirectionally coded pictures in between a spatially coded picture (*I*) and a forward predicted picture (*P*). Note how for the same quality the system which only uses spatial coding needs two and a half times the bit rate that the bidirectionally coded system needs.

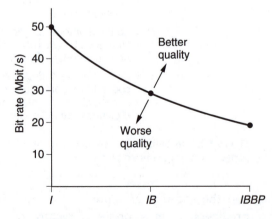

Figure 5.26 Bidirectional coding is very powerful as it allows the same quality with only 40 per cent of the bit rate of intra-coding. However, the encoding and decoding delays must increase. Coding over a longer time span is more efficient but editing is more difficult.

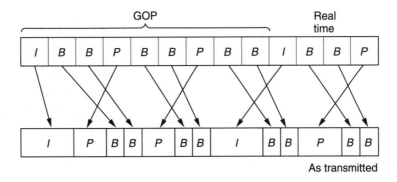

Figure 5.27 Comparison of pictures before and after compression showing sequence change and varying amount of data needed by each picture type. *I, P, B* pictures use unequal amounts of data.

Clearly information in the future has yet to be transmitted and so is not normally available to the decoder. MPEG gets around the problem by sending pictures in the wrong order. Picture reordering requires delay in the encoder and a delay in the decoder to put the order right again. Thus the overall codec delay must rise when bidirectional coding is used. This is quite consistent with Figure 1.6 which showed that as the compression factor rises the latency must also rise.

Figure 5.27 shows that although the original picture sequence is *IBBPBBPBBIBB . . .*, this is transmitted as *IPBBPBBIBB . . .* so that the future picture is already in the decoder before bidirectional decoding begins. Note that the *I* picture of the next GOP is actually sent before the last *B* pictures of the current GOP.

Figure 5.27 also shows that the amount of data required by each picture is dramatically different. *I* pictures have only spatial redundancy and so need a lot of data to describe them. *P* pictures need fewer data because they are created by shifting the *I* picture with vectors and then adding a prediction error picture. *B* pictures need the least data of all because they can be created from *I* or *P*.

With pictures requiring a variable length of time to transmit, arriving in the wrong order, the decoder needs some help. This takes the form of picture-type flags and time stamps which will be described in section 6.2.

5.10 Coding applications

Figure 5.28 shows a variety of possible GOP (group of pictures in MPEG-1 and MPEG-2) or GOV (group of video object planes in MPEG-4) structures. The simplest is the *III . . .* sequence in which every picture (or object in MPEG-4) is intra-coded. These can be fully decoded without reference to any other picture or object and so editing is straightforward.

I I I I I I ...	*I* only freely editable, needs high bit rate
I P P P P I P ...	Forward predicted only, needs less decoder memory, used in Simple Profile
I B B P B B P B ...	Forward and bidirectional, best compression factor, needs large decoder memory, hard to edit
I B I B I B ...	Lower bit rate than *I* only, editable with moderate processing

Figure 5.28 Various possible GOP structures used with MPEG. See text for details.

However, this approach requires about two-and-one-half times the bit rate of a full bidirectional system.

Bidirectional coding is most useful for final delivery of post-produced material either by broadcast or on prerecorded media as there is then no editing requirement. As a compromise the *IBIB* ... structure can be used which has some of the bit rate advantage of bidirectional coding but without too much latency. It is possible to edit an *IBIB* stream by performing some processing. If it is required to remove the video following a *B* picture, that *B* picture could not be decoded because it needs *I* pictures either side of it for bidirectional decoding. The solution is to decode the *B* picture first, and then re-encode it with forward prediction only from the previous *I* picture. The subsequent *I* picture can then be replaced by an edit process. Some quality loss is inevitable in this process but this is acceptable in applications such as ENG and industrial video.

5.11 Intra-coding

Intra-coding or spatial compression in MPEG is used in *I* pictures on actual picture data and in *P* and *B* pictures on prediction error data. MPEG-1 and MPEG-2 use the discrete cosine transform described in section 3.13. In still pictures, MPEG-4 may also use the wavelet transform described in section 3.14.

Entering the spatial frequency domain has two main advantages. It allows dominant spatial frequencies which occur in real images to be efficiently coded, and it allows noise shaping to be used. As the eye is not uniformly sensitive to noise at all spatial frequencies, dividing the information up into frequency bands allows a different noise level to be produced in each.

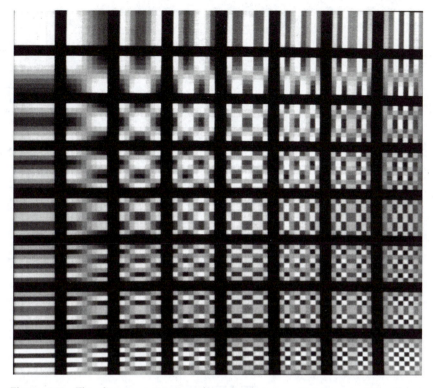

Figure 5.29 The discrete cosine transform breaks up an image area into discrete frequencies in two dimensions. The lowest frequency can be seen here at the top-left corner. Horizontal frequency increases to the right and vertical frequency increases downwards.

The DCT works on blocks and in MPEG these are 8×8 pixels. Section 5.7 showed how the macroblocks of the motion-compensation structure are designed so they can be broken down into 8×8 DCT blocks. In a 4:2:0 macroblock there will be six DCT blocks whereas in a 4:2:2 macroblock there will be eight.

Figure 5.29 shows the table of basis functions or *wave table* for an 8×8 DCT. Adding these two-dimensional waveforms together in different proportions will give any original 8×8 pixel block. The coefficients of the DCT simply control the proportion of each wave which is added in the inverse transform. The top-left wave has no modulation at all because it conveys the DC component of the block. This coefficient will be a unipolar (positive only) value in the case of luminance and will typically be the largest value in the block as the spectrum of typical video signals is dominated by the DC component.

Increasing the DC coefficient adds a constant amount to every pixel. Moving to the right the coefficients represent increasing horizontal spatial frequencies and moving downwards the coefficients represent increasing vertical spatial frequencies. The bottom-right coefficient

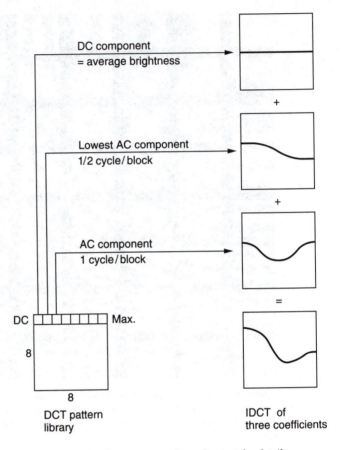

Figure 5.30 A one-dimensional inverse transform. See text for details.

represents the highest diagonal frequencies in the block. All these coefficients are bipolar, where the polarity indicates whether the original spatial waveform at that frequency was inverted.

Figure 5.30 shows a one-dimensional example of an inverse transform. The DC coefficient produces a constant level throughout the pixel block. The remaining waves in the table are AC coefficients. A zero coefficient would result in no modulation, leaving the DC level unchanged. The wave next to the DC component represents the lowest frequency in the transform which is half a cycle per block. A positive coefficient would make the left side of the block brighter and the right side darker whereas a negative coefficient would do the opposite. The magnitude of the coefficient determines the amplitude of the wave which is added. Figure 5.30 also shows that the next wave has a frequency of one cycle per block, i.e. the block is made brighter at both sides and darker in the middle. Consequently an inverse DCT is no more than a process of mixing various pixel patterns from the wave table where the relative amplitudes and polarity of these patterns are controlled by the

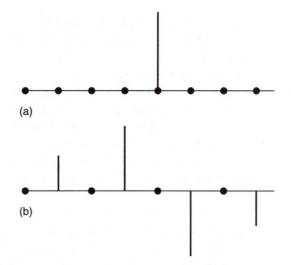

Figure 5.31 At (a) the DCT of a cosine wave has one dominant coefficient whereas at (b), with a sine wave input, a large number of coefficients will result. Thus the DCT is not really a spectral analyser.

coefficients. The original transform is simply a mechanism which finds the coefficient amplitudes from the original pixel block.

It should be noted that the DCT is not a true spectral analysis like the DFT. If a cosine waveform enters a DCT the behaviour is DFT-like, but the DCT handles a sine waveform by generating a larger number of coefficients. This is shown in Figure 5.31.

The DCT itself achieves no compression at all. Sixty-four pixels are converted to sixty-four coefficients. However, in typical pictures, not all coefficients will have significant values; there will often be a few dominant coefficients. The coefficients representing the higher two-dimensional spatial frequencies will often be zero or of small value in large areas, due to blurring or simply plain undetailed areas before the camera.

Statistically, the further from the top-left corner of the wave table the coefficient is, the smaller will be its magnitude. Coding gain (the technical term for reduction in the number of bits needed) is achieved by transmitting the low-valued coefficients with shorter wordlengths. The zero-valued coefficients need not be transmitted at all. Thus it is not the DCT which compresses the data, it is the subsequent processing. The DCT simply expresses the data in a form that makes the subsequent processing easier.

Higher compression factors require the coefficient wordlength to be further reduced using requantizing. Coefficients are divided by some factor which increases the size of the quantizing step. The smaller number of steps which results permits coding with fewer bits, but of course with an increased quantizing error. The coefficients will be multiplied by a reciprocal factor in the decoder to return to the correct magnitude.

Inverse transforming a requantized coefficient means that the frequency it represents is reproduced in the output with the wrong amplitude. The difference between original and reconstructed amplitude is regarded as a noise added to the wanted data. Figure 5.10 showed that the visibility of such noise is far from uniform. The maximum sensitivity is found at DC and falls thereafter. As a result the top-left coefficient is often treated as a special case and left unchanged. It may warrant more error protection than other coefficients.

Transform coding takes advantage of the falling sensitivity to noise. Prior to requantizing, each coefficient is divided by a different weighting constant as a function of its frequency. Figure 5.32 shows a typical weighting process. Naturally the decoder must have a corresponding inverse weighting. This weighting process has the effect of reducing the magnitude of high-frequency coefficients disproportionately. Clearly different weighting will be needed for colour difference data as colour is perceived differently.

P and *B* pictures are decoded by adding a prediction error image to a reference image. That reference image will contain weighted noise. One purpose of the prediction error is to cancel that noise to prevent tolerance build-up. If the prediction error were also to contain weighted noise this

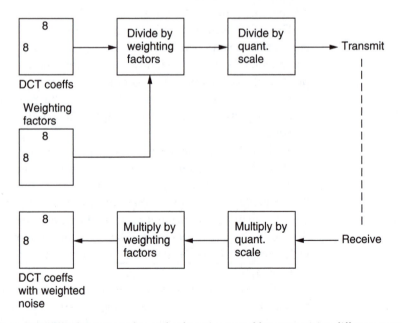

Figure 5.32 Weighting is used to make the noise caused by requantizing different at each frequency.

result would not be obtained. Consequently prediction error coefficients are flat weighted.

When forward prediction fails, such as in the case of new material introduced in a *P* picture by a pan, *P* coding would set the vectors to zero and encode the new data entirely as an unweighted prediction error. In this case it is better to encode that material as an *I* macroblock because then weighting can be used and this will require fewer bits.

Requantizing increases the step size of the coefficients, but the inverse weighting in the decoder results in step sizes which increase with frequency. The larger step size increases the quantizing noise at high frequencies where it is less visible. Effectively the noise floor is shaped to match the sensitivity of the eye. The quantizing table in use at the encoder can be transmitted to the decoder periodically in the bitstream.

5.12   Intra-coding in MPEG-1 and MPEG-2

Study of the signal statistics gained from extensive analysis of real material is used to measure the probability of a given coefficient having a given value. This probability turns out to be highly non-uniform suggesting the possibility of a variable-length encoding for the coefficient values. On average, the higher the spatial frequency, the lower the value of a coefficient will be. This means that the value of a coefficient tends to fall as a function of its radius from the DC coefficient. DC coefficients also have certain characteristics. As they represent the average brightness of a block, in many picture areas, adjacent blocks will have similar DC coefficient values. This can be exploited using differential coding which will be dealt with in section 5.14. However, errors in the magnitude of DC coefficients cause wide area flicker in the picture and so the coding must be accurate.

Typical material often has many coefficients which are zero valued, especially after requantizing. The distribution of these also follows a pattern. The non-zero values tend to be found in the top-left-hand corner of the DCT block, but as the radius increases, not only do the coefficient values fall, but it becomes increasingly likely that these small coefficients will be interspersed with zero-valued coefficients. As the radius increases further it is probable that a region where all coefficients are zero will be entered.

MPEG uses all these attributes of DCT coefficients when encoding a coefficient block. By sending the coefficients in an optimum order, by describing their values with Huffman coding and by using run-length encoding for the zero-valued coefficients it is possible to achieve a significant reduction in coefficient data which remains entirely lossless. Despite the complexity of this process, it does contribute to improved

Start

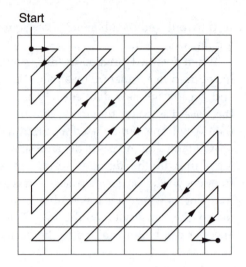

Figure 5.33 The zig-zag scan for a progressively scanned image.

picture quality because for a given bit rate lossless coding of the coefficients must be better than requantizing, which is lossy. Of course, for lower bit rates both will be required.

It is an advantage to scan in a sequence where the largest coefficient values are scanned first. Then the next coefficient is more likely to be zero than the previous one. With progressively scanned material, a regular zigzag scan begins in the top-left corner and ends in the bottom-right corner as shown in Figure 5.33. Zig-zag scanning means that significant values are more likely to be transmitted first, followed by the zero values. Instead of coding these zeros, a unique 'end of block' (EOB) symbol is transmitted instead.

As the zig-zag scan approaches the last finite coefficient it is increasingly likely that some zero value coefficients will be scanned. Instead of transmitting the coefficients as zeros, the *zero-run-length*, i.e. the number of zero-valued coefficients in the scan sequence, is encoded into the next non-zero coefficient which is itself variable-length coded. This combination of run-length and variable-length coding is known as RLC/VLC in MPEG.

The DC coefficient is handled separately because it is differentially coded and this discussion relates to the AC coefficients. Three items need to be handled for each coefficient: the zero-run-length prior to this coefficient, the wordlength and the coefficient value itself. The wordlength needs to be known by the decoder so that it can correctly parse the bitstream. The wordlength of the coefficient is expressed directly as an integer called the *size*.

Figure 5.34(a) shows that a two-dimensional run/size table is created. One dimension expresses the zero-run-length; the other the size. A run

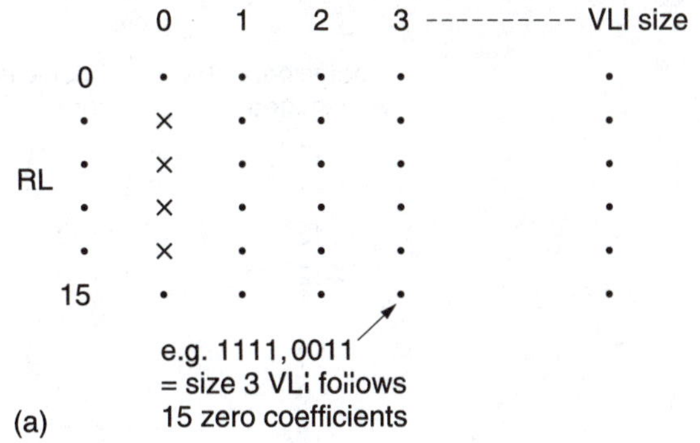

(a)

Run \ Size	0	1	2	3 → etc.
0	1010 (EOB)	00	01	100
1	–	1100	11011	
2	–	11100	11111001	
3	–	111010	111110111	
4	–	111011	1111111000	
5 ↓ etc.	–	1111010		

(b)

Figure 5.34 Run-length and variable-length coding simultaneously compresses runs of zero-valued coefficients and describes the wordlength of a non-zero coefficient. (Continued on page 268.)

length of zero is obtained when adjacent coefficients are non-zero, but a code of 0/0 has no meaningful run/size interpretation and so this bit pattern is used for the end-of-block (EOB) symbol.

In the case where the zero-run-length exceeds 14, a code of 15/0 is used signifying that there are fifteen zero-valued coefficients. This is then followed by another run/size parameter whose run-length value is added to the previous fifteen.

The run/size parameters contain redundancy because some combinations are more common than others. Figure 5.34(b) shows that each run/size value is converted to a variable-length Huffman codeword for transmission. As was shown in section 1.5, the Huffman codes are designed so that short codes are never a prefix of long codes so that the decoder can deduce the parsing by testing an increasing number of bits until a match with the look-up table is found. Having parsed and etc.

Coefficient to be transmitted	Coefficient code	Size parameter
15	1 1 1 1	
14	1 1 1 0	
13	1 1 0 1	
12	1 1 0 0	4
11	1 0 1 1	
10	1 0 1 0	
9	1 0 0 1	
8	1 0 0 0	
7	1 1 1	
6	1 1 0	3
5	1 0 1	
4	1 0 0	
3	1 1	2
2	1 0	
1	1	1
−1	0	
−2	0 1	2
−3	0 0	
−4	0 1 1	
−5	0 1 0	3
−6	0 0 1	
−7	0 0 0	
−8	0 1 1 1	
−9	0 1 1 0	
−10	0 1 0 1	
−11	0 1 0 0	4
−12	0 0 1 1	
−13	0 0 1 0	
−14	0 0 0 1	
−15	0 0 0 0	

(c)   etc.

Figure 5.34 Continued.

decoded the Huffman run/size code, the decoder then knows what the coefficient wordlength will be and can correctly parse that.

The variable-length coefficient code has to describe a bipolar coefficient, i.e. one which can be positive or negative. Figure 5.34(c) shows that for a particular size, the coding scale has a certain gap in it. For example, all values from −7 to +7 can be sent by a size 3 code, so a size 4 code only has to send the values of −15 to −8 and +8 to +15. The coefficient code is sent as a pure binary number whose value ranges from all zeros to all ones where the maximum value is a function of the size.

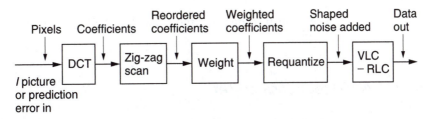

Figure 5.35 A complete spatial coding system which can compress an *I* picture or the prediction error in *P* and *B* pictures. See text for details.

The number range is divided into two, the lower half of the codes specifying negative values and the upper half specifying positive.

In the case of positive numbers, the transmitted binary value is the actual coefficient value, whereas in the case of negative numbers a constant must be subtracted which is a function of the size. In the case of a size 4 code, the constant is 15_{10}. Thus a size 4 parameter of 0111_2 (7_{10}) would be interpreted as $7 - 15 = -8$. A size of 5 has a constant of 31 so a transmitted coded of 01010_2 (10_2) would be interpreted as $10 - 31 = -21$.

This technique saves a bit because, for example, 63 values from -31 to $+31$ are coded with only five bits having only 32 combinations. This is possible because that extra bit is effectively encoded into the run/size parameter.

Figure 5.35 shows the entire MPEG-1 and MPEG-2 spatial coding subsystem. Macroblocks are subdivided into DCT blocks and the DCT is calculated. The resulting coefficients are multiplied by the weighting matrix and then requantized. The coefficients are then reordered by the zig-zag scan so that full advantage can be taken of run-length and variable-length coding. The last non-zero coefficient in the scan is followed by the EOB symbol.

In predictive coding, sometimes the motion-compensated prediction is nearly exact and so the prediction error will be almost zero. This can also happen on still parts of the scene. MPEG takes advantage of this by sending a code to tell the decoder there is no prediction error data for the macroblock concerned.

The success of temporal coding depends on the accuracy of the vectors. Trying to reduce the bit rate by reducing the accuracy of the vectors is false economy as this simply increases the prediction error. Consequently for a given GOP structure it is only in the spatial coding that the overall bit rate is determined. The RLC/VLC coding is lossless and so its contribution to the compression cannot be varied. If the bit rate is too high, the only option is to increase the size of the coefficient-requantizing steps. This has the effect of shortening the wordlength of large coefficients, and rounding small coefficients to zero, so that the bit rate goes down. Clearly if taken too far the picture quality will also suffer because at some point the noise floor will become visible as some form of artifact.

5.13 A bidirectional coder

MPEG does not specify how an encoder is to be built or what coding decisions it should make. Instead it specifies the protocol of the bitstream at the output. As a result the coder shown in Figure 5.36 is only an example. Conceptually MPEG-2 Main Profile coding with a progressive scan input is almost identical to that of MPEG-1 as the differences are to be found primarily in the picture size and the resulting bit rate. The coder

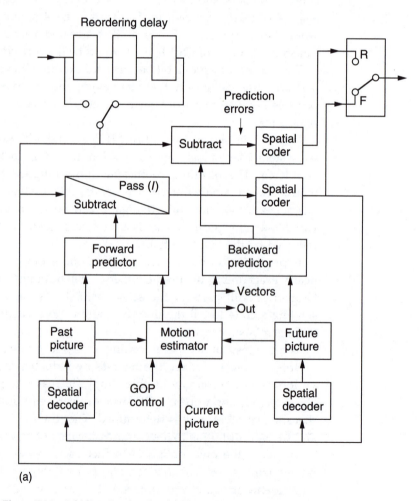

(a)

Figure 5.36 A bidirectional coder. (a) The essential components.

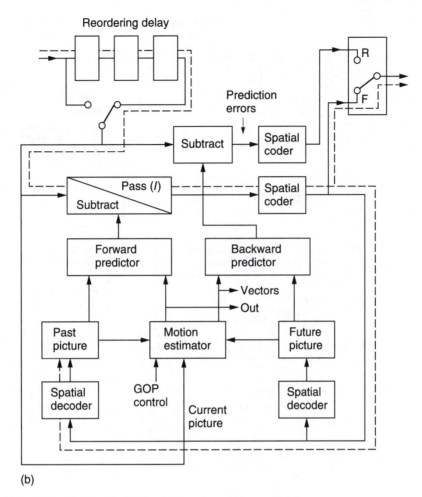

Figure 5.36 Continued. (b) Signal flow when coding an *I* picture.

shown here will create MPEG-1 and MPEG-2 bidirectionally coded bitstreams from progressively scanned inputs. It also forms the basis of interlaced MPEG-2 coding and for MPEG-4 texture coding, both of which will be considered later.

Figure 5.36(a) shows the component parts of the coder. At the input is a chain of picture stores which can be bypassed for reordering purposes. This allows a picture to be encoded ahead of its normal timing when bidirectional coding is employed.

At the centre is a dual-motion estimator which can simultaneously measure motion between the input picture, an earlier picture and a later picture. These reference pictures are held in frame stores. The vectors from the motion estimator are used locally to shift a picture in a frame store to form a predicted picture. This is subtracted from the input picture to produce a prediction error picture which is then spatially

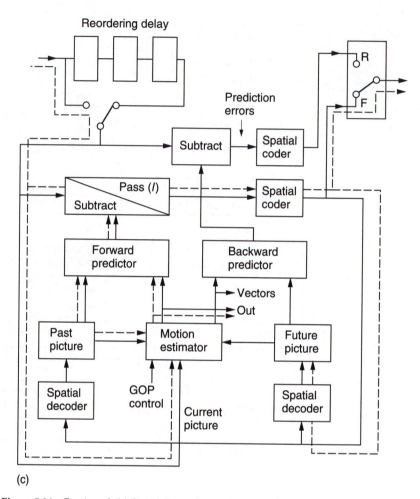

Figure 5.36 Continued. (c) Signal flow when coding a *P* picture.

coded. The bidirectional encoding process will now be described. A GOP begins with an *I* picture which is intra-coded. In Figure 5.36(b) the *I* picture emerges from the reordering delay. No prediction is possible on an *I* picture so the motion estimator is inactive. There is no predicted picture and so the prediction error subtractor is set simply to pass the input. The only processing which is active is the forward spatial coder which describes the picture with DCT coefficients. The output of the forward spatial coder is locally decoded and stored in the past picture frame store.

The reason for the spatial encode/decode is that the past picture frame store now contains exactly what the decoder frame store will contain, including the effects of any requantizing errors. When the same picture is used as a reference at both ends of a differential coding system, the errors will cancel out.

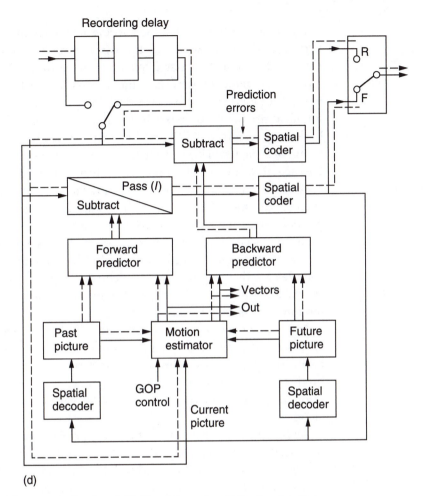

Figure 5.36 Continued. (d) Signal flow when bidirectional coding.

Having encoded the *I* picture, attention turns to the *P* picture. The input sequence is *IBBP*, but the transmitted sequence must be *IPBB*. Figure 5.36(c) shows that the reordering delay is bypassed to select the *P* picture. This passes to the motion estimator which compares it with the *I* picture and outputs a vector for each macroblock. The forward predictor uses these vectors to shift the *I* picture so that it more closely resembles the *P* picture. The predicted picture is then subtracted from the actual picture to produce a forward prediction error. This is then spatially coded. Thus the *P* picture is transmitted as a set of vectors and a prediction error image.

The *P* picture is locally decoded in the right-hand decoder. This takes the forward-predicted picture and adds the decoded prediction error to obtain exactly what the decoder will obtain.

Figure 5.36(d) shows that the encoder now contains an *I* picture in the left store and a *P* picture in the right store. The reordering delay is reselected so that the first *B* picture can be input. This passes to the motion estimator where it is compared with both the *I* and *P* pictures to produce forward and backward vectors. The forward vectors go to the forward predictor to make a *B* prediction from the *I* picture. The backward vectors go to the backward predictor to make a *B* prediction from the *P* picture. These predictions are simultaneously subtracted from the actual *B* picture to produce a forward prediction error and a backward prediction error. These are then spatially encoded. The encoder can then decide which direction of coding resulted in the best prediction, i.e. the smallest prediction error.

In the encoder shown, motion estimation sometimes takes place between an input picture and a decoded picture. With increased complexity, the original input pictures may be stored for motion-estimation purposes. As these contain no compression artifacts the motion vectors may be more accurate.

Not shown in the interests of clarity is a third signal path which creates a predicted *B* picture from the average of forward and backward predictions. This is subtracted from the input picture to produce a third prediction error. In some circumstances this prediction error may use fewer data than either forward of backward prediction alone.

As *B* pictures are never used to create other pictures, the decoder does not locally decode the *B* picture. After decoding and displaying the *B* picture the decoder will discard it. At the encoder the *I* and *P* pictures remain in their frame stores and the second *B* picture is input from the reordering delay.

Following the encoding of the second *B* picture, the encoder must reorder again to encode the second *P* picture in the GOP. This will be locally decoded and will replace the *I* picture in the left store. The stores and predictors switch designation because the left store is now a future *P* picture and the right store is now a past *P* picture. *B* pictures between them are encoded as before.

5.14 Slices

In MPEG-1 and MPEG-2 *I* pictures and in MPEG-4 *I-VOPs*, the DC coefficient describes the average brightness of an entire DCT block. In real video the DC component of adjacent blocks will be similar much of the time. A saving in bit rate can be obtained by differentially coding the DC coefficient.

In *P* and *B* pictures this is not done because these are prediction errors, not actual images, and the statistics are different. However, *P* and *B* pictures send vectors and instead the redundancy in these is explored. In a large moving object, many macroblocks will be moving at the same velocity and their vectors will be the same. Thus differential vector coding will be advantageous.

As has been seen above, differential coding cannot be used indiscriminately as it is prone to error propagation. Periodically absolute DC coefficients and vectors must be sent and the *slice* is the logical structure which supports this mechanism. In *I* coding, the first DC coefficient in a slice is sent in absolute form, whereas the subsequent coefficients are sent differentially. In *P* or *B* coding, the first vector in a slice is sent in absolute form, but the subsequent vectors are differential.

Slices are horizontal picture strips which are one macroblock (16 pixels) high and which proceed from left to right across the screen and may run on to the next horizontal row. The encoder is free to decide how big slices should be and where they begin and end.

In the case of a central dark building silhouetted against the bright sky, there would be two large changes in the DC coefficients, one at each edge of the building. It may be advantageous to the encoder to break the width of the picture into three slices, one each for the left and right areas of sky and one for the building. In the case of a large moving object, different slices may be used for the object and the background.

Each slice contains its own synchronizing pattern, so following a transmission error, correct decoding can resume at the next slice. Slice size can also be matched to the characteristics of the transmission channel. For example, in an error-free transmission system the use of a large number of slices in a packet simply wastes data capacity on surplus synchronizing patterns. However, in a non-ideal system it might be advantageous to have frequent resynchronizing. In DVB, for example, additional constraints are placed on the slice size.

5.15   Handling interlaced pictures

MPEG-1 does not support interlace, whereas MPEG-2 and MPEG-4 do. Spatial coding, predictive coding and motion compensation can still be performed using interlaced source material at the cost of considerable complexity. Despite that complexity, MPEG cannot be expected to perform as well with interlaced material.

Figure 5.37 shows that in an incoming interlaced frame there are two fields each of which contains half of the lines in the frame. In MPEG-2 and MPEG-4 these are known as the *top field* and the *bottom field*. In video from a camera, these fields represent the state of the image at two

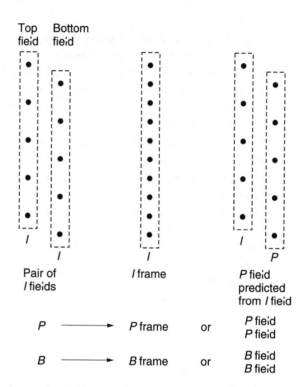

Figure 5.37   An interlaced frame consists of top and bottom fields. MPEG-2 can code a frame in the ways shown here.

different times. Where there is little image motion, this is unimportant and the fields can be combined, obtaining more effective compression. However, in the presence of motion the fields become increasingly decorrelated because of the displacement of moving objects from one field to the next.

This characteristic determines that MPEG must be able to handle fields independently or together. This dual approach permeates all aspects of MPEG and affects the definition of pictures, macroblocks, DCT blocks and zig-zag scanning.

Figure 5.37 also shows how MPEG-2 designates interlaced fields. In picture types *I*, *P* and *B*, the two fields can be superimposed to make a *frame-picture* or the two fields can be coded independently as two *field-pictures*. As a third possibility, in *I* pictures only, the bottom field-picture can be predictively coded from the top field-picture to make an *IP* frame picture.

A frame-picture is one in which the macroblocks contain lines from both field types over a picture area 16 scan lines high. Each luminance macroblock contains the usual four DCT blocks but there are two ways in which these can be assembled. Figure 5.38(a) shows how a frame is

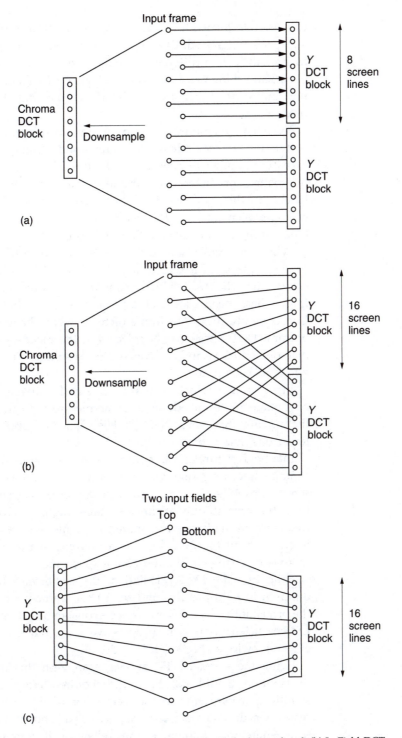

Figure 5.38 (a) In Frame-DCT, a picture is effectively de-interlaced. (b) In Field-DCT, each DCT block only contains lines from one field, but over twice the screen area. (c) The same DCT content results when field-pictures are assembled into blocks.

divided into *frame DCT* blocks. This is identical to the progressive scan approach in that each DCT block contains eight contiguous picture lines. In 4:2:0, the colour difference signals have been downsampled by a factor of two and shifted as was shown in Figure 2.18. Figure 5.38(a) also shows how one 4:2:0 DCT block contains the chroma data from 16 lines in two fields.

Even small amounts of motion in any direction can destroy the correlation between odd and even lines and a frame DCT will result in an excessive number of coefficients. Figure 5.38(b) shows that instead the luminance component of a frame can also be divided into *field DCT* blocks. In this case one DCT block contains odd lines and the other contains even lines. In this mode the chroma still produces one DCT block from both fields as in Figure 5.38(a).

When an input frame is designated as two *field-pictures*, the macro-blocks come from a screen area which is 32 lines high. Figure 5.38(c) shows that the DCT blocks contain the same data as if the input frame had been designated a *frame-picture* but with *field DCT*. Consequently it is only frame-pictures which have the option of field or frame DCT. These may be selected by the encoder on a macroblock-by-macroblock basis and, of course, the resultant bitstream must specify what has been done.

In a frame which contains a small moving area, it may be advantageous to encode as a frame-picture with frame DCT except in the moving area where field DCT is used. This approach may result in fewer bits than coding as two field-pictures.

In a field-picture and in a frame-picture using field DCT, a DCT block contains lines from one field type only and this must have come from a screen area 16 scan lines high, whereas in progressive scan and frame DCT the area is only eight scan lines high. A given vertical spatial frequency in the image is sampled at points twice as far apart which is interpreted by the field DCT as a doubled spatial frequency, whereas there is no change in the horizontal spectrum.

Following the DCT calculation, the coefficient distribution will be different in field-pictures and field DCT frame-pictures. In these cases, the probability of coefficients is not a constant function of radius from the DC coefficient as it is in progressive scan, but is elliptical where the ellipse is twice as high as it is wide.

Using the standard 45° zig-zag scan with this different coefficient distribution would not have the required effect of putting all the significant coefficients at the beginning of the scan. To achieve this requires a different zig-zag scan, which is shown in Figure 5.39. This scan, sometimes known as the Yeltsin walk, attempts to match the elliptical probability of interlaced coefficients with a scan slanted at 67.5° to the vertical.

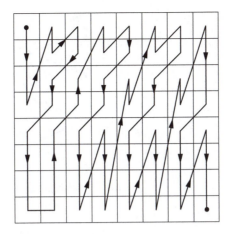

Figure 5.39 The zig-zag scan for an interlaced image has to favour vertical frequencies twice as much as horizontal.

Motion estimation is more difficult in an interlaced system. Vertical detail can result in differences between fields and this reduces the quality of the match. Fields are vertically subsampled without filtering and so contain alias products. This aliasing will mean that the vertical waveform representing a moving object will not be the same in successive pictures and this will also reduce the quality of the match.

Even when the correct vector has been found, the match may be poor so the estimator fails to recognize it. If it is recognized, a poor match means that the quality of the prediction in *P* and *B* pictures will be poor and so a large prediction error or residual has to be transmitted. In an attempt to reduce the residual, MPEG-2 allows field-pictures to use motion-compensated prediction from either the adjacent field or from the same field type in another frame. In this case the encoder will use the better match. This technique can also be used in areas of frame-pictures which use field DCT.

The motion compensation of MPEG-2 has half-pixel resolution and this is inherently compatible with an interlace because an interpolator must be present to handle the half-pixel shifts. Figure 5.40(a) shows that in an interlaced system, each field contains half of the frame lines and so interpolating half-way between lines of one field type will actually create values lying on the sampling structure of the other field type. Thus it is equally possible for a predictive system to decode a given field type based on pixel data from the other field type or of the same type.

If when using predictive coding from the other field type the vertical motion vector contains a half-pixel component, then no interpolation is

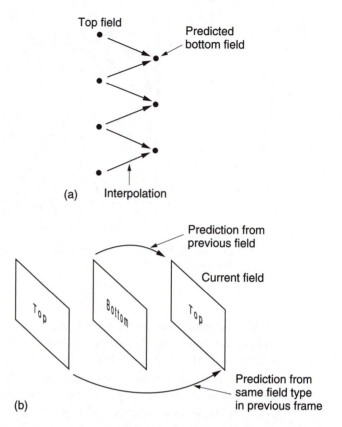

Figure 5.40 (a) Each field contains half of the frame lines and so interpolation is needed to create values lying on the sampling structure of the other field type. (b) Prediction can use data from the previous field or the one before that.

needed because the act of transferring pixels from one field to another results in such a shift.

Figure 5.40(b) shows that a macroblock in a given *P* field-picture can be encoded using a vector which shifts data from the previous field or from the field before that, irrespective of which frames these fields occupy. As noted above, field-picture macroblocks come from an area of screen 32 lines high and this means that the vector density is halved, resulting in larger prediction errors at the boundaries of moving objects.

As an option, field-pictures can restore the vector density by using 16×8 motion compensation where separate vectors are used for the top and bottom halves of the macroblock. Frame-pictures can also use 16×8 motion compensation in conjunction with field DCT. Whilst the 2×2 DCT block luminance structure of a macroblock can easily be divided vertically in two, in 4:2:0 the same screen area is represented by only one chroma macroblock of each component type. As it cannot be divided in half, this chroma is deemed to belong to the luminance DCT blocks of the upper field. In 4:2:2 no such difficulty arises.

MPEG supports interlace simply because interlaced video exists in legacy systems and there is a requirement to compress it. However, where the opportunity arises to define a new system, interlace should be avoided. Legacy interlaced source material should be handled using a motion-compensated de-interlacer prior to compression in the progressive domain.

5.16   MPEG-1 and MPEG-2 coders

Figure 5.41 shows a complete coder. The bidirectional coder outputs coefficients and vectors, and the quantizing table in use. The vectors of P and B pictures and the DC coefficients of I pictures are differentially encoded in slices and the remaining coefficients are RLC/VLC coded. The multiplexer assembles all these data into a single bitstream called an elementary stream. The output of the encoder is a buffer which absorbs the variations in bit rate between different picture types. The buffer output has a constant bit rate determined by the demand clock. This comes from the transmission channel or storage device. If the bit rate is low, the buffer will tend to fill up, whereas if it is high the buffer will tend to empty. The buffer content is used to control the severity of the requantizing in the spatial coders. The more the buffer fills, the bigger the requantizing steps get.

The buffer in the decoder has a finite capacity and the encoder must model the decoder's buffer occupancy so that it neither overflows nor underflows. An overflow might occur if an I picture is transmitted when

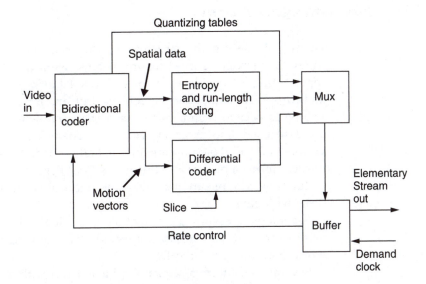

Figure 5.41   An MPEG-2 coder. See text for details.

the buffer content is already high. The buffer occupancy of the decoder depends somewhat on the memory access strategy of the decoder. Instead of defining a specific buffer size, MPEG-2 defines the size of a particular mathematical model of a hypothetical buffer. The decoder designer can use any strategy which implements the model, and the encoder can use any strategy which doesn't overflow or underflow the model. The elementary stream has a parameter called the video buffer verifier (VBV) which defines the minimum buffering assumptions of the encoder.

As was seen in Chapter 1, buffering is one way of ensuring constant quality when picture entropy varies. An intelligent coder may run down the buffer contents in anticipation of a difficult picture sequence so that a large amount of data can be sent.

MPEG-2 does not define what a decoder should do if a buffer underflow or overflow occurs, but since both irrecoverably lose data it is obvious that there will be more or less of an interruption to the decoding. Even a small loss of data may cause loss of synchronization and in the case of long GOP the lost data may make the rest of the GOP undecodable. A decoder may choose to repeat the last properly decoded picture until it can begin to operate correctly again.

Buffer problems occur if the VBV model is violated. If this happens then more than one underflow or overflow can result from a single violation. Switching an MPEG bitstream can cause a violation because the two encoders concerned may have radically different buffer occupancy at the switch.

5.17   The elementary stream

Figure 5.42 shows the structure of the elementary stream from an MPEG-2 encoder. The structure begins with a set of coefficients representing a DCT block. Six or eight DCT blocks form the luminance and chroma content of one macroblock. In *P* and *B* pictures a macroblock will be associated with a vector for motion compensation. Macroblocks are associated into slices in which DC coefficients of *I* pictures and vectors in *P* and *B* pictures are differentially coded. An arbitrary number of slices forms a picture and this needs *I/P/B* flags describing the type of picture it is. The picture may also have a global vector which efficiently deals with pans.

Several pictures form a group of pictures (GOP). The GOP begins with an *I* picture and may or may not include *P* and *B* pictures in a structure which may vary dynamically.

Several GOPs form a sequence which begins with a sequence header containing important data to help the decoder. It is possible to repeat the

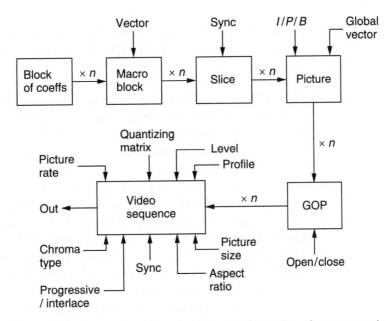

Figure 5.42 The structure of an elementary stream. MPEG defines the syntax precisely.

header within a sequence, and this helps lock-up in random access applications. The sequence header describes the MPEG-2 profile and level, whether the video is progressive or interlaced, whether the chroma is 4:2:0 or 4:2:2, the size of the picture and the aspect ratio of the pixels. The quantizing matrix used in the spatial coder can also be sent. The sequence begins with a standardized bit pattern which is detected by a decoder to synchronize the deserialization.

5.18 An MPEG-2 decoder

The decoder is only defined by implication from the definitions of syntax and any decoder which can correctly interpret all combinations of syntax at a particular profile will be deemed compliant however it works. Compliant MPEG-2 decoders must be able to decode an MPEG-1 elementary stream. This is not particularly difficult as MPEG-2 uses all the tools of MPEG-1 and simply adds more of its own. Consequently an MPEG-1 bitstream can be thought of as a subset of an MPEG-2 bitstream.

The first problem a decoder has is that the input is an endless bitstream which contains a huge range of parameters many of which have variable length. Unique synchronizing patterns must be placed periodically throughout the bitstream so that the decoder can identify known starting points. The pictures which can be sent under MPEG are so flexible that the decoder must first find a sequence header so that it can establish the size of the picture, the frame rate, the colour coding used, etc.

The decoder must also be supplied with a 27 MHz system clock. In a DVD player, this would come from a crystal, but in a transmission system this would be provided by a numerically locked loop running from a clock reference parameter in the bitstream (see Chapter 6). Until this loop has achieved lock the decoder cannot function properly.

Figure 5.43 shows a bidirectional decoder. The decoder can only begin decoding with an *I* picture and as this only uses intra-coding there will be no vectors. An *I* picture is transmitted as a series of slices which begin with subsidiary synchronizing patterns. The first macroblock in the slice contains an absolute DC coefficient, but the remaining macroblocks code the DC coefficient differentially so the decoder must subtract the differential values from the previous value to obtain the absolute value.

The AC coefficients are sent as Huffman coded run/size parameters followed by coefficient value codes. The variable-length Huffman codes are decoded by using a look-up table and extending the number of bits considered until a match is obtained. This allows the zero-run-length and the coefficient size to be established. The right number of bits is taken from the bitstream corresponding to the coefficient code and this is decoded to the actual coefficient using the size parameter.

If the correct number of bits has been taken from the stream, the next bit must be the beginning of the next run/size code and so on until the EOB symbol is reached. The decoder uses the coefficient values and the zero-run-lengths to populate a DCT coefficient block following the appropriate zig-zag scanning sequence. Following EOB, the bitstream then continues with the next DCT block. Clearly this Huffman decoding will work perfectly or not at all. A single bit slippage in synchronism or a single corrupted data bit can cause a spectacular failure.

Once a complete DCT coefficient block has been received, the coefficients need to be inverse quantized and inverse weighted. Then an inverse DCT can be performed and this will result in an 8×8 pixel block. A series of DCT blocks will allow the luminance and colour information for an entire macroblock to be decoded and this can be placed in a frame store. Decoding continues in this way until the end of the slice when an absolute DC coefficient will once again be sent. Once all the slices have been decoded, an entire picture will be resident in the frame store.

The amount of data needed to decode the picture is variable and the decoder just keeps going until the last macroblock is found. It will obtain data from the input buffer. In a constant bit rate transmission system, the decoder will remove more data to decode an *I* picture than has been

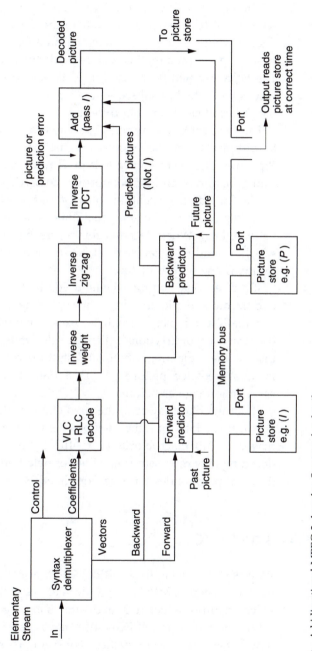

Figure 5.43 A bidirectional MPEG-2 decoder. See text for details.

received in one picture period, leaving the buffer emptier than it began. Subsequent *P* and *B* pictures need much fewer data and allow the buffer to fill again.

The picture will be output when the time stamp (see Chapter 6) sent with the picture matches the state of the decoder's time count.

Following the *I* picture may be another *I* picture or a *P* picture. Assuming a *P* picture, this will be predictively coded from the *I* picture. The *P* picture will be divided into slices as before. The first vector in a slice is absolute, but subsequent vectors are sent differentially. However, the DC coefficients are not differential.

Each macroblock may contain a forward vector. The decoder uses this to shift pixels from the *I* picture into the correct position for the predicted *P* picture. The vectors have half-pixel resolution and where a half-pixel shift is required, an interpolator will be used.

The DCT data are sent much as for an *I* picture. It will require inverse quantizing, but not inverse weighting because *P* and *B* coefficients are flat-weighted. When decoded this represents an error-cancelling picture which is added pixel-by-pixel to the motion-predicted picture. This results in the output picture.

If bidirectional coding is being used, the *P* picture may be stored until one or more *B* pictures have been decoded. The *B* pictures are sent essentially as a *P* picture might be, except that the vectors can be forward, backward or bidirectional. The decoder must take pixels from the *I* picture, the *P* picture, or both, and shift them according to the vectors to make a predicted picture. The DCT data decode to produce an error-cancelling image as before.

In an interlaced system, the prediction mechanism may alternatively obtain pixel data from the previous field or the field before that. Vectors may relate to macroblocks or to 16×8 pixel areas. DCT blocks after decoding may represent frame lines or field lines. This adds up to a lot of different possibilities for a decoder handling an interlaced input.

5.19   MPEG-4 and AVC

As was seen in Chapter 1, MPEG-4 advances the coding art in a number of ways. Whereas MPEG-1 and MPEG-2 were directed only to coding the video pictures which resulted after shooting natural scenes or from computer synthesis, MPEG-4 also moves further back in the process of how those scenes were created. For example, the rotation of a detailed three-dimensional object before a video camera produces huge changes in the video from picture to picture which MPEG-2 would find difficult to code. Instead, if the three-dimensional object is re-created at the

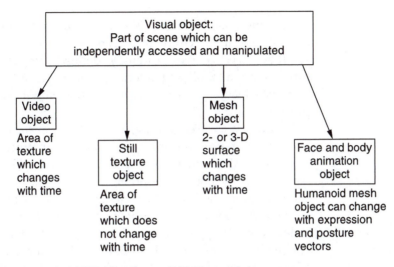

Figure 5.44 In MPEG-4 four types of *objects* are coded.

decoder, rotation can be portrayed by transmitting a trivially small amount of vector data.

If the above object is synthetic, effectively the synthesis or rendering process is completed in the decoder. However, a suitable if complex image processor at the encoder could identify such objects in natural scenes. MPEG-4 objects are defined as a part of a scene that can independently be accessed or manipulated. An object is an entity that exists over a certain time span. The pictures of conventional imaging become *object planes* in MPEG-4. Where an object intersects an object plane, it can be described by the coding system using intra-coding, forward prediction or bidirectional prediction.

Figure 5.44 shows that MPEG-4 has four object types. A video object is an arbitrarily shaped planar pixel array describing the appearance or *texture* of part of a scene. A still texture object or *sprite* is a planar video object in which there is no change with respect to time. A mesh object describes a two- or three-dimensional shape as a set of points. The shape and its position can change with respect to time. Using computer graphics techniques, texture can be mapped onto meshes, a process known as warping, to produce rendered images.

Using two-dimensional warping, a still texture object can be made to move. In three-dimensional graphic rendering, mesh coding allows an arbitrary solid shape to be created which is then covered with texture. Perspective computation then allows this three-dimensional object to be viewed in correct perspective from any viewpoint. MPEG-4 provides tools to allow two- or three-dimensional meshes to be created in the decoder and then oriented by vectors. Changing the vectors then allows realistic moving images to be created with an extremely low bit rate.

Face and body animation is a specialized subset of three-dimensional mesh coding in which the mesh represents a human face and/or body. As the subject moves, carefully defined vectors carry changes of expression which allow rendering of an apparently moving face and/or body which has been almost entirely synthesized from a single still picture.

In addition to object coding, MPEG-4 refines the existing MPEG tools by increasing the efficiency of a number of processes using lossless prediction. AVC extends this concept further still. This improves the performance of both the motion compensation and coefficient coding allowing either a lower bit rate or improved quality. MPEG-4 also extends the idea of scaleability introduced in MPEG-2. Multiple scaleability is supported, where a low-bit-rate base-level picture may optionally be enhanced by adding information from one or more additional bitstreams. This approach is useful in network applications where the content creator cannot know the bandwidth which a particular user will have available. Scaleability allows the best quality in the available bandwidth.

Although most of the spatial compression of MPEG-4 is based on the DCT as in earlier MPEG standards, MPEG-4 also introduces wavelet coding of still objects. Wavelets are advantageous in scaleable systems because they naturally decompose the original image into various resolutions.

In contrast to the rest of MPEG-4, AVC is intended for use with entire pictures and as such is more of an extension of MPEG-2. AVC adds refinement to the existing coding tools of MPEG and also introduces some new ones. The emphasis is on lossless coding to obtain similar performance to MPEG-2 at around half the bit rate.

5.20 Video objects

Figure 5.45 shows an example of a video object intersecting *video object planes*, or VOPs. At each plane, the shape and the texture of the object must be portrayed. Figure 5.46 shows this can be done using appropriate combinations of intra- and inter-coding as described for the earlier standards. This gives rise to I-VOPs, P-VOPs and B-VOPs. A group of VOPs is known as a GOV.

Figure 5.47 shows how video objects are handled at the decoder which effectively contains a multi-layer compositing stage. The shape of each object is transmitted using *alpha data* which is decoded to produce a key signal. This has the effect of keying the texture data into the overall picture. Several objects can be keyed into the same picture. The

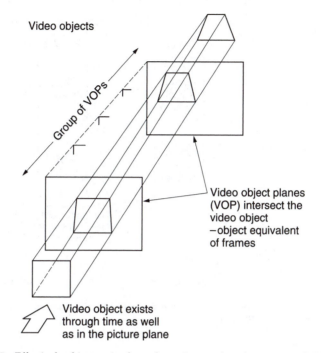

Video objects

Group of VOPs

Video object planes
(VOP) intersect the
video object
—object equivalent
of frames

Video object exists
through time as well
as in the picture plane

Figure 5.45 Effectively objects exist through continuous time, but are sampled for display purposes. A video object plane (VOP) is a temporal sample of an object. VOPs correspond to pictures of MPEG-1 and MPEG-2.

background may be yet another video object or a still texture object which can be shifted by vectors in the case of pans etc.

Figure 5.48 shows that MPEG-4 codes each arbitrarily shaped video object by creating a *bounding rectangle* within which the object resides. The shape and the texture of each video object are re-created at the decoder by two distinct but interrelated processes. The bounding rectangle exists on macroblock boundaries and can change from VOP to VOP. At each VOP, the bitstream contains horizontal and vertical references specifying the position of the top-left corner of the bounding rectangle and its width and height.

Within the bounding rectangle are three kinds of macroblock. *Transparent macroblocks* are entirely outside the object and contain no texture data. The shape data are identical over the entire block and result in a key signal which deselects this block in the compositing process. Such shape data are trivial to compress. *Opaque macroblocks* are entirely within the object and are full of texture data. The shape data are again identical over the entire block and result in the block being keyed at the compositor. *Boundary macroblocks* are blocks through which the edge of the object passes. They contain essentially all the shape information and somewhat fewer texture data than an opaque macroblock.

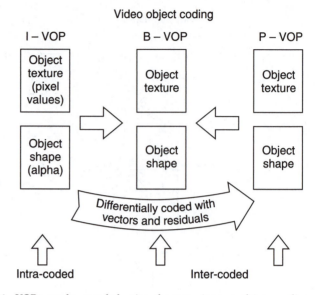

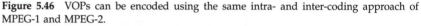

Figure 5.46 VOPs can be encoded using the same intra- and inter-coding approach of MPEG-1 and MPEG-2.

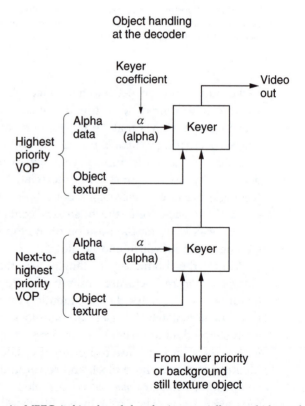

Figure 5.47 An MPEG-4 object-based decoder is essentially a multi-layered compositing device, using keying to give the illusion that objects are in front of a background.

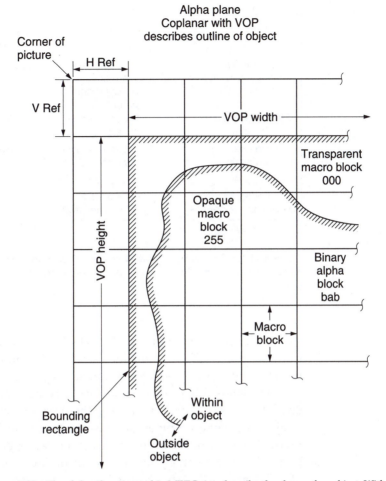

Figure 5.48 The alpha plane is used in MPEG-4 to describe the shape of an object. Within a bounding rectangle are three different types of macroblock: those within the object, those outside and those which are intersected by the boundary.

5.21 Texture coding

In MPEG-1 and MPEG-2 the only way of representing an image is with pixels and this requires no name. In MPEG-4 there are various types of image description tools and it becomes necessary to give the pixel representation of the earlier standards a name. This is *texture coding* which is that part of MPEG-4 that operates on pixel-based areas of image.

Coming later than MPEG-1 and MPEG-2, the MPEG-4 and AVC texture-coding systems can afford additional complexity in the search for higher performance. Figure 5.49 contrasts MPEG-2, MPEG-4 and AVC. Figure 5.49(a) shows the texture decoding system of MPEG-2 whereas (b)

MPEG-2	MPEG-4	AVC
DCT	DCT	Small block size integer coefficient transform
DC coefficient prediction in slice	DC coefficient prediction AC coefficient prediction	Spatial prediction with edge direction adaptation
Single coefficient scan	3 × coefficient scans	Multiple coefficient scans
Fixed resolution weighting	Reduced resolution weighting	Reduced resolution weighting
VLC/RLC	VLC/RLC	
Differential vectors in slice one vector/MB	Vector prediction up to 4 vectors/MB	Vector prediction up to 16 vectors/MB
(a)	(b)	(c)

Figure 5.49 (a) The texture coding system of MPEG-2. (b) Texture coding in MPEG-4. (c) Texture coding in AVC. Note a steady process of refinement with the penalty of increased complexity.

shows MPEG-4 and (c) shows AVC. The latter two are refinements of the earlier technique. These refinements are lossless in that the reduction in bit rate they allow does not result in a loss of quality.

When inter-coding, there is always a compromise needed over the quantity of vector data. Clearly if the area steered by each vector is smaller, the motion compensation is more accurate, but the reduction in residual data is offset by the increase in vector data. In MPEG-1 and MPEG-2 only a small amount of vector compression is used. In contrast, MPEG-4 and AVC use advanced forms of lossless vector compression which can, without any bit rate penalty, increase the vector density to one vector per DCT block in MPEG-4 and to one vector per 4×4 pixel block in AVC. AVC also allows quarter-pixel accurate vectors. In inter-coded pictures the prediction of the picture is improved so that the residual to be coded is smaller.

When intra-coding, MPEG-4 looks for further redundancy between coefficients using prediction. When a given DCT block is to be intra-coded, certain of its coefficients will be predicted from adjacent blocks.

The choice of the most appropriate block is made by measuring the picture gradient, defined as the rate of change of the DC coefficient. Figure 5.50(a) shows that the three adjacent blocks, A, B and C, are analysed to decide whether to predict from the DCT block above (vertical prediction) or to the left (horizontal prediction). Figure 5.50(b) shows that in vertical prediction the top row of coefficients is predicted from the block above so that only the differences between them need to be coded.

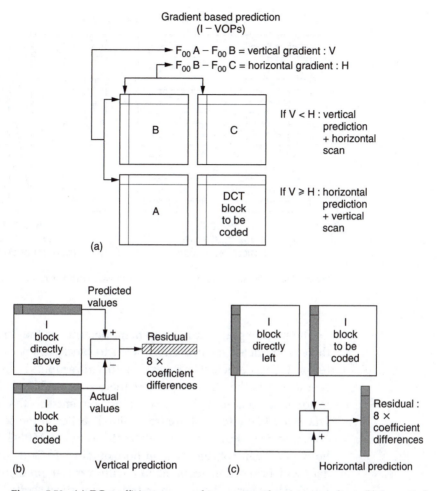

Figure 5.50 (a) DC coefficients are used to measure the picture gradient. (b) In vertical prediction the top row of coefficients are predicted using those above as a basis. (c) In horizontal prediction the left column of coefficients is predicted from those to the left.

Figure 5.50(c) shows that in horizontal prediction the left column of coefficients is predicted from the block on the left so that again only the differences need be coded.

Choosing the blocks above and to the left is important because these blocks will already be available in both the encoder and decoder. By making the same picture gradient measurement, the decoder can establish whether vertical or horizontal prediction has been used and so no flag is needed in the bitstream.

Some extra steps are needed to handle the top row and the left column of a picture or object where true prediction is impossible. In these cases both encoder and decoder assume standardized constant values for the missing prediction coefficients.

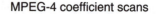

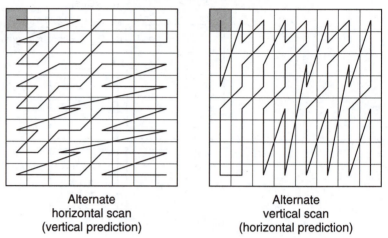

Alternate
horizontal scan
(vertical prediction)

Alternate
vertical scan
(horizontal prediction)

Figure 5.51 The alternate zig-zag scans employed with vertical or horizontal prediction.

The picture gradient measurement determines the direction in which there is the least change from block to block. There will generally be fewer DCT coefficients present in this direction. There will be more coefficients in the other axis where there is more change. Consequently it is advantageous to alter the scanning sequence so that the coefficients which are likely to exist are transmitted earlier in the sequence.

Figure 5.51 shows the two alternate scans for MPEG-4. The alternate horizontal scan concentrates on horizontal coefficients early in the scan and will be used in conjunction with vertical prediction. Conversely the alternate vertical scan concentrates on vertical coefficients early in the scan and will be used in conjunction with horizontal prediction. The decoder can establish which scan has been used in the encoder from the picture gradient.

Coefficient prediction is not employed when inter-coding because the statistics of residual images are different. Instead of attempting to predict residual coefficients, in inter-coded texture, pixel-based prediction may be used to reduce the magnitude of texture residuals. This technique is known as *overlapped block motion compensation* (OBMC) which is only used in P-VOPs. With only one vector per DCT block, clearly in many cases the vector cannot apply to every pixel in the block. If the vector is considered to describe the motion of the centre of the block, the vector accuracy falls towards the edge of the block. A pixel in the corner of a block is almost equidistant from a vector in the centre of an adjacent block.

OBMC uses vectors from adjacent blocks, known as *remote vectors*, in addition to the vector of the current block for prediction. Figure 5.52

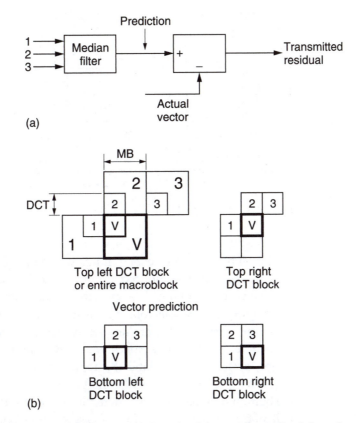

Figure 5.52 (a) MPEG-4 inter-coded pixel values may be predicted from three remote vectors as well as the true vector. (b) The three remote vectors are selected according to the macroblock quadrant. Macroblocks may have one or four vectors and the prediction mechanism allows prediction between blocks of either type.

shows that the motion-compensation process of MPEG-1 and MPEG-2 which uses a single vector is modified by the addition of the pixel prediction system which considers three vectors. A given pixel in the block to be coded is predicted from the weighted sum of three motion-compensated pixels taken from the previous I- or P-VOP. One of these pixels is obtained in the normal way by accessing the previous VOP with a shift given by the vector of this block. The other two are obtained by accessing the same VOP pixels using the remote vectors of two adjacent blocks.

The remote vectors which are used and the weighting factors are both a function of the pixel position in the block. Figure 5.52 shows that the block to be coded is divided into quadrants. The remote vectors are selected from the blocks closest to the quadrant in which the pixel resides. For example, a pixel in the bottom-right quadrant would be predicted using remote vectors from the DCT block immediately below and the block immediately to the right.

4	5	5	5	5	5	5	4
5	5	5	5	5	5	5	5
5	5	6	6	6	6	5	5
5	5	6	6	6	6	5	5
5	5	6	6	6	6	5	5
5	5	6	6	6	6	5	5
5	5	5	5	5	5	5	5
4	5	5	5	5	5	5	4

2	2	2	2	2	2	2	2
1	1	2	2	2	2	1	1
1	1	1	1	1	1	1	1
1	1	1	1	1	1	1	1
1	1	1	1	1	1	1	1
1	1	1	1	1	1	1	1
1	1	2	2	2	2	1	1
2	2	2	2	2	2	2	2

2	1	1	1	1	1	1	2
2	2	1	1	1	1	2	2
2	2	1	1	1	1	2	2
2	2	1	1	1	1	2	2
2	2	1	1	1	1	2	2
2	2	1	1	1	1	2	2
2	2	1	1	1	1	2	2
2	1	1	1	1	1	1	2

(a) Weighting values for use with motion vector of current Y block (true vector)

(b) Weighting values for use with motion vector of Y blocks above or below current Y block (remote vector)

(c) Weighting values for use with motion vectors of Y blocks left or right of current Y block (remote vector)

Figure 5.53 Vector prediction.

Not all blocks can be coded in this way. In P-VOPs it is permissible to have blocks which are not coded or intra-blocks which contain no vector. Remote vectors will not all be available at the boundaries of a VOP. In the normal sequence of macroblock transmission, vectors from macroblocks below the current block are not yet available. Some additional steps are needed to handle these conditions. Adjacent to boundaries where a remote vector is not available it is replaced by a copy of the actual vector. This is also done where an adjacent block is intra-coded and for blocks at the bottom of a macroblock where the vectors for the macroblocks below will not be available yet. In the case of non-coded blocks the remote vector is set to zero.

Figure 5.53(a) shows that the weighting factors for pixels near the centre of a block favour that block. In the case of pixels at the corner of the block, the weighting is even between the value obtained from the true vector and the sum of the two pixel values obtained from remote vectors.

The weighted sum produces a predicted pixel which is subtracted from the actual pixel in the current VOP to be coded to produce a residual pixel. Blocks of residual pixels are DCT coded as usual. OBMC reduces the magnitude of residual pixels and gives a corresponding reduction in the number or magnitude of DCT coefficients to be coded.

OBMC is lossless because the decoder already has access to all the vectors and knows the weighting tables. Consequently the only overhead is the transmission of a flag which enables or disables the mechanism.

MPEG-4 also has the ability to downsample prediction error or residual macroblocks which contain little detail. A 16×16 macroblock block is downsampled to 8×8 and flagged. The decoder will identify the flag and interpolate back to 16×16.

In vector prediction, each macroblock may have only one or four vectors as the coder decides. Consequently the prediction of a current vector may have to be done from either macroblock or DCT block vectors. In the case of predicting one vector for an entire macro-block, or the top-left DCT block vector, the process shown in Figure 5.52(b) is used. Three earlier vectors, which may be macroblock or DCT block vectors, as available, are used as the input to the prediction process. In the diagram the large squares show the macroblock vectors to be selected and the small squares show the DCT block vectors to be selected. The three vectors are passed to a median filter which outputs the vector in the centre of the range unchanged.

A median filter is used because the same process can be performed in the decoder with no additional data transmission. The median vector is used as a prediction, and comparison with the actual vector enables a residual to be computed and coded for transmission. At the decoder the same prediction can be made and the received residual is added to recreate the original vector.

The remaining parts of Figure 5.52(b) show how the remaining three DCT block vectors are predicted from adjacent DCT block vectors. If the relevant block is only macroblock coded, that vector will be substituted.

5.22 Shape coding

Shape coding is the process of compressing alpha or keying data. Most objects are opaque and so a binary alpha signal is adequate for the base-level shape system. For each texture pixel, an alpha bit exists forming a *binary alpha map* which is effectively a two-dimensional mask through which the object can be seen. At the decoder binary alpha data are converted to 000 or 255 levels in an eight-bit keying system.

Optionally the object can be faded in the compositing process by sending a *constant alpha value* at each VOP. As a further option, variable transparency can be supported by sending *alpha texture data*. This is coded using the usual MPEG spatial coding tools such as DCT and scanning etc.

Binary data such as alpha data do not respond to DCT coding, and another compression technique has been developed for binary alpha blocks (bab). This is known as *context-based coding* and it effectively codes the location of the boundary between alpha one bits and alpha zero bits. Clearly once the boundary is located the values of all remaining alpha bits are obvious.

The babs are raster scanned into a serial bitstream. Context coding works by attempting to predict the state of the current bit from a set of bits which have already been decoded. Figure 5.54(a) shows the set of bits, known as a context, used in an intra-coded VOP. There are ten bits in the context and so there can be 1024 different contexts. Extensive analysis of real shapes shows that for each context there is a certain probability

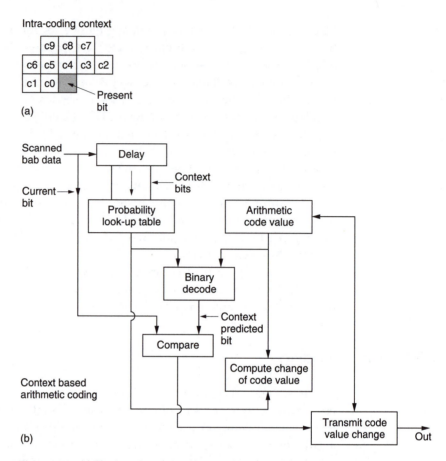

Figure 5.54 (a) The context is a set of bits used for prediction of the current bab bit. (b) The encoder compares the actual bit with the predicted value and modifies the arithmetic code in order to make the prediction correct at the decoder.

that the current bit will be zero. This probability exists as a standardized look-up table in the encoder and decoder.

Figure 5.54(b) shows that the encoder compares the probability with a parameter called the arithmetic code value to predict the value of the alpha bit. If the prediction is correct, the arithmetic code value needs no change and nothing needs to be transmitted. However, if the predicted bit is incorrect, a change to the arithmetic code value must be transmitted, along with the position of the bit in the scan to which it applies. This change is calculated to be just big enough to make the prediction correct. In this way only prediction errors, which represent the boundary location where alpha changes, are transmitted and the remaining bits self-predict.

Figure 5.55 shows that the spatial extent of the context requires alpha bits from adjacent babs to code the present bab. This results in the concept of the *bordered bab* which incorporates a two-pixel deep border of

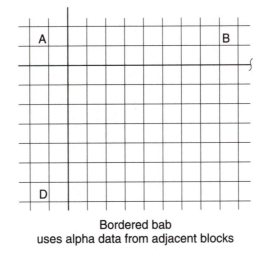

Bordered bab
uses alpha data from adjacent blocks

Figure 5.55 A bordered bab contains bits from adjacent babs so that context bits are available.

alpha bits above and to each side. In the case of babs adjacent to the top or sides of the bounding rectangle, some of the bounding bits are outside that rectangle and their value is obviously always zero.

Shape data can also be inter-coded. This is handled using a context which spreads across two VOPs. As Figure 5.56 shows, four context bits are in the current VOP, whereas five context bits are in a previous VOP. This nine-bit context requires a different probability table, but otherwise coding proceeds as before. If the shape changes from one VOP to another, motion compensation can be used. A shape vector is transmitted. It will be seen from Figure 5.56(b) that this vector shifts the context relative to the previous VOP, thus altering (hopefully improving) the chances of correctly predicting the current bit.

Within a boundary block, shape vectors are highly redundant with the motion vectors of texture and texture vectors may be used to predict shape vectors.

It might be thought that binary shape data would result in objects having ratcheted edges because the key signal can only exist in pixel steps. However, texture coding can overcome this problem. If a binary keyed image is used as a predictor, the texture prediction error will deliver the necessary accuracy in the final image.

5.23   Padding

The peculiar conditions in boundary macroblocks where some of the block is inside the object and some outside requires special handling and

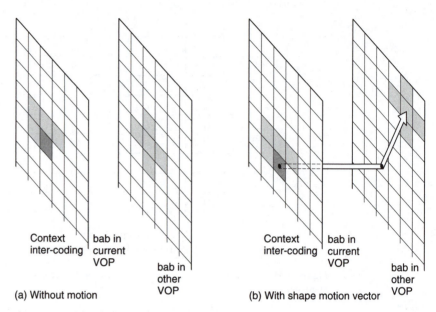

Figure 5.56 (a) In bab inter-coding, the context spreads over the current and the previous VOP. (b) Shape motion vectors shift the context with respect to the reference VOP to improve the accuracy of prediction.

this is the function of padding. There are two types of padding which perform distinct functions; texture padding and motion compensation (MC) padding.

Texture padding makes the spatial coding of boundary blocks more efficient. As the frequency coefficients of the DCT relate to the entire block area, detail outside the object can result in coefficients which are not due to the object itself. Texture padding consists of replacing those pixels in a boundary block which are outside the object with pixel values that are selected to minimize the amount of coefficient data. The exact values are unimportant as they will be discarded in the decoder.

When objects move they may also change their shape. Motion compensation will be used whereby texture and shape from another VOP is used to predict texture and shape in the current VOP. If there is a small error in the boundary data, background pixels could leak into the object causing a large prediction error. MC padding is designed to prevent this. In the case of VOPs used as anchors for inter-coding, in boundary blocks, after decoding, texture padding is replaced with MC padding. In MC padding, pixel values at the very edge of the object are copied to pixels outside the object so that small shape errors can be corrected with minor residual data.

5.24   Video object coding

Figure 5.57 shows the video object coding process. At the encoder, image analysis dissects the images into objects, in this case one small object (1) and a background object (2). The picture and shape data for object 1 are used to create a bounding rectangle whose co-ordinates are coded. Pixel values outside the boundary are replaced with texture padding. The texture macroblocks are then DCT coded and the shape babs are context coded. This can be on an intra- or motion-compensated inter-basis according to the type of VOP being coded. Background data are coded by another process and multiplexed into the bitstream as another object.

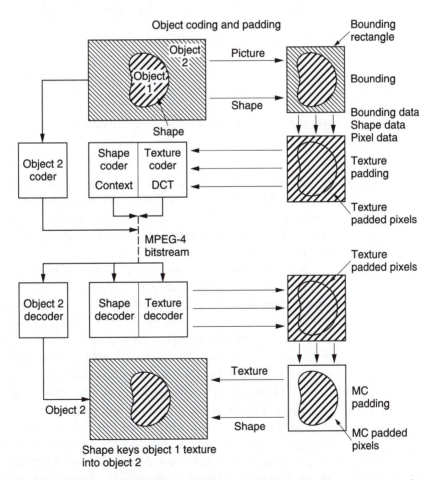

Figure 5.57   The video object coding process. Each object requires shape and texture data. One or more objects and a background are transmitted.

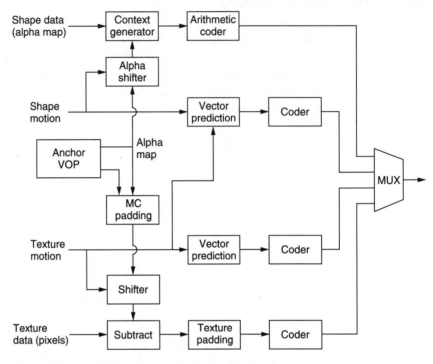

Figure 5.58 An MPEG-4 object coder. See text for details.

At the decoder the texture and shape data are decoded, and in anchor VOPs the shape data are used to strip off the texture padding and replace it with MC padding. MC padded object data are used to predict intra-coded objects. Finally the shape data key the object into the background.

Figure 5.58 shows an object coder. The object analysis of the incoming image provides texture and texture motion as well as object shape and shape motion. Texture coding takes place in much the same way as MPEG picture coding. Intra-VOPs are spatially coded, whereas P- and B-VOPs use motion-compensated prediction and a spatially coded residual is transmitted. The vectors in MPEG-4 are subject to a prediction process not found in MPEG-2. Note the use of texture padding before the coder. As the decoder will use MC padding in the course of prediction, the encoder must also use it to prevent drift.

The shape data are context coded in I-VOPs and the coding will be motion compensated in P- and B-VOPs. However, the shape vectors can be predicted from other shape vectors or from the texture motion vectors where these exist. These shape vectors are coded as prediction residuals. Figure 5.59 shows how the shape vector prediction works. Around the

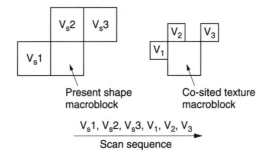

Figure 5.59 Shape vectors may be coded or taken from texture vectors. The decoder scans vectors in the sequence shown and takes the first ones available.

bab to be coded are three designated shape vectors and three designated texture vectors. The six designated vectors are scanned in the order shown and the first one which is defined will be used as the predictor. Consequently if no shape vectors are defined, the texture vectors will be used automatically since these are later in the scan.

Shape babs can exist in a variety of forms as Figure 5.48 showed. Opaque and transparent blocks are easily and efficiently coded. Intra babs have no shape vector but need a lot of data. Inter babs may or may not contain a shape vector according to object motion and only a residual is sent. On the other hand, under certain object conditions, sufficient shape accuracy may result by sending only the shape vector.

5.25 Two-dimensional mesh coding

Mesh coding was developed in computer graphics to aid the rendering of synthetic images with perspective. As Figure 5.60 shows, as a three-dimensional body turns, its two-dimensional appearance changes. If the body has a flat side square-on to the optical axis whose texture is described by uniformly spaced pixels, after a rotation the pixels will no longer be uniformly spaced. Nearly every pixel will have moved, and clearly an enormous amount of data would be needed to describe the motion of each one. Fortunately this is not necessary; if the geometry of the object is correctly sampled before and after the motion, then the shift of every pixel can be computed.

The geometric sampling results in a structure known as a mesh. Effectively a mesh is a sampled surface. The smoother the surface, the fewer samples are necessary because the remainder of the surface can be interpolated. In MPEG-4, meshes can be two or three dimensional. Figure 5.61 shows a two-dimensional mesh which is a set of points known as *nodes* which must remain in the video object plane. Figure 5.62

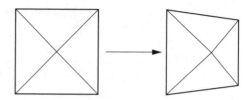

Figure 5.60 As a body turns, its shape on a two-dimensional screen may change.

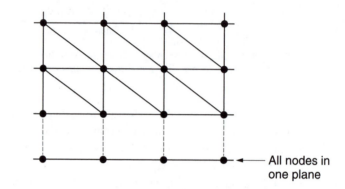

All nodes in
one plane

Figure 5.61 All the nodes of a two-dimensional mesh lie in the same plane.

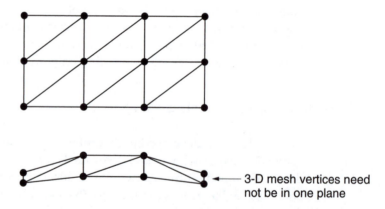

3-D mesh vertices need
not be in one plane

Figure 5.62 A three-dimensional mesh samples the surface of a solid body.

shows a three-dimensional mesh which is a set of nodes describing a non-flat surface.

Like other MPEG-4 parameters, meshes can be scaleable. A base mesh has relatively few nodes; adding enhancement data will increase the number of nodes so that the shape is better described.

Figure 5.63 shows an example of how two-dimensional meshes are used to predict an object from a previous VOP. The first object may be sent as an I-VOP, including texture and alpha outline data, both of which will be intra-coded. The texture pixels in the I-VOP are uniformly spaced

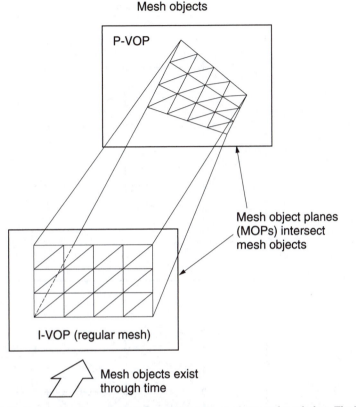

Mesh objects

P-VOP

Mesh object planes
(MOPs) intersect
mesh objects

I-VOP (regular mesh)

Mesh objects exist
through time

Figure 5.63 In mesh coding, an object is coded as texture, shape and mesh data. The I-VOP mesh may be regular and need few data to code it.

and so a uniform mesh can be sent as a further part of the same I-VOP. Uniform meshes require very few data. Figure 5.64(a) shows that little more than the co-ordinates of the top-left corner of the mesh and the mesh pitch need be sent. There are also some choices of how the mesh boxes are divided into triangles.

As an alternative to a regular mesh, an irregular or *Delaunay* mesh may be created by specifying the location of each vertex. This will require more data initially, but may prove to be more efficient in the case of an irregular object which exists for a long time.

Figure 5.64(b) shows how the shape of the mesh can be changed by transmitting mesh vectors in P-VOPs. These specify the new position of each vertex with respect to the original position. The mesh motion vectors are predictively coded as shown in Figure 5.65. In two adjacent triangles there are two common nodes. If the first triangle has been fully coded, only one node of the second triangle remains to be coded. The vector for the remaining node is predicted by taking the average of the two common nodes and rounding to half-pixel accuracy. This prediction is subtracted from the actual vector to produce a residual which is then

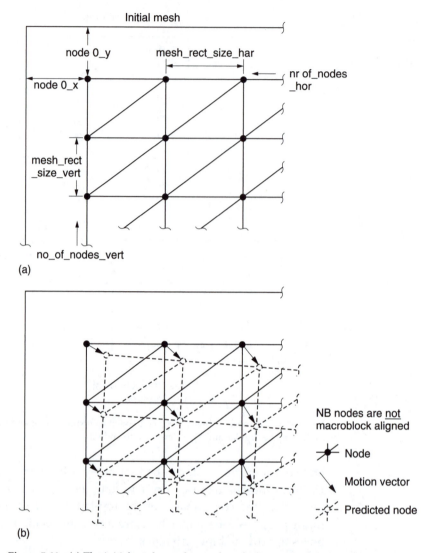

Figure 5.64 (a) The initial mesh may be regular which requires few data. (b) A mesh may be warped by transmitting vectors which displace the nodes.

variable-length coded for transmission. As each node is coded, another triangle is completed and a new pair of common nodes become available for further prediction.

Figure 5.66 shows an object coding system using meshes. At (a), following the transmission of the I-VOP containing shape, outline and a regular mesh, the I-VOP and the next VOP, which will be a P-VOP, are supplied to a motion estimator. The motion estimator will determine the motion of the object from one VOP to the next. As the object moves and turns, its shape and perspective will change. The new shape may be encoded using differential alpha data which the decoder uses to change

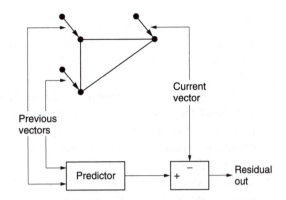

Figure 5.65 Mesh vectors are predicted from the previous two vertices of the triangle concerned.

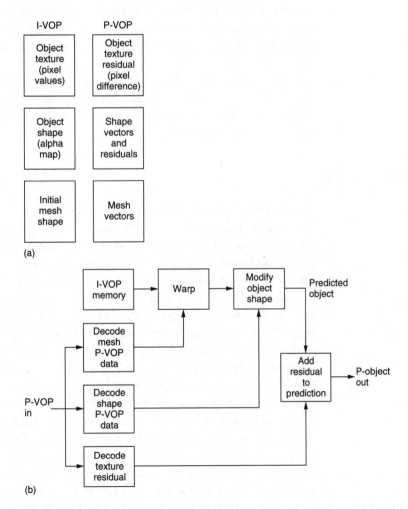

Figure 5.66 (a) Mesh coding requires texture, shape and mesh data to be multiplexed into the bitstream. (b) An object coding system using meshes. See text.

the previous shape into the current shape. The motion may also result in a perspective change. The motion estimator may recognize features in the object which are at a new location and this information is used to create mesh vectors.

At the encoder, mesh vectors are used to warp the pixels in the I-VOP to predict the new perspective. The differential shape codes are used to predict the new shape of the object. The warped, reshaped object is then compared with the actual object, and the result is a texture residual which will be DCT coded.

At the decoder, (b), the I-VOP is in memory and the mesh motion, the shape difference and the texture residual arrive as a P-VOP. The mesh motion is decoded and used to warp the object pixels taken from the I-VOP memory. The shape difference is decoded to produce a new shape around the warped pixels, resulting in a predicted object. The texture residual is decoded and added to the predicted object to produce the final decoded object which is then composited into the output picture along with other objects.

It should be clear that by transmitting warping vectors the pixels from the I-VOP can be used to create a very accurate prediction of the texture of the P-VOP. The result is that the texture residual can be encoded with a very small number of bits.

5.26   Sprites

Sprites are images or parts of images which do not change with time. Such information only needs to be sent once and is obviously attractive for compression. However, it is important to appreciate that it is only the transmitted sprite which doesn't change. The decoder may manipulate the sprite in a different way for each picture, giving the illusion of change.

Figure 5.67 shows the example of a large sprite used as a background. The pixel array size exceeds the size of the target picture. This can be sent as an I-VOP (*intra-coded video object plane*). Once the texture of the sprite is available at the decoder, vectors can be sent to move or warp the picture. These instructions are sent as S-VOPs (*static video object planes*). Using S-VOP vectors, a different part of the sprite can be delivered to the display at each picture, giving the illusion of a moving background. Other video objects can then be keyed over the background.

Sending a large background sprite in one I-VOP may cause difficulty at high compression factors because the one-off image distorts the bit rate. The solution here is *low-latency* sprite coding. Although the sprite is a single still texture object, it need not all be transmitted at once. Instead the sprite is transmitted in *pieces*. The first of these is an *object piece*, whereas subsequently *update pieces* may be sent.

Large sprite (S-VOP)

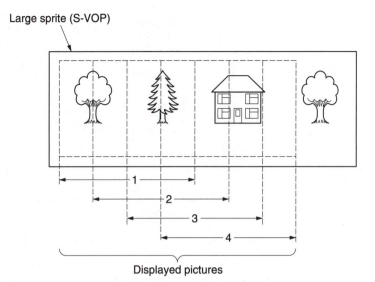

Displayed pictures

Figure 5.67 A large sprite used as a background may be bigger than the screen. If shifted by vectors, the illusion of a moving background is given.

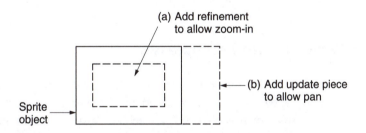

Figure 5.68 An object piece may be used in several VOPs. (a) To allow a zoom-in, part of the sprite object may have its resolution enhanced by an additional object piece. (b) An additional object piece may extend an object to allow a pan.

Update pieces may coincide spatially with the object piece and result in a refinement of image quality, or may be appended spatially to increase the size of a sprite. Figure 5.68 shows the example of an object piece which is transmitted once but used in a series of pictures. In Figure 5.68(a) an update piece is transmitted which improves the quality of the sprite so that a zoom-in can be performed.

Figure 5.68(b) shows a large sprite sent to create a moving background. Just before the edge of the sprite becomes visible, the sprite is extended by sending an update piece. Update pieces can be appended to pixel accuracy because they are coded with offset parameters which show where the update fits with respect to the object piece.

Figure 5.69 shows a sprite decoder. The basic sprite is decoded from an I-VOP and placed in the sprite buffer. It does not become visible until

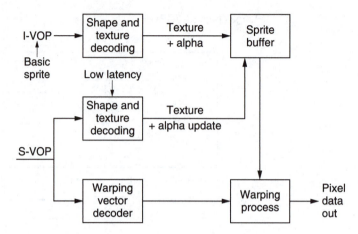

Figure 5.69 An MPEG-4 sprite decoder. See text for details.

an S-VOP arrives carrying shifting and warping instructions. Low-latency decoding sends sprite pieces as S-VOPs which are assembled in the buffer as each sprite piece arrives.

5.27 Wavelet-based compression

MPEG-4 introduces the use of wavelets in still picture object coding. Wavelets were introduced in Chapter 3 where it was shown that the transform itself does not achieve any compression. Instead the picture information is converted to a form in which redundancy is easy to find. Figure 5.70 shows three of the stages in a wavelet transform. Each of these represents more detail in the original image, assuming, of course, that there was any detail there to represent. In real images, the highest spatial frequencies may not be present except in localized areas such as edges or in detailed objects. Consequently many of the values in the highest resolution difference data will be zero or small. An appropriate coding scheme can achieve compression on data of this kind. As in DCT coding, wavelet coefficients can be quantized to shorten their word-length, advantageous scanning sequences can be employed and arithmetic coding based on coefficient statistics can be used.

MPEG-4 provides standards for scaleable coding. Using scaleable coding means that images can be reproduced both at various resolutions and with various noise levels. In one application a low-cost simple decoder will decode only the low-resolution noisy content of the bitstream whereas a more complex decoder may use more or all of the data to enhance resolution and to lower the noise floor. In another application where the bit rate is severely limited, the early part of a

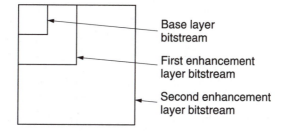

Figure 5.70 Three of the stages in a wavelet transform in which different levels of detail exist.

transmission may be decoded to produce a low-resolution image whose resolution increases as further detail arrives.

The wavelet transform is naturally a multi-resolution process and it is easy to see how a resolution scaleable system could be built from Figure 5.70 by encoding the successive difference images in separate bitstreams. As with DCT-based image compression, the actual bit rate reduction in wavelet compression is achieved by a combination of lossy and lossless coding. The lossless coding consists of scanning the parameters in a manner which reflects their statistics, followed by variable-length coding.

The lossy coding consists of quantizing the parameters to reduce their wordlength. Coarse quantization may be employed on a base-level bitstream, whereas an enhancement bitstream effectively transmits the quantizing error of that coarse quantization.

The wavelet transform produces a decomposition of the image which is ideal for compression. Each sub-band represents a different band of spatial frequencies, but in the form of a spatial array. In real images, the outline of every object consists of an edge which will contain a wide range of frequencies. There will be energy in all sub-bands in the case of a sharp edge. As each sub-band is a spatial array, edge information will be found in the same place in each sub-band. For example, an edge placed one quarter of the way across the picture will result in energy one quarter of the way across each sub-band.

This characteristic can be exploited for compression if the sequence in which the coefficients are coded starts at a given coefficient in the lowest sub-band and passes through each sub-band in turn. Figure 5.71 shows that for each coefficient in a given sub-band there will be four *children* in the next, sixteen *descendants* in the next and so on, in a tree structure. In the case of a sharp edge, all the relevant coefficients will generally lie on a single route through the tree. In plain areas containing only low frequencies, the corollary of this characteristic is that generally if a given coefficient has value zero, then all of the coefficients in higher sub-bands will frequently also have value zero, producing a *zerotree*.[3] Zerotrees are

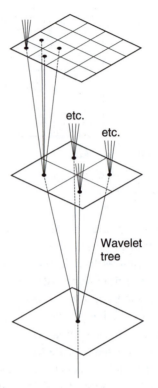

Figure 5.71 In wavelet coding, every coefficient at a given resolution corresponds to four coefficients at the next highest level.

easy to code because they simply need a bit pattern which is interpreted as meaning there are no further non-zero coefficients up this tree.

Figure 5.72 shows how zerotree coding works. Zero frequency coefficients are coded separately using predictive coding, so zerotree coding starts with coefficients in the lowest AC sub-band. Each coefficient represents the root of a tree and leads to four more nodes in the next sub-band and so on. At nodes, one of four codes may be applied. ZTR means that this node is at the bottom of a zerotree and that all further coefficients up the tree are zero and need not be coded. VZTR means that this coefficient is non-zero but all its descendants are. In this case only the valid coefficient at the foot of the tree is sent. IZ means that this coefficient is zero but it has non-zero descendants and the scan must continue. Finally VAL means a non-zero coefficient with non-zero descendants. This coefficient and subsequent ones must be coded.

Zerotree coding is efficient because in real images the energy is concentrated at low frequency and most trees do not need to be coded as far as the leaf node.

It is important to appreciate that the scanning order in which zerotree coding takes place must go from the lowest AC sub-band upwards.

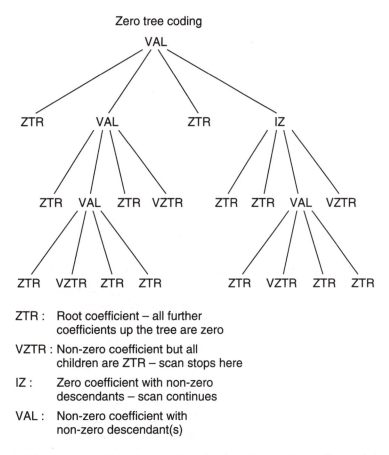

ZTR : Root coefficient – all further
coefficients up the tree are zero

VZTR : Non-zero coefficient but all
children are ZTR – scan stops here

IZ : Zero coefficient with non-zero
descendants – scan continues

VAL : Non-zero coefficient with
non-zero descendant(s)

Figure 5.72 Zerotree coding relies on the redundancy in wavelet coefficients from the lowest resolution upwards in a tree structure.

However, when the coefficients have been designated by the zerotree coder into the four categories above, they can be transmitted in any order which is convenient. MPEG-4 supports either tree depth scanning or band-by-band scanning. Figure 5.73(a) shows that in tree-depth scanning the coefficients are transmitted one tree at a time from the lowest spatial frequency to the highest. The coding is efficient but the picture will not be available until all the data have been received. Figure 5.73(b) shows that in band-by-band scanning the coefficients are transmitted in order of ascending spatial frequency. At the decoder a soft picture becomes available first, and the resolution gradually increases as more sub-bands are decoded. This coding scheme is less efficient but the decoding latency is reduced which may be important in image database browsing applications.

Figure 5.74(a) shows a simple wavelet coder operating in single-quant mode. After the DWT, the DC or root coefficients are sent to a predictive coder where the values of a given coefficient are predicted from adjacent

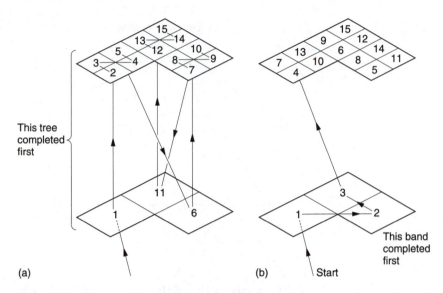

Figure 5.73 (a) In tree-depth scanning the coefficients are scanned up each tree in turn. (b) In band-by-band scanning the coefficients are transmitted in order of increasing resolution.

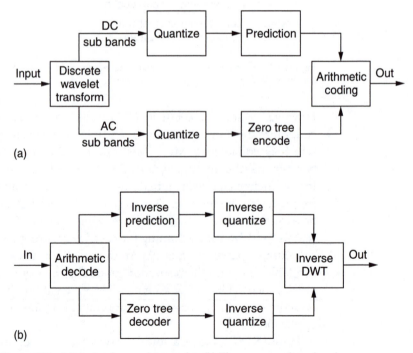

Figure 5.74 (a) A simple wavelet encoder. (b) The corresponding decoder.

coefficients. The AC coefficients are zerotree coded. Coefficients are then quantized and arithmetic coded. The decoder is shown in (b). After arithmetic decoding, the DC coefficients are obtained by inverse prediction and the AC coefficients are re-created by zerotree decoding. After inverse quantizing the coefficients control an inverse DWT to re-create the texture.

MPEG-4 supports scaleable wavelet coding in multi-quant and bilevel-quant modes. Multi-quant mode allows resolution and noise scaleability. In the first layer, a low-resolution and/or noisy texture is encoded. The decoder will buffer this texture and optionally may display it. Higher layers may add resolution by delivering higher sub-band coefficients or reduce noise by delivering the low-order bits removed by the quantizing of the first layer. These refinements are added to the contents of the buffer.

In bilevel-quant mode the coefficients are not sent as binary numbers, but are sent bitplane-by-bitplane. In other words the MSBs of all coefficients are sent first followed by all the second bits and so on. The decoder would reveal a very noisy picture at first in which the noise floor falls as each enhancement layer arrives. With enough enhancement layers the compression could be lossless.

5.28 Three-dimensional mesh coding

In computer-generated images used, for example, in simulators and virtual reality, the goal is to synthesize the image which would have been seen by a camera or a single eye at a given location with respect to the virtual objects. Figure 5.75 shows that this uses a process known as *ray*

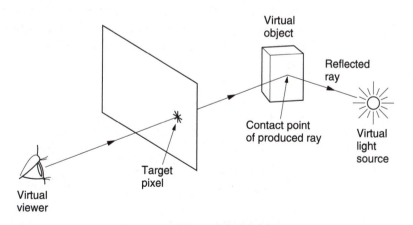

Figure 5.75 In ray tracing, imaginary rays are projected from the viewer's eye through each screen pixel in turn to points on the scene to be rendered. The characteristics of the point in the scene are transferred to the pixel concerned.

tracing. From a fixed point in the virtual camera, a ray is projected outwards through every pixel in the image to be created. These rays will strike either an object or the background. Rays which strike an object must result in pixels which represent that object. Objects which are three dimensional will reflect the ray according to their geometry and reflectivity, and the reflected ray has to be followed in case it falls on a source of light which must appear as a reflection in the surface of the object. The reflection may be sharp or diffuse according to the surface texture of the object. The colour of the reflection will be a function of the spectral reflectivity of the object and the spectrum of the incident light.

If the geometry, surface texture and colour of all objects and light sources are known, the image can be computed in a process called *rendering*. If any of the objects are moving, or if the viewpoint of the virtual camera changes, then a new image will need to be rendered for each video frame. If such synthetic video were to be compressed by, say, MPEG-2, the resultant bit rate would reflect the large number of pixels changing from frame to frame. However, the motion of virtual objects can be described by very few bits. A solid object moves in three dimensions and can rotate in three axes and this is trivial to transmit. A flexible object such as a jellyfish requires somewhat more information to describe how its geometry changes with time, but still much less than describing the changes in the rendered video.

Figure 5.76 shows that in MPEG-4, the rendering process is transferred to the decoder. The bitstream describes objects to the decoder which then renders the virtual image. The bitstream can then describe the motion of the objects with a very low bit rate, and the decoder will render a new image at each frame. In interactive applications such as simulators, CAD and video games, the user may change the viewpoint of the virtual camera and/or the position of virtual objects and result in a unique rendering. This does not require any communication between the user and the encoder because the user is only interacting with the rendering process.

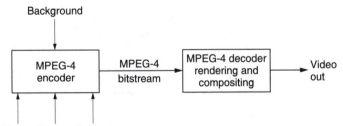

Figure 5.76 Three-dimensional mesh coding allows the rendering process to be completed in the decoder.

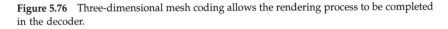

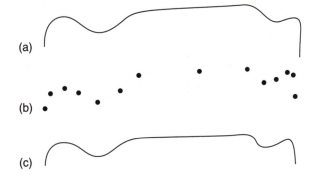

Figure 5.77 (a) An arbitrary body with variable curvature. (b) The surface can be sampled by vertices which are not necessarily evenly spaced. (c) Filtering the vertices re-creates the shape of the body.

Transmitting raw geometry requires a large amount of data. Space is quantized in three axes and for every location in, say, the x-axis, the y and z co-ordinates of the surface must be transmitted. Three-dimensional mesh coding is an efficient way of describing the geometry and properties of bodies in a compressed bitstream. Audio and video compression relies upon the characteristics of sounds, images and the human senses, whereas three-dimensional mesh coding relies on the characteristics of topology.[4]

Figure 5.77(a) shows a general body in which the curvature varies. Sampling this body at a constant spacing is obviously inefficient because if the samples are close enough together to describe the sharply curved areas, the gently curved areas will effectively be heavily oversampled. Three-dimensional mesh coding uses irregular sampling locations called *vertices* which can be seen in Figure 5.77(b). A vertex is a point in the surface of an object which has a unique position in x, y and z. Shape coding consists of efficiently delivering the co-ordinates of a number of vertices to the decoder. Figure 5.77(c) shows that the continuous shape can then be reconstructed by filtering as all sampled processes require.

Filtering of irregularly spaced samples is more complex than that of conventional reconstruction filters and uses algorithms called splines.[5] Failure correctly to filter the shape results in synthetic objects which appear multi-faceted instead of smoothly curved.

Figure 5.78(a) shows that a set of three vertices may be connected by straight lines called *edges* to form a triangle. In fact this is how the term 'vertex' originates. Note that these edges are truly straight and are thus not necessarily on the surface of the object except at the vertices. There are a number of advantages to creating these triangles. Wherever the vertices are, a triangle is always flat, which is not necessarily the case for shapes with four or more sides. A flat surface needs no

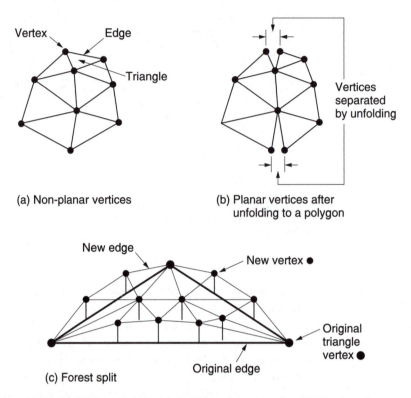

(a) Non-planar vertices

(b) Planar vertices after unfolding to a polygon

(c) Forest split

Figure 5.78 (a) Vertices are joined by edges to form triangles. (b) Hinging along some edges and opening others allow the triangles to be unfolded into a plane. (c) Greater resolution can be obtained by locating additional vertices with respect to each triangle in a forest split operation.

further description because it can be interpolated from the vertices. Figure 5.78(b) shows that by cutting along certain edges and hinging along others, a triangulated body can be transformed into a plane. (A knowledge of origami is useful here.) Figure 5.78(c) shows that once a triangle has been transmitted to the decoder, it can be used as the basis for further information about the surface geometry. In a process known as a *forest split operation*, new vertices are located with respect to the original triangle.[6]

Forest split operations are efficient because the displacements of the new vertices from the original triangle plane are generally small. Additionally a forest split is only needed in triangles in the vicinity of sharp changes. Forest splits can be cascaded allowing the geometry to be reconstructed to arbitrary accuracy. By encoding the forest split data in different layers, a scaleable system can be created where a rough shape results from the base layer which can be refined by subsequent layers.

Figure 5.79 shows an MPEG-4 three-dimensional mesh coding system at high level. The geometry of the object is coded by the vertices which are points, whereas the properties are coded with respect to the triangles

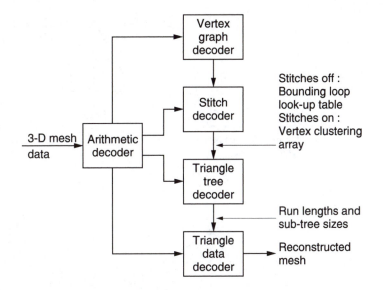

Figure 5.79 An MPEG-4 three-dimensional mesh coder. See text for details.

between the vertices. The dual relationship between the triangles and the vertices which they share is known as the *connectivity*. Geometry is compressed using topological principles and properties are compressed by quantizing. These parameters are then subject to entropy (variable-length) coding prior to multiplexing into a bitstream. At the decoder the three information streams are demultiplexed and decoded to drive the rendering and composition process. The connectivity coding is logical and must be lossless whereas the vertex positions and triangle properties may be lossy or lossless according to the available bit rate.

Generic geometry coding is based on meshes using polygons. Each polygon is defined by the position of each vertex and its surface properties. MPEG-4 breaks such polygons down into triangles for coding the vertices and associates the properties with the correct triangles at the decoder using the connectivity data so that the polygons can be re-created. The geometry coding is based on triangles because they have useful properties.

Figure 5.80 shows that triangles are fundamentally binary. Digital transmission is serial, and compression works by finding advantageous sequences in which to send information, for example the scanning of DCT coefficients. When scanning triangles, if a scan enters via one edge, there are then only two sides by which to exit. This decision can be represented by a single bit for each triangle, known as a *marching* bit.

Figure 5.81(a) shows a representative object, in this case a spheroid. Its surface has been roughly sampled to create twelve vertices, and edges are drawn between the vertices to create triangles. The flat triangles

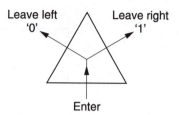

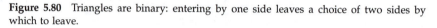

Figure 5.80 Triangles are binary: entering by one side leaves a choice of two sides by which to leave.

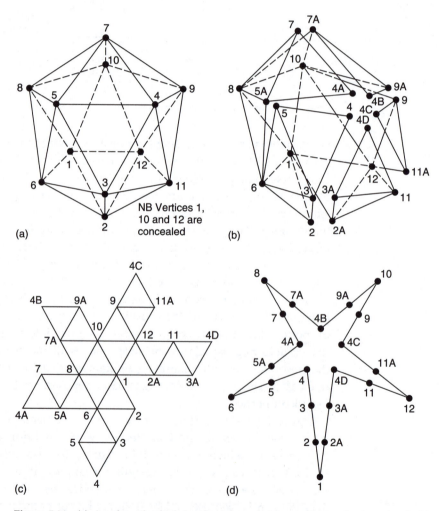

Figure 5.81 (a) A spheroid which has been sampled by vertices and triangulated. (b) Partially unfolding the triangles. (c) Completely unfolded triangles form a planar polygon. (d) The vertex loop which drives the vertex look-up process in order to link the vertices which were disconnected during unfolding.

create a dodecahedron, and this may later be refined more closely to the spheroid with a forest split operation. For the moment the goal is to transmit the vertices so that the triangles can be located. As adjacent triangles share vertices, there are fewer vertices than triangles. In this example there are twenty triangles but only twelve vertices.

When a vertex is transmitted, the information may be required by more than one triangle. Transferring this information to the next triangle in the scan sequence is obvious, but where the scan branches it is non-obvious and a structure known as *vertex loop look-up table* is needed to connect vertex data. Only one vertex needs to have its absolute co-ordinates transmitted. This is known as the *root vertex*. The remaining vertices can be coded by prediction from earlier vertices so that only the residual needs to be sent.

In general it is impossible for a continuous scan sequence to visit all of the triangles. Figure 5.81(b) shows that if cuts are made along certain edges, the triangles can be hinged at their edges. This is continued until they all lie in the same plane to form a polygon (c). This process has created a binary tree along which the triangles can be scanned, but it has also separated some of the vertices. Figure 5.81(c) apparently has 22 vertices, but ten of these are redundant because they simply repeat the locations of the real vertices. Figure 5.81(d) shows how the vertex loop look-up process can connect a single coded vertex to all its associated triangles.

In graphics terminology, the edges along which the polyhedron was cut form a rooted vertex tree. Each run of the vertex tree terminates at a point where a cut ended. The extremities of the vertex tree correspond to the concavities in the polygon. When the vertex loop is collapsed to zero area in the process of folding the polygon into a solid body it becomes a vertex tree.

A solid body such as a spheroid is described as *manifold* because its surface consists of a continuous layer of faces with a regular vertex at each corner. However, some bodies which need to be coded are not manifold. Figure 5.82 shows a non-manifold body consisting of a pair of intersecting planes. The two planes share an edge joining shared vertices. The two planes can be coded separately and joined using *stitches* which indicate common vertices.

Stitches can also be used to transmit meshes in discrete stages known as *partitions*. Partitions can be connected together by stitches such that the result is indistinguishable from a mesh coded all at once. There are many uses of mesh partitions, but an example is in the coding of a rotating solid body. Only the part of the body which is initially visible needs to be transmitted before decoding can begin. Extra partitions can be transmitted which describe that part of the surface of the body that will come into view as the rotation continues. This approach is the three-

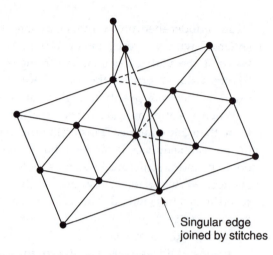

Figure 5.82 A non-manifold body in which planes are joined by stitches.

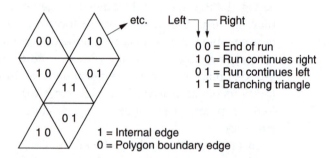

Figure 5.83 The four types of triangle which can be encountered when scanning.

dimensional equivalent of transmitting static sprites as pieces; both allow the bit rate to remain more constant.

Figure 5.83 shows that when scanning, it is possible to enter four types of triangle. Having entered by one edge, the other two edges will either be internal edges, leading to another triangle, or a boundary edge. This can be described with a two-bit code; one bit for the left edge and one bit for the right. The scanning process is most efficient if it can create long *runs* which are linear sequences of triangles between nodes. Starting at a boundary edge, the run will continue as long as type 01 or 10 triangles are found. If a type 11 triangle is found, there are two runs from this node.

The encoder must remember the existence of nodes in a stack, and pick one run until it ends at a type 00 triangle. It must then read the stack and encode the other run. When the current run has reached a 00 triangle and the stack is empty, all the triangles must have been coded.

There is redundancy in the two-bit code describing the triangles. Except for the end triangles, the triangles in a run will have the value 01

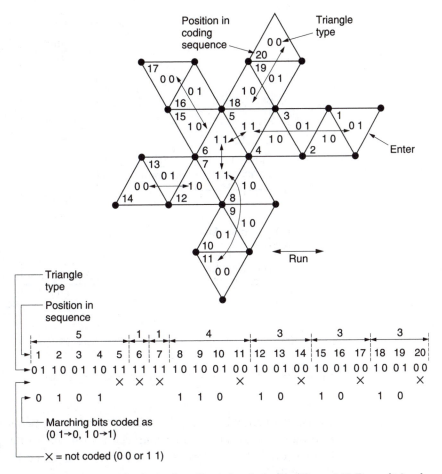

Figure 5.84 An example of triangle coding using the body of Figure 5.81. Runs of triangles are created. See text for details.

or 10. By transmitting the *run length*, the decoder knows where the run ends. As only two values are possible in the run, 01 can be coded as 0 and 10 can be coded as 1 and only this needs to be coded for each triangle. This bit is, of course, the marching bit which determines whether the run leaves the triangle by the left edge or the right. Clearly in type 00 or 11 triangles there is no marching bit.

Figure 5.84 shows how the triangles are coded. There are seven runs in the example shown, and so seven run lengths are transmitted. Marching bits are only transmitted for type 01 or 10 triangles and the decoder can determine how the sequence of marching bits is to be decoded using the run lengths.

Figure 5.85 shows a three-dimensional mesh codec. This decoder demultiplexes the mesh object bitstream into data types and reverses the arithmetic coding. The first item to be decoded is the vertex graph which

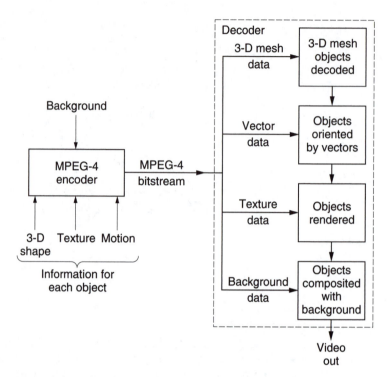

Figure 5.85 A three-dimensional mesh codec. See text for details.

creates the vertex loop look-up table. If stitches are being used these will also be decoded so that in conjunction with the vertex graph look-up table a complete list of how triangles are to be joined to create the body will result.

The triangle topology is output by the triangle tree decoder. This decodes the run lengths and the marching bits of the runs which make up the polygon. Finally the triangle data are decoded to produce the vertex co-ordinates. The co-ordinates are linked by the connectivity data to produce the finished mesh (or partition).

The faces of the mesh then need to be filled in with properties so that rendering can take place.

5.29 Animation

In applications such as videophones and teleconferencing the images to be coded frequently comprise the human face in close-up or the entire body. Video games may also contain virtual human actors. Face and body animation (FBA) is a specialized subset of mesh coding which may be used in MPEG-4 for coding images of, or containing, humans at very low bit rate.

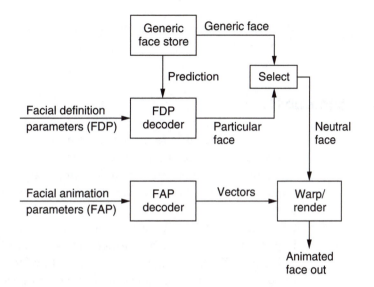

Figure 5.86 Face animation decoder used facial definition parameters (FDP) to create a neutral face. Facial animation parameters (FAPs) are specialized vectors which move the face vertices to reproduce expressions.

In face coding, the human face is constructed in the decoder as a three-dimensional mesh onto which the properties of the face to be coded are mapped. Figure 5.86 shows a facial animation decoder. As all faces have the same basic layout, the decoder contains a generic face which can be rendered immediately. Alternatively the generic face can be modified by *facial definition parameters* (FDP) into a particular face. The data needed to do this can be moderate.

The FDP decoder creates what is known as a neutral face; one which carries no expression. This face is then animated to give it dynamically changing expressions by moving certain vertices and re-rendering. It is not necessary to transmit data for each vertex. Instead face-specific vectors known as *face animation parameters* (FAPs) are transmitted. As certain combinations of vectors are common in expressions such as a smile, these can be coded as *visemes* which are used either alone or as predictions for more accurate FAPs. The resulting vectors control algorithms which are used to move the vertices to the required places. The data rate needed to do this is minute; 2–3 kilobits per second is adequate.

In body animation, the three-dimensional mesh created in the decoder is a neutral human body, i.e. one with a standardized posture. All the degrees of freedom of the body can be replicated by transmitting codes corresponding to the motion of each joint.

In both cases if the source material is video from a camera, the encoder will need sophisticated algorithms which recognize the human features and output changing animation parameters as expression and posture change.

5.30 Scaleability

MPEG-4 offers extensive support for scaleability. Given the wide range of objects which MPEG-4 can encode, offering scaleability for virtually all of them must result in considerable complexity. In general, scaleability requires the information transmitted to be decomposed into a base layer along with one or more enhancement layers. The base layer alone can be decoded to obtain a picture of a certain quality. The quality can be improved in some way by adding enhancement information.

Figure 5.87 shows a generic scaleable decoder. There is a decoder for the base layer information and a decoder for the enhancement layer. For efficient compression, the enhancement layer decoder will generally require a significant number of parameters from the base layer to assist with predictively coded data. These are provided by the *mid-processor*. Once the base and enhancement decoding is complete, the two layers are combined in a post-processor.

Figure 5.88 shows a spatial scaleability system in which the enhancement improves resolution. Spatial scaleability may be applied to rectangular VOPs or to arbitrarily shaped objects using alpha data. In the case of irregular objects the alpha data will also need to be refined. The mid-processor will upsample the base layer images to provide base pixel data at the new, higher resolution, sampling grid. With respect to a sampling array upsampled by a factor of two, motion vectors appear half as accurate and there are one quarter as many as are needed. Consequently to improve prediction in the enhancement layer, the motion compensation must be made more accurate.

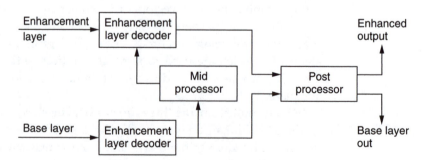

Figure 5.87 A generic scaleable decoder contains decoding for base and enhancement layers as well as a mid-processor which adapts the base layer data to the needs of the enhancement process.

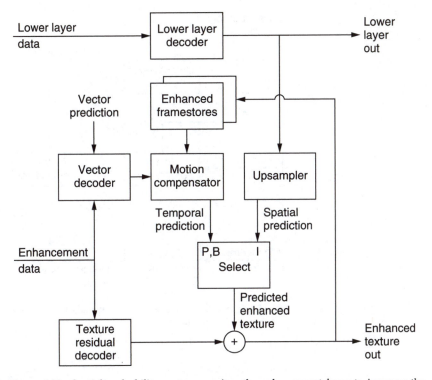

Figure 5.88 Spatial scaleability system requires the enhancement layer to improve the vector density in order to minimize the residual bit rate.

The output of the base level decoder is considered to be a spatial prediction by the enhancement process. This may be shifted by vectors from the enhancement bitstream. Figure 5.89 shows that a base level macroblock of 16×16 pixels predicted with one vector is upsampled to four macroblocks, each of which can be shifted with its own enhancement vector. Upsampled base layer pixels which have been shifted by enhancement vectors form a new high-resolution prediction. The encoder transmits the spatial residual from this prediction.

Temporally scaleable decoding allows new VOPs to be created in between the VOPs of the base layer to increase the frame rate. Figure 5.90 shows that enhancement I-VOPs are intra-coded and so are decoded without reference to any other VOP just like a base I-VOP. P- and B-VOPs in the enhancement layer are motion predicted from other VOPs. These may be in the base layer or the enhancement layer according to prediction reference bits in the enhancement data. Base layer B-VOPs are never used as enhancement references, but enhancement B-VOPs can be references for other enhancement VOPs.

Figure 5.91 shows the example of an enhancement B-VOP placed between two VOPs in the base layer. Enhancement vectors are used to

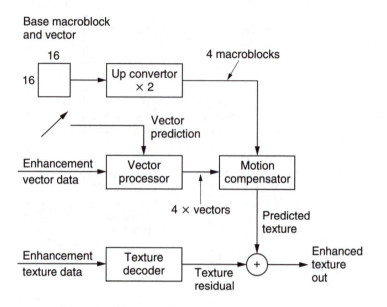

Figure 5.89 Each base level macroblock corresponds to four enhancement macroblocks. Base vectors are used to predict enhancement vectors.

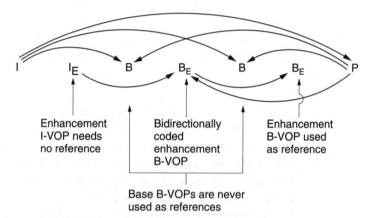

Figure 5.90 Temporal scaleability allows new VOPs to be created between base layer VOPs thereby increasing the picture rate.

shift base layer pixels to new locations in the enhancement VOP. The enhancement residual is then added to these predictions to create the output VOP.

5.31 Advanced Video Coding (AVC)

AVC (Advanced Video Coding), or H.264, is intended to compress moving images that take the form of eight-bit 4:2:0 coded pixel arrays.

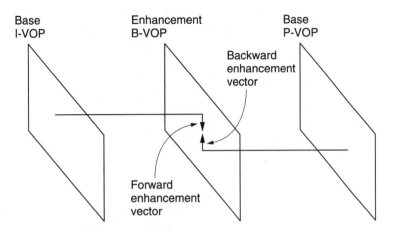

Figure 5.91 This enhancement B-VOP contains vectors to shift base level anchor VOPs. Residuals are then added to correct the prediction error.

Although complex, AVC offers between two and two and a half times the compression factor of MPEG-2 for the same quality.[7]

As in MPEG-2 these may be pixel arrays or fields from an interlaced signal. It does not support object-based coding. Incoming pixel arrays are subdivided into 16×16 pixel macroblocks as in previous MPEG standards. In those previous standards, macroblocks were transmitted only in a raster scan fashion. Whilst this is fine where the coded data are delivered via a reliable channel, AVC is designed to operate with imperfect channels that are subject to error or packet loss. One mechanism that supports this is known as FMO (Flexible Macroblock Ordering).

When FMO is in use, the picture can be divided into different areas along horizontal or vertical macroblock boundaries. Figure 5.92(a) shows an approach in which macroblocks are chequerboarded. If the shaded macroblocks are sent in a different packet to the unshaded macroblocks, the loss of a packet will result in a degraded picture rather than no picture. Figure 5.92(b) shows another approach in which the important elements of the picture are placed in one area and less important elements in another. The important data may be afforded higher priority in a network. Note that when interlaced input is being coded, it may be necessary to constrain the FMO such that the smallest element becomes a macroblock pair in which one macroblock is vertically above the other.

In FMO these areas are known as *slice groups* that contain integer numbers of slices. Within slice groups, macroblocks are always sent in raster scan fashion with respect to that slice group. The decoder must be able to establish the position of every received macroblock in the picture. This is the function of the *macroblock to slice group map*

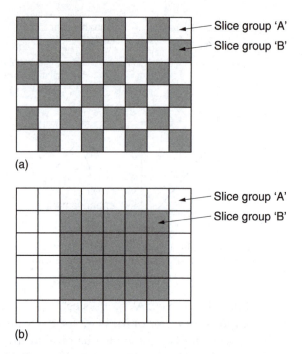

(a)

(b)

Figure 5.92 (a) Chequerboarded macroblocks which have come from two different slice groups. Loss of one slice group allows a degraded picture to be seen. (b) Important picture content is placed in one slice whereas background is in another.

which can be deduced by the decoder from picture header and slice header data.

Another advantage of AVC is that the bitstream is designed to be transmitted or recorded in a greater variety of ways having distinct advantages in certain applications. AVC may convert the output of the Video Coding Layer (VCL) in a Network Application Layer (NAL) that formats the date in an appropriate manner. This chapter covers the Video Coding Layer, whereas the AVC NAL is considered in Chapter 6.

AVC is designed to operate in multi-rate systems where the same program material is available at different bit rates depending on the bandwidth available at individual locations. Frequently available bandwidth varies and the situation will arise where a decoder needs to switch to a lower or higher bit rate represention of the same video sequence without a visible disturbance. In the case of MPEG-2 such switching could only be done at an *I* frame in the incoming bitstream. However, the frequent insertion of such *I* frames would reduce the quality of that bitstream. AVC overcomes the problem by the introduction of two new slice coding types, SI and SP.[8] These are switching slices that use intra- or inter-coding. Switching slices are inserted by the encoder that is creating both the high and low bit rate streams to facilitate switching between them. With switching slices, switching can take place at an arbitrary location in the GOP without waiting for an *I* picture or artificially inserting one. Ordinarily such switching would be impossible because of temporal coding. Lacking the history of the bitstream, a decoder switching into the middle of a GOP would not be able to function. The function of the switching slices is now clear. When a switch is to be performed, the decoder adds decoded switching slice(s) data to the last decoded picture of the old bitstream and this converts the picture into what it would have been if the decoder had been decoding the new bitstream since the beginning of the GOP. Armed with a correct previous picture, the decoder simply decodes the MC and residual data of the new bitstream and produces correct output pictures.

In previous MPEG standards, prediction was used primarily between pictures. In MPEG-2 *I* pictures the only prediction was in DC coefficients whereas in MPEG-4 some low frequency coefficients were predicted. In AVC, *I* pictures are subject to spatial prediction and it is the prediction residual that is transform coded, not pixel data.

In I PCM mode, the prediction and transform stages are both bypassed and actual pixel values enter the remaining stages of the coder. In non-typical images such as noise, PCM may be more efficient. In addition, if the channel bit rate is high enough, a truly lossless coder may be obtained by the use of PCM.

Figure 5.93 shows that the encoder contains a spatial predictor that is switched in for *I* pictures whereas for *P* and *B* pictures the temporal

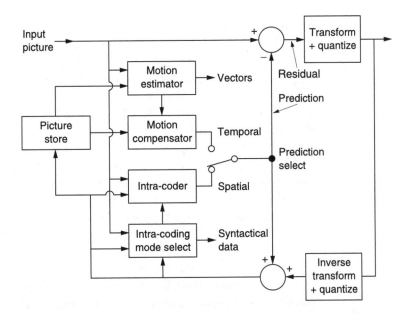

Figure 5.93 AVC encoder has a spatial predictor as well as a temporal predictor.

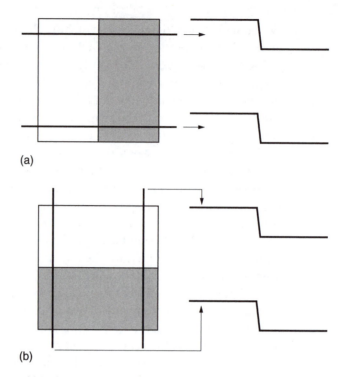

(a)

(b)

Figure 5.94 (a) In the case of a strong vertical edge, pixel values in rows tend to be similar. (b) Horizontal edges result in columns of similar values.

predictor operates. The predictions are subtracted from the input picture and the residual is coded.

Spatial prediction works in two ways. In featureless parts of the picture, the DC component, or average brightness is highly redundant. Edges between areas of differing brightness are also redundant. Figure 5.94(a) shows that in a picture having a strong vertical edge, rows of pixels traversing the edge are highly redundant, whereas (b) shows that in the case of a strong horizontal edge, columns of pixels are redundant. Sloping edges will result in redundancy on diagonals.

According to picture content, spatial prediction can operate on 4×4 pixel blocks or 16×16 blocks. Figure 5.95(a) shows eight of the nine spatial prediction modes for 4×4 blocks. Mode 2, not shown, is the DC prediction that is directionless. Figure 5.95(b) shows that in 4×4 prediction, up to 13 pixel values above and to the left of the block will be used. This means that these pixel values are already known by the decoder because of the order in which decoding takes place. Spatial prediction cannot take place between different slices because the error recovery capability of a slice would be compromised if it depended on an earlier one for decoding.

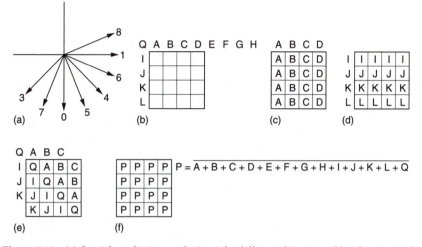

Figure 5.95 (a) Spatial prediction works in eight different directions. (b) Adjacent pixels from which predictions will be made. (c) Vertical prediction copies rows of pixels downwards. (d) Horizontal prediction copies columns of pixels across. (e) Diagonal prediction. (f) DC prediction copies the average of the reference pixels into every predicted pixel location.

Figure 5.95(c) shows that in vertical prediction (Mode 0), four pixel values above the block are copied downwards so that all four rows of the predicted block are identical. Figure 5.95(d) shows that in horizontal prediction (Mode 1) four pixel values to the left are copied across so that all four columns of the predicted block are identical. Figure 5.95(e) shows how in diagonal prediction (Mode 4) seven pixel values are copied diagonally. Figure 5.95(f) shows that in DC prediction (Mode 2) pixel values above and to the left are averaged and the average value is copied into all 16 predicted pixel locations.

With 16 × 16 blocks, only four modes are available: vertical, horizontal, DC and plane. The first three of these are identical in principle to Modes 0, 1 and 2 with 4 × 4 blocks. Plane mode is a refinement of DC mode. Instead of setting every predicted pixel in the block to the same value by averaging the reference pixels, the predictor looks for trends in changing horizontal brightness in the top reference row and similar trends in vertical brightness in the left reference column and computes a predicted block whose values lie on a plane which may be tilted in the direction of the trend.

Clearly it is necessary for the encoder to have circuitry or software that identifies edges and their direction (or the lack of them) in order to select the appropriate mode. The standard does not suggest how this should work; only how its outputs should be encoded. In each case the predicted pixel block is subtracted from the actual pixel block to produce a residual.

Spatial prediction is also used on chroma data.

$$H = \begin{bmatrix} 1 & 1 & 1 & 1 \\ 2 & 1 & -1 & -2 \\ 1 & -1 & -1 & 1 \\ 1 & -2 & 2 & -1 \end{bmatrix}$$

Figure 5.96 The transform matrix used in AVC. The coefficients are all integers.

When spatial prediction is used, the statistics of the residual will be different to the statistics of the original pixels. When the prediction succeeds, the lower frequencies in the image are largely taken care of and so only higher frequencies remain in the residual. This suggests the use of a smaller transform than the 8×8 transform of previous systems. AVC uses a 4×4 transform. It is not, however a DCT, but a DCT-like transform using coefficients that are integers. This gives the advantages that coding and decoding requires only shifting and addition and that the transform is perfectly reversible even when limited wordlength is used. Figure 5.96 shows the transform matrix of AVC.

One of the greatest deficiencies of earlier coders was blocking artifacts at transform block boundaries. AVC incorporates a de-blocking filter. In operation, the filter examines sets of pixels across a block boundary. If it finds a step in value, this may or may not indicate a blocking artifact. It could be a genuine transition in the picture. However, the size of pixel value steps can be deduced from the degree of quantizing in use. If the step is bigger than the degree of quantizing would suggest, it is left alone. If the size of the step corresponds to the degree of quantizing, it is filtered or smoothed.

The adaptive de-blocking algorithm is deterministic and must be the same in all decoders. This is because the encoder must also contain the same de-blocking filter to prevent drift when temporal coding is used. This is known as in-loop de-blocking. In other words when, for example, a P picture is being predicted from an I picture, the I picture in both encoder and decoder will have been identically de-blocked. Thus any errors due to imperfect de-blocking are cancelled out by the P picture residual data. De-blocking filters are modified when interlace is used because the vertical separation of pixels in a field is twice as great as in a frame.

Figure 5.97 shows an in-loop de-blocking system. The I picture is encoded and transmitted and is decoded and de-blocked identically at both encoder and decoder. At the decoder the de-blocked I picture forms the output as well as the reference with which a future P or I picture can be decoded. Thus when the encoder sends a residual, it will send the difference between the actual input picture and the de-blocked I picture. The decoder adds this residual to its own de-blocked I picture and recovers the actual picture.

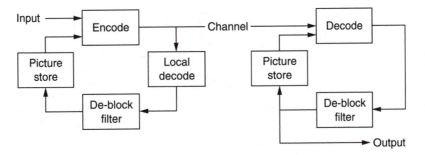

Figure 5.97 The in-loop de-blocking filter exists at both encoder and decoder to prevent drift.

5.32 Motion compensation in AVC

AVC has a more complex motion-compensation system than previous standards. Smaller picture areas are coded using vectors that may have quarter pixel accuracy. The interpolation filter for sub-pixel MC is specified so that the same filter is present in all encoders and decoders. The interpolator is then effectively in the loop like the de-blocking filter. Figure 5.98 shows that more than one previous reference picture may be used to decode a motion-compensated picture. A larger number of future pictures are not used as this would increase latency. The ability to select a number of previous pictures is advantageous when a single non-typical picture is found inserted in normal material. An example is the white frame that results from a flashgun firing. MPEG-2 deals with this poorly, whereas AVC could deal with it well simply by decoding the picture after the flash from the picture before the flash. Bidirectional coding is enhanced because the weighting of the contribution from earlier and later pictures can now be coded. Thus a dissolve between two pictures could be coded efficiently by changing the weighting. In previous standards a *B* picture could not be used as a basis for any further decoding but in AVC this is allowed.

AVC macroblocks may be coded with between one and sixteen vectors. Prediction using 16×16 macroblocks fails when the edge of a moving object intersects the macroblock as was shown in Figure 5.20. In such cases it may be better to divide the macroblock up according to the angle and position of the edge. Figure 5.99(a) shows the number of ways a 16×16 macroblock may be partitioned in AVC for motion-compensation purposes. There are four high-level partition schemes, one of which is to use four 8×8 blocks. When this mode is selected, these 8×8 blocks may be further partitioned as shown. This finer subdivision requires additional syntactical data to specify to the decoder what has

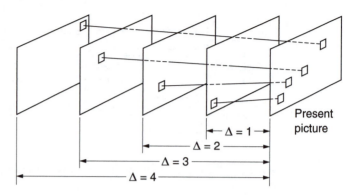

Figure 5.98 The motion compensation of AVC allows a picture to be built up from more than one previous picture.

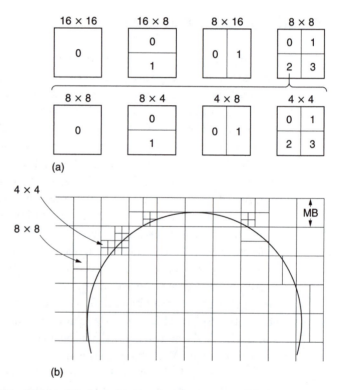

Figure 5.99 (a) Macroblock partitioning for motion compensation in AVC. (b) How an encoder might partition macroblocks at the boundary of a moving object.

been done. It will be self-evident that if more vectors have to be transmitted, there must be a greater reduction in the amount of residual data to be transmitted to make it worthwhile. Thus the encoder needs intelligently to decide the partitioning to be used. Figure 5.99(b) shows an example. There also needs to be some efficient vector coding scheme.

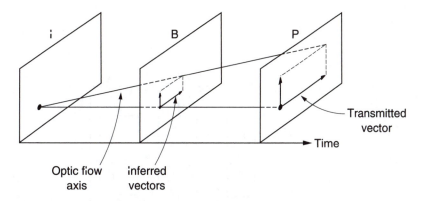

Figure 5.100 Vector inference. By assuming the optic flow axis to be straight, the vector for a B block can be computed from the vector for a P block.

In P coding, vectors are predicted from those in macroblocks already sent, provided that slice independence is not compromised. The predicted vector is the median of those on the left, above and above right of the macroblock to be coded. A different prediction is used if 16×8 or 8×16 partitions are used. Only the prediction error needs to be sent. In fact if nothing is sent, as in the case of a skipped block, the decoder can predict the vector for itself.

In B coding, the vectors are predicted by inference from the previous P vectors. Figure 5.100 shows the principle. In order to create the P picture from the I picture, a vector must be sent for each moving area. As the B picture is at a known temporal location with respect to these anchor pictures, the vector for the corresponding area of the B picture can be predicted by assuming the optic flow axis is straight and performing a simple linear interpolation.

5.33   An AVC codec

Figure 5.101 shows an AVC coder–decoder pair. There is a good deal of general similarity with the previous standards. In the case of an I picture, there is no motion compensation and no previous picture is relevant. However, spatial prediction will be used. The prediction error will be transformed and quantized for transmission, but is also locally inverse quantized and inverse transformed prior to being added to the prediction to produce an unfiltered reconstructed macroblock. Thus the encoder has available exactly what the decoder will have and both use the same data to make predictions to avoid drift. The type of intra-prediction used is determined from the characteristics of the input picture.

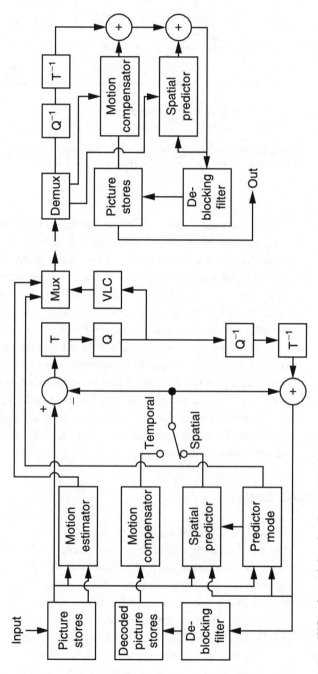

Figure 5.101 AVC coder and decoder. See text for details.

The locally reconstructed macroblocks are also input to the de-blocking filter. This is identical to the decoder's de-blocking filter and so the output will be identical to the output of the decoder. The de-blocked, decoded *I* picture can then be used as a basis for encoding a *P* picture. Using this architecture the de-blocking is in-loop for inter-coding purposes, but does not interfere with the intra-prediction.

Operation of the decoder should be obvious from what has gone before as the encoder effectively contains a decoder.

Like earlier formats, AVC uses lossless arithmetic coding, or entropy coding, to more efficiently pack the data. However, AVC takes the principle further. Arithmetic coding is used to compress syntax data as well as coefficients. Syntax data take a variety of forms: vectors, slice headers etc. A common exp-Golomb variable length arithmetic code is used for all syntax data. The different types of data are mapped appropriately for their statistics before that code. Coefficients are coded using a system called CAVLC (context adaptive variable length coding).

Optionally, a further technique known as CABAC (context adaptive binary arithmetic coding) may be used in some profiles. This is a system which adjusts the coding dynamically according to the local statistics of the data instead of relying on statistics assumed at the design stage. It is more efficient and allows a coding gain of about 15 per cent with more complexity.

CAVLC performs the same function as RLC/VLC in MPEG-2 but it is more efficient. As in MPEG-2 it relies on the probability that coefficient values fall with increasing spatial frequency and that at the higher frequencies coefficients will be spaced apart by zero values. The efficient prediction of AVC means that coefficients will typically be smaller than in earlier standards. It becomes useful to have specific means to code coefficients of value ± 1 as well as zero. These are known as trailing ones (T1s). Figure 5.102 shows the parameters used in CAVLC.

The coefficients are encoded in the reverse order of the zig-zag scan. The number of non-zero coefficients N and the number of trailing ones are encoded into a single VLC symbol. The TotalZeros parameter defines the number of zero coefficients between the last non-zero coefficient and its start. The difference between N and TotalZeros must be the number of

Trailing 1s (T1s)
Non-zero coefficients (*N*)
Value of coefficients
Sign
Total number of zero coefficients (TotalZeros)
Distribution of zeros (RunBefore)

Figure 5.102 CAVLC parameters used in AVC. See text for details.

zeros within the transmitted coefficient sequence but does not reveal where they are. This is the function of the RunBefore parameter which is sent prior to any coefficient that is preceded by zeros in the transmission sequence. If N is sixteen the TotalZeros must be zero and will not be sent. RunBefore parameters will not occur.

Coefficient values for trailing ones need only a single bit to denote the sign. Values above 1 embed the polarity into the value input to the VLC.

CAVLC obtains extra coding efficiency because it can select different codes according to circumstances. For example, if in a sixteen coefficient block N is 7, then TotalZeros must have a value between zero and nine. The encoder selects a VLC table optimized for nine values. The decoder can establish what table has been used by subtracting N from 16 so no extra data need be sent to switch tables. The N and T1s parameter can be coded using one of four tables selected using the values of N and T1 in nearby blocks. Six code tables are available for adaptive coefficient encoding.

5.34   AVC profiles and levels

Like earlier standards, AVC is specified at various profiles and levels and these terms have the same meaning as they do elsewhere. There are three profiles: Baseline, Main and Extended. The Baseline profile supports all of the features of AVC, except for bidirectional coding, interlace, weighted prediction, SP and SI slices and CABAC. FMO is supported, but the number of slices per picture cannot exceed eight. The Main profile supports all features except FMO and SP and SI slices. The extended profile supports all features except CABAC and macroblock adaptive switching between field and frame coding.

AVC levels are defined by various requirements for decoder memory and processing power and are defined as sets of maxima such as picture size, bit rate and vector range. Figure 5.103 shows the levels defined for AVC.

5.35   Coding artifacts

This section describes the visible results of imperfect coding. This may be where the coding algorithm is sub-optimal, where the coder latency is too short or where the compression factor in use is simply too great for the material.

Figure 5.104 shows that all MPEG coders can be simplified to the same basic model in which the predictive power of the decoder is modelled in the encoder. The current picture/object is predicted as well as possible,

Level number	Max macroblock processing rate MaxMBPS (MB/s)	Max frame size MaxFS (MBs)	Max decoded picture buffer size MaxDPB (1024 bytes)	Max video bit rate MaxBR (1000 bits/s or 1200 bits/s)	Max CPB size MaxCPB (1000 bits or 1200 bits)	Vertical MV component range MaxVmvR (luma frame samples)	Min compression ratio MinCR	Max number of motion vectors per two consecutive MBs MaxMvsPer2Mb
1	1 485	99	148.5	64	175	[−64, +63.75]	2	
1.1	3 000	396	337.5	192	500	[−128, +127.75]	2	
1.2	6 000	396	891.0	384	1 000	[−128, +127.75]	2	
1.3	11 880	396	891.0	768	2 000	[−128, +127.75]	2	
2	11 880	396	891.0	2 000	2 000	[−128, +127.75]	2	
2.1	19 800	792	1782.0	4 000	4 000	[−256, +255.75]	2	
2.2	20 250	1 620	3037.5	4 000	4 000	[−256, +255.75]	2	
3	40 500	1 620	3037.5	10 000	10 000	[−256, +255.75]	2	32
3.1	108 000	3 600	6750.0	14 000	14 000	[−512, +511.75]	4	16
3.2	216 000	5 120	7680.0	20 000	20 000	[−512, +511.75]	4	16
4	245 760	8 192	12 288.0	20 000	25 000	[−512, +511.75]	4	16
4.1	245 760	8 192	12 288.0	50 000	62 500	[−512, +511.75]	2	16
4.2	491 520	8 192	12 288.0	50 000	62 500	[−512, +511.75]	2	16
5	589 824	22 080	41 310.0	135 000	135 000	[−512, +511.75]	2	16
5.1	983 040	36 864	69 120.0	240 000	240 000	[−512, +511.75]	2	16

Figure 5.103 Different levels available in AVC.

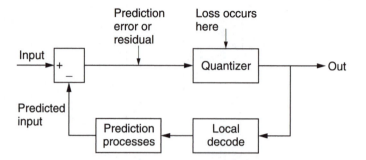

Figure 5.104   All MPEG codecs can be reduced to a lossless prediction process and a lossy coding of the prediction error or residual.

and the prediction error or residual is transmitted. As the decoder can make the same prediction, if the residual is correctly transmitted, the decoded output will be lossless.

The MPEG coding family contains a large number of compression tools and many of these are lossless. Lossless coding tools include the motion compensation, zig-zag scanning and run-length coding of MPEG-1 and MPEG-2 and the context coding and various types of predictive coding used in MPEG-4 and AVC. It is a simple fact that the more sophisticated the prediction, the fewer data will be needed to transmit the residual.

However, in many, perhaps most, applications of MPEG, the bit rate is not decided by the encoder, but by some other decision process which may be economically biased. All MPEG coders contain an output buffer, and if the allocated bit rate is not adequate, this will start to fill up. To prevent data loss and decoder crashes, the encoder must reduce its bit rate.

It cannot make any economy in the lossless coding. Reducing the losslessly coded information would damage the prediction mechanism and *increase* the residual. Reducing the accuracy of vectors, for example, is counterproductive. Consequently all that can be done is to reduce the bit rate of the residual. This must be done where the transform coefficients are quantized because this is the only variable mechanism at the encoder's disposal. When in an unsympathetic environment, the coder has to reduce the bit rate the best it can.

The result is that the output pictures are visually different from the input pictures. The difference between the two is classified as *coding noise*. This author has great difficulty with this term, because true noise should be decorrelated from the message whereas the errors of MPEG coders are signal dependent and the term *coding distortion* is more appropriate. This is supported by the fact that the subjective visual impact of coding errors is far greater than would be caused by the same level of true noise. Put another way, quantizing distortion is irritating and pretending that it is noise gives no assistance in determining how bad it will look.

In motion-compensated systems such as MPEG, the use of periodic intra-fields means that the coding error may vary from picture to picture and this may be visible as *noise pumping*. The designer of the coder is in a difficult position as the user reduces the bit rate. If the I data are excessive, the P and B data will have to be heavily quantized resulting in errors. However, if the data representing the I pictures/objects is reduced too much, P and B pictures may look better than the I pictures. Consequently it is necessary to balance the requantizing in the I, P and B pictures/objects so that the level of visible artifacts in each remains roughly the same in each.

Noise pumping may also be visible where the amount of motion changes. If a pan is observed, as the pan speed increases the motion vectors may become less accurate and reduce the quality of the prediction processes. The prediction errors will get larger and will have to be more coarsely quantized. Thus the picture gets noisier as the pan accelerates and the noise reduces as the pan slows down. The same result may be apparent at the edges of a picture during zooming. The problem is worse if the picture contains fine detail. Panning on grass or trees waving in the wind taxes most coders severely. Camera shake from a hand-held camera also increases the motion vector data and results in more noise, as does film weave.

Input video noise or film grain degrades inter-coding as there is less redundancy between pictures and the difference data become larger, requiring coarse quantizing and adding to the existing noise.

Where a codec is really fighting the quantizing may become very coarse and as a result the video level at the edge of one DCT block may not match that of its neighbour. As a result the DCT block structure becomes visible as a mosaicking or tiling effect. MPEG-4 introduces some decoding techniques to filter out blocking effects and in principle these could be applied to MPEG-1 and MPEG-2 decoders. AVC has the best solution, namely to insert the de-blocking filter into the encoding loop to prevent drift as was described above. Consequently the blocking performance of AVC is exceptional.

Coarse quantizing also causes some coefficients to be rounded up and appear larger than they should be. High-frequency coefficients may be eliminated by heavy quantizing and this forces the DCT to act as a steep-cut low-pass filter. This causes fringing or ringing around sharp edges and extra shadowy edges which were not in the original and is most noticeable on text.

Excess compression may also result in colour bleed where fringing has taken place in the chroma or where high-frequency chroma coefficients have been discarded. Graduated colour areas may reveal banding or posterizing as the colour range is restricted by requantizing. These artifacts are almost impossible to measure with conventional test gear.

Neither noise pumping nor blocking are visible on analog video recorders and so it is nonsense to liken the performance of a codec to the quality of a VCR. In fact noise pumping is extremely objectionable because, unlike steady noise, it attracts attention in peripheral vision and may result in viewing fatigue.

In addition to highly detailed pictures with complex motion, certain types of video signal are difficult for MPEG to handle and will usually result in a higher level of artifacts than usual. Noise has already been mentioned as a source of problems. Timebase error from, for example, VCRs is undesirable because this puts successive lines in different horizontal positions. A straight vertical line becomes jagged and this results in high spatial frequencies in the transform process. Spurious coefficients are created which need to be coded.

Much archive video is in composite form and MPEG can only handle this after it has been decoded to components. Unfortunately many general-purpose composite decoders have a high level of residual subcarrier in the outputs. This is normally not a problem because the subcarrier is designed to be invisible to the naked eye. Figure 5.105 shows that in PAL and NTSC the subcarrier frequency is selected so that a phase reversal is achieved between successive lines and frames.

Whilst this makes the subcarrier invisible to the eye, it is not invisible to an MPEG decoder. The subcarrier waveform is interpreted as a

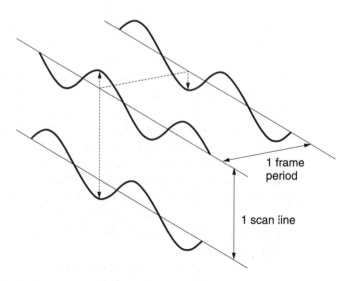

Figure 5.105 In composite video the subcarrier frequency is arranged so that inversions occur between adjacent lines and pictures to help reduce the visibility of the chroma.

horizontal frequency, the vertical phase reversals are interpreted as a vertical spatial frequency and the picture-to-picture reversals increase the magnitude of the prediction errors. The subcarrier level may be low but it can be present over the whole screen and require an excess of coefficients to describe it.

Composite video should not in general be used as a source for MPEG encoding, but where this is inevitable the standard of the decoder must be much higher than average, especially in the residual subcarrier specification. Some MPEG preprocessors support high-grade composite decoding options.

Judder from conventional linear standards convertors degrades the performance of MPEG. The optic flow axis is corrupted and linear filtering causes multiple images which confuse motion estimators and result in larger prediction errors. If standards conversion is necessary, the MPEG system must be used to encode the signal in its original format and the standards convertor should be installed after the decoder. If a standards convertor has to be used before the encoder, then it must be a type which has effective motion compensation.

Film weave causes movement of one picture with respect to the next and this results in more vector activity and larger prediction errors. Movement of the centre of the film frame along the optical axis causes magnification changes which also result in excess prediction error data. Film grain has the same effect as noise: it is random and so cannot be compressed.

Perhaps because it is relatively uncommon, MPEG-2 cannot handle image rotation well because the motion-compensation system is only designed for translational motion. Where a rotating object is highly detailed, such as in certain fairground rides, the motion compensation failure requires a significant amount of prediction error data and if a suitable bit rate is not available the level of artifacts will rise. The additional coding tools of MPEG-4 allow rotation be handled more effectively. Meshes can be rotated by repositioning their vertices with a few vectors and this improves the prediction of rotations dramatically.

Flashguns used by still photographers are a serious hazard to MPEG especially when long GOPs are used. At a press conference where a series of flashes may occur, the resultant video contains intermittent white frames. These are easy enough to code, but a huge prediction error is required to return the white frame to the next picture. The output buffer fills and heavy requantizing is employed. After a few flashes the picture has generally gone to tiles. AVC can handle a single flash by using an earlier picture as the basis for decoding thereby bypassing the white picture.

5.36 MPEG and concatenation

Concatenation loss occurs when the losses introduced by one codec are compounded by a second codec. All practical compressers, MPEG included, are lossy because what comes out of the decoder is not bit-identical to what went into the encoder. The bit differences are controlled so that they have minimum visibility to a human viewer.

MPEG is a toolbox which allows a variety of manipulations to be performed in both the spatial and temporal domains. MPEG-2 has more tools than MPEG-1 and MPEG-4 has more still. There is a limit to the compression which can be used on a single picture/object, and if higher compression factors are needed, temporal coding will have to be used. The longer the run of time considered, the lower the bit rate needed, but the harder it becomes to edit.

The most editable form of MPEG is to use *I* data only. As there is no temporal coding, pure cut edits can be made between pictures. The next best thing is to use a repeating *IB* structure which is locked to the odd/even field structure. Cut edits cannot be made as the *B* pictures are bidirectionally coded and need data from both adjacent *I* pictures for decoding. The *B* picture has to be decoded prior to the edit and re-encoded after the edit. This will cause a small concatenation loss.

Beyond the *IB* structure processing gets harder. If a long GOP is used for the best compression factor, an *IBBPBBP*... structure results. Editing this is very difficult because the pictures are sent out of order so that bidirectional decoding can be used. MPEG allows closed GOPs where the last *B* picture is coded wholly from the previous pictures and does not need the *I* picture in the next GOP. The bitstream can be switched at this point but only if the GOP structures in the two source video signals are synchronized (makes colour framing seem easy). Consequently in practice a long GOP bitstream will need to be decoded prior to any production step. Afterwards it will need to be re-encoded.

This is known as *naive* concatenation and an enormous pitfall awaits. Unless the GOP structure of the output is identical to and synchronized with the input the results will be disappointing. The worst case is where an *I* picture is encoded from a picture which was formerly a *B* picture. It is easy enough to lock the GOP structure of a coder to a single input, but if an edit is made between two inputs, the GOP timings could well be different.

As there are so many structures allowed in MPEG, there will be a need to convert between them. If this has to be done, it should only be in the direction which increases the GOP length and reduces the bit rate. Going the other way is inadvisable. The ideal way of converting from, say, the *IB* structure of a news system to the *IBBP* structure of an emission system is to use a recompressor. This is a kind of standards convertor which will give better results than a decode followed by an encode.

The DCT part of MPEG itself is lossless. If all the coefficients are preserved intact an inverse transform yields the same pixel data. Unfortunately this does not yield enough compression for many applications. In practice the coefficients are made less accurate by removing bits starting at the least significant end and working upwards. This process is weighted, or made progressively more aggressive as spatial frequency increases.

Small-value coefficients may be truncated to zero and large-value coefficients are most coarsely truncated at high spatial frequencies where the effect is least visible.

Figure 5.106(a) shows what happens in the ideal case where two *identical* coders are put in tandem and synchronized. The first coder quantizes the coefficients to finite accuracy and causes a loss on decoding. However, when the second coder performs the DCT calculation, the coefficients obtained will be identical to the quantized coefficients in the first coder and so if the second weighting and requantizing step is identical the same truncated coefficient data will result and there will be no further loss of quality.[9]

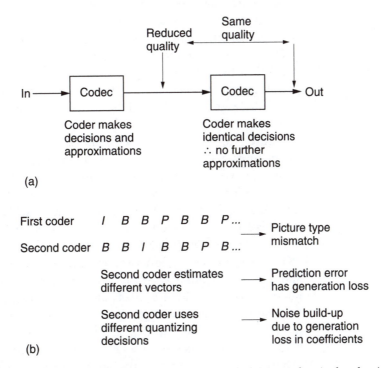

(a)

(b)

Figure 5.106 (a) Two identical coders in tandem which are synchronized make similar coding decisions and cause little loss. (b) There are various ways in which concatenated coders can produce non-ideal performance.

In practice this ideal situation is elusive. If the two DCTs become non-identical for any reason, the second requantizing step will introduce further error in the coefficients and the artifact level goes up. Figure 5.106(b) shows that non-identical concatenation can result from a large number of real-world effects.

An intermediate processing step such as a fade will change the pixel values and thereby the coefficients. A DVE resize or shift will move pixels from one DCT block to another. Even if there is no processing step, this effect will also occur if the two codecs disagree on where the MPEG picture boundaries are within the picture. If the boundaries are correct there will still be concatenation loss if the two codecs use different weighting.

One problem with MPEG is that the compressor design is unspecified. Whilst this has advantages, it does mean that the chances of finding identical coders is minute because each manufacturer will have his own views on the best compression algorithm. In a large system it may be worth obtaining the coders from a single supplier.

It is now increasingly accepted that concatenation of compression techniques is potentially damaging, and results are worse if the codecs are different. Clearly feeding a digital coder such as MPEG-2 with a signal which has been subject to analog compression comes into the category of worse. Using interlaced video as a source for MPEG coding is sub-optimal and using decoded composite video is even worse.

One way of avoiding concatenation is to stay in the compressed data domain. If the goal is just to move pictures from one place to another, decoding to traditional video so that an existing router can be used is not ideal, although it is substantially better than going through the analog domain.

Figure 5.107 shows some possibilities for picture transport. Clearly if the pictures exist as a compressed file on a server, a file transfer is the right way to do it as there is no possibility of loss because there has been no concatenation. File transfer is also quite indifferent to the picture format. It doesn't care about the frame rate, whether the pictures are interlaced or not or whether the colour is 4:2:0 or 4:2:2.

Decoding to SDI (serial digital interface) standard is sometimes done so that existing serial digital routing can be used. This is concatenation and has to be done carefully. The compressed video can only use interlace with non-square pixels and the colour coding has to be 4:2:2 because SDI only allows that. If a compressed file has 4:2:0 the chroma has to be interpolated up to 4:2:2 for SDI transfer and then subsampled back to 4:2:0 at the second coder and this will cause generation loss. An SDI transfer also can only be performed in real time, thus negating one of the advantages of compression. In short traditional SDI is not really at home with compression.

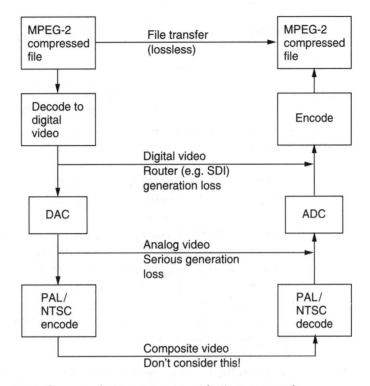

Figure 5.107 Compressed picture transport mechanisms contrasted.

As 4:2:0 progressive scan gains popularity and video production moves steadily towards non-format-specific hardware using computers and data networks, use of the serial digital interface will eventually decline. In the short term, if an existing SDI router has to be used, one solution is to produce a bitstream which is sufficiently similar to SDI that a router will pass it. One example of this is known as SDTI. The signal level, frequency and impedance of SDTI is pure SDI, but the data protocol is different so that a bit accurate file transfer can be performed. This has two advantages over SDI. First, the compressed data format can be anything appropriate and non-interlaced and/or 4:2:0 can be handled in any picture size, aspect ratio or frame rate. Second, a faster than real-time transfer can be used depending on the compression factor of the file.

Equipment which allows this is becoming available and its use can mean that the full economic life of an SDI routing installation can be obtained.

An improved way of reducing concatenation loss has emerged from the ATLANTIC research project.[10] Figure 5.108 shows that the second encoder in a concatenated scheme does not make its own decisions from the incoming video, but is instead steered by information from the first bitstream. As the second encoder has less intelligence, it is known as a *dim* encoder.

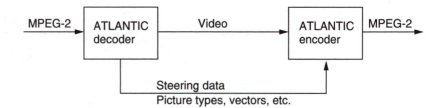

Figure 5.108 In an ATLANTIC system, the second encoder is steered by information from the decoder.

The information bus carries all the structure of the original MPEG-2 bitstream which would be lost in a conventional decoder. The ATLANTIC decoder does more than decode the pictures. It also places on the information bus all parameters needed to make the dim encoder re-enact what the initial MPEG-2 encode did as closely as possible.

The GOP structure is passed on so that pictures are re-encoded as the same type. Positions of macroblock boundaries become identical so that DCT blocks contain the same pixels and motion vectors relate to the same screen data. The weighting and quantizing tables are passed so that coefficient truncation is identical. Motion vectors from the original bitstream are passed on so that the dim encoder does not need to perform motion estimation. In this way predicted pictures will be identical to the original prediction and the prediction error data will be the same.

One application of this approach is in recompression, where an MPEG-2 bitstream has to have its bit rate reduced. This has to be done by heavier requantizing of coefficients, but if as many other parameters as possible can be kept the same, such as motion vectors, the degradation will be minimized. In a simple recompressor just requantizing the coefficients means that the predictive coding will be impaired. In a proper encode, the quantizing error due to coding say an I picture is removed from the P picture by the prediction process. The prediction error of P is obtained by subtracting the decoded I picture rather than the original I picture.

In simple recompression this does not happen and there may be a tolerance build-up known as drift.[11] A more sophisticated recompressor will need to repeat the prediction process using the decoded output pictures as the prediction reference.

MPEG-2 bitstreams will often be decoded for the purpose of switching. Local insertion of commercial breaks into a centrally originated bitstream is one obvious requirement. If the decoded video signal is switched, the information bus must also be switched. At the switch point identical re-encoding becomes impossible because prior pictures required for predictive coding will have disappeared. At this point the dim encoder has to become bright again because it has to create an MPEG-2 bitstream without assistance.

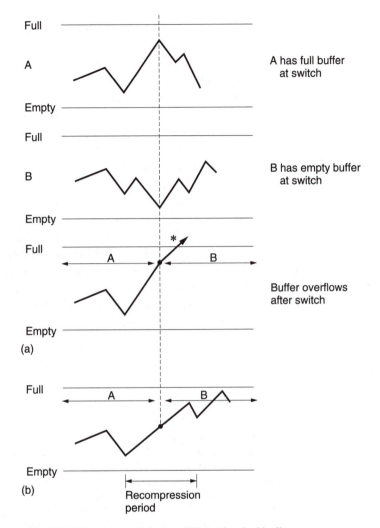

Figure 5.109 (a) A bitstream switch at a different level of buffer occupancy can cause a decoder to overflow. (b) Recompression after a switch to return to correct buffer occupancy.

It is possible to encode the information bus into a form which allows it to be invisibly carried in the serial digital interface. Where a production process such as a vision mixer or DVE performs no manipulation, i.e. becomes bit transparent, the subsequent encoder can extract the information bus and operate in 'dim' mode. Where a manipulation is performed, the information bus signal will be corrupted and the encoder has to work in 'bright' mode. The encoded information signal is known as a 'mole'[12] because it burrows through the processing equipment!

There will be a generation loss at the switch point because the re-encode will be making different decisions in bright mode. This may be difficult to detect because the human visual system is slow to react to a vision cut and defects in the first few pictures after a cut are masked.

In addition to the video computation required to perform a cut, the process has to consider the buffer occupancy of the decoder. A downstream decoder has finite buffer memory, and individual encoders model the decoder buffer occupancy to ensure that it neither overflows nor underflows. At any instant the decoder buffer can be nearly full or nearly empty without a problem provided there is a subsequent correction. An encoder which is approaching a complex *I* picture may run down the buffer so it can send a lot of data to describe that picture. Figure 5.109(a) shows that if a decoder with a nearly full buffer is suddenly switched to an encoder which has been running down its buffer occupancy, the decoder buffer will overflow when the second encoder sends a lot of data.

An MPEG-2 switcher will need to monitor the buffer occupancy of its own output to avoid overflow of downstream decoders. Where this is a possibility the second encoder will have to recompress to reduce the output bit rate temporarily. In practice there will be a recovery period where the buffer occupancy of the newly selected signal is matched to that of the previous signal. This is shown in Figure 5.109(b).

References

1. Kelly, D.H., Visual processing of moving stimuli. *J. Opt. Soc. America*, **2**, 216–225 (1985)
2. Uyttendaele, A., Observations on scanning formats. Presented at HDTV '97 Montreux (June 1997)
3. Shapiro, J.M., Embedded image coding using zerotrees of wavelet coefficients. *IEEE Trans. SP*, **41**, 3445–3462 (1993)
4. Taubin, G. and Rossignac, J., Geometric compression through topological surgery. *ACM Trans. on Graphics*, 88–115 (April 1998)
5. de Boor, C., *A Practical Guide to Splines*. Berlin: Springer (1978)
6. Taubin, G., Guezic, A., Horn, W.P. and Lazarus, F., *Progressive forest split compression, Proc. Siggraph '98*, 123–132 (1998)
7. ITU-T Recommendation H.264, *Advanced video coding for generic audiovisual services*.
8. Karczewicz, M. and Kurceren, R., The SP and SI frames design for H.264/AVC. *IEEE Trans. on Circuits and Systems for Video Technology* (July 2003)
9. Stone, J. and Wilkinson, J., Concatenation of video compression systems. Presented at 37th SMPTE Tech. Conf., New Orleans (1995)
10. Wells, N.D., The ATLANTIC project: models for programme production and distribution. *Proc. Euro. Conf. Multimedia Applications Services and Techniques (ECMAST)*, 243–253 (1996)
11. Werner, O., Drift analysis and drift reduction for multiresolution hybrid video coding. *Image Communication*, **8**, 387–409 (1996)
12. Knee, M.J. and Wells, N.D., Seamless concatenation – a 21st century dream. Presented at Int. Television. Symp., Montreux (1997)

6

MPEG bitstreams

After compression, audio and video signals are simply data and only differ from generic data in that they relate to real-time signals. MPEG bitstreams are basically means of transporting data whilst allowing the time axis of the original signal to be re-created at the decoder.

6.1   Introduction

There are two basic applications of MPEG bitstreams – recording and transmission – and these have quite different requirements. In the multichannel recording application the encoders and decoders can all share the same clock. The read data rate of the storage device can be adjusted so that the decoded frame rate or audio sampling rate can be slaved to any required reference signal. In the case of multichannel transmission, such as a digital television service, the program sources are not necessarily synchronous. The source of timing is the encoder and the decoder must synchronize or genlock to that. Thus the difference between a program stream and a transport stream is that the latter must contain additional synchronizing information to lock the encoder and decoder clocks together independently in each program.

Transmission techniques are steadily becoming more complex as new applications are found. In the earliest systems a dedicated signal path with constant bandwidth was specified and one compression factor would be employed. The use of statistical multiplexing allowed variable compression factors to be used subject to the overall bit rate of the multiplex remaining the same.

In network applications different users have access to different bit rates according to geographic and economic constraints. Further factors, such as network congestion or file server capacity may mean that the

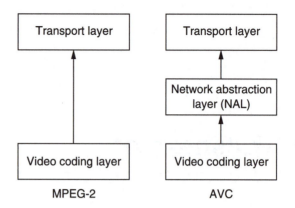

Figure 6.1 A comparison of MPEG-2 and AVC shows that the latter has an additional layer.

available bit rate is less than the capacity of the terminal equipment. One solution to this is the use of multi-rate compression, in which the same program material is compressed to a number of different bit rates. A given connection will be provided with a data rate that does not exceed the steady capacity of the terminal equipment or the instantaneous capacity of the network. In practice this may require the decoder to switch between different bit-rate versions of the same material. Whilst MPEG-2 can do this, there is little flexibility in the times at which such a switch can be made. A distinct advantage of AVC is that it is designed to allow multi-rate operation.

Figure 6.1 shows the basic difference between MPEG-2 and AVC. In MPEG-2 there is a video coding layer, which outputs an elementary stream to a transport layer. In AVC there is an additional layer, known as the *Network Abstraction Layer* (NAL), between the coding layer and the transport layer. This allows more flexible packaging of the elementary stream for network applications.

Clearly in any bit serial recording or transmission application there must be some means to parse the bitstream by locating symbol boundaries. This is the function of synchronizing patterns. Not all channels are true bitstreams. In many systems, especially where Reed–Solomon error correction is used, the system operates one byte at a time and the parsing of the bitstream into bytes is already performed as a necessary step in error correction and demultiplexing. ATM works in this way, as does DVB and DVD. Thus the output of such a channel would be a bytestream in which word boundaries are already known and the synchronization problem is then to locate a specific byte.

In a packetized multiplexed transmission of several programs, the packets are small so that each program receives frequent updates, reducing buffering requirements. The drawback is that each packet requires a synchronization mechanism and the smaller the packets the more bit rate is lost to synchronizing. Thus for recording it is advantageous to have a different approach in which larger packets are used to cut down synchronizing overhead.

6.2 Packets and time stamps

The video elementary stream is an endless bitstream representing pictures which are not necessarily in the correct order and which take a variable length of time to transmit. Storage and transmission systems prefer discrete blocks of data. In MPEG-2 elementary streams are packetized to form a PES (packetized elementary stream). Audio elementary streams are also packetized. A packet is shown in Figure 6.2. It begins with a header containing an unique packet start code and a code which identifies the type of data stream. Optionally the packet header also may contain one or more time stamps which are used for synchronizing the video decoder to real time and for obtaining lip-sync.

Figure 6.3 shows that a time stamp is a sample of the state of a counter which is driven by a 90 kHz clock. This is obtained by dividing down the master 27 MHz clock of MPEG-2. There are two types of time stamp: PTS and DTS. These are abbreviations for presentation time stamp and decode time stamp. A presentation time stamp determines when the associated picture should be displayed on the screen, whereas a decode

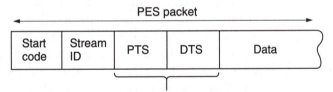

PTS/DTS need not be in every PES packet.
Can be up to 700 milliseconds apart in program
streams or 100 milliseconds apart in transport streams
Decoder interpolates stamps

Figure 6.2 A PES packet structure is used to break up the continuous elementary stream.

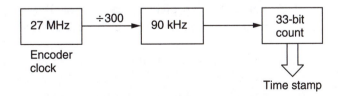

Figure 6.3 Time stamps are the result of sampling a counter driven by the encoder clock.

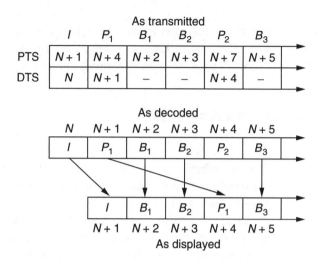

Figure 6.4 An example of using PTS/DTS to synchronize bidirectional decoding.

time stamp determines when it should be decoded. In bidirectional coding these times can be quite different.

Audio packets only have presentation time stamps. Clearly if lip-sync is to be obtained, the audio and the video streams of a given program must have been locked to the same master 27 MHz clock and the time stamps must have come from the same counter driven by that clock.

With reference to Figure 6.4, the GOP begins with an *I* picture, and then *P1* is sent out of sequence prior to the *B* pictures. *P1* has to be decoded before *B1* and *B2* can be decoded. As only one picture can be decoded at a time, the *I* picture is decoded at time *N*, but not displayed until time $N+1$. As the *I* picture is being displayed, *P1* is being decoded at $N+1$. *P1* will be stored in RAM. At time $N+2$, *B1* is decoded and displayed immediately. For this reason *B* pictures need only PTS. At $N+3$, *B2* is decoded and displayed. At $N+4$, *P1* is displayed, hence the large difference between PTS and DTS in *P1*. Simultaneously *P2* is decoded and stored ready for the decoding of *B3* and so on.

In practice the time between input pictures is constant and so there is a certain amount of redundancy in the time stamps. Consequently PTS/DTS need not appear in every PES packet. Time stamps can be up to 700 ms apart in program streams and up to 100 ms apart in transport streams. As each picture type (*I*, *P* or *B*) is flagged in the bitstream, the decoder can infer the PTS/DTS for every picture from the ones actually transmitted.

Figure 6.5 shows that one or more PES packets can be assembled in a pack whose header contains a sync pattern and a system clock reference code which allows the decoder to re-create the encoder clock. Clock reference operation is described in section 6.4.

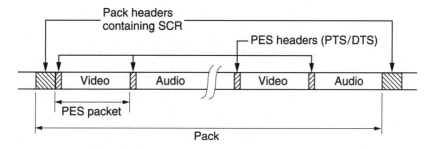

Figure 6.5 A pack is a set of PES packets. The pack header contains a clock reference code.

In AVC the rigid structure of MPEG-2 is relaxed somewhat. Temporal coding relies on identification of reference pictures and MPEG-2 does this with the combination of PTS/DTS and the known group structure. AVC allows the reference order of coded pictures to be decoupled from the display order. Thus encoded pictures can be sent in any order within buffering constraints. The encoder can select the order that minimizes overall bit rate. This requires a different picture identification mechanism. AVC uses frame number and Picture Order Count (POC). The frame number is a count which increments in the order of decoding whereas POC increments in the order of display. Note that these are picture counts, not time counts. These counts can be converted to time stamps by mutiplication by the period of each frame which is a constant for a given video format.

POC may be sent explicitly for each picture in slice headers, or it may be compressed. Where a repeating group structure is used, this will be sent in the sequence parameters and the decoder can compute the POC from the picture type and its transmitted position in the group. AVC encoders may change the group structure temporarily by sending delta POCs to change the decoder POCs from the predicted value to the actual value. In the event that the display order is the same as the decoding order the POC can be obtained from the frame number.

6.3 Transport streams

The MPEG-2 transport stream is intended to be a multiplex of many TV programs with their associated sound and data channels, although a single program transport stream (SPTS) is possible. The transport stream is based upon packets of constant size so that adding error-correction codes and interleaving[1] in a higher layer is eased. Figure 6.6 shows that these are always 188 bytes long. Transport stream packets should not be confused with PES packets which are larger and vary in size.

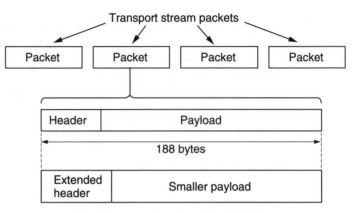

Packet is always 188 bytes long

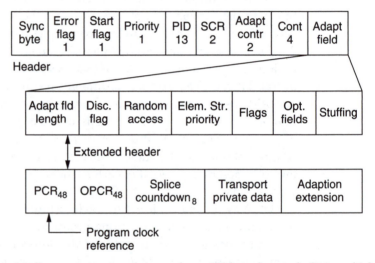

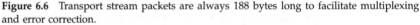

Figure 6.6 Transport stream packets are always 188 bytes long to facilitate multiplexing and error correction.

Transport stream packets always begin with a header. The remainder of the packet carries data known as the payload. For efficiency, the normal header is relatively small, but for special purposes the header may be extended. In this case the payload gets smaller so that the overall size of the packet is unchanged.

The header begins with a sync byte which is a unique pattern detected by a demultiplexer. A transport stream may contain many different elementary streams and these are identified by giving each a unique 13-bit Packet Identification Code or PID which is included in the header. A multiplexer seeking a particular elementary stream simply checks the PID of every packet and accepts those that match, rejecting the rest.

In a multiplex there may be many packets from other programs in between packets of a given PID. To help the demultiplexer, the packet header contains a continuity count. This is a four-bit value which increments at each new packet having a given PID.

This approach allows statistical multiplexing as it does not matter how many or how few packets have a given PID; the demux will still find them. Statistical multiplexing has the problem that it is virtually impossible to make the sum of the input bit rates constant. Instead the multiplexer aims to make the average data bit rate slightly less than the maximum and the overall bit rate is kept constant by adding stuffing or null packets. These packets have no meaning, but simply keep the bit rate constant. Null packets always have a PID of 8191 (all ones) and the demultiplexer discards them.

6.4   Clock references

A transport stream is a multiplex of several TV programs and these may have originated from widely different locations. It is impractical to expect all the programs in a transport stream to be synchronous and so the stream is designed from the outset to allow asynchronous programs. A decoder running from a transport stream has to genlock to the encoder and the transport stream has to have a mechanism to allow this to be done independently for each program. The synchronizing mechanism is called Program Clock Reference (PCR).

In program streams all the programs must be synchronous so that only one clock is required at the decoder. In this case the synchronizing mechanism is called System Clock Reference (SCR).

Figure 6.7 shows how the PCR/SCR system works. The goal is to re-create at the decoder a 27 MHz clock which is synchronous with that at the encoder. The encoder clock drives a forty-eight-bit counter which continuously counts up to the maximum value before overflowing and beginning again.

A transport stream multiplexer will periodically sample the counter and place the state of the count in an extended packet header as a PCR (see Figure 6.6). The demultiplexer selects only the PIDs of the required program, and it will extract the PCRs from the packets in which they were inserted. In a program stream the count is placed in a pack header as an SCR which the decoder can identify.

The PCR/SCR codes are used to control a numerically locked loop (NLL). This is similar to a phase-locked loop, except that the two phases concerned are represented by the state of a binary number. The NLL contains a 27 MHz VCXO (voltage controlled crystal oscillator), a variable-frequency oscillator based on a crystal which has a relatively small frequency range.

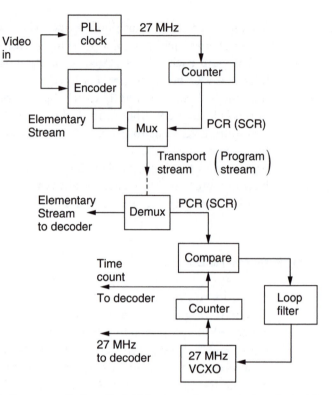

Figure 6.7 Program or System Clock Reference codes regenerate a clock at the decoder. See text for details.

The VCXO drives a forty-eight-bit counter in the same way as in the encoder. The state of the counter is compared with the contents of the PCR/SCR and the difference is used to modify the VCXO frequency. When the loop reaches lock, the decoder counter would arrive at the same value as is contained in the PCR/SCR and no change in the VCXO would then occur. In practice the transport stream packets will suffer from transmission jitter and this will create phase noise in the loop. This is removed by the loop filter so that the VCXO effectively averages a large number of phase errors.

A heavily damped loop will reject jitter well, but will take a long time to lock. Lock-up time can be reduced when switching to a new program if the decoder counter is jammed to the value of the first PCR received in the new program. The loop filter may also have its time constants shortened during lock-up. Once a synchronous 27 MHz clock is available at the decoder, this can be divided down to provide the 90 kHz clock which drives the time stamp mechanism. The entire timebase stability of the decoder is no better than the stability of the clock derived from PCR/SCR. MPEG-2 sets standards for the maximum amount of jitter which can be present in PCRs in a real transport stream.

6.5   Program Specific Information (PSI)

In a real transport stream, each elementary stream has a different PID, but the demultiplexer has to be told what these PIDs are and what audio belongs with what video before it can operate. This is the function of PSI. Figure 6.8 shows the structure of PSI. When a decoder powers up, it knows nothing about the incoming transport stream except that it must search for all packets with a PID of zero. PID zero is reserved for the Program Association Table (PAT). The PAT is transmitted at regular intervals and contains a list of all the programs in this transport stream. Each program is further described by its own Program Map Table (PMT) and the PIDs of the PMTs are contained in the PAT.

Figure 6.8 also shows that the PMTs fully describe each program. The PID of the video elementary stream is defined, along with the PID(s) of the associated audio and data streams. Consequently when the viewer selects a particular program, the demultiplexer looks up the program number in the PAT, finds the right PMT and reads the audio, video and data PIDs. It then selects elementary streams having these PIDs from the transport stream and routes them to the decoders.

Program 0 of the PAT contains the PID of the Network Information Table (NIT). This contains information about what other transport

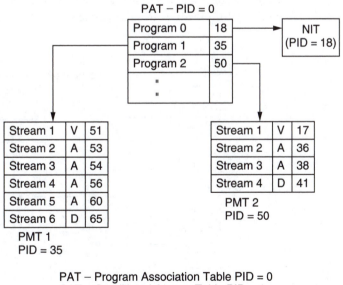

PAT – Program Association Table PID = 0
CAT – Conditional Access Table PID = 1
NIT – Network Information Table
Null packets – PID = 8191

Figure 6.8   MPEG-2 Program Specific Information (PSI) is used to tell a demultiplexer what the transport stream contains.

streams are available. For example, in the case of a satellite broadcast, the NIT would detail the orbital position, the polarization, carrier frequency and modulation scheme. Using the NIT a set-top box could automatically switch between transport streams.

Apart from 0 and 8191, a PID of 1 is also reserved for the Conditional Access Table (CAT). This is part of the access control mechanism needed to support pay per view or subscription viewing.

6.6   Multiplexing

A transport stream multiplexer is a complex device because of the number of functions it must perform. A fixed multiplexer will be considered first. In a fixed multiplexer, the bit rate of each of the programs must be specified so that the sum does not exceed the payload bit rate of the transport stream. The payload bit rate is the overall bit rate less the packet headers and PSI rate.

In practice the programs will not be synchronous to one another, but the transport stream must produce a constant packet rate given by the bit rate divided by 188 bytes, the packet length. Figure 6.9 shows how this is handled. Each elementary stream entering the multiplexer passes through a buffer which is divided into payload-sized areas. Note that MPEG-2 decoders also have a quantity of buffer memory. The challenge to the multiplexer is to take packets from each program in such a way

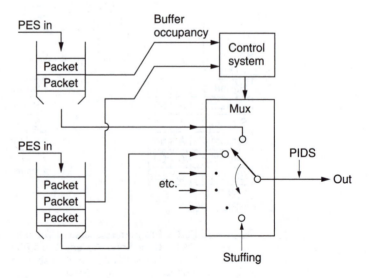

Figure 6.9 A transport stream multiplexer can handle several programs which are asynchronous to one another and to the transport stream clock. See text for details. Periodically the payload area is made smaller because of the requirement to insert PCR.

that neither its own buffers nor the buffers in any decoder either overflow or underflow. This requirement is met by sending packets from all programs as evenly as possible rather than bunching together a lot of packets from one program. When the bit rates of the programs are different, the only way this can be handled is to use the buffer contents indicators. The fuller a buffer is, the more likely it should be that a packet will be read from it. This buffer content arbitrator can decide which program should have a packet allocated next.

If the sum of the input bit rates is correct, the buffers should all slowly empty because the overall input bit rate has to be less than the payload bit rate. This allows for the insertion of Program Specific Information. While PATs and PMTs are being transmitted, the program buffers will fill up again. The multiplexer can also fill the buffers by sending more PCRs as this reduces the payload of each packet. In the event that the multiplexer has sent enough of everything but still cannot fill a packet then it will send a null packet with a PID of 8191. Decoders will discard null packets and as they convey no useful data, the multiplexer buffers will all fill while null packets are being transmitted.

In a statistical multiplexer or statmux, the bit rate allocated to each program can vary dynamically. Figure 6.10 shows that there must be a tight connection between the statmux and the associated compressors. Each compressor has a buffer memory which is emptied by a demand clock from the statmux. In a normal, fixed bit rate, coder the buffer contents feed back and control the requantizer. In statmuxing this process is less severe and only takes place if the buffer is very close to full, because the buffer content is also fed to the statmux.

The statmux contains an arbitrator which allocates packets to the program with the fullest buffer. Thus if a particular program encounters difficult material it will produce large prediction errors and begin to fill

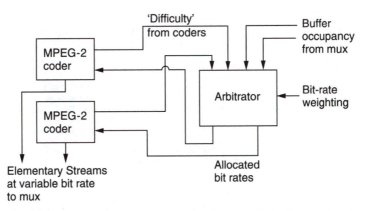

Figure 6.10 A statistical multiplexer contains an arbitrator which allocates bit rate to each program as a function of program difficulty.

its output buffer. This will cause the statmux to allocate more packets to that program. In order to fill more packets, the statmux clocks more data out of that buffer, causing the level to fall again. Of course, this is only possible if the other programs in the transport stream are handling typical video.

In the event that several programs encounter difficult material at once, clearly the buffer contents will rise and the requantizing mechanism will have to operate.

6.7   Remultiplexing

In real life a program creator may produce a transport stream which carries all its programs simultaneously. A service provider may take in several such streams and create its own transport stream by selecting different programs from different sources. In an MPEG-2 environment this requires a remultiplexer, also known as a transmultiplexer. Figure 6.11 shows what a remultiplexer does.

Remultiplexing is easier when all the incoming programs have the same bit rate. If a suitable combination of programs is selected it is obvious that the output transport stream will always have sufficient bit rate. Where statistical multiplexing has been used, there is a possibility that the sum of the bit rates of the selected programs will exceed the bit rate of the output transport stream. To avoid this, the remultiplexer will have to employ recompression.

Recompression requires a partial decode of the bitstream to identify the DCT coefficients. These will then be requantized to reduce the bit rate until it is low enough to fit the output transport stream.

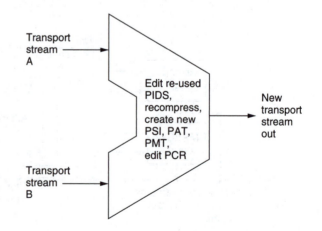

Figure 6.11 A remultiplexer creates a new transport stream from selected programs in other transport streams.

Remultiplexers have to edit the Program Specific Information (PSI) such that the Program Association Table (PAT) and the Program Map Tables (PMT) correctly reflect the new transport stream content. It may also be necessary to change the packet identification codes (PIDs) since the incoming transport streams could have inadvertently used the same values.

When Program Clock Reference (PCR) data are included in an extended packet header, they represent a real-time clock count and if the associated packet is moved in time the PCR value will be wrong. Remultiplexers have to recreate a new multiplex from a number of other multiplexes and it is inevitable that this process will result in packets being placed in different locations in the output transport stream than they had in the input. In this case the remultiplexer must edit the PCR values so that they reflect the value the clock counter would have had at the location at which the packet now resides.

Reference

1. Watkinson, J.R., *The Art of Digital Video*, second edition, Ch. 6. Oxford: Focal Press (1994)

7

MPEG applications

7.1　Introduction

It should be borne in mind that however exciting it may be, MPEG is only a technology. Technology *per se* is not useful and only becomes useful when it is incorporated into an appropriate and affordable product or service. If the use is not appropriate or affordable, there is no point in blaming the technology.

In this chapter a number of useful applications of MPEG are outlined. In most cases designers have followed the rules of high technology to design systems which maximize the potential of the technology whilst protecting against its weaknesses.

MPEG is an information technology. It cannot deliver anything physical: you get the movie but no popcorn. The strength of MPEG is that it delivers audio-visual material with economy of bandwidth. Its weaknesses are sensitivity to bit errors and the requirement for near-real-time transmission. The variable-length coding of MPEG can lose synchronization in the presence of a single bit error. Decoders can take a considerable time to recover from a buffer underflow or overflow. Wherever bandwidth or storage capacity is in short supply, MPEG is useful. Where bandwidth is plentiful, as in optical fibre networks, MPEG is pointless. As the capacity and economics of storage devices continue to increase, MPEG becomes less important.

MPEG will remain important in any area where there will be a permanent shortage of bandwidth; this includes any mobile equipment or service which must use radio communication.

Figure 7.1 shows that well-engineered applications of MPEG will always include an error-correction system appropriate for the characteristics of the channel and suitable mechanisms to ensure that decoder buffers neither overflow nor underflow. Constant-bit rate channels

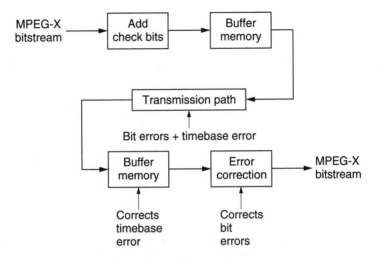

Figure 7.1 Any real-time MPEG delivery system must include means to maintain a low error rate and buffering to deliver data within the decoder's time window.

having constant delay are easy to implement because the buffering mechanisms of the standard MPEG encoders and decoders are able to operate with no further assistance. Digital TV transmitters provide essentially constant bit-rate because this is related to the standardized (and regulated) channel bandwidth allowed.

In packet networks the delivery delay is not constant because other types of messages are multiplexed with the audio-visual message of interest. Variable delay channels cause MPEG decoders difficulty. Not only is there a greater danger of buffer overflow or underflow, but the program clock reference information is no longer correct if a packet is received with a time shift. In this case additional buffering is needed at both ends of the channel so that the variable delay characteristic of the channel is invisible to the MPEG layer.

There are now many members of the MPEG family and it can be difficult to decide which type of MPEG coding to use. Figure 7.2 shows some general guidelines. As a decoder becomes more complex, the bit rate which can be used for a given quality will fall. However, this will be accompanied by an increase in power consumption at the encoder and decoder as well as an increased delay. The designer will have to balance the cost of the bandwidth with the cost of the encoding and decoding equipment and the power consumed.

7.2 Telephones

The telephone is a classic example of limited bandwidth. If there is a market for video phones, then compression is the only way forward.

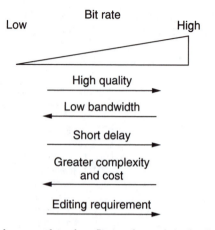

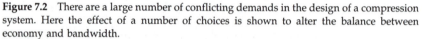

Figure 7.2 There are a large number of conflicting demands in the design of a compression system. Here the effect of a number of choices is shown to alter the balance between economy and bandwidth.

The facial animation coding developed for MPEG-4 is an obvious contender as it allows a reasonable reproduction of the caller's face with a data rate of only a few kilobits per second. This is considerably less than the data rate needed for the speech. Video telephony is relatively easy between desk-based equipment, where the camera can be mounted on top of the display, but it is not clear how this can be implemented in a cellular telephone which is held against the user's ear. At the time of writing the cellular telephone appears to be degenerating into a cross between a fashion statement and a feature contest as manufacturers pack in more and more gadgets to lure customers. Cellular telephones incorporating CCD cameras that can transmit and receive images rely heavily on compression technology, although pixel counts are low and the quality is poor.

Another important issue for cellular telephones is the amount of signal processing needed to decode and display image related data. Whilst LSI chips can easily perform these tasks in very small physical space, this is only practicable in a portable product if the current consumption is within the range of available battery technology. Battery life is marginal in some of the more complex products.

7.3 Digital television broadcasting

Digital television broadcasting relies on the combination of a number of fundamental technologies. These are: MPEG-2 compression to reduce the bit rate, multiplexing to combine picture and sound data into a common bitstream, digital modulation schemes to reduce the RF bandwidth needed by a given bit rate and error correction to reduce the error statistics of the channel down to a value acceptable to MPEG data. MPEG is a compression and multiplexing standard and does not specify how error correction should be performed. Consequently a transmission standard must define a system which has to correct essentially all errors such that the delivery mechanism is transparent.

DVB (digital video broadcasting)[1] is a standard which incorporates MPEG-2 picture and sound coding but which also specifies all the additional steps needed to deliver an MPEG transport stream from one place to another. This transport stream will consist of a number of elementary streams of video and audio, where the audio may be coded according to MPEG audio standard or AC-3. In a system working within its capabilities, the picture and sound quality will be determined only by the performance of the compression system and not by the RF transmission channel. This is the fundamental difference between analog and digital broadcasting. In analog television broadcasting, the picture quality may be limited by composite video encoding artifacts as well as transmission artifacts such as noise and ghosting. In digital television broadcasting the picture quality is determined instead by the compression artifacts and interlace artifacts if interlace has been retained.

If the received error rate increases for any reason, once the correcting power is used up, the system will degrade rapidly as uncorrected errors enter the MPEG decoder. In practice decoders will be programmed to recognize the condition and blank or mute to avoid outputting garbage. As a result digital receivers tend either to work well or not at all.

It is important to realize that the signal strength in a digital system does not translate directly to picture quality. A poor signal will increase the number of bit errors. Provided that this is within the capability of the error-correction system, there is no visible loss of quality. In contrast, a very powerful signal may be unusable because of similarly powerful reflections due to multipath propagation.

Whilst in one sense an MPEG transport stream is only data, it differs from generic data in that it must be presented to the viewer at a particular rate. Generic data are usually asynchronous, whereas baseband video and audio are synchronous. However, after compression and multiplexing audio and video are no longer precisely synchronous and so the term *isochronous* is used. This means a signal which was at one time synchronous and will be displayed synchronously, but which uses buffering at transmitter and receiver to accommodate moderate timing errors in the transmission.

Clearly another mechanism is needed so that the time axis of the original signal can be re-created on reception. The time stamp and program clock reference system of MPEG does this.

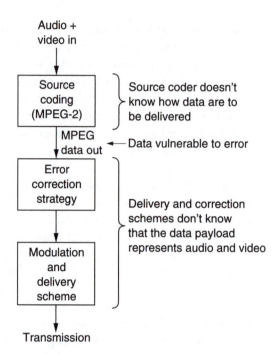

Figure 7.3 Source coder doesn't know the delivery mechanism and delivery doesn't need to know what the data mean.

Figure 7.3 shows that the concepts involved in digital television broadcasting exist at various levels which have an independence not found in analog technology. In a given configuration a transmitter can radiate a given payload data bit rate. This represents the useful bit rate and does not include the necessary overheads needed by error correction, multiplexing or synchronizing. It is fundamental that the transmission system does not care what this payload bit rate is used for. The entire capacity may be used up by one high-definition channel, or a large number of heavily compressed channels may be carried. The details of this data usage are the domain of the *transport stream*. The multiplexing of transport streams is defined by the MPEG standards, but these do not define any error correction or transmission technique.

At the lowest level in Figure 7.3 is the source coding scheme, in this case MPEG-2 compression results in one or more elementary streams, each of which carries a video or audio channel. Figure 7.4 shows that elementary streams are multiplexed into a transport stream. The viewer then selects the desired elementary stream from the transport stream. Metadata in the transport stream ensure that when a video elementary stream is chosen, the appropriate audio elementary stream will automatically be selected.

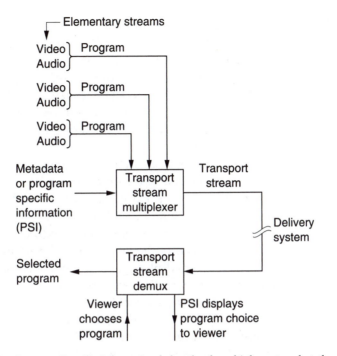

Figure 7.4 Program Specific Information helps the demultiplexer to select the required program.

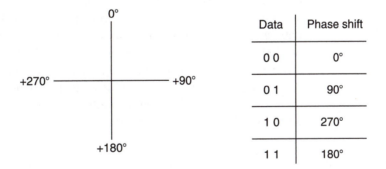

Data	Phase shift
0 0	0°
0 1	90°
1 0	270°
1 1	180°

Figure 7.5 Differential quadrature phase-shift keying (DQPSK).

A key difference between analog and digital transmission is that the transmitter output is switched between a number of discrete states rather than continuously varying. The process is called channel coding which is the digital equivalent of modulation.[2] A good code minimizes the channel bandwidth needed for a given bit rate. This quality of the code is measured in bits/s/Hz.

Where the SNR is poor, as in satellite broadcasting, the amplitude of the signal will be unstable, and phase modulation is used. Figure 7.5 shows that phase-shift keying (PSK) can use two or more phases. When four phases in quadrature are used, the result is quadrature phase-shift keying or QPSK. Each period of the transmitted waveform can have one of four phases and therefore conveys the value of two data bits. 8-PSK uses eight phases and can carry three bits per symbol where the SNR is adequate. PSK is generally encoded in such a way that a knowledge of absolute phase is not needed at the receiver. Instead of encoding the signal phase directly, the data determine the magnitude of the phase shift between symbols.

In terrestrial transmission more power is available than, for example, from a satellite and so a stronger signal can be delivered to the receiver. Where a better SNR exists, an increase in data rate can be had using multi-level signalling instead of binary. Figure 7.6 shows that the ATSC system uses an eight-level signal (8-VSB) allowing three bits to be sent per symbol. Four of the levels exist with normal carrier phase and four exist with inverted phase so that a phase-sensitive rectifier is needed in the receiver. Clearly the data separator must have a three-bit ADC which can resolve the eight signal levels. The gain and offset of the signal must be precisely set so that the quantizing levels register precisely with the centres of the eyes. The transmitted signal contains sync pulses which are encoded using specified code levels so that the data separator can set its gain and offset.

Multi-level signalling systems have the characteristic that the bits in the symbol have different error probability. Figure 7.7 shows that a small noise level will corrupt the low-order bit, whereas twice as much noise will be needed to corrupt the middle bit and four times as much will be needed to corrupt the high-order bit. In ATSC the solution is that the lower two bits are encoded together in an inner error-correcting scheme so that they represent only one bit with similar reliability to the top bit. As a result the 8-VSB system actually delivers two data bits per symbol even though eight-level signalling is used.

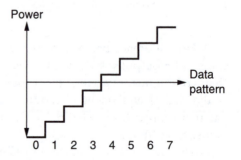

Figure 7.6 In 8-VSB the transmitter operates in eight different states enabling three bits to be sent per symbol.

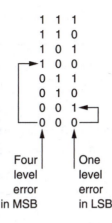

Figure 7.7 In multi-level signalling the error probability is not the same for each bit.

Multi-level signalling can be combined with PSK to obtain multi-level quadrature amplitude modulation (QUAM). Figure 7.8 shows the example of 64-QUAM. Incoming six-bit data words are split into two three-bit words and each is used to amplitude modulate a pair of sinusoidal carriers which are generated in quadrature. The modulators are four-quadrant devices such that 23 amplitudes are available, four which are in phase with the carrier and four which are antiphase. The two AM carriers are linearly added and the result is a signal which has 26 or 64 combinations of amplitude and phase. There is a great deal of similarity between QUAM and the colour subcarrier used in analog television in which the two colour difference signals are encoded into one amplitude- and phase-modulated waveform. On reception, the waveform is sampled twice per cycle in phase with the two original carriers and the result is a pair of eight-level signals. 16-QUAM is also possible, delivering only four bits per symbol but requiring a lower SNR.

The data bit patterns to be transmitted can have any combinations whatsoever, and if nothing were done, the transmitted spectrum would be non-uniform. This is undesirable because peaks cause interference with other services, whereas energy troughs allow external interference in. A randomizing technique known as energy dispersal is used to overcome the problem. The signal energy is spread uniformly throughout the allowable channel bandwidth so that it has less energy at a given frequency.

A pseudo-random sequence (PRS) generator is used to generate the randomizing sequence. Figure 7.9 shows the randomizer used in DVB. This sixteen-bit device has a maximum sequence length of 65 535 bits, and is preset to a standard value at the beginning of each set of eight transport stream packets. The serialized data are XORed with the sequence, which randomizes the output that then goes to the modulator.

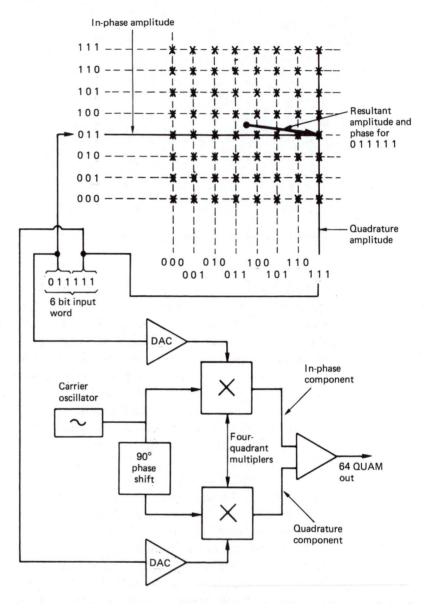

Figure 7.8 In 64-QUAM, two carriers are generated with a quadrature relationship. These are independently amplitude modulated to eight discrete levels in four quadrant multipliers. Adding the signals produces a QUAM signal having 64 unique combinations of amplitude and phase. Decoding requires the waveform to be sampled in quadrature like a colour TV subcarrier.

The spectrum of the transmission is now determined by the spectrum of the PRS.

On reception, the de-randomizer must contain the identical ring counter which must also be set to the starting condition to bit accuracy.

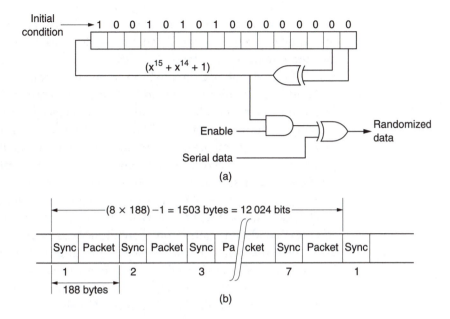

Figure 7.9 The randomizer of DVB is pre-set to the initial condition once every eight transport stream packets (a). The maximum length of the sequence is 65 535 bits, but only the first 12 024 bits are used before resetting again (b).

Its output is then added to the data stream from the demodulator. The randomizing will effectively then have been added twice to the data in modulo-2, and as a result is cancelled out leaving the original serial data.

The way that radio signals interact with obstacles is a function of the relative magnitude of the wavelength and the size of the object. AM sound radio transmissions with a wavelength of several hundred metres can easily diffract around large objects. The shorter the wavelength of a transmission, the larger objects in the environment appear to it and these objects can then become reflectors. Reflecting objects produce a delayed signal at the receiver in addition to the direct signal. In analog television transmissions this causes the familiar ghosting. In digital transmissions, the symbol rate may be so high that the reflected signal may be one or more symbols behind the direct signal, causing intersymbol interference. As the reflection may be continuous, the result may be that almost every symbol is corrupted. No error-correction system can handle this. Raising the transmitter power is no help at all as it simply raises the power of the reflection in proportion.

The only solution is to change the characteristics of the RF channel in some way either to prevent the multipath reception or to prevent it being a problem. The RF channel includes the modulator, transmitter, antennae, receiver and demodulator.

As with analog UHF TV transmissions, a directional antenna is useful with digital transmission as it can reject reflections. However, directional antennae tend to be large and they require a skilled permanent installation. Mobile use on a vehicle or vessel is simply impractical.

Another possibility is to incorporate a ghost canceller in the receiver. The transmitter periodically sends a standardized known waveform known as a training sequence. The receiver knows what this waveform looks like and compares it with the received signal. In theory it is possible for the receiver to compute the delay and relative level of a reflection and so insert an opposing one. In practice if the reflection is strong it may prevent the receiver finding the training sequence.

The most elegant approach is to use a system in which multipath reception conditions cause only a small increase in error rate which the error-correction system can manage. This approach is used in DVB. Figure 7.10(a) shows that when using one carrier with a high bit rate, reflections can easily be delayed by one or more bit periods, causing interference between the bits. Figure 7.10(b) shows that instead, OFDM

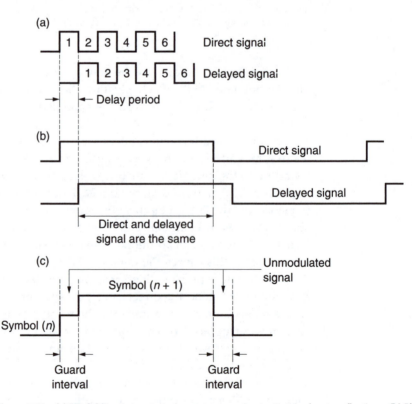

Figure 7.10 (a) High bit rate transmissions are prone to corruption due to reflections. (b) If the bit rate is reduced the effect of reflections is eliminated, in fact reflected energy can be used. (c) Guard intervals may be inserted between symbols.

sends many carriers each having a low bit rate. When a low bit rate is used, the energy in the reflection will arrive during the same bit period as the direct signal. Not only is the system immune to multipath reflections, but the energy in the reflections can actually be used. This characteristic can be enhanced by using guard intervals shown in Figure 7.10(c). These reduce multipath bit overlap even more.

Note that OFDM is not a modulation scheme, and each of the carriers used in an OFDM system still needs to be modulated using any of the digital coding schemes described above. What OFDM does is to provide an efficient way of packing many carriers close together without mutual interference.

A serial data waveform basically contains a train of rectangular pulses. The transform of a rectangle is the function $\sin x/x$ and so the baseband pulse train has a $\sin x/x$ spectrum. When this waveform is used to modulate a carrier the result is a symmetrical $\sin x/x$ spectrum centred on the carrier frequency. Figure 7.11(a) shows that nulls in the spectrum appear spaced at multiples of the bit rate away from the carrier.

Further carriers can be placed at spacings such that each is centred at the nulls of the others as is shown in Figure 7.11(b). The distance between the carriers is equal to 90° or one quadrant of $\sin x$. Owing to the quadrant spacing, these carriers are mutually orthogonal, hence the term orthogonal frequency division. A large number of such carriers (in practice several thousand) will be interleaved to produce an overall spectrum which is almost rectangular and which fills the available transmission channel.

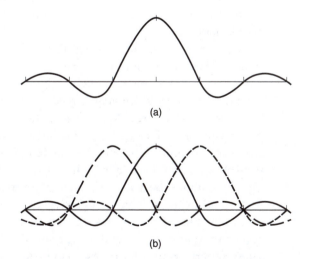

(a)

(b)

Figure 7.11 In OFDM the carrier spacing is critical, but when correct the carriers become independent and most efficient use is made of the spectrum. (a) Spectrum of bitstream has regular nulls. (b) Peak of one carrier occurs at null of another.

When guard intervals are used, the carrier returns to an unmodulated state between bits for a period which is greater than the period of the reflections. Then the reflections from one transmitted bit decay during the guard interval before the next bit is transmitted. The use of guard intervals reduces the bit rate of the carrier because for some of the time it is radiating carrier, not data. A typical reduction is to around 80 per cent of the capacity without guard intervals.

This capacity reduction does, however, improve the error statistics dramatically, such that much less redundancy is required in the error-correction system. Thus the effective transmission rate is improved. The use of guard intervals also moves more energy from the sidebands back to the carrier. The frequency spectrum of a set of carriers is no longer perfectly flat but contains a small peak at the centre of each carrier.

The ability to work in the presence of multipath cancellation is one of the great strengths of OFDM. In DVB, more than 2000 carriers are used in single transmitter systems. Provided there is exact synchronism, several transmitters can radiate exactly the same signal so that a single-frequency network can be created throughout a whole country. SFNs require a variation on OFDM which uses over 8000 carriers.

With OFDM, directional antennae are not needed and, given sufficient field strength, mobile reception is perfectly feasible. Of course, directional antennae may still be used to boost the received signal outside of normal service areas or to enable the use of low-powered transmitters.

An OFDM receiver must perform fast Fourier transforms (FFTs) on the whole band at the symbol rate of one of the carriers. The amplitude and/or phase of the carrier at a given frequency effectively reflects the state of the transmitted symbol at that time slot and so the FFT partially demodulates as well.

In order to assist with tuning in, the OFDM spectrum contains pilot signals. These are individual carriers which are transmitted with slightly more power than the remainder. The pilot carriers are spaced apart through the whole channel at agreed frequencies which form part of the transmission standard. Practical reception conditions, including multipath reception, will cause a significant variation in the received spectrum and some equalization will be needed. Figure 7.12 shows what the possible spectrum looks like in the presence of a powerful reflection. The signal has almost been cancelled at certain frequencies. However, the FFT performed in the receiver is effectively a spectral analysis of the signal and so the receiver computes for free the received spectrum. As in a flat spectrum the peak magnitude of all the coefficients would be the same (apart from the pilots), equalization is easily performed by multiplying the coefficients by suitable constants until this characteristic is obtained.

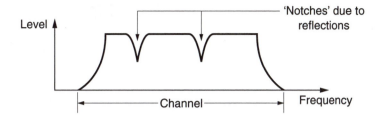

Figure 7.12 Multipath reception can place notches in the channel spectrum. This will require equalization at the receiver.

Although the use of transform-based receivers appears complex, when it is considered that such an approach simultaneously allows effective equalization the complexity is not significantly higher than that of a conventional receiver which needs a separate spectral analysis system just for equalization purposes. The only drawback of OFDM is that the transmitter must be highly linear to prevent intermodulation between the carriers. This is readily achieved in terrestrial transmitters by derating the transmitter so that it runs at a lower power than it would in analog service. This is not practicable in satellite transmitters which are optimized for efficiency, so OFDM is not really suitable for satellite use.

Broadcast data suffer from both random and burst errors and the error correction strategies of digital television broadcasting have to reflect that. Figure 7.13 shows a typical system in which inner and outer codes are employed. The Reed–Solomon codes are universally used for burst correcting outer codes, along with an interleave which will be convolutional rather than the block-based interleave used in recording media. The inner codes will not be R–S, as more suitable codes exist for the statistical conditions prevalent in broadcasting. DVB uses a parity-based variable-rate system in which the amount of redundancy can be adjusted according to reception conditions.

Figure 7.14 shows a block diagram of a DVB-T (terrestrial) transmitter. Incoming transport stream packets of 188 bytes each are first subject to R–S outer coding. This adds 16 bytes of redundancy to each packet, resulting in 204 bytes. Outer coding is followed by interleaving. The interleave mechanism is shown in Figure 7.15. Outer code blocks are commutated on a byte basis into twelve parallel channels. Each channel contains a different amount of delay, typically achieved by a ring-buffer RAM. The delays are integer multiples of 17 bytes, designed to skew the data by one outer block ($12 \times 17 = 204$). Following the delays, a commutator reassembles interleaved outer blocks. These have 204 bytes as before, but the effect of the interleave is that adjacent bytes in the input are 17 bytes apart in the output. Each output block contains data from twelve input blocks making the data resistant to burst errors.

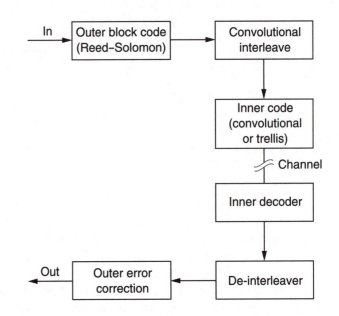

Figure 7.13 Error-correcting strategy of digital television broadcasting systems.

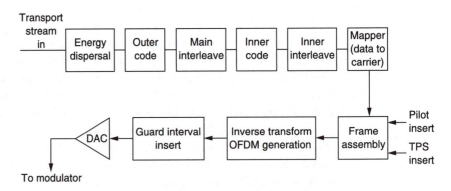

Figure 7.14 DVB-T transmitter block diagram. See text for details.

Following the interleave, the energy-dispersal process takes place. The pseudo-random sequence runs over eight outer blocks and is synchronized by inverting the transport stream packet sync symbol in every eighth block. The packet sync symbols are not randomized.

The inner coding process of DVB is convolutional. The output bit rate of the inner coder is twice the input bit rate. Under the worst reception conditions, this 100 per cent redundancy offers the most powerful correction with the penalty that a low data rate is delivered. However, a variety of inner redundancy factors can be used from 1/2 down to 1/8 of the transmitted bit rate.

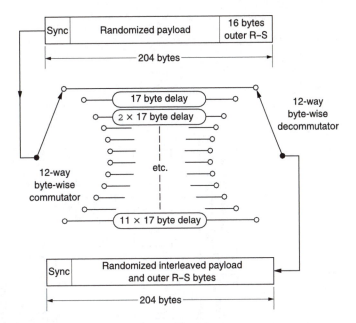

Figure 7.15 The interleaver of DVB uses 12 incrementing delay channels to reorder the data. The sync byte passes through the undelayed channel and so is still at the head of the packet after interleave. However, the packet now contains non-adjacent bytes from 12 different packets.

The DVB standard allows the use of QPSK, 16-QUAM or 64-QUAM coding in an OFDM system. There are five possible inner code rates, and four different guard intervals which can be used with each modulation scheme. Thus for each modulation scheme there are twenty possible transport stream bit rates in the standard DVB channel, each of which requires a different receiver SNR. The broadcaster can select any suitable balance between transport stream bit rate and coverage area. For a given transmitter location and power, reception over a larger area may require a channel code with a smaller number of bits/s/Hz and this reduces the bit rate which can be delivered in a standard channel.

Alternatively a higher amount of inner redundancy means that the proportion of the transmitted bit rate which is data goes down. Thus for wider coverage the broadcaster will have to send fewer programs in the multiplex or use higher compression factors.

7.4 The DVB receiver

Figure 7.16 shows a block diagram of a DVB receiver. The off-air RF signal is fed to a mixer driven by the local oscillator. The IF output of

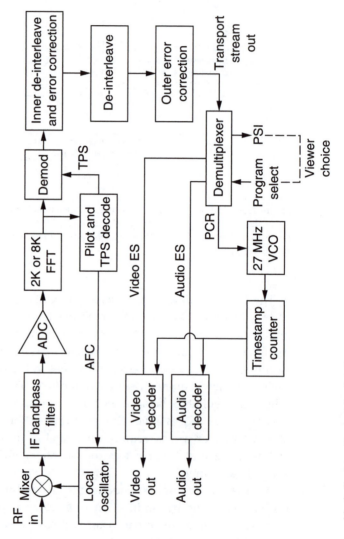

Figure 7.16 DVB receiver block diagram. See text for details.

the mixer is bandpass filtered and supplied to the ADC which outputs a digital IF signal for the FFT stage. The FFT is analysed initially to find the higher-level pilot signals. If these are not in the correct channels the local oscillator frequency is incorrect and it will be changed until the pilots emerge from the FFT in the right channels. The data in the pilots will be decoded in order to tell the receiver how many carriers, what inner redundancy rate, guard band rate and modulation scheme are in use in the remaining carriers. The FFT magnitude information is also a measure of the equalization required.

The FFT outputs are demodulated into 2 K or 8 K bitstreams and these are multiplexed to produce a serial signal. This is subject to inner error correction which corrects random errors. The data are then de-interleaved to break up burst errors and then the outer R–S error correction operates. The output of the R–S correction will then be de-randomized to become an MPEG transport stream once more. The de-randomizing is synchronized by the transmission of inverted sync patterns.

The receiver must select a PID of 0 and wait until a Program Association Table (PAT) is transmitted. This will describe the available programs by listing the PIDs of the Program Map Tables (PMT). By looking for these packets the receiver can determine what PIDs to select to receive any video and audio elementary streams.

When an elementary stream is selected, some of the packets will have extended headers containing Program Clock Reference (PCR). These codes are used to synchronize the 27 MHz clock in the receiver to the one in the MPEG encoder of the desired program. The 27 MHz clock is divided down to drive the time stamp counter so that audio and video emerge from the decoder at the correct rate and with lip-sync.

It should be appreciated that time stamps are relative, not absolute. The time stamp count advances by a fixed amount each picture, but the exact count is meaningless. Thus the decoder can only establish the frame rate of the video from time stamps, but not the precise timing. In practice the receiver has finite buffering memory between the demultiplexer and the MPEG decoder. If the displayed video timing is too late, the buffer will tend to overflow whereas if the displayed video timing is too early the decoding may not be completed. The receiver can advance or retard the time stamp counter during lock-up so that it places the output timing mid-way between these extremes.

7.5   ATSC

The ATSC system is an alternative way of delivering a transport stream, but it is considerably less sophisticated than DVB, and supports only

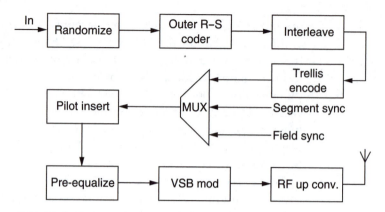

Figure 7.17 Block diagram of ATSC transmitter. See text for details.

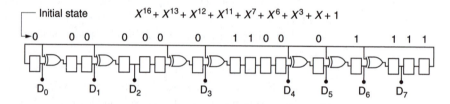

Figure 7.18 The randomizer of ATSC. The twisted ring counter is pre-set to the initial state shown each data field. It is then clocked once per byte and the eight outputs D_0–D_7 are X-ORed with the data byte.

one transport stream bit rate of 19.28 Mbits/s. If any change in the service area is needed, this will require a change in transmitter power.

Figure 7.17 shows a block diagram of an ATSC transmitter. Incoming transport stream packets are randomized, except for the sync pattern, for energy dispersal. Figure 7.18 shows the randomizer.

The outer correction code includes the whole packet except for the sync byte. Thus there are 187 bytes of data in each codeword and 20 bytes of R–S redundancy are added to make a 207-byte codeword. After outer coding, a convolutional interleaver shown in Figure 7.19 is used. This reorders data over a time span of about 4 ms. Interleave simply exchanges content between packets, but without changing the packet structure.

Figure 7.20 shows that the result of outer coding and interleave is a data frame which is divided into two fields of 313 segments each. The frame is transmitted by scanning it horizontally a segment at a time. There is some similarity with a traditional analog video signal here, because there is a sync pulse at the beginning of each segment and a field sync which occupies two segments of the frame. Data segment sync repeats every 77.3 µs, a segment rate of 12 933 Hz, whereas a frame has

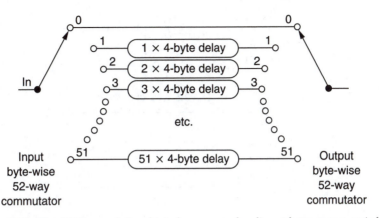

Figure 7.19 The ATSC convolutional interleaver spreads adjacent bytes over a period of about 4 ms.

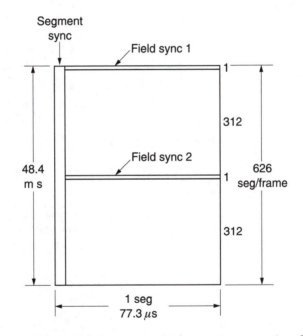

Figure 7.20 The ATSC data frame is transmitted one segment at a time. Segment sync denotes the beginning of each segment and the segments are counted from the field sync signals.

a period of 48.4 ms. The field sync segments contain a training sequence to drive the adaptive equalizer in the receiver.

The data content of the frame is subject to trellis coding which converts each pair of data bits into three channel bits inside an inner interleave. The trellis coder is shown in Figure 7.21 and the interleave in Figure 7.22. Figure 7.21 also shows how the three channel bits map to the eight signal levels in the 8-VSB modulator.

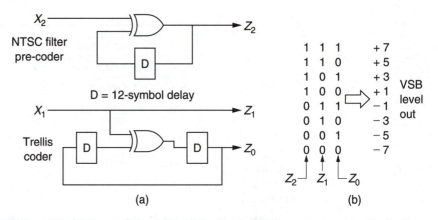

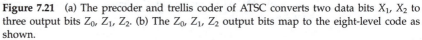

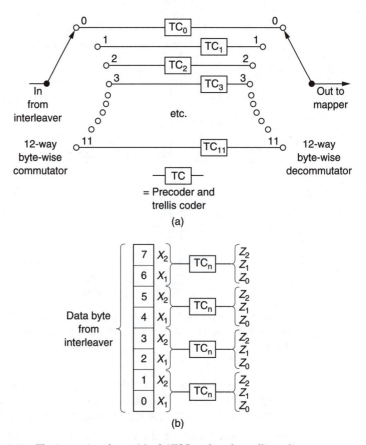

Figure 7.21 (a) The precoder and trellis coder of ATSC converts two data bits X_1, X_2 to three output bits Z_0, Z_1, Z_2. (b) The Z_0, Z_1, Z_2 output bits map to the eight-level code as shown.

Figure 7.22 The innter interleave (a) of ATSC makes the trellis coding operate as twelve parallel channels working on every twelfth byte to improve error resistance. The interleave is byte-wise, and, as (b) shows, each byte is divided into four di-bits for coding into the tri-bits Z_0, Z_1, Z_2.

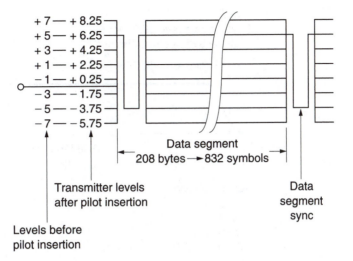

Figure 7.23 ATSC data segment. Note the sync pattern which acts as a timing and amplitude reference. The 8 levels are shifted up by 1.25 to create a DC component resulting in a pilot at the carrier frequency.

Figure 7.23 shows the data segment after eight-level coding. The sync pattern of the transport stream packet, which was not included in the error-correction code, has been replaced by a segment sync waveform. This acts as a timing reference to allow deserializing of the segment, but as the two levels of the sync pulse are standardized, it also acts as an amplitude reference for the eight-level slicer in the receiver.

The eight-level signal is subject to a DC offset so that some transmitter energy appears at the carrier frequency to act as a pilot. Each eight-level symbol carries two data bits and so there are 832 symbols in each segment. As the segment rate is 12 933 Hz, the symbol rate is 10.76 MHz and so this will require 5.38 MHz of bandwidth in a single sideband.

Figure 7.24 shows the transmitter spectrum. The lower sideband is vestigial and an overall channel width of 6 MHz results.

Figure 7.25 shows an ATSC receiver. The first stages of the receiver are designed to lock to the pilot in the transmitted signal. This then allows the eight-level signal to be sampled at the right times. This process will allow location of the segment sync and then the field sync signals. Once the receiver is synchronized, the symbols in each segment can be decoded. The inner or trellis coder corrects for random errors, then following de-interleave the RS coder corrects burst errors, After de-randomizing, standard transport stream sync patterns are added to the output data.

In practice ATSC transmissions will experience co-channel interference from NTSC transmitters and the ATSC scheme allows the use of an NTSC rejection filter. Figure 7.26 shows that most of the energy of NTSC

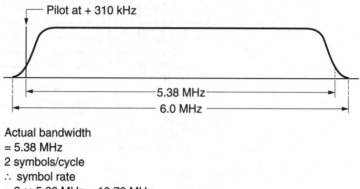

ATSC
Payload data rate: 19.28 Mb/s
Channel bandwidth: 6MHz nom.

Pilot at + 310 kHz

5.38 MHz
6.0 MHz

Actual bandwidth
= 5.38 MHz
2 symbols/cycle
∴ symbol rate
= 2 × 5.38 MHz = 10.76 MHz

Figure 7.24 The spectrum of ATSC and its associated bit and symbol rates. Note pilot at carrier frequency created by DC offset in multi-level coder.

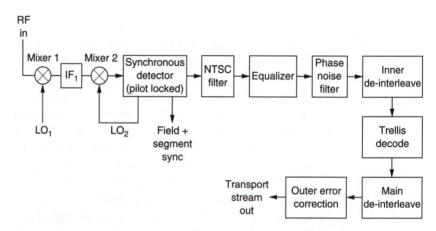

Figure 7.25 An ATSC receiver. Double conversion can be used so that the second conversion stage can be arranged to lock to the transmitted pilot.

is at the carrier, subcarrier and sound carrier frequencies. A comb filter with a suitable delay can produce nulls or notches at these frequencies. However, the delay-and-add process in the comb filter also causes another effect. When two eight-level signals are added together, the result is a sixteen-level signal. This will be corrupted by noise of half the level that would corrupt an eight-level signal. However, the sixteen-level signal contains redundancy because it corresponds to the combinations of four bits whereas only two bits are being transmitted. This allows a form of error correction to be used.

The ATSC inner precoder results in a known relationship existing between symbols independent of the data. The time delays in the inner

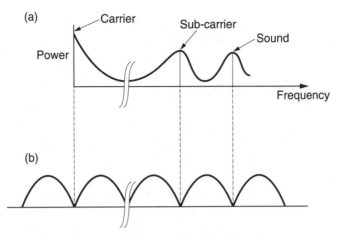

Figure 7.26 Spectrum of typical analog transmitter showing (a) maximum power carrier, subcarrier and audio carrier. A comb filter (b) with a suitable delay can notch out NTSC interference. The pre-coding of ATSC is designed to work with the necessary receiver delay.

interleave are designed to be compatible with the delay in the NTSC rejection comb filter. This limits the number of paths the received waveform can take through a time/voltage graph called a trellis. Where a signal is in error it takes a path sufficiently near to the correct one that the correct one can be implied.

ATSC uses a training sequence sent once every data field, but is otherwise helpless against multipath reception as tests have shown. In urban areas, ATSC must have a correctly oriented directional antenna to reject reflections. Unfortunately the American viewer has been brought up to believe that television reception is possible with a pair of 'rabbit's ears' on top of the TV set and ATSC will not work like this. Mobile reception is not practicable. As a result the majority of the world's broadcasters appear to be favouring an OFDM-based system.

7.6   CD-Video and DVD

CD-Video and DVD are both digital optical disks which store video and audio program material. CD-Video is based on the Compact Disc, with, which it shares the same track dimensions and bit rate. MPEG-1 coding is used on video signals adhering to the common intermediate format (CIF – see Chapter 1). The input subsampling needed to obtain the CIF imaging and the high compression factor needed to comply with the low bit rate of a digital audio disk mean that the quality of CD-Video is marginal.

DVD is based on the same concepts as Compact Disc, but with a number of enhancements. The laser in the pickup has a shorter wavelength. In conjunction with a larger lens aperture this allows the readout spot significantly to be reduced in size. This in turn allows the symbols on the tracks to be shorter as well as allowing the track spacing to be reduced. The EFM code of CD is modified to EFMPlus which improves the raw error rate.

The greatly increased capacity of DVD means that moderate compression factors can be employed. MPEG-2 coding is used, so that progressively scanned or interlaced material can be handled. As most DVDs are mastered from movie film, the use of progressive scan is common.

The perceived quality of DVDs can be very high indeed. This is partly due to the fact that a variable bit rate is supported. When difficult frames are encountered, the bit rate can rise above the average. Another advantage of DVD is that it can be mastered in non-real time. This allows techniques such as aligning cuts with *I*-pictures to be used. Also the quality obtained can be assessed and if artifacts are observed the process can be modified.

Figure 7.27 shows the block diagram of a typical DVD player, and illustrates the essential components. A CD-Video player is similar. The most natural division within the block diagram is into the control/ servo system and the data path. The control system provides the interface between the user and the servo mechanisms, and performs the logical interlocking required for safety and the correct sequence of operation.

The servo systems include any power-operated loading drawer and chucking mechanism, the spindle-drive servo, and the focus and tracking servos already described.

Power loading is usually implemented on players where the disk is placed in a drawer. Once the drawer has been pulled into the machine, the disk is lowered onto the drive spindle, and clamped at the centre, a process known as chucking. In the simpler top-loading machines, the disk is placed on the spindle by hand, and the clamp is attached to the lid so that it operates as the lid is closed. The lid or drawer mechanisms have a safety switch which prevents the laser operating if the machine is open. This is to ensure that there can be no conceivable hazard to the user. In actuality there is very little hazard in a DVD pickup. This is because the beam is focused a few millimetres away from the objective lens, and beyond the focal point the beam diverges and the intensity falls rapidly. It is almost impossible to position the eye at the focal point when the pickup is mounted in the player, but it would be foolhardy to attempt to disprove this.

The data path consists of the data separator, the de-interleaving and error-correction process followed by a RAM buffer which supplies the MPEG decoder.

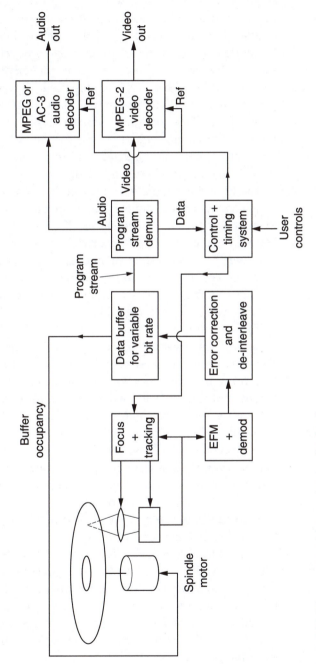

Figure 7.27   A DVD player's essential parts. See text for details.

The data separator converts the EFMplus readout waveform into data. Following data separation the error-correction and de-interleave processes take place. Because of the interleave system, there are two opportunities for correction, first, using the inner code prior to de-interleaving, and second, using the outer code after de-interleaving.

Interleaving is designed to spread the effects of burst errors among many different codewords, so that the errors in each are reduced. However, the process can be impaired if a small random error, due perhaps to an imperfection in manufacture, occurs close to a burst error caused by surface contamination. The function of the inner redundancy is to correct single-symbol errors, so that the power of interleaving to handle bursts is undiminished, and to generate error flags for the outer system when a gross error is encountered.

The EFMplus coding is a group code which means that a small defect which changes one channel pattern into another could have corrupted up to eight data bits. In the worst case, if the small defect is on the boundary between two channel patterns, two successive bytes could be corrupted. However, the final odd/even interleave on encoding ensures that the two bytes damaged will be in different inner codewords; thus a random error can never corrupt two bytes in one inner codeword, and random errors are therefore always correctable.

The de-interleave process is achieved by writing sequentially into a memory and reading out using a sequencer. The outer decoder will then correct any burst errors in the data. As MPEG data are very sensitive to error the error-correction performance has to be extremely good. Following the de-interleave and outer error-correction process an MPEG program stream (see Chapter 6) emerges. Some of the program stream data will be video, some will be audio and this will be routed to the appropriate decoder. It is a fundamental concept of DVD that the bit rate of this program stream is not fixed, but can vary with the difficulty of the program material in order to maintain consistent image quality. However, the disk uses constant linear velocity rather than constant angular velocity. It is not possible to obtain a particular bit rate with a fixed spindle speed.

The solution is to use a RAM buffer between the transport and the MPEG decoders. The RAM is addressed by counters which are arranged to overflow, giving the memory a ring structure. Writing into the memory is done using clocks derived from the disk whose frequency rises and falls with runout, whereas reading is done by the decoder which, for each picture, will take as much data as is required from the buffer.

The buffer will only function properly if the two addresses are kept apart. This implies that the amount of data read from the disk over the long term must equal the amount of data used by the MPEG decoders.

This is done by analysing the address relationship of the buffer. If the bit rate from the disk is too high, the write address will move towards the read address; if it is too low, the write address moves away from the read address. Subtraction of the two addresses produces an error signal which can be fed to the drive.

In some DVD drives, the disk spins at a relatively high speed, resulting in an excessively high continuous data rate. However, this is reduced by jumping the pickup back. Repeating a previous track does not produce any new data and so the average rate falls. As all the disk blocks are labelled it is a simple matter to reassemble the discontinuous bitstream in memory.

The exact speed of the motor is unimportant. The important factor is that the data rate needed by the decoder is correct, and the system will skip the pickup as often as necessary so that the buffer neither underflows nor overflows.

The MPEG-2 decoder will convert the compressed elementary streams into PCM video and audio and place the pictures and audio blocks into RAM. These will be read out of RAM whenever the time stamps recorded with each picture or audio block match the state of a time stamp counter. If bidirectional coding is used, the RAM readout sequence will convert the recorded picture sequence back to the real-time sequence. The time stamp counter is derived from a crystal oscillator in the player which is divided down to provide the 90 kHz time stamp clock. As a result the frame rate at which the disk was mastered will be replicated as the pictures are read from RAM. Once a picture buffer is read out, this will trigger the decoder to decode another picture. It will read data from the buffer until this has been completed and thus indirectly influence the disk bit rate.

Owing to the use of constant linear velocity, the disk speed will be wrong if the pickup is suddenly made to jump to a different radius using manual search controls. This may force the data separator out of lock, or cause a buffer overflow and the decoder may freeze briefly until this has been remedied. The control system of a DVD player is inevitably microprocessor-based, and as such does not differ greatly in hardware terms from any other microprocessor-controlled device. Operator controls will simply interface to processor input ports and the various servo systems will be enabled or overridden by output ports. Software, or more correctly firmware, connects the two. The necessary controls are Play and Eject, with the addition in most players of at least Pause and some buttons which allow rapid skipping through the program material.

Although machines vary in detail, the flowchart of Figure 7.28 shows the logic flow of a simple player, from start being pressed to pictures and sound emerging. At the beginning, the emphasis is on bringing the

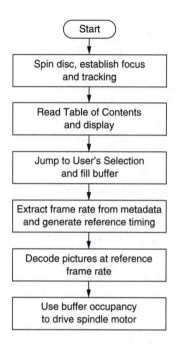

Figure 7.28 Simple processes required for a DVD player to operate.

various servos into operation. Towards the end, the disk subcode is read in order to locate the beginning of the first section of the program material.

When track following, the tracking-error feedback loop is closed, but for track crossing, in order to locate a piece of music, the loop is opened, and a microprocessor signal forces the laser head to move. The tracking error becomes an approximate sinusoid as tracks are crossed. The cycles of tracking error can be counted as feedback to determine when the correct number of tracks has been crossed. The 'mirror' signal obtained when the readout spot is half a track away from target is used to brake pickup motion and re-enable the track following feedback.

7.7   Personal video recorders

The development of the consumer VCR was a small step to end the linearity of commercial television. Increasing numbers of viewers use VCRs not just as time shifters but also as a means of fast-forwarding through the commercial breaks. The non-linear storage of video was until recently restricted by economics to professional applications. However, with the falling cost of hard disk drives and the availability

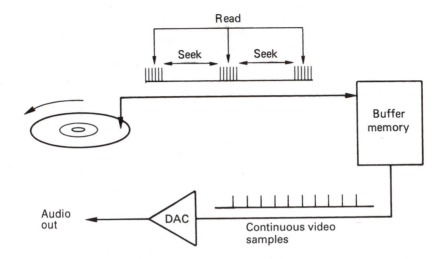

Figure 7.29 In a hard disk recorder, a large-capacity memory is used as a buffer or timebase corrector between the convertors and the disk. The memory allows the convertors to run constantly despite the interruptions in disk transfer caused by the head moving between tracks.

of MPEG compression, non-linear video storage is now a consumer product.

The personal video recorder (PVR) is based on the random access storage of a hard disk drive. As disk drives can move their heads from track to track across the disk surface, they can access data anywhere very quickly. Unlike tape, which can only record or play back but not both at the same time, a PVR can do both simultaneously at arbitrary points on a time line.

Figure 7.29 shows that the disk drive can transfer data much faster than the required bit rate, and so it transfers data in bursts which are smoothed out by RAM buffers. It is straightforward to interleave read and write functions so that it gives the impression of reading and writing simultaneously. The read and write processes can take place from anywhere on the disk.

Although the PVR can be used as an ordinary video recorder, it can do some other tricks. Figure 7.30 shows the most far-reaching trick. The disk drive starts recording an off-air commercial TV station. A few minutes later the viewer starts playing back the recording. When the commercial break is transmitted, the disk drive may record it, but the viewer can skip over it using the random access of the hard drive. With suitable software the hard drive could skip over the commercial break automatically by simply not recording it.

When used with digital television systems, the PVR can simply record the transmitted transport stream data and replay it into an MPEG

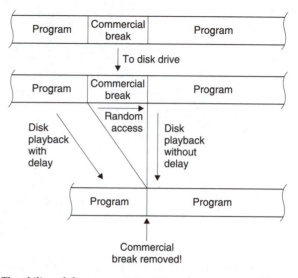

Figure 7.30 The ability of the consumer to use random access to skip over commercial breaks may destroy commercial television as it exists today.

decoder. In this way the PVR has no quality loss whatsoever. The picture quality will be the same as off-air. Optionally PVRs may also have MPEG encoders so that they can record analog video inputs.

Real-time playback in a PVR is trivial as it is just a question of retrieving recorded data as the decoder buffer demands it. However, the consumer is accustomed to the ability of the VCR to produce a picture over a range of speeds as well as a freeze frame. PVRs incorporate additional processing which modifies the recorded MPEG bitstream on playback so that a standard MPEG decoder will reproduce it with a modified timebase. Figure 7.31 shows that a typical off-air MPEG elementary stream uses bidirectional coding with a moderately long GOP structure. An increase in apparent playback speed can be obtained by discarding some of the pictures in the group. This has to be done with caution as the pictures are heavily interdependent. However, if the group is terminated after a P picture, all pictures up to that point are decodable.

The resultant motion portrayal will not be smooth because pictures are being omitted, but the goal is simply to aid the viewer in finding the right place in the recording so this is of no consequence. In practice the results are good, not least because the noise bar of the analog VCR is eliminated.

High forward speeds can be obtained by selecting only the I pictures from the recorded bitstream. These cannot be transmitted to the decoder directly, because the I pictures contain a lot of data and the decoder buffer might overflow. Consequently the data rate is diluted by sending null P pictures. These are P pictures in which all of the vectors are zero and the residual data are also zero. Null P pictures require very few data but have the effect of converting an I picture into another identical

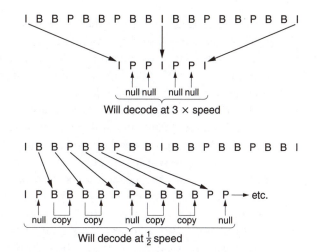

Figure 7.31 By manipulating the elementary stream, a compliant bitstream can be produced which will play at a different speed from the original.

picture. A similar technique can be used to decode in reverse. With a normal MPEG bidirectionally coded bitstream, reverse decoding is impossible, but by taking *I* pictures in reverse order and padding them with null-*P* pictures a reverse replay is obtained.

7.8   Networks

A network is basically a communication resource which is shared for economic reasons. Like any shared resource, decisions have to be made somewhere and somehow about how the resource is to be used. In the absence of such decisions the resultant chaos will be such that the resource might as well not exist.

In communications networks the resource is the ability to convey data from any node or port to any other. On a particular cable, clearly only one transaction of this kind can take place at any one instant even though in practice many nodes will simultaneously be wanting to transmit data. Arbitration is needed to determine which node is allowed to transmit.

Data networks originated to serve the requirements of computers and it is a simple fact that most computer processes don't need to be performed in real time or indeed at a particular time at all. Networks tend to reflect that background as many of them, particularly the older ones, are asynchronous. Asynchronous means that the time taken to deliver a given quantity of data is unknown. A TDM system may chop the data into several different transfers and each transfer may experience delay according to what other transfers the system is engaged in. Ethernet and most storage system buses are asynchronous. For broadcasting purposes an asynchronous delivery system is no use at all, but for copying an MPEG data file between two storage devices an asynchronous system is perfectly adequate.

The opposite extreme is the synchronous system in which the network can guarantee a constant delivery rate and a fixed and minor delay. An AES/EBU digital audio router or an SDI digital video router is a synchronous network. In between asynchronous and synchronous networks reside the isochronous approaches which cause a fixed moderate delay. These can be thought of as sloppy synchronous networks or more rigidly controlled asynchronous networks.

These three different approaches are needed for economic reasons. Asynchronous systems are very efficient because as soon as one transfer completes another one can begin. This can only be achieved by making every device wait with its data in a buffer so that transfer can start immediately. Asynchronous systems also make it possible for low bit rate devices to share a network with high bit rate devices. The low bit rate device will only need a small buffer and will send few cells, whereas the high bit rate device will send more cells.

Isochronous systems try to give the best of both worlds, generally by sacrificing some flexibility in block size. Modern networks are tending to be part isochronous and part asynchronous so that the advantages of both are available.

There are a number of different arbitration protocols and these have evolved to support the needs of different types of network. In small networks, such as LANs, a single point failure which halts the entire network may be acceptable, whereas in a public transport network owned by a telecommunications company, the network will be redundant so that if a particular link fails data may be sent via an alternative route.

A link which has reached its maximum capacity may also be supplanted by transmission over alternative routes.

In physically small networks, arbitration may be carried out in a single location. This is fast and efficient, but if the arbitrator fails it leaves the system completely crippled. The processor buses in computers work in this way.

In centrally arbitrated systems the arbitrator needs to know the structure of the system and the status of all the nodes. Following a configuration change, due perhaps to the installation of new equipment, the arbitrator needs to be told what the new configuration is, or have a mechanism which allows it to explore the network and learn the configuration. Central arbitration is only suitable for small networks that change their configuration infrequently.

In other networks the arbitration is distributed so that some decision-making ability exists in every node. This is less efficient but is does allow at least some of the network to continue operating after a component failure.

Distributed arbitration also means that each node is self-sufficient and so no changes need to be made if the network is reconfigured by adding or deleting a node. This is the only possible approach in wide area networks where the structure may be very complex and changes dynamically in the event of failures or overload.

Ethernet uses distributed arbitration. FireWire is capable of using both types of arbitration. A small amount of decision-making ability is built into every node so that distributed arbitration is possible. However, if one of the nodes happens to be a computer, it can run a centralized arbitration algorithm.

The physical structure of a network is subject to some variation as Figure 7.32 shows. In radial networks, (a), each port has a unique cable connection to a device called a *hub*. The hub must have one connection for every port and this limits the number of ports. However, a cable failure will only result in the loss of one port. In a ring system (b) the nodes are connected like a daisy chain with each node acting as a feedthrough. In this case the arbitration requirement must be distributed. With some protocols, a single cable break doesn't stop the network

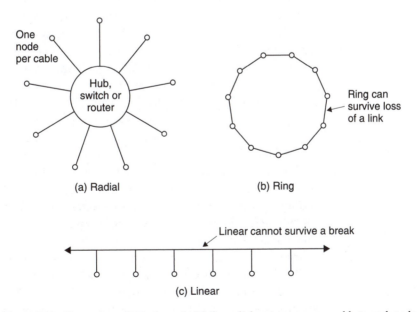

Figure 7.32 Network configurations. At (a) the radial system uses one cable to each node. (b) Ring system uses less cable than radial. (c) Linear system is simple but has no redundancy.

operating. Depending on the protocol, simultaneous transactions may be possible provided they don't require the same cable. For example, in a storage network a disk drive may be outputting data to an editor whilst another drive is backing up data to a tape streamer. For the lowest cost, all nodes are physically connected in parallel to the same cable. Figure 7.32(c) shows that a cable break would divide the network into two halves, but it is possible that the impedance mismatch at the break could stop both halves working.

One of the concepts involved in arbitration is priority which is fundamental to providing an appropriate quality of service. If two processes both want to use a network, the one with the highest priority would normally go first.

Attributing priority must be done carefully because some of the results are non-intuitive. For example, it may be beneficial to give a high priority to a humble device which has a low data rate for the simple reason that if it is given use of the network it won't need it for long. In a television environment transactions concerned with on-air processes would have priority over file transfers concerning production and editing.

When a device gains access to the network to perform a transaction, generally no other transaction can take place until it has finished. Consequently it is important to limit the amount of time that a given port can stay on the bus. In this way when the time limit expires, a further arbitration must take place. The result is that the network resource rotates between transactions rather than one transfer hogging the resource and shutting everyone else out. It follows from the presence of a time (or data quantity) limit that ports must have the means to break large files up into frames or cells and reassemble them on reception. This process is sometimes called *adaptation*. If the data to be sent originally exist at a fixed bit rate, some buffering will be needed so that the data can be time-compressed into the available frames. Each frame must be contiguously numbered and the system must transmit a file size or word count so that the receiving node knows when it has received every frame in the file.

The error-detection system interacts with this process because if any frame is in error on reception, the receiving node can ask for a retransmission of the frame. This is more efficient than retransmitting the whole file. Figure 7.33 shows the mechanism of retransmission where one packet has been lost or is in error. The retransmitted packet is inserted at the correct place in the bitstream by the receiver.

Breaking files into frames helps to keep down the delay experienced by each process using the network. Figure 7.34 shows a frame-multiplexed transmission. Each frame may be stored ready for transmission in a silo memory. It is possible to make the priority a function of the number of frames in the silo, as this is a direct measure

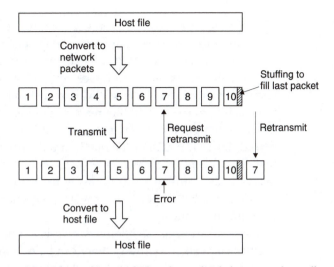

Figure 7.33 Receiving a file which has been divided into packets allows for the retransmission of just the packet in error.

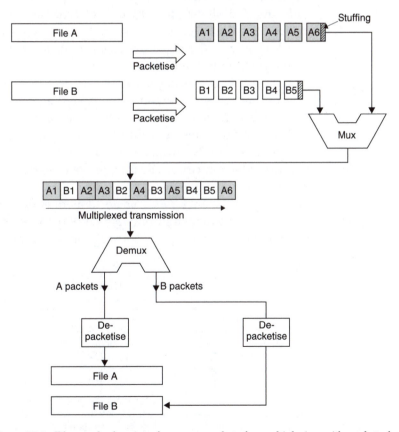

Figure 7.34 Files are broken into frames or packets for multiplexing with packets from other users. Short packets minimize the time between the arrival of successive packets. The priority of the multiplexing must favour isochronous data over asynchronous data.

of how long a process has been kept waiting. Isochronous systems must do this in order to meet maximum delay specifications.

When delivering an MPEG bitstream over an isochronous network, the network transmitter and receiver will require buffering over and above that provided in the MPEG encoder and decoder. This will enable the receiver to re-create a bitstream at the decoder which has essentially the same temporal characteristics as that leaving the encoder, except for a fixed delay. The greater the maximum delay of the network, the greater that fixed delay will have to be. Providing buffering is expensive and delays cause difficulty in applications such as videoconferencing. In this case it is better to use a network protocol which can limit delay by guaranteeing bandwidth.

A central arbitrator is relatively simple to implement because when all decisions are taken centrally there can be no timing difficulty (assuming a well-engineered system). In a distributed system, there is an extra difficulty due to the finite time taken for signals to travel down the data paths between nodes.

Figure 7.35 shows the structure of Ethernet which uses a protocol called CSMA/CD (carrier sense multiple access with collision detect) developed by DEC and Xerox. This is a distributed arbitration network where each node follows some simple rules. The first of these is not to transmit if an existing bus signal is detected. The second is not to transmit more than a certain quantity of data before releasing the bus. Devices wanting to use the bus will see bus signals and so will wait until the present bus transaction finishes. This must happen at some point because of the frame size limit. When the frame is completed, signalling on the bus should cease. The first device to sense the bus becoming free and to assert its own signal will prevent any other nodes transmitting according to the first rule. Where numerous devices are present it is possible to give them a priority structure by providing a delay between sensing the bus coming free and beginning a transaction. High-priority

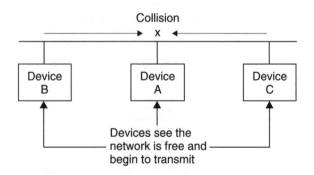

Figure 7.35 In Ethernet collisions can occur because of the finite speed of the signals. A 'back-off' algorithm handles collisions, but they do reduce the network throughput.

devices will have a short delay so they get in first. Lower-priority devices will only be able to start a transaction if the high-priority devices don't need to transfer.

It might be thought that these rules would be enough and everything would be fine. Unfortunately the finite signal speed means that there is a flaw in the system. Figure 7.35 shows why. Device A is transmitting and devices B and C both want to transmit and have equal priority. At the end of A's transaction, devices B and C see the bus become free at the same instant and start a transaction. With two devices driving the bus, the resultant waveform is meaningless. This is known as a collision and all nodes must have means to recover from it. First, each node will read the bus signal at all times. When a node drives the bus, it will also read back the bus signal and compare it with what was sent. Clearly if the two are the same all is well, but if there is a difference, this must be because a collision has occurred and two devices are trying to determine the bus voltage at once.

If a collision is detected, both colliding devices will sense the disparity between the transmitted and readback signals, and both will release the bus to terminate the collision. However, there is no point is adhering to the simple protocol to reconnect because this will simply result in another collision. Instead each device has a built-in delay which must expire before another attempt is made to transmit. This delay is not fixed, but is controlled by a random number generator and so changes from transaction to transaction.

The probability of two node devices arriving at the same delay is infinitesimally small. Consequently if a collision does occur, both devices will drop the bus, and they will start their back-off timers. When the first timer expires, that device will transmit and the other will see the transmission and remain silent. In this way the collision is not only handled, but is prevented from happening again.

The performance of Ethernet is usually specified in terms of the bit rate at which the cabling runs. However, this rate is academic because it is not available all of the time. In a real network bit rate is lost by the need to send headers and error-correction codes and by the loss of time due to interframe spaces and collision handling. As the demand goes up, the number of collisions increases and throughput goes down. Collision-based arbitrators do not handle congestion well.

An alternative method of arbitration developed by IBM is shown in Figure 7.36. This is known as a *token ring* system. All the nodes have an input and an output and are connected in a ring which must be complete for the system to work. Data circulate in one direction only. If data are not addressed to a node which receives it, the data will be passed on. When the data arrive at the addressed node, that node will capture the data as well as passing them on with an acknowledge added.

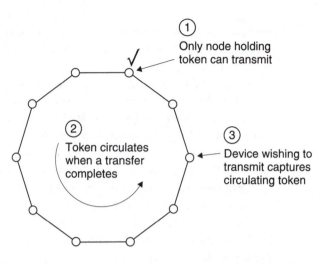

Figure 7.36 In a token ring system only the node in possession of the token can transmit so collisions are impossible. In very large rings the token circulation time causes loss of throughput.

Thus the data packet travels right around the ring back to the sending node. When the sending node receives the acknowledge, it will transmit a token packet. This token packet passes to the next node, which will pass it on if it does not wish to transmit. If no device wishes to transmit, the token will circulate endlessly. However, if a device has data to send, it simply waits until the token arrives again and captures it. This node can now transmit data in the knowledge that there cannot be a collision because no other node has the token.

In simple token ring systems, the transmitting node transmits idle characters after the data packet has been sent in order to maintain synchronization. The idle character transmission will continue until the acknowledge arrives. In the case of long packets the acknowledge will arrive before the packet has all been sent and no idle characters are necessary. However, with short packets idle characters will be generated. These idle characters use up ring bandwidth.

Later token ring systems use *early token release* (ETR). After the packet has been transmitted, the sending node sends a token straight away. Another node wishing to transmit can do so as soon as the current packet has passed. It might be thought that the nodes on the ring would transmit in their physical order, but this is not the case because a priority system exists. Each node can have a different priority if necessary. If a high-priority node wishes to transmit, as a packet from elsewhere passes through that node, the node will set *reservation bits* with its own priority level. When the sending node finishes and transmits a token, it will copy that priority level into the token.

In this way nodes with a lower priority level will pass the token on instead of capturing it. The token will ultimately arrive at the high-priority node.

The token ring system has the advantage that it does not waste throughput with collisions and so the full capacity is always available. However, if the ring is broken the entire network fails.

In Ethernet the performance is degraded by the number of transactions, not the number of nodes, whereas in token ring the performance is degraded by the number of nodes.

7.9 FireWire

FireWire[3] is actually an Apple Computers Inc. trade name for the interface which is formally known as IEEE 1394–1995. It was originally intended as a digital audio network, but grew out of recognition. FireWire is more than just an interface as it can be used to form networks and if used with a computer effectively extends the computer's data bus. Figure 7.37 shows that devices are simply connected together as any combination of daisychain or star network.

Any pair of devices can communicate in either direction, and arbitration ensures that only one device transmits at once. Intermediate devices simply pass on transmissions. This can continue even if the intermediate device is powered down as the FireWire carries power to keep repeated functions active.

Communications are divided into *cycles* which have a period of 125 µs. During a cycle, there are 64 time slots. During each time slot, any one

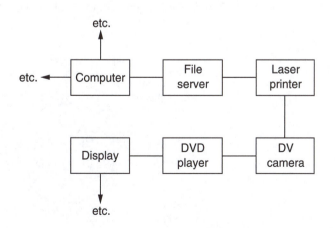

Figure 7.37 FireWire supports radial (star) or daisy-chain connection. Two-port devices pass on signals destined for a more distant device – they can do this even when powered down.

node can communicate with any other, but in the next slot, a different pair of nodes may communicate. Thus FireWire is best described as a time division multiplexed (TDM) system. There will be a new arbitration between the nodes for each cycle.

FireWire is eminently suitable for video/computer convergent applications because it can simultaneously support asynchronous transfers of non-real-time computer data and isochronous transfers of real-time audio/video data. It can do this because the arbitration process allocates a fixed proportion of slots for isochronous data (about 80 per cent) and these have a higher priority in the arbitration than the asynchronous data. The higher the data rate a given node needs, the more time slots it will be allocated. Thus a given bit rate can be guaranteed throughout a transaction; a prerequisite of real-time A/V data transfer.

It is the sophistication of the arbitration system which makes FireWire remarkable. Some of the arbitration is in hardware at each node, but some is in software which only needs to be at one node. The full functionality requires a computer somewhere in the system which runs the isochronous bus management arbitration. Without this only asynchronous transfers are possible. It is possible to add or remove devices whilst the system is working. When a device is added the system will recognize it through a periodic learning process. Essentially every node on the system transmits in turn so that the structure becomes clear.

The electrical interface of FireWire is shown in Figure 7.38. It consists of two twisted pairs for signalling and a pair of power conductors. The twisted pairs carry differential signals of about 220 mV swinging around a common mode voltage of about 1.9 V with an impedance of 112 Ω. Figure 7.39 shows how the data are transmitted. The host data are simply serialized and used to modulate twisted pair A. The other twisted pair

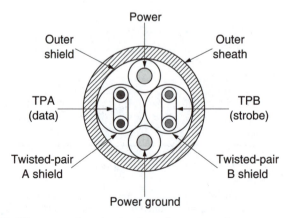

Figure 7.38 FireWire uses twin twisted pairs and a power pair.

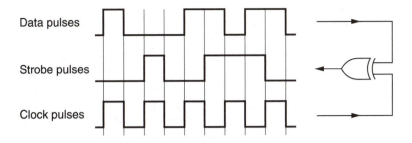

Figure 7.39 The strobe signal is the X-OR of the data and the bit clock. The data and strobe signals together form a self-clocking system.

(B) carries a signal called *strobe*, which is the exclusive-OR of the data and the clock. Thus whenever a run of identical bits results in no transitions in the data, the strobe signal will carry transitions. At the receiver another exclusive-OR gate adds data and strobe to re-create the clock.

This signalling technique is subject to skew between the two twisted pairs and this limits cable lengths to about 10 metres between nodes. Thus FireWire is not a long-distance interface technique, instead it is very useful for interconnecting a large number of devices in close proximity. Using a copper interconnect, FireWire can run at 100, 200 or 400 megabits/s, depending on the specific hardware. It is proposed to create an optical fibre version which would run at gigabit speeds.

7.10 Broadband networks and ATM

Broadband ISDN (B-ISDN) is the successor to N-ISDN and in addition to providing more bandwidth, offers practical solutions to the delivery of any conceivable type of data. The flexibility with which ATM operates means that intermittent or one-off data transactions which only require asynchronous delivery can take place alongside isochronous MPEG video delivery. This is known as *application independence* whereby the sophistication of isochronous delivery does not raise the cost of asynchronous data. In this way, generic data, video, speech and combinations of the above can co-exist.

ATM is multiplexed, but it is not time-division multiplexed. TDM is inefficient because if a transaction does not fill its allotted bandwidth, the capacity is wasted. ATM does not offer fixed blocks of bandwidth, but allows infinitely variable bandwidth to each transaction. This is done by converting all host data into small fixed size cells at the adaptation layer. The greater the bandwidth needed by a transaction, the more cells per second are allocated to that transaction. This approach is superior to the fixed bandwidth approach, because if the bit rate of a particular transaction falls, the cells released can be used for other transactions so that the full bandwidth is always available.

As all cells are identical in size, a multiplexer can assemble cells from many transactions in an arbitrary order. The exact order is determined by the quality of service required, where the time positioning of isochronous data would be determined first, with asynchronous data filling the gaps.

Figure 7.40 shows how a broadband system might be implemented. The transport network would typically be optical fibre based, using SONET (synchronous optical network) or SDH (synchronous digital hierarchy). These standards differ in minor respects. Figure 7.41 shows the bit rates available in each. Lower bit rates will be used in the access networks which will use different technology such as xDSL.

SONET and SDH assemble ATM cells into a structure known as a *container* in the interests of efficiency. Containers are passed intact between exchanges in the transport network. The cells in a container need not belong to the same transaction, they simply need to be going the same way for at least one transport network leg.

The cell-routing mechanism of ATM is unusual and deserves explanation. In conventional networks, a packet must carry the complete destination address so that at every exchange it can be routed closer to its destination. The exact route by which the packet travels cannot be anticipated and successive packets in the same transaction may take different routes. This is known as a *connectionless* protocol.

In contrast, ATM is a *connection oriented* protocol. Before data can be transferred, the network must set up an end-to-end route. Once this is done, the ATM cells do not need to carry a complete destination address. Instead they only need to carry enough addressing so that an exchange or switch can distinguish between all of the expected transactions.

The end-to-end route is known as a *virtual channel* which consists of a series of *virtual links* between switches. The term virtual channel is used because the system acts like a dedicated channel even though physically it is not. When the transaction is completed the route can be dismantled so that the bandwidth is freed for other users. In some cases, such as delivery of a TV station's output to a transmitter, or as a replacement for analog cable TV the route can be set up continuously to form what is known as a *permanent virtual channel*.

The addressing in the cells ensures that all cells with the same address take the same path, but owing to the multiplexed nature of ATM, at other times and with other cells a completely different routing scheme may exist. Thus the routing structure for a particular transaction always passes cells by the same route, but the next cell may belong to another transaction and will have a different address causing it to be routed in another way.

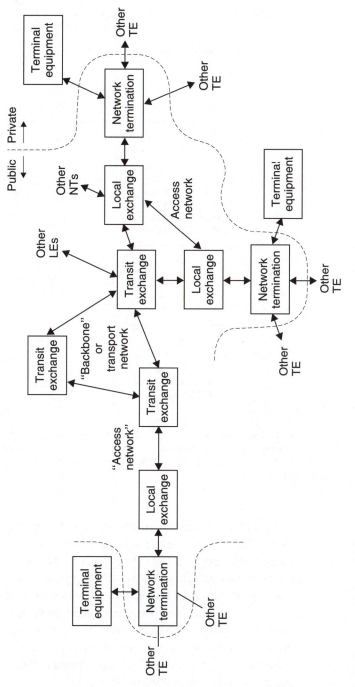

Figure 7.40 Structure and terminology of a broadband network. See text.

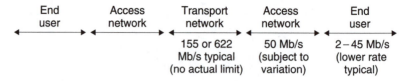

Figure 7.41 Bit rates available in SONET and SDH.

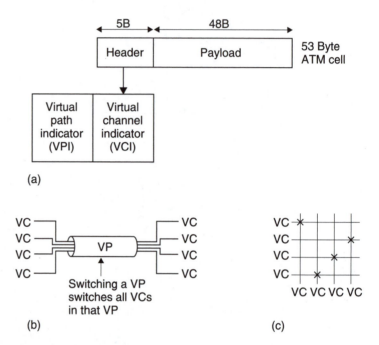

Figure 7.42 The ATM cell (a) carries routing information in the header. ATM paths carrying a group of channels can be switched in a virtual path switch (b). Individual channel switching requires a virtual channel switch which is more complex and causes more delay (c).

The addressing structure is hierarchical. Figure 7.42(a) shows the ATM cell and its header. The cell address is divided into two fields, the virtual channel identifier and the virtual path identifier. Virtual paths are logical groups of virtual channels which happen to be going the same way. An example would be the output of a video-on-demand server travelling to the first switch. The virtual path concept is useful because all cells in the same virtual path can share the same container in a transport network. A virtual path switch shown in Figure 7.42(b) can operate at the container level whereas a virtual channel switch (c) would need to dismantle and reassemble containers.

When a route is set up, at each switch a table is created. When a cell is received at a switch the VPI and/or VCI code is looked up in the table and used for two purposes. First, the configuration of the switch is obtained, so that this switch will correctly route the cell. Second, the VPI and/or VCI codes may be updated so that they correctly control the next switch. This process repeats until the cell arrives at its destination.

In order to set up a path, the initiating device will initially send cells containing an ATM destination address, the bandwidth and quality of service required. The first switch will reply with a message containing the VPI/VCI codes which are to be used for this channel. The message from the initiator will propagate to the destination, creating look-up tables in each switch. At each switch the logic will add the requested bandwidth to the existing bandwidth in use to check that the requested quality of service can be met. If this succeeds for the whole channel, the destination will reply with a connect message which propagates back to the initiating device as confirmation that the channel has been set up. The connect message contains a unique call reference value which identifies this transaction. This is necessary because an initiator such as a file server may be initiating many channels and the connect messages will not necessarily return in the same order as the set-up messages were sent. The last switch will confirm receipt of the connect message to the destination and the initiating device will confirm receipt of the connect message to the first switch.

7.11 ATM AALs

ATM works by dividing all real data messages into cells of 48 bytes each. At the receiving end, the original message must be re-created. This can take many forms and Figure 7.43 shows some possibilities. The message may be a generic data file having no implied timing structure, a serial bitstream with a fixed clock frequency, known as UDT (unstructured data transfer) or a burst of data bytes from a TDM system.

The application layer in ATM has two sublayers shown in Figure 7.44. The first is the segmentation and reassembly (SAR) sublayer which must

Generic data file having no timebase
Constant bit rate serial data stream
Audio/video data requiring a timebase
Compressed A/V data with fixed bit rate
Compressed A/V data with variable bit rate

Figure 7.43 Types of data which may need adapting to ATM.

ATM Application Layer	Convergence sublayer	Recovers timing of original data
	Segmentation and reassembly	Divides data into cells for transport Reassembles original data format

Figure 7.44   ATM adaption layer has two sublayers, segmentation and convergence.

divide the message into cells and rebuild it to get the binary data right. The second is the convergence sublayer (CS) which recovers the timing structure of the original message. It is this feature which makes ATM so appropriate for delivery of audio/visual material. Conventional networks such as the Internet don't have this ability.

In order to deliver a particular quality of service, the adaptation layer and the ATM layer work together. Effectively the adaptation layer will place constraints on the ATM layer, such as cell delay, and the ATM layer will meet those constraints without needing to know why. Provided the constraints are met, the adaptation layer can rebuild the message. The variety of message types and timing constraints leads to the adaptation layer having a variety of forms. The adaptation layers which are most relevant to MPEG applications are AAL-1 and AAL-5. AAL-1 is suitable for transmitting MPEG-2 multi-program transport streams at constant bit rate and is standardized for this purpose in ETS 300814 for DVB application. AAL-1 has an integral forward error-correction (FEC) scheme. AAL-5 is optimized for single-program transport streams (SPTS) at a variable bit rate and has no FEC.

AAL-1 takes as an input the 188-byte transport stream packets which are created by a standard MPEG-2 multiplexer. The transport stream bit rate must be constant but it does not matter if statistical multiplexing has been used within the transport stream.

The Reed–Solomon FEC of AAL-1 uses a codeword of size 128 so that the codewords consist of 124 bytes of data and 4 bytes of redundancy, making 128 bytes in all. Thirty-one 188-byte TS packets are restructured into this format. The 256-byte codewords are then subject to a block interleave. Figure 7.45 shows that 47 such codewords are assembled in rows in RAM and then columns are read out. These columns are 47 bytes long and, with the addition of an AAL header byte, make up a 48-byte ATM packet payload. In this way the interleave block is transmitted in 128 ATM cells.

The result of the FEC and interleave is that the loss of up to four cells in 128 can be corrected, or a random error of up to two bytes can be corrected in each cell. This FEC system allows most errors in the ATM layer to be corrected so that no retransmissions are needed. This is important for isochronous operation.

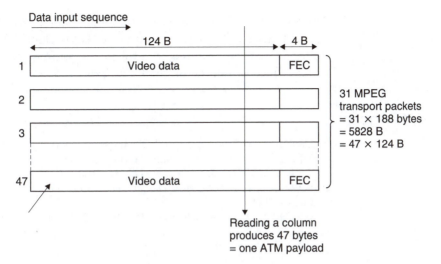

Figure 7.45 The interleave structure used in AAL-1.

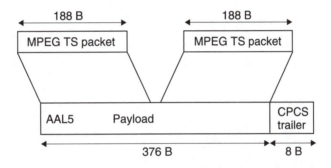

Figure 7.46 The AAL-5 adaptation layer can pack MPEG transport packets in this way.

The AAL header has a number of functions. One of these is to identify the first ATM cell in the interleave block of 128 cells. Another function is to run a modulo-8 cell counter to detect missing or out-of sequence ATM cells. If a cell simply fails to arrive, the sequence jump can be detected and used to flag the FEC system so that it can correct the missing cell by erasure. In a manner similar to the use of program clock reference (PCR) in MPEG, AAL-1 embeds a timing code in ATM cell headers. This is called the synchronous residual time stamp (SRTS) and in conjunction with the ATM network clock allows the receiving AAL device to reconstruct the original data bit rate. This is important because in MPEG applications it prevents the PCR jitter specification being exceeded.

In AAL-5 there is no error correction and the adaptation layer simply reformats MPEG TS blocks into ATM cells. Figure 7.46 shows one way in which this can be done. Two TS blocks of 188 bytes are associated with an 8-byte trailer known as CPCS (common part convergence sublayer).

The presence of the trailer makes a total of 384 bytes which can be carried in eight ATM cells. AAL-5 does not offer constant delay and external buffering will be required, controlled by reading the MPEG PCRs in order to reconstruct the original time axis.

References

1. Digital Video Broadcasting (DVB); Implementation guidelines for the use of MPEG-2 systems, video and audio in satellite and cable broadcasting applications. *ETSI Tech. Report ETR 154* (1996)
2. Watkinson, J.R., *The Art of Digital Video*, third edition, Ch. 8. Oxford: Focal Press (2000)
3. Wicklegren, I.J., The facts about FireWire. *IEEE Spectrum,* 19–25 (1997)

Index